NEW APPROACHES TO
COMPARATIVE EDUCATION

NEW APPROACHES TO COMPARATIVE EDUCATION

Edited by Philip G. Altbach and Gail P. Kelly

The University of Chicago Press
Chicago and London

The essays in this volume originally appeared in various issues of
Comparative Education Review. Acknowledgments of the original
publications can be found on the first page of each chapter.
© 1978, 1979, 1980, 1982, 1983, 1984, 1985, and 1986 by the
Comparative and International Education Society.

The University of Chicago Press, Chicago 60637
The University of Chicago Press, Ltd., London

Library of Congress Cataloging-in-Publication Data
Main entry under title:

New approaches to comparative education.

    "The essays in this volume originally appeared in
various issues of Comparative education review"—CIP
prelim p.
    Bibliography: p.
    Includes index.
    1. Comparative education—Addresses, essays,
lectures.   I. Altbach, Philip G.   II. Kelly, Gail
Paradise.
LA133.N48   1986   370.19′5   85-24523
ISBN 0-226-01525-4
ISBN 0-226-01526-2 (pbk.)

The paper used in this publication meets the
minimum requirements of American National Standard
for Information Sciences—Permanence of Paper for
Printed Library Materials, ANSI Z39.48-1984.

Contents

Introduction:
Perspectives on Comparative Education

PHILIP G. ALTBACH AND GAIL P. KELLY

This volume, *New Approaches to Comparative Education*, has a unique purpose. We have carefully selected articles published in the *Comparative Education Review* to illuminate the diversity of perspectives on research in comparative education that has emerged in recent years and provides new visions for the field. Our intention is to present an array of new viewpoints, orientations, and approaches that have arisen since the "State of the Art" issue of the *Comparative Education Review* was published in 1977.[1] All the essays included here have appeared in the *Review* since that time. The 1977 "State of the Art," for the most part, focused on comparative education from the vantage of the social sciences and stressed the contribution of those disciplines to the field. Such an orientation to the field reflected but one in a long research tradition; but it dominated North American scholarship at that time. This volume departs significantly from that presentation of the field. We do not ask here how the social sciences can guide research; rather, our intent is to draw attention to the new and diverse currents of thought about comparative education, the use of the field, regional variation and world systems analysis, the theories undergirding comparative studies and paradigm shifts, and the debates over ideology and scholarship that give the field vitality and strength.

Since 1977 the field of comparative education has broadened its research orientation. As some of the essays in this book indicate, there is no one method of study in the field; rather, the field increasingly is characterized by a number of different research orientations. No longer are there attempts to define a single methodology of comparative education, and none of our contributors argues that one single method be developed as a canon. Scholars in comparative education have recently adopted a range of methodologies and approaches to develop innovative ways of dealing with complex research issues and in analyzing educational data creatively in a cross-cultural frame. The new approaches reflect eclectic and creative ways of dealing with a broad spectrum of issues. Prior to 1977, comparative education was, in general, concerned with national educational policies. Since that time, the questions scholars address have turned to intranational comparisons as well as analysis of transnational trends. Research has also been guided by a broad range of different theories. Since 1977 we have seen the application of conflict theories to the field's scholarship. The

[1] "The State of the Art: Twenty Years of Comparative Education," *Comparative Education Review*, vol. 21, nos. 2–3 (June/October 1977).

emergence of this literature had lead to a set of lively debates about the relation of theory to research and theory to developing prescriptions for educational policy.

This book is not a handbook of comparative education methodology. Rather, it presents a range of orientations toward the conduct of research in the field. The articles we present reflect diverse thinking on the use of the field, methods for comparison, and theories guiding scholarship that have come to the fore since 1977. This volume coincides with the beginning of the thirtieth year of publication of the *Comparative Education Review;* it is fitting that in it we explore future research directions and reflect on the debates in our field that are germane to the diverse clientele and uses of the field.

Internationalization and Expansion

In the 30 years since the founding of the *Comparative Education Review,* the field has expanded from a small enclave of scholars mainly in North America and Great Britain to a worldwide "invisible college" of scholars, teachers, policymakers, and students concerned with the cross-cultural understanding of education in an increasingly complex world. The growth of the field has been impressive and has added tremendous diversity and strength to it. Comparative education organizations were established first in Western Europe, and the Comparative Education Society in Europe (CESE) now has branches in a large number of countries including France, Great Britain, the Netherlands, Belgium, the German Federal Republic, and Spain. Japan has an active and long-standing comparative education organization, and recently China, India, and South Korea have established organizations. Comparative education as a field has become truly international, and this will have an impact on scholarship as researchers in the Third World begin to publish their work.

The development of the infrastructures of the field has also been impressive. When the *Comparative Education Review* was founded, it was joined only by the *International Review of Education.* The number of journals in English has grown impressively—*Comparative Education, Compare,* and *Canadian and International Education* are among the key publications. *Prospects,* published in four languages by Unesco, features work on comparative education. In addition, journals exist in French, German, Spanish, and Chinese. Books on comparative education are published regularly by such publishers as Praeger and Pergamon in English. In short, the scholarly infrastructure has grown impressively. Research and scholarship is still dominated by the English-speaking countries, but with the growth of interest in the field in other parts of this world, this domination may in time be broken.

The Origins and Development of the Field

It is not possible to present a complete history of the field of comparative education. This has been done by J. Trethewey and by Harold Noah and Max Eckstein,[2] although a definitive history of the field has yet to be written. Nor is it possible to provide a description of the multifaceted substantive contributions of the field. It is our purpose here to provide a brief overview of the development and scope of the field in order to situate comparative education as a field of study. Comparative education, unlike most other fields in educational studies, has encompassed a large variety of disciplinary and methodological approaches and has covered many substantive topics. This is a very important strength of the field in that it has from time to time attracted able scholars from many fields and has used research paradigms from a variety of disciplines. But it does create certain definitional problems. Over time, this has made the development of a distinct methodology in comparative education impossible— and probably undesirable as well.[3] Comparative education has been increasingly marked by considerable diversity in approaches to research and analysis. Given the range of concerns of the field, this diversity is natural. Comparative education, after all, takes the world as its research base and can encompass virtually any methodology that can help to understand an education-related topic in cross-cultural perspective.

Historically, comparative education has encompassed many research traditions. One of the most long-standing of these has been that of "travelers' tales"—descriptions of educational practices in other countries. Frequently such descriptions became the basis for inducing changes at home. For example, many scholars and policymakers were interested in the development of German education in the nineteenth century; Urie Bronfenbrenner's work on socialization of Soviet children in the 1960s became a way of criticizing American child-rearing and school practices.[4]

Another tradition in the field is educational "lending and borrowing," which aims at transferring practices from one country to another in the hopes of reforming education for the better. Flexner's famous study of higher education fits this category as does much contemporary scholarship on educational achievement and on school practices in Japan.[5] The im-

---

[2] J. Trethewey, *Comparative Education* (Elmsford, N.Y.: Pergamon, 1976); Harold Noah and Max Eckstein, *Toward a Science of Comparative Education* (New York: Macmillan, 1969).

[3] For a bibliographical guide to the field, see Philip G. Altbach, Gail P. Kelly, and David H. Kelly, *International Bibliography of Comparative Education* (New York: Praeger, 1981).

[4] Urie Bronfenbrenner, *Two Worlds of Childhood: USA and USSR* (New York: Pocket, 1973).

[5] Abraham Flexner, *Universities: American, English, German* (New York: Oxford University Press, 1930); on Japan, see William Cummings, *Education and Equality in Japan* (Princeton, N.J.: Princeton University Press, 1980), and Nobuo Shimahara, *Adaptation and Education in Japan* (New York: Praeger, 1979).

position of educational models from one country to another is part of this tradition as well. Much of comparative education evolved in the context of colonialism. Britain, France, and other colonial powers imposed educational models on their overseas colonies, often displacing indigenous forms and without consultation with the colonized. Educational "lending" in much of the world included elements of coercion.[6]

Another major research tradition in comparative education is that of historical/cultural studies. Such work was pioneered in the field by Issac Kandel and taken up by Robert Ulich. Their works sought to understand how history and culture influenced the evolution of contemporary education. Although Kandel and some of his followers, notably Vernon Mallinson, developed national character as a construct to guide understanding of contemporary educational practices, the research tradition in the field often uses no such construct; it does seek to understand, for example, how language and culture affect what children learn in school.[7] An example of such work is Gay and Cole's study of mathematics instruction among the Kpelle of Liberia and John Ogbu's recent work on caste and class in education.[8]

The improvement of international understanding in general and education in particular is a long-standing tradition in the field. There has always been and, we hope, will continue to be a humanitarian and ameliorative element that has impelled many comparative educators to become involved in international programs to improve aspects of education and to encourage increased international understanding, particularly in the schools, as a contribution to world peace and development. This trend, which can be seen in the writing of Kandel and Mallinson in an earlier period, is reflected in the involvement of comparative educators in efforts to improve education in Third World nations and to teach about human rights today.

In the 1960s a new tradition emerged that attempted to build a "science of comparative education." George Bereday's classic volume marked the beginning of such a trend. Noah, Eckstein, and C. Arnold Anderson contributed much to developing it to a point where the "scientific" approach to comparative education dominated the field in North America through the 1970s. Bereday tried to develop a methodology for conducting research that was distinctly comparative; Noah and Eckstein, as well as Anderson,

---

[6] See Philip G. Altbach and Gail P. Kelly, eds., *Education and the Colonial Experience* (New Brunswick, N.J.: Transaction, 1982).

[7] Isaac L. Kandel, "Problems of Comparative Education," *International Review of Education* 2, no. 1 (1956): 1–15; Vernon Mallinson, *An Introduction to the Study of Comparative Education* (London: Heinemann, 1975).

[8] John Gay and Michael Cole, *The New Mathematics in an Old Culture* (New York: Holt, Rinehart & Winston, 1967); John U. Ogbu, *Caste and Class in Comparative Perspective* (in press).

believed that a "science" could be developed only through use of methodologies borrowed from the social sciences that consisted of hypothesis formulation and testing and the use of quantification and statistics in the conduct of scholarship.[9] The goal was to discover scientific laws governing school/society relations that could guide policy decisions. While North American scholars focused on discovering scientific laws, in Great Britain scholars such as Brian Holmes and Edmund King doubted the possibility of being able to do so. However, they attempted to develop scientific approaches to the field that could guide educational decision making.[10] It will be clear from the essays in this volume that in the 1980s the field of comparative education has departed in some significant ways from earlier traditions and that new ones are appearing. New research topics have emerged, and the field increasingly has come to discuss the underlying assumptions guiding research methods as well as choice of research questions in ways that in the past were muted.

Trends in Research

Comparative education not only has a range of research traditions but has also covered many substantive fields and topics. This brief summary is intended to provide a sense of the range of studies that have been undertaken in recent years rather than a bibliographical guide to the literature.[11] Our special interest is to indicate the richness of the research that has emerged in recent years.

It is fair to say that in the major expansion of comparative education in the 1950s and 1960s, sociology and economics were the main disciplines that formed the basis of much of the research. Attention was focused on societal outcomes of education. Much of it was informed exclusively by human capital theory. This was particularly the case with scholarship in Third World countries. Interest in education became almost exclusively an interest in production and individual income. Other educational outcomes—social, political, and cognitive—seemingly became devalued. The focus on production and individual income also denied complex social relations and the obvious effect of class, race, gender, and ethnicity on who got and who could use education in what context. By the late 1970s, voices within the field argued forcefully that human capital theory, like

---

[9] George Z. F. Bereday, *Comparative Method in Education* (New York: Holt, Rinehart & Winston, 1964); Harold Noah and Max Eckstein, *Toward a Science of Comparative Education* (New York: Macmillan, 1969); Max Eckstein and Harold Noah, eds., *Scientific Investigations in Comparative Education* (New York: Macmillan, 1969); C. Arnold Anderson, "Methodology of Comparative Education," *International Review of Education* 7 (1961): 1–23.

[10] See, e.g., Brian Holmes, *Problems in Education: A Comparative Approach* (London: Routledge & Kegan Paul, 1965); Edmund King, *Comparative Studies and Educational Decision* (London: Methuen, 1968).

[11] For a guide to the literature in specific areas of comparative education, see Altbach, Kelly, and Kelly.

structural functionalism of which it was a variant, had blinded research to the key educational issues facing the Third World in particular and most countries in general. They argued that education had political and social outcomes in many instances in contradiction to economic ones. In addition, they argued that schools have *educational* outcomes, which the field largely ignored and which were of central concern to policymakers and educators.

The critiques of the 1970s gave rise to a literature that began to look at *who* went to school—and at the differential opportunities, experiences, and outcomes of women, ethnic and racial minorities, and social strata. Such research often did not dwell on comparison of nations; instead, it compared women, minorities, and various social strata's experience with schooling.

A concern with remaining social inequalities and a realization that educational "inputs" at the micro level did not necessarily lead to the solution of educational problems or to socioeconomic development led researchers to look more deeply at precisely what schools taught and how the quality and content of education affected its use by different categories of students. Research has turned in the 1980s to tracing the processes of education to a wide array of educational, personal, and social outcomes, and innovative research strategies have begun to enter the field as such research progresses.

A research direction that was pioneered in the late 1960s, but remained for some time the domain of psychometricians, has been the study of educational achievement. The research done by the International Association for the Study of Educational Achievement (IEA) has been influential in making the field of comparative education orient research toward an understanding of the educational outcomes of schooling, an area that the field had generally neglected up to that time in favor of focusing on social and economic outcomes. As more scholarship has appeared on the achievement outcomes of education, the field has begun to ask about the effect of culture, politics, and social structure on the ways in which students perform in schools. Additionally, it has stimulated a series of lively debates between psychometricians and comparativists on the meaning of cross-national comparisons of educational achievement data.

Specific crises have traditionally stimulated research on particular subjects in the field. In the 1960s, the worldwide wave of student political activism stimulated research on student politics. Today, given the world food crisis and the economic recession that has affected many countries in the world, the field has increasingly become concerned with issues of educational efficiency.[12] Scholars recently have begun to ask how greater

---

[12] See Philip H. Coombs, *The World Crisis in Education: The View from the Eighties* (New York: Oxford University Press, 1985).

quality of education can be achieved without greater increases in expenditure. They have also begun to question the wisdom of educational expansion and the trend toward comprehensive, common schooling for all, which had preoccupied much research in the 1960s and 1970s. Some have begun to look at alternative modes of educational finance and delivery of educational services.

While a large part of the field has turned to new ways of looking at schooling and its relation to the world outside the school, another new current in the field has been self-reflective and has asked how scholarship in the field has evolved and the relation to the questions scholars ask to how research is funded and sponsored. In addition, they have asked how the priorities of funding agencies—be they public or private, bilateral or multilateral—affect what questions comparativists ask and how their research is used. Much of this scholarship has been critical of funding agencies and aid policies; for the most part, such scholarship has raised a series of controversies in the field about the nature of comparative education.

We have discussed some of the new research trends to emerge over the past years; elsewhere in this volume we will discuss in greater detail the challenges that we believe face the field in the 1980s. Without question, we believe that the emergence of these new trends represents vitality in the field and a self-conscious attempt to make the field relevant to a vast and diverse constituency. The field in the 1980s has matured and has begun to arrive at a deeper understanding of the complexity of drawing relations between the meaning of education in today's world.

Conclusion

This volume, which focuses on recent developments in comparative education, must be seen in the broader context of the development of the field. We have provided an overview of some of what we consider to be important elements in the field. Historical origins and research directions are important elements to consider when analyzing the contemporary status of comparative education.

Comparative education has surmounted many obstacles in its short history as a self-conscious academic specialization in North American colleges and universities. It has at first surmounted the ever-present parochialism of American education: the field has in fact contributed significantly to an international consciousness in the study of education in the United States and Canada. Comparative educators were able to build the institutional structures and develop the expertise necessary to maintain a variety of centers and institutes and to develop appropriate library and other resources. When research and consulting funds were readily available, the field drew on them to further develop a cadre of educators with overseas experience. Academic programs, although working with various advising projects, were not swallowed up by them. Somewhat later, when social science methodology became the generally accepted way of looking at research questions in comparative education, the field did not lose its self-consciousness to the "parent" social sciences and continued to develop as an independent but related academic specialty.

Perhaps the most important challenge came in the 1970s, when external funding all but disappeared in the United States and comparative educators were virtually thrown back on their own resources. The number of American graduate students choosing to specialize in the field dwindled as funding opportunities disappeared and jobs became scarce. But the field managed to maintain its viability in most of the institutions in which it had established itself. To some extent, foreign students replaced Americans in doctoral specializations. Students and faculty became adept in choosing research topics that could be done on a small scale or from relevant documentary sources in the United States. A trickle of money from external sources continued to be available; generally, however, this was earmarked for evaluation or other projects directly related to ongoing assistance or other programs of the major funding agencies such as the World Bank or USAID.

Comparative education in the 1980s is a healthy, intellectually viable field of study. Its problems remain, but it has successfully built the infra-structures necessary to ensure survival. Indeed, on a very small scale, the field has flourished. Its "invisible college" of scholars and students, its journals and book publishers, and its regional and national organizations all testify to an active community of scholars. The thirtieth anniversary of the *Comparative Education Review* is not merely an appropriate chrono-logical occasion to look at the methodological and research directions of the field; it is a watershed and a symbol of the impressive development of comparative education in North America in the past 3 decades.

Overview of This Volume

This book concentrates on current and future trends in comparative education. We have organized the volume to begin with a look forward, followed by a series of reflections on the field by a group of distinguished scholars. We conclude with some methodological considerations. Our final chapter is an overview of current trends and the responses by scholars in the field to these trends. All the chapters have appeared as articles in the *Comparative Education Review*.

The first section, "New Currents and Critiques," includes chapters dealing with recent reflections by comparative educators on a variety of topics related to the development of the field and the interpretation of major educational issues of contemporary importance. From quite different perspectives, John Boli and his colleagues and Mary Jean Bowman look at educational expansion and the spread of schooling worldwide, certainly the key international trend of the past half-century. The underlying fact of educational systems in every country has been rapid expansion. In the Third World, this expansion continues while demographic trends and fiscal problems have slowed growth in most industrialized nations. These two chapters look at broad trends, going beyond analysis at the nation-state level.

Several of the chapters in the first section stress alternative ideological perspectives in the comparative analysis. Martin Carnoy and Michael W. Apple utilize Marxist approaches to the study of educational issues and show that this perspective can provide some important insights into key questions in the field. Both authors question many of the assumptions on which much "mainstream" research is based. Without question, Marxist and other critical perspectives can help to illuminate educational questions. Vandra Lea Masemann argues that comparative educators must go beyond the traditional "macro" research approaches and focus more on in-school and ethnographic methodologies. She shows in her chapter that ethnographic research can be very important in permitting a deeper understanding of some questions. Gary L. Theisen and his colleagues urge us to look critically at important trends in research in comparative education by focusing critical attention on the influential international studies of educational achievement. "New Currents and Critiques" is intended to show how comparative education has broken new ground in recent years and how alternative approaches to research can be used to look both on broad international issues such as questions of school expansion and in depth on in-school questions that can be looked at in comparative perspective. The chapters in this section do not cover all new approaches, nor do they thoroughly critique existing trends in research and analysis. Our intention is not to argue that comparative education requires a revolution in analysis but only to point out that there have been significant, exciting, and useful new developments in the field that are worthy of careful consideration.

In the second major section, "Reflections on the Field," several senior scholars analyze the field from the perspective of long experience of research and analysis. Harold Noah, a former editor of the *Comparative Education Review,* provides a wide-ranging discussion of the use and abuse of the field. Max Eckstein, in an intellectually stimulating discussion of the use of metaphor in comparative education, asks us to consider the use of language and of logic in the way that we think about comparative education. His discussion has relevance for the nature of comparative analysis and goes to the heart of some of the unexamined assumptions of thought in the field. Brian Holmes and Lê Thành Khôi, both senior

European scholars of comparative education, write from quite different perspectives on some key aspects of the field. Each reflects some of the ways of thinking about the field from the perspective, respectively, of British and French scholarship. Joseph Farrell deals with some of the broader issues of comparison and perspective on the conduct of comparative research. Erwin Epstein, discussing "Currents Left and Right," decries what he sees as increasing "ideological influences" in the field and urges comparative educators to try to develop a consensus about both the nature of the field and research perspectives to be used. In this sense, he harks back to an earlier period in the development of the field when it was felt that a common approach was possible. While Epstein's points are valuable in terms of pointing out that there are hotly contested viewpoints, it is clear that, in some cases, ideological as well as methodological concerns are part of this debate.

The final section deals with methodological issues. Its purpose is not to provide a guide to methods in the field, or even to articulate the new methodological approaches that have arisen in recent years, but rather to focus on how methodology impinges on research questions. The purpose of the section is to raise large issues of the use of methods, and the three chapters we have included each deal with this broad concern. Reijo Raivola deals with some of the basic philosophical assumptions of the nature of comparison. Frederick M. Wirt and Richard H. Pfau are concerned with the methodological implications of particular research areas in comparative education—educational policy analysis and classroom behaviors, respectively. This section provides some important insights into the nature and uses of methodology in general and as applied to specific research issues in the field.

Comparative education is a field with considerable intellectual vigor. This volume reflects much of that vigor, at least as reflected by North American scholarship. We have not tried to develop a consensus or a new perspective or direction because we feel that the field is much too complex and diverse. This volume celebrates diversity, a range of perspectives, and the variety of new directions that have emerged in the past decade. No doubt the agenda reflected in a volume like this written at the end of this century—only 14 years away—will focus on quite different concerns. Well it should. This is the sign of a field that is alive and relevant.

Critical Ethnography in the Study of Comparative Education

VANDRA LEA MASEMANN

In this essay I consider recent perspectives in educational research and in particular the use of critical ethnography in the study of comparative education. Since the term is relatively new, some introduction will first be given to other approaches, their origins, and their relationship to critical approaches in the field. The parameters of several approaches and their implications for the study of comparative education will be discussed, and suggestions will be made throughout for research applications of these approaches in comparative education.

"Critical ethnography" refers to studies which use a basically anthropological, qualitative, participant-observer methodology but which rely for their theoretical formulation on a body of theory deriving from critical sociology and philosophy.[1] The theoretical forebears in this area date back to Marx, with his critique of bourgeois theories of society, and the positivist sociology of Comte.[2] The fundamental criticism of positivist social science embodied in Marx's approach was that the distinction between the objective and subjective could not bring together the "is" and the "ought" in a way that made possible the construction of a theory of ethics and politics.[3] These questions come down to us today in modern guise when we consider problems in educational research, but their basic core remains the same: Is it the task of social scientists to seek ever more diligently to define objective methods of researching the social world (or education), with possibilities for change seen as simply the result of "reading out the data" and making choices on the basis of some cost-efficient or technological rationale? Or is it their task to attempt to understand as accurately as possible the subjective understandings that actors have of their own version of "social reality"? Or, third, is there some way of seeing social science in Marx's terms that would forever blur the objective/subjective distinction and thus make necessary the redefinition of social research itself? These questions lie at the heart of any discussion of research methodology

---

[1] See Michael Apple, *Ideology and Curriculum* (London: Routledge & Kegan Paul, 1979), for an orientation to this approach.

[2] "I shall use the term 'positivism' . . . to characterise an approach to the social sciences which regards them as being the same as the natural sciences, aiming at the formulation of general causal laws, resting their claims to valid knowledge upon the analysis of some empirical reality, not upon philosophical intuition, and thus asserting the unity of scientific method, and which makes a sharp distinction between scientific statements and value judgements" (Thomas Bottomore, *Marxist Sociology* [London: Macmillan, 1975], p. 9, n).

[3] Ibid., p. 10.

Reprinted from *Comparative Education Review,* vol. 26, no. 1 (February 1982).

in social science in general as well as in the study of comparative education with which we are concerned here. The history of the development of educational research demonstrates the interplay of thought on these three questions.

Sociological Approaches

A very useful summary of sociological approaches to educational research is given by Karabel and Halsey.[4] They document the rise of functionalist approaches in sociology which attempted to legitimize the study of education as a scientific endeavor. However, the definition of functionalism itself does not necessarily carry with it the notion of objectivity with regard to mode of research. Radcliffe-Brown's original definition of "function" makes no mention of it: "The concept of functions as here defined thus involves the notion of a *structure* consisting of a *set of relations* amongst *unit entities*, the *continuity* of the structure being maintained by a *life-process* made up of the *activities* of the constituent units."[5] Nonetheless, the analogy of the social functioning of society with the biological functioning of the human body makes it clear that Radcliffe-Brown was using positivist conceptions of social science.

Such conceptions of society and its institutions, such as education or the family, were increasingly common throughout the 80 years of this century and gained far more currency in social science than did Marx's attempt to see a social science as ultimately ethical. Several reasons for the nondiffusion of Marx's ideas have been advanced. Mafeje, an African anthropologist, suggests, for example, that positivist functionalist ideas were the ultimate bourgeois conceptions of society which kept the proletariat from realizing their condition. He suggests that, in America particularly, the legacy of nineteenth- and twentieth-century French and British positivist philosophy was accentuated by the historical relativism of Max Weber in his separation of normative judgments from factual statements, a separation which "made it possible for him and his future American followers to think of science as autonomous and morally neutral."[6] Moreover, he also attributes to Weber the relativizing and abstracting of ideology "in such a way that it ceased to be a question of class conflict and became merely a problem of interpreting individual intellectual reflexes under determinate social conditions."[7] The legacy of such an approach is clearly seen in the development of American "scientific" sociology and psychol-

[4] Jerome Karabel and A. H. Halsey, *Power and Ideology in Education* (New York: Oxford University Press, 1977).
[5] A. R. Radcliffe-Brown, *Structure and Function in Primitive Society* (London: Cohen & West, 1964), p.180.
[6] Archie Mafeje, "The Problem of Anthropology in Historical Perspective: An Inquiry into the Growth of the Social Sciences, *Canadian Journal of African Studies* 10 (1976): 313.
[7] Ibid.

ogy and their influence on the direction of educational research with its strong emphasis on the individual as the unit of analysis and on the collection of objective data on a large scale.

Thomas Bottomore, a sociologist, concurs that such objective approaches may well have been buttressed by their place in the reproduction of bourgeois culture, but he also suggests that there is much evidence of "the obstacles that have been put in the way of Marxist social science in the universities of many Western countries."[8] Moreover, he views the creation of the Marxist political orthodoxy in the USSR as a deterrent to the development of Marxist conceptions of social science there and elsewhere.

Comparative education as a field of research has largely reflected these currents of thought. Early research in the field focused on typologies of national educational systems and paralleled attempts in anthropology and sociology to define societies by their "type."[9] As interest developed in empirical research, attention shifted to large-scale survey-type comparisons of educational outcomes or effects.[10] Karabel and Halsey discuss the development of the "human-capital" approach to education, with its emphasis on the post-1945 expansion and diffusion of educational systems, and the concomitant development of the human capital (skills and knowledge) of the person becoming educated.[11] This approach turns away from interest in typologies of educational systems, or even schools as such, to the individuals as products of a system. The recent "equality" research in the United States reflects such concerns, although recent writers have tended to stress the importance of school processes which are left unresearched in such studies.[12]

Anthropological Approaches

During these same 80 years, there was a parallel development in the history of ethnographic (anthropological) approaches to the study of society. The major shift from the typologies of anthropologists such as Tylor or Fraser[13] occurred with the rise of functionalist anthropology in the early years of this century.[14] However, whereas sociology became a science which examines large-scale societies and developed research strategies which could manage large amounts of data, anthropology tended to remain rooted in small-scale participant-observation modes of research. The theo-

[8] Bottomore, p. 30.

[9] Edward B. Tylor, *Primitive Culture* (London: Murray, 1871).

[10] E.g., the International Association for the Evaluation of Educational Achievement studies (see *Comparative Education Review*, vol. 18 [June 1974]).

[11] Karabel and Halsey, pp. 12–16.

[12] Christopher Jencks et al., *Inequality: A Reassessment of the Effect of Family and Schooling in America* (New York: Basic, 1972).

[13] James Frazer, *The Golden Bough* (New York: Macmillan, 1928).

[14] Radcliffe-Brown; Bronislaw Malinowski, "The Group and the Individual in Functional Analysis," *American Journal of Sociology* 44 (1939): 938–64.

retical underpinnings of anthropology remained firmly functionalist. If the perspectives of sociology were linked to the ruling classes in the mother society, Mafeje linked them to the colonizing activities of Europeans.[15]

Until the last decade or so the use of traditional anthropological methods in educational research has been sporadic. More complete summaries of the relationship of anthropological studies to comparative education already exist.[16] Suffice it to say here that the interest of early anthropologists was in the socialization of children as part of the ongoing functioning of a small-scale society.[17] The influence of Freud led later to the development of an interest in how culture influenced personality.[18] With the post-1945 establishment of schools in newly independent areas, interest turned to the role of schools as agents of modernization and value change. A few ethnographic studies were published of schools in (formerly) British-controlled areas.[19] In America, George Spindler and his students produced the most voluminous literature on educational ethnography in the 1960s and 1970s.[20] Some attempts at theory formulation have been advanced more recently,[21] although generally in a functionalist framework, with an emphasis on transaction. A Marxist anthropology of education is far less advanced than Marxist sociology of education, while both exist in a predominantly functionalist environment.[22] The most frequent use made of ethnographic research in the 1970s was in evaluation research, where it was an adjunct to sociological and psychological data gathering concerning school or program effects.[23] Very little has been done to develop a "critical ethnography" which could transcend the limitations of a functionalist social science. I shall return to this discussion later.

Before I leave this discussion of ethnographic approaches, they should be discussed in terms of the subjective/objective dichotomy. Within the framework of functionalist anthropology, considerable effort has been ex-

[15] Mafeje, pp. 317-22.
[16] Vandra Masemann, "Anthropological Approaches to Comparative Education," *Comparative Education Review* 20 (1976): 368-80; Douglas Foley, "Anthropological Studies of Schooling in Developing Countries: Some Recent Findings and Trends," *Comparative Education Review* 21 (1977): 311-28.
[17] Margaret Read, *Children of Their Fathers: Growing Up among the Ngoni of Nyasaland* (New Haven, Conn.: Yale University Press, 1960); John Middleton, *From Child to Adult* (New York: Natural History Press, 1971); Margaret Mead, *Coming of Age in Samoa* (New York: Morrow, 1928).
[18] Clyde Kluckhohn, Henry Murray, and David Schneider, *Personality in Nature, Society, and Culture* (New York: Knopf, 1964).
[19] G. Waton, *Passing for White* (London: Tavistock, 1970); F. Musgrove, "A Uganda Secondary School as a Field of Social Change," *Africa* 22 (1952): 234-48.
[20] George Spindler, *Education and Cultural Process* (New York: Holt, Rinehart & Winston, 1974). For a review of the socialization literature, see Patricia Draper, "Comparative Studies of Socialization," *Annual Review of Anthropology* (Palo Alto, Calif.: Annual Reviews, 1974), pp. 263-77.
[21] Frederick O. Gearing and B. Allan Tindall, "Anthropological Studies of the Educational Process," *Annual Review of Anthropology* (Palo Alto, Calif.: Annual Reviews, 1973); also recent issues of *Anthropology and Education Quarterly*.
[22] Apple.
[23] See any collection of work on evaluation of U.S. bilingual education programs; e.g., F. Cordasco, *Bilingual Schooling in the United States* (New York: McGraw-Hill, 1976).

pended by anthropologists to define "whose" definition of reality they are discussing.[24] It has been considered debatable whether researchers should be searching for an objectively analyzable set of phenomena or whether they should seek to discover the models of, for example, kinship in the informants' minds. Generally, however, even such "subjective" accounts from an informant have been considered as "objective" data for the anthropologist. It becomes a very interesting point to ponder the extent to which the anthropologist can acquire an inside understanding of the subjective reality of the informant, even if he/she is adept at "personally replicating appropriate language and behaviour in another culture."[25] Such problems in research lead directly to a discussion of the more subjective philosophical and symbolic interactionist approaches.

Interpretative Approaches

The several approaches under this rubric have been variously called symbolic interactionist, phenomenological, ethnomethodological, and the "new" sociology of education. Their fundamental assumption is that it is inadequate to study either the formal structure of social institutions (educational systems) or to survey the effects of such institutions in terms predefined by the researcher. Rather, the task is to uncover the workings of, for example, educational systems in terms of their meanings for the participants, either as teachers or learners. This approach derives from a sociology of knowledge perspective which exemplified itself in a predominantly phenomenological approach in Europe and an ethnomethodological approach in America.[26] The phenomenological approach ultimately defines as the researchable question the meaning of events and processes. The ethnomethodologist is primarily interested in demonstrating "the fragility of tacit understandings underlying daily social interactions" as these are negotiated by people in their daily lives.[27]

Richard Heyman has written recently on the utility of such approaches in comparative education.[28] He strongly criticizes the taken-for-grantedness of many of the concepts used previously in comparative educational research (e.g., political socialization, economic development, and elite formation). He argues that "the macroanalysis characterizing most of comparative education research must be replaced by the systematic obser-

---

[24] Michael Banton, ed., *The Relevance of Models for Social Anthropology* (London: Tavistock, 1964).

[25] Foley, p. 313.

[26] Karl Mannheim, *Essays on the Sociology of Knowledge* (London: Routledge & Kegan Paul, 1952); Thomas S. Kuhn, *The Structure of Scientific Revolutions* (Chicago: University of Chicago Press, 1970).

[27] Karabel and Halsey, p. 49.

[28] Richard Heyman, "Comparative Education from an Ethnomethodological Perspective," *Comparative Education* 15 (1979): 241–49.

vation and analysis of the microcosmic world of everyday life."[29] He criticizes the supposed objectivity of various categories of measurement used in macrocosmic research and the use of large-scale questionnaire surveys, since they are conceived and carried out without reference to people's subjective interpretation of them. His suggestions as to future directions for comparative education are that it should "(1) . . . focus its attention on the problem of describing how the social reality called education exists in the lived world (2) . . . study those aspects of social reality which are directly *observable* and therefore *recordable* . . . (3) concentrate on the detailed analysis of social interaction as the most obvious source of the social reality of education."[30] Moreover, he advocates that it be microscopic in its analyses, and be based on the interpretation of audio- and/or video-taped interaction.

The ethnomethodological approach can thus be distinguished by its efforts to be rigorous in the microanalysis of small segments of interaction, whereas phenomenology comprehends a far larger philosophical orientation toward understanding the subjective interpretation of events.

Related to such approaches are developments in other interpretative approaches in Britain and, more recently, North America. The work of Michael Young and Basil Bernstein laid the foundations for an interpretation of school life and the use of language which lent a more complex (and largely unresearched) theoretical framework to educational research.[31] Bernstein's work exists somewhere between the "given" categories of so-called objective social science and the essentially fluid and subjective interpretations of the phenomenologists. Young's contribution in particular was to question the "givenness" of categories of school organization such as curriculum or discipline and to relate them to the interests of those who controlled the structure of school organization (a somewhat Weberian notion). Bernstein's contribution was to attempt to delineate the ways in which language was used, taught, and learned (or resisted) by those within that educational and social framework. Bernstein's early analyses were somewhat static, his later work provides an adequate framework for seeing language as controlled by particular class interests.

Young's and Bernstein's work was accompanied by the rise of an interpretative approach used by several researchers.[32] Many studies have been published which document the "problematic" definition of the reality of

[29] Ibid., p. 245.

[30] Ibid., p. 248.

[31] Michael Young, *Knowledge and Control* (London: Collier Macmillan, 1971); Basil Bernstein, *Class, Codes and Control*, vol. 1, *Theoretical Studies towards a Sociology of Language* (London: Routledge & Kegan Paul, 1971), vol.2, *Applied Studies towards a Sociology of Language* (London: Routledge & Kegan Paul, 1973), and vol.3, *Towards a Theory of Educational Transmissions* (London: Routledge & Kegan Paul, 1977).

[32] Michael Flude and John Ahier, *Educability, Schools, and Ideology* (New York: Wiley, 1974); Peter Woods and Martyn Hammersley, *School Experience: Explorations in the Sociology of Education* (New York: St. Martin's, 1977).

schooling and particularly curriculum. These interpretative studies share with the ethnomethodologists the emphasis on the subjective interpretation of events by the actors and the necessity to interpret the meaning of sequences of interaction.

These scholars, who are beginning to have an impact on thinking in North America, all emerged from the British research tradition.[33] Their views on primary education were influenced by the long history of progressivism in English education, and particularly in that period by the abolition of the 11+ examination for secondary school entrance.[34] Thus, they were particularly receptive to ideas of spontaneity, flexibility, and openness in curriculum and definitions of curriculum as "negotiable" or "created" by teacher-student interaction. Whitty has termed this mode of thinking "possibilitarian," in that researchers and teachers-in-training alike thought that the "new" sociology could open up new possibilities for improving classroom life and education in general.[35]

The values and limitations of the "new" sociology for comparative education are difficult to discern and complex in their nature. The drawbacks of doing classroom research with little reference to the surrounding social structure are again evident as with other phenomenological approaches. However, it seems even more difficult to consider curriculum or school organization as problematic in countries with (a) either strong centralized political control as in France, or (b) a history of dependence on and veneration of colonial education, or (c) a strong religious orientation to education. I would argue that the new sociology in England was itself a historically and socially specific development. It arose in a country with a strongly decentralized educational system in which teachers had a strong autonomous professional association (the National Union of Teachers) and a great deal of control over curricular innovation, and in which the elite private educational sector was performing the task of cultural reproduction for the elite.[36] In comparative studies, one would need to examine the cultural context of studies of classroom interaction and language use. In countries in which formal education is a scarce and valued good, it seems unlikely that a high degree of flexibility would exist in classroom organization. In ex-colonial countries (which often have ties to the metropole), where schools are derived from foreign models and where the syllabus has strong external roots, a spontaneous approach to the curriculum is unlikely. Moreover, where high school entrance is controlled through a

[33] Margaret Archer, *Social Origins of Educational Systems* (London and Beverly Hills, Calif.: Sage, 1979), pp. 567–68.

[34] Richard J. W. Selleck, *English Primary Education and the Progressives 1914–1939* (London: Routledge & Kegan Paul, 1972).

[35] Geoff Whitty, "Schools and the Problem of Radical Educational Change," in Flude and Ahier, pp. 112–37.

[36] Archer, chap. 8.

bottleneck by nationally administered examinations, the primary school pupils' parents are unlikely to want them to "learn at their own pace." Last, the blurring of the work/play distinction in philosophies of progressive education would clearly find an unsympathetic audience in parents who perceive a highly structured formal education as the key to their children's future. Thus a comparative study of teacher education in many countries would probably not uncover the same extent of "possibilitarian" thinking as in the English setting.

This raises another topic of concern for comparative education: the implicit evolutionary thinking about pedagogy in which teaching is conceived as progressing from "rote" to "structured" to "open." The view is supported by the educational literature on innovation and diffusion in which more modern or sophisticated methods are seen as diffusing to Third World countries or to more "rigid" systems.[37] An interpretative analysis of the adoption of various kinds of educational innovation would yield extemely interesting data (for example, in attempts to teach the New Math in West Africa).[38] However, it is important to understand to what extent such interpretative analysis, itself the product of a particular social and political climate, would serve to mask the social context of educational innovation in economically dependent, neocolonial, highly structured educational systems.

To end this section on interpretative approaches, one can consider a few issues in comparative education and how they might be illuminated by such approaches. Far too often the trivia of everyday school life are put into the "taken-for-granted" categories of questionnaires or checkoff observation sheets. These interpretative approaches could be used to advantage to dissect the taken-for-grantedness of such terms as social stratification, achievement, curriculum, pedagogy, school discipline, innovation, teacher training, and now such newer terms as competency-based evaluation, behavioral objectives, therapeutic intervention, change agent, and so on. Some useful comparative interpretative studies could be done on receptivity to new curriculum units, to students' perceptions of the scholastic achievement hierarchy, or of the education/employment relationship. However, from a noninterpretative standpoint all such studies are inherently limited by their lack of generalizability, their lack of connection to a wider theoretical framework, and their essentially (suppressed) functionalist analysis of social relations. While they give insights into the workings of an educational reality, the sum of all such realities does not add up to a study of comparative education which would satisfy those interested in a more general theory of school/society relationships.

[37] Douglas Foley, "Colonialism and Schooling in the Philippines from 1898 to 1970," in P. Altbach and G. Kelly, eds., *Education and Colonialism* (New York: Longman, 1978).

[38] John Gay and Michael Cole, *The New Mathematics and an Old Culture* (New York: Holt, Rinehart & Winston, 1967).

Critical Approaches

Critical approaches are distinguished from interpretative approaches primarily by their connection to theoretical perspectives which are linked to a general theory of society and a concept of social structure which exists beyond the actor's perception of it. Conflict sociology can be seen as a first step away from functionalist approaches, while recent structuralist and neo-Marxist approaches are somewhat further removed, or are indeed antithetical. Critical approaches emphasize class conflict, the dissimilar interests of various classes, and their differing relationship to (and benefits from) the workings of the educational system.

Conflict approaches in sociology generally parade under the guise of an inverted functionalism. In the writings of Weber and Durkheim, the emphasis was still on social integration rather than on basic contradictions or a social dialectic. The legacy of such thinking in conflict approaches in the sociology of education has been a search for trivial arenas of conflict (e.g., teacher-student interaction as in Lacey's or Hargreaves's studies), and the ignoring of massive contradictions in the relationship between schools and student culture.[39] Bowles and Gintis, who claim to be not only conflict theorists but neo-Marxists, carry this sort of analysis somewhat further.[40] They use statistical analysis in an attempt to demonstrate that social class structure is reproduced by schools which prepare various classes of children for their roles in the workplace by reinforcing class-based personality traits. Not enough critical analysis has been done of their study, except for attempts by Michael Apple to analyze the categories of personality traits that actually exist in the workplace.[41] Other analyses, such as Olneck and Bills's, use essentially similar statistical techniques to demonstrate the accuracy (or lack thereof) of Bowles and Gintis's analysis.[42]

Probably of greater utility than the emphasis on personality traits is Bowles and Gintis's "theory of correspondence," that the social relations of production are mirrored in the social relations of education. Even in complex industrialized societies, with reasonably indigenous educational systems, a one-to-one correspondence between the functions and practices of the schools and their relationship to the economic system and to social class relationships often does not exist. From a comparativist's point of view, it is an even more complex issue to examine the school's role in class/status legitimation in former colonial countries with nonuniversal education and competing indigenous status systems. Few studies have ex-

[39] Colin Lacey, *Hightown Grammar* (Manchester: Manchester University Press, 1970); David H. Hargreaves, *Social Relations in a Secondary School* (London: Routledge & Kegan Paul, 1967).
[40] Samuel Bowles and Herbert Gintis, *Schooling in Capitalist America* (New York: Basic, 1976).
[41] Michael Apple, "The Other Side of the Hidden Curriculum: Correspondence Theories and the Labour Process," *Journal of Education* 162, no.1 (Winter 1980): 47–66.
[42] Michael R. Olneck and David B. Bills, "What Makes Sammy Run?: An Empirical Assessment of the Bowles-Gintis Correspondence Theory" (Discussion Paper no. 574-79, Institute for Research on Poverty, Madison, Wis., 1979).

amined "resistance" to Western education except as some kind of example of "failed" foreign aid, and there is only one that I can cite that examines the contradictions that students experience in certain aspects of the curriculum or school organization.[43] The greater task posed in Bowles and Gintis's work, however, would be to examine correspondence in countries where the social relations of industrial production are basically foreign owned. One place to start on this task is, for example, Canada. The 1976 OECD report on Canadian education clearly documents its lack of national purpose and its continuing reliance on American pedagogical models.[44] Another area of investigation that would tie in to Bowles and Gintis's work is the study of higher education in Third World countries and its reliance on the "social relations of higher education" of the metropole. Such work has been and is being done by Philip Altbach and Robert Arnove, and several of these issues are briefly taken up in the volume on colonial education edited by Altbach and Kelly.[45] However, they need to be set in a theoretical framework in which colonialism is examined not *sui generis,* but as part of a larger theory of social relations.

A work of far more structuralist derivation is that of Pierre Bourdieu in France, but its implications for comparative education may be similar to those of Bowles and Gintis.[46] Bourdieu postulates that the educational system reproduces in stratified form the cultural capital (in the form of ideas, rather than physical capital) of the dominant class. He shows how children come to acquire the correct framework of thinking about the material they are learning.[47] In a way similar to the British "new" sociology of education, however, the very rigid French structuralist approach could be viewed as itself a cultural product compatible with the highly centralized French educational system. Thus to apply such an analysis comparatively, one would have to fit it to a similar type of system. It would probably be useful to have such an analysis, for example, of the Russian educational system, with particular reference to ethnic minorities and cultural reproduction. Another interesting comparative analysis would be of cultural reproduction in former French colonies. In this way the data from Clignet and Foster's "Fortunate Few" in the Ivory Coast could be seen in

[43] Philip Wexler, "Educational Change and Social Contradiction: An Example," *Comparative Education Review* 23 (1979): 240-55.

[44] Organization for Economic Co-operation and Development, *Reviews of National Policies for Education: Canada* (Paris: OECD, 1976).

[45] Philip Altbach and Gail Kelly, eds., *Education and Colonialism* (New York: Longman, 1978); Robert Arnove, "Comparative Education and World-Systems Analysis," *Comparative Education Review* 24 (1980): 48-62.

[46] Pierre Bourdieu and Jean-Claude Passeron, *Reproduction in Education, Society, and Culture* (London: Sage, 1977).

[47] Pierre Bourdieu, "Systems of Education and Systems of Thought," in Roger Dale, ed., *Schooling and Capitalism* (London: Routledge & Kegan Paul, with the Open University Press, 1976), pp. 192-200.

an entirely new light.[48] The role of higher education in Third World countries could also be usefully viewed from such a perspective, which would greatly enhance the "elite formation" or "student aspirations" literature.

One note of caution concerning structuralist approaches. An overemphasis on the formal properties of educational systems can lead back to the classic definition of comparative education as the comparison of national systems of education and their structures. It seems important not to forget that formal systems do not necessarily operate in a flawless manner to dispense cultural capital in prescribed doses, nor do they need to in order to fulfill their function. Archer, for example, documents how regional, class, and ethnic interests are so poorly served in centralized educational systems, and yet this is not apparently undermining the legitimacy of the education endeavor itself.[49]

Neo-Marxist approaches, unlike structuralist approaches, are far removed from postulating a simple correspondence between the formal properties of systems and their ideal workings. As Young's and Bernstein's work presaged, neo-Marxist interpretations of school life have questioned the established categories of education and have raised fundamental questions about the social control functions of schools and the social contradictions they create or participate in. Sharp and Green's study of progressive primary education in an English school uses a Marxist framework in which to insert an ethnographic account of teachers' use of the rhetoric of progressivism to control working-class students.[50] However, their analysis, while referring briefly to the social class composition of the surrounding community, does not go much beyond the classroom.

Paul Willis's account of the school experiences of a group of working-class "lads" in the English Midlands goes further toward tying together the world of control in school and in the workplace.[51] He postulates that working-class resistance to middle-class control, which legitimates the lads' identity in their own eyes, seals their destiny as manual workers in the capitalist system. Willis seeks to explore the social relations which exist beyond the lads' perceptions of them. As he expresses it: "This most central point of reference is an absent or at least silent centre beneath the splendid bedizenment of a culture. It is impossible to prove its rationality. . . . That is why the ethnography of visible forms is limited."[52]

[48] Remi Clignet and Philip Foster, *The Fortunate Few* (Evanston, Ill.: Northwestern University Press, 1966).

[49] See n. 33 above.

[50] Rachel Sharp and Anthony Green, *Education and Social Control* (London: Routledge & Kegan Paul, 1975).

[51] Paul Willis, *Learning to Labour: How Working Class Kids Get Working Class Jobs* (Westmead: Saxon House, 1977).

[52] Ibid., p. 121.

Michael Apple has taken Willis's analysis further in his examination of resistance among workers and among teachers themselves.[53] He argues that the increasing professionalism of teachers' jobs removes increasingly more of the task-related decisions from their immediate ken, as in the use of prepackaged curriculum materials with the directions outlined in the minutest detail. This process is analogous to that in the factory, where workers are being deskilled by highly sophisticated machinery which removes their decision-making capacity for even the simplest tasks. Apple refers also to the deskilling of women workers in computerized "word processing centres" (formerly known as typing pools). In addition, the deskilling of parenthood has occurred as more reliance was placed on outside experts and child-rearing manuals and that of housework with the invention by men of labor-saving devices for women.[54]

To place this analysis in comparative perspective, it is not difficult to view the diffusion of Western education intenationally as part of a massive deskilling process of Third World populations in terms of indigenous systems of language, symbols, art, folklore, music, and knowledge itself. Moreover, indigenous systems of technology and "science" have been particularly undermined, so much so that anthropologists have debated for some years as to whether indigenous "science" ever existed.[55] The underlying ethos of "development education" itself was the assumption that economic systems and thus, automatically, knowledge systems, were undeveloped. The protests of those who resist the label of "undeveloped" are largely squelched or muted in the colonial experience. If one views the persistence of Koranic schooling as a form of cultural resistance, one has only to look at Western distrust of the Moslem world to understand how threatening is the refusal of many to be called "undeveloped."

Thus the comparative study of the worldwide trend toward educational entropy, formerly thought to be "enlightenment," would be an interesting one. The progressive deskilling of teachers and students alike in computer-assisted, packaged, individualized learning systems in North American schools and the diffusion of such techniques to countries effectively controlled economically from outside present a rich field for research.

Critical Ethnography

The final topic for discussion in this essay is the specific utility to the study of comparative education of critical ethnography. What particular aspects of ethnography and critical perspectives are embodied in such an approach?

[53] Michael Apple, "Curricular Form and the Logic of Technical Control: Building the Possessive Individual," mimeographed (Madison: University of Wisconsin, 1979).
[54] Christopher Lasch, *The Culture of Narcissism* (New York: Warner, 1979).
[55] Claude Lévi-Strauss, *The Savage Mind* (Chicago: University of Chicago Press, 1966).

From ethnography, the main emphases are on participant-observation of the small scale as a method, with an attempt to understand the culture and symbolic life of the actors involved. Willis points out that "participant-observation, and the methods under its aegis, display a tendency towards naturalism and therefore to conservatism. . . . Still we cannot invent a form out of its time. . . . The ethnographic account, for all its faults, records a critical level of experience and through its very biases insists on a level of human agency which is persistently overlooked or denied. . . ."[56] Willis places such a study firmly within a wider theoretical framework of cultural forms and reproduction in which the researcher can make statements about the researched that they themselves would never say: "Capitalist freedoms are potentially real freedoms, and capitalism takes the wager, which is the essence of reproduction, that the freedoms will be used for self-damnation. The dominant class could never batten down the hatch on these freedoms without help from below."[57]

Thus Willis uses a language and concepts derived from perspectives that are not ultimately the actors', even though the method he uses to gather their perceptions is very similar to that used by the phenomenologists or the symbolic interactionists. In the study of comparative education, it should also be possible to use such a method to investigate the lived life in schools while not necessarily limiting the analysis to the actors' perceptions of their situation. Arnove's work on world systems analysis demonstrates the interlinkage of life chances for students in all countries, depending on their particular position in the hegemonic structure, as recipients of educational "aid" or as potential elites.[58] It should be possible to ground theoretical perspectives on such problems in ethnographic studies of educational innovation (or conservatism). Detailed studies of curricular diffusion from the metropole and cultural reproduction in the recipient countries could be carried out. Studies of the diffusion of educational television might be even more important.

Diffusion studies of "information" have, however, generally been done on the assumption that the intent of the information senders was to enlighten, or at least to convince, the recipients. Foley's recent work on critical ethnography based on Habermas's work on miscommunication questions this assumption. The concepts which he sees most useful in investigating by critical ethnography are those of labor in the schools, student alienation, reification and fetishization of ideas, and commodification of many aspects of educational life such as curriculum "packages," educational credentials, subject credits, and ultimately the educational life

[56] Willis, p. 194.
[57] Ibid., p. 175.
[58] See n. 45 above.

itself. Foley sees the need to uncover the basic contradictions in the aspects of school existence and in the school/work dichotomy.

Foley's suggestions for a "description of alienated communication in a school" are the study of the conditions of production and nature of work in schools and of the concomitant social relations of production. These relations give rise to certain patterns of socialization and (mis) communication which occur in classrooms. Teachers and students "manipulate and transform managerial norms of production and techniques of control" by various tactics, such as work avoidance, trivialization by cheating, distancing work by "cool demeanor," playing with work, escaping work by absenteeism or ritual disruptions, literalizing work by "mindless anality," or rebelling against work.[59]

In such a setting, students learn "the set of dispositions and communicative incompetencies needed to legitimate post-industrial capitalism."[60] Under the label of "technological rationality," teachers and students learn to transform questions of ethics into questions of technique, and schooling becomes an attempt to carve up knowledge into manageable curriculum pieces. Knowledge becomes conceived as "(1) form with little immediate substance or use value and (2) a commodity with considerable exchange value through the organization's credit and credentialling system."[61] Such knowledge also becomes theoretical and disassociated from praxis; indeed praxis itself becomes irrelevant, as knowledge and credentials are hoarded for future "use."

Foley notes that the only way of studying the techniques that schools and teachers use to organize, model, practice, and reward the behaviors that socialize students into the technological rationality is in critical ethnography.[62]

The implications of such an approach in comparative education are profound. It would be possible to study village schools in any country in terms of socialization into preferred language dialects or national language, for example. At the secondary school level, various forms of socialization into the national political culture could be examined. At the university level, socialization of elites and concomitant value orientations could be studied. In general, all forms of penetration of dominant ideology or imported innovative "rationality" could be studied in a comparative sense. Systems of student credentialling, the socialization of Third World graduate students in the universities of the metropole, and the penetration of computer technologies into high school classrooms are all topics that

[59] Douglas Foley, "Labour and Legitimation in Schools: Notes on Doing Ethnography " (revised version of paper presented at the Comparative and International Education Society meeting, Ann Arbor, Mich., 1979), mimeographed (University of Texas at Austin, Department of Anthropology, 1980), p.31.
[60] Ibid., p. 34.
[61] Ibid., p. 35.
[62] Ibid., p. 38.

could be studied ethnographiclly and also in macrolevel surveys. Ultimately, the process of educational entropy which consists of the ever more effective spread of certain old and new forms of "rationality" could be a most challenging new field of research in comparative education.

The Underachievement of Cross-national Studies of Achievement

GARY L. THEISEN, PAUL P. W. ACHOLA, AND FRANCIS MUSA BOAKARI

Comparative studies of the determinants or correlates of academic achievement, including those carried out by the International Project for the Evaluation of Educational Achievement (IEA), have perhaps, without intending it, encouraged what Inkeles has referred to as engaging in "olympic gamesmanship" with national achievement results. National aggregations of data that focus on explaining state profiles of academic achievement often fall short of accounting for within-country factors that may affect standard measures of scholastic performance. Yet these are precisely the variables with the most policy relevance for enhancing student learning.

A great deal of painstaking attention has been given by measurement and curriculum specialists and statisticians to problems of test reliability and validity. The same is true for issues surrounding the standardized testing of students who are exposed to nonstandardized curricula. However, despite these laudable and ground-breaking efforts, structural and cultural determinants of within-country variances in achievement have eluded the careful attention of most of these same large-scale investigations.

Sampling strategies for cross-national studies generally have been designed to reflect aggregate levels of achievement; individual students, not school systems or districts, have been the unit of measurement, and national systems have been the unit of analysis. Under most sampling schemes, one or two schools from a defined geographical or administrative boundary are selected in the first stage of a multistage sampling process. Subsequently, a handful of individual students are chosen randomly from these schools for inclusion in the final sample. As a result of the low number of students drawn from each school and because of randomly distributed variations in ability among the sampled elements, achievement data may only marginally reflect the importance of school and community characteristics on learning.

Furthermore, the statistics resulting from those samples may be highly unstable as a result of the small numbers of cases taken from each school. Frequently, few questions related to the social, demographic, and envi-

We would like to thank C. Arnold Anderson, Steve Arum, Scott McNabb, John Meyer, and two anonymous reviewers for their helpful criticisms and suggestions. Responsibility for the content, however, lies solely with the authors.

Reprinted from *Comparative Education Review*, vol. 27, no. 1 (February 1983).

ronmental characteristics associated with specific learning settings are introduced into analysis. For example, the final pretest version of the questionnaire designed by the U.S. component of the Second International Mathematics Study (SIMS is being administered in a host of countries during 1980–82) contained only one question related to the social environment of the school (Is it rural or urban?). Conspicuously missing are items dealing with school selectivity, general level of district resources, local occupational opportunities, socioeconomic status of local residents, school learning environment, or related indicators of economic/cultural context. The SIMS students are being asked to provide four bits of background information on themselves: age, sex, parental education, and occupational status. This represents a rather limited range of sociopsychological and socioeconomic measures that may have some relationship to academic achievement.

From the outset, we wish to emphasize that the following critique is not intended to draw into question the utilitarian purposes for which most of the cross-national studies were originally designed, among the most important of which are: (1) comparisons of relative achievement status by subject and country; (2) gleaning policy implications in one nation from the determinants of achievement registered in others; and (3) reassessments of in-country expenditure priorities to boost achievement scores. Rather, our concern is focused on the methodological and logical shortcomings attendant to the design and analysis components of such studies and on examining the range of applications to which these findings can be applied usefully. We have already alluded to the temptation for policymakers to measure the effectiveness of their educational plans, the quality of their schooling, and even the efficacy of their sociopolitical system by the yardstick of national achievement scores. An even more irresistible allure is prescribing local panaceas on the basis of national level diagnoses.

Formulating policy from indicators of achievement that emerge from national settings that are different from one's own is problematic at best because of the danger of predicting the impact of causal variables outside of their cultural context. Frequently forgotten by analysts is that differences in the variable configuration or combinations subject to analysis may in themselves produce variability in the explanatory power of the individual determinants under question; cross-national regression models designed to explain variance in achievement are difficult to standardize in terms of both variable inclusion and measurement. Because of the sampling restrictions forced on cross-societal studies in the quest for national representativeness, regional and more localized achievement measures are difficult to ascertain, yet it is at this level that educational policies, if they are to be effective, must be designed and implemented.

In this paper, we review key determinants of achievement in formal schooling, some of which have been glossed over, if not systematically ignored, in cross-national studies, and we discuss the implications of this oversight. Several sets of variables that we feel merit scrutiny in future studies are also examined. Our concern is to make recommendations on ways to use existing data better and to provide guidelines for future studies that may help national educational planners and policymakers. The thrust of our position is that we concur with Richard Wolf's important but neglected recommendation concerning the design and subsequent utility of cross-national achievement studies:

> The sample design must be arranged to facilitate within-country analysis. This may be more important than provision of national summaries or international comparisons. . . . National centers need to be directed, encouraged, and assisted in determining substantively relevant major stratification for their studies. Certainly in all countries there are important regions, types of communities, or teachers for which nationally important educational policy questions need to be answered. A process at the national level of discussion and debate needs to be carried out to decide what the critical strata are. In one country these may be regional, while in another they may be according to school stream.[1]

Only by thus shifting the level of analysis from national, aggregate, social indicators to micro-level, contextual, and individual variables can determinants of academic achievement be better understood and policymakers be better informed.

In the final analysis, our comments in this paper are directed toward substantiating three critical propositions. First, most national systems of education are highly complex, extremely heterogeneous agglomerations of students, schools, and administrators; hence, achievement attributions made to local populations on the basis of national test results are encumbered by an ecological fallacy. Second, because of the variability in educational context, the configurations that achievement-related variables will exhibit are multitudinous; consequently, policymaking and intervention strategies should be targeted at the unit or local level, not the national level. And third, in light of the two previous contentions, cross-national comparisons of aggregate data are of extremely limited utility in planning and policy intervention unless comparable contextual controls are applied first to the findings.

Background

The sociopsychological literature dealing with achievement has identified four general types of explanatory variables: the background characteristics

[1] R. Wolf, "Sampling," in *Bulletin 4: Secondary Study of Mathematics* (Urbana, Ill.: SIMS, December 1979).

of the learner, school resources, school and classroom environment, and the general social and cultural context in which instruction takes place. The literature on the first two sets of variables is by far the most extensive and well established. Although these two blocks of determinants have consistently generated the highest amount of explained variance in achievement, cross-national analyses utilizing them as key explanatory measures suffer from errors of aggregation. That is, in utilizing aggregated data such as economic indicators like GNP per capita and averaged number of books per school, researchers employ "manufactured" general socio-economic indexes for what may be highly specific, individualized, or at least localized variations in these determinants of achievement.

Although school effect variables, such as teacher quality and school resources on the one hand and socioeconomic and home environment variables on the other, explain substantial variance in achievement, their impact varies according to the context of the general level of economic development in which achievement is measured. On the whole, home background variables tend to account for more variance in the more industrialized countries,[2] whereas school resources tend to account for more variance in the less industrialized countries (LICs).[3]

However, in most studies, the vast majority of difference in achievement remains unaccounted for. Furthermore, the 30 or more variables that have been identified as having a causal relationship to academic achievement seem to vary in their importance, depending on the specific achievement variables in question (math, science, language, etc.),[4] the cultural milieu, and perhaps even the educational level of the sampled students.

Tables 1 and 2 contain a summary of the findings of a number of studies regarding the relationships between academic achievement and selected background, school, and classroom variables. The studies show rather lucidly that in the LICs the relationships between academic achievement and given variables are inconsistent. That is, in some instances the relationships with background, school, and classroom variables are sta-

[2] James S. Coleman and Ernest Q. Campbell, *Equality of Educational Opportunity* (Washington, D.C.: Government Printing Office, 1966); Christopher Jencks and Marshall Smith, *Inequality* (New York: Basic, 1972); and Marion F. Shaycroft, *The High School Years: Growth in Cognitive Skills* (Pittsburgh: American Institute for Research and Project Talent, 1967).

[3] Throughout this paper we will refer to the LDCs as less industrialized countries (LICs). This distinction removes at least a part of the negative value connotation of the former designation. Joseph P. Farrell, "The IEA Studies: Factors That Affect Achievement, in Six Subjects in Twenty-one Countries," *Teachers College Record* 79 (December 1977): 289–97; Stephen P. Heyneman and William Loxley, "Influences on Academic Achievement across High and Low Income Countries: A Re-Analysis of I.E.A. Data," *Sociology of Education* 55 (January 1982): 13–21; and Stephen P. Heyneman, "Influence on Academic Achievement: A Comparison of Results from Uganda and More Industrialized Societies," *Sociology of Education* 49 (July 1976): 200–11.

[4] Max A. Eckstein, "Comparative Study of Educational Achievement," *Comparative Education Review* 21 (1977): 345–57; and John Bibby and Margaret Peil, "Secondary Education in Ghana: Private Enterprise and Social Selection," *Sociology of Education* 47 (Summer 1974): 399–418.

TABLE 1

RESULTS OF EDUCATIONAL PRODUCTION FUNCTION STUDIES FOR POOR COUNTRIES
FOR BACKGROUND VARIABLES AND SCHOOLING VARIABLES

Variable and Its Relationship (+, −, or ?) to Student Performance	Statistically Significant with Expected Sign	Not Statistically Significant or with Opposite Sign
SES has strong effect at primary and lower secondary grades for all subjects (+)	Epstein Simmons-Askoy Schiefelbein-Farrell Carnoy (R.F.) Beebout IEA science IEA reading	Carnoy-Thias (grade 7) Carnoy (S.F.)
SES has less effect in developing countries than developed countries	Schiefelbein-Farrell IEA science IEA reading	
SES has diminished effect throughout secondary cycle	Carnoy-Thias Carnoy Beebout (English) IEA science IEA reading Simmons (1975)	Beebout (Malay)
Schooling variables have some effect at lower grades, but a stronger effect in upper secondary grades(?)	Carnoy-Thias Carnoy IEA science IEA reading	
Schooling variables have some effect on native language beyond primary grades (+)	IEA reading	Simmons-Askoy

SOURCE.—Adapted largely from Karl Alexander and John Simmons, "The Determinants of School Achievement in Developing Countries: The Educational Production Function," IBRD Working Paper no. 210 (March 1975), pp. 57–59.

NOTE.—The countries in which the studies were conducted are: Beebout (Malaysia), Carnoy (Puerto Rico), Carnoy-Thias (Tunisia), Epstein (St. Lucia), Haddad, 1978 (international), Heyneman (Uganda), Heyneman et al., 1978 (international), IEA science and reading (international), Levy (international), Noonan (IEA) (Israel and Japan), Schiefelbein-Farrell (Chile), Simmons, 1975 (IEA data—international), Simmons-Askoy (Tunisia), Thias-Carnoy, grades 7 and 11 (Kenya).

tistically significant and positive; however, in some instances the relationships are statistically insignificant and/or negative. That such variability exists may in itself be a more interesting finding than one that might have pointed to cross-national consistency! The question that remains unanswered, of course, is why, despite the laborious attempts to standardize measures and procedures, are the data so exasperatingly unpredictable from one context to the next?

Table 1 shows that the inconsistent findings are quite frequent in the cases involving teacher-specific variables and such "exposure to learning" variables as boarding at the secondary level, grade repetition, double sessions, and size of school enrollment. It is not clear why these variables relate this way to achievement, except to suggest that perhaps academic performance is extremely susceptible to indigenous, situational factors that escape detection in macro-level studies.

TABLE 2
RESULTS OF EDUCATIONAL PRODUCTION FUNCTION STUDIES FOR POOR COUNTRIES FOR INDIVIDUAL SCHOOLING VARIABLES

Variable and Its Relationship (+, −, or ?) to Student Performance	Statistically Significant with Expected Sign	Not Statistically Significant or with Opposite Sign
Per-pupil expenditures on school facilities or teachers (+)		Levy Thias-Cornoy (grade 11) Beebout Noonan (IEA)
Average class size, or pupil–teacher ratio (−)	Carnoy Beebout	Levy Thias-Carnoy (grade 7) Schiefelbein-Farrell IEA science IEA reading Haddad
Teacher certification and academic qualification at primary and lower secondary grades (+)	Carnoy	Levy Thias-Carnoy (grade 7) Schiefelbein-Farrell
Teacher certification and academic qualifications at upper secondary grades (+)	Beebout IEA science	Carnoy-Thias Carnoy
Teacher contract (tenure) at upper secondary grades (+)	Carnoy	Carnoy-Thias
Teacher experience at primary and lower secondary grades (+)	Thias-Carnoy (grade 7) Schiefelbein-Farrell Carnoy	Carnoy-Thias
Teacher experience at upper secondary grades (−)	Beebout Simmons (1975)	Carnoy-Thias Carnoy
Teacher sex—males at primary and lower secondary grades; females at upper secondary grades (+)	Carnoy-Thias Beebout IEA science IEA reading	Thias-Carnoy (grade 7) Carnoy
Teacher motivation (−)	IEA science	
Textbook availability at primary grades (+)	Schiefelbein-Farrell IEA science Heyneman et al. Heyneman	
Availability and use of library (+)	Beebout IEA reading	
Homework and free reading at home (+)	Schiefelbein-Farrell Simmons-Askoy IEA science IEA reading	
Boarding at secondary grades (+)	Thias-Carnoy (grade 11) Carnoy-Thias	Beebout
Grade repetition (−)	Levy Thias-Carnoy (grade 7) Simmons-Askoy	Beebout
Double sessions (−)	Beebout	Schiefelbein-Farrell
Size of school enrollment at upper secondary grades (?)	Thias-Carnoy (grade 11) (+) IEA science (+)	Beebout (−)
Performance and attitudes of classroom peer group (+)	Carnoy-Thias Schiefelbein-Farrell	

SOURCE.—See table 1.

NOTE.—See note to table 1 for countries in which the studies were conducted.

The studies summarized in tables 1 and 2 were conducted in different countries; therefore it is possible the inconsistent findings may emanate from the differences in sociocultural context and attendant educational policies and practices.[5] The possibility that these factors "contaminate" the correlates of academic achievement underscores the pitfalls of aggregating countries under the simple rubric of "developed versus developing."

Tables 1 and 2 also indicate that home background or parental socioeconomic status has a significant impact on a student's academic performance in primary and lower secondary grades irrespective of the academic subject tested. Nonetheless, there is strong support for a point made earlier that home background factors account for more variance in academic achievement in the industrialized countries than they do in the LICs. Two reasons have been advanced to explain this finding. First, there is a smaller range of differences of home conditions in the LICs; in rural areas in the Third World, background differences may be measured by whether a family has a private well or uses a communal one, has a thatch or tile roof, owns 2 hectares of land or works as tenant farmers. Status inequality may be measured more in terms of differences in power and lineage than material possessions and monetary resources. A second reason is the greater importance of the schooling process than the home in mastering certain subjects.[6] With few learning resources at home and low levels of parental education, most academic learning takes place in the only facility conducive to it—the village school.

In short, not only do the measured causal determinants of achievement vary by level of education and subject matter; the impact of the same variables appears to be positive in some countries and negative in others! Either measures of the dependent variable suffer from serious problems of validity or, more likely, sampling strata or the elements within them (cultural, structural, and contextual) have not been made comparable across the countries studied.

Methodological and Theoretical Caveats

Our criticisms of existing comparative investigations of achievement must be tempered somewhat by the great distance our knowledge base has advanced in the past 15 years. Yet, despite the abundance of cross-sectional, within-country studies, few convincing comparisons of a longitudinal sort exist that examine the reliability and/or validity of the initial findings (not the instruments themselves).

[5] Karl Alexander and John Simmons, "The Determinants of School Achievement in Developing Countries: The Educational Production Function," IBRD Working Paper 210 (Washington, D.C.: World Bank, March 1975), pp. 57–59.

[6] Ibid., p. 2.

Several factors account for the paucity of high-quality, valid, and reliable comparative data. First, large-scale in-country achievement studies are very expensive; cross-national administration is almost prohibitively so. Second, language differences and variations in curricular emphasis introduce variance into both the measurement of the verbally based variables and the academic preparation of students prior to the administration of achievement questionnaires. Third, students vary widely in their familiarity with testing procedures both within and among societies. Hence, performance may be a measure of exposure to the procedures of the system as well as an index of mastery of the material.[7] Fourth, because education is tied to the political organization of a country, achievement is sometimes seen as a surrogate measure of political effectiveness. Hence, the collection of national data may be discouraged, or, worse, the data may be adjusted for reasons of political expediency. (Data received from cooperating countries and reported by Unesco are filled with curious statistical anomalies; certain data collected as part of IEA studies have also been labeled suspect.) And finally, logistical problems and methodological variations among test administrations may reduce the comparability of scores and measures.

Despite these limitations, however, family background and school resources repeatedly show modest correlations with achievement. This consistency, however, belies the ease of interpreting and generalizing from them.

Family Background

Family background measures, such as parental education and occupation, income, possessions, and the influence and expectations of family members, pose fewer analytical problems in comparisons made among industrialized countries than among LICs. In the former, the labor force is typically composed of people engaging in a broad range of occupations graded by technical skill level with a normally distributed array of incomes associated with the skill gradients. The occupational profiles of the LICs, however, are much less varied; they are usually characterized by a large peasant sector with an extended kinship labor network, an almost nonexistent middle class, and a small professional elite. As a result, the effect of SES on achievement may be diminished (or at least rendered incomparable to its effect in industrialized nations) because of the relative homogeneity of its components in LICs. Since there is a polar distribution of occupation and income in the population, the strength of the *average* correlation between status and achievement is effectively suppressed. The relationship between these two variables may be misrepresented even further if kinship resources are not included in construction of the SES

[7] Alex Inkeles, "National Differences in Scholastic Performance," *Comparative Education Review* 23 (1979): 386–407.

index. In extended family systems found in many Third World countries, using a single family's resources as a measure of status and an implicit index of values and achievement orientation betrays not only a Western bias but also a naive set of social science assumptions. Indeed, it may be the poor family that is willing to borrow from kin that is most likely to have the motivation and value orientation conducive to academic success that we most frequently identify with high-status families in the industrialized world.

Regional Resources

Regional resources may define inequities in sectoral levels of academic achievement for several reasons. The richer regions of a country normally have a greater financial capacity to support more and perhaps better educational resources for teachers and students; the richer regions, ceteris paribus, are more likely than the poor ones to have physically superior schools, large stockpiles of educationally relevant texts, and related materials as well as better trained or better qualified teachers. Studies in a number of African countries have found a strong association between region on the one hand and school quality on the other.[8] How easily these resources are translated into higher achievement scores for students is still a matter of some controversy.[9]

Concurrent, and frequently overlapping, with geographical variations in resources are ethnic inequalities in wealth and subsequent access to educational benefits. The more prosperous ethnic groups are usually better able to turn their relative affluence into educational advantage. Wealth can be converted into the acquisition of relevant instructional materials, the hiring of private tutors, the organization of educational tours, and perhaps also the inculcation of a strong and pervasive achievement orientation.

The upshot of educational competition is that ethnic groups with disproportionately large shares of the national elite population among their ranks tend to be increasingly overrepresented in the student population at all levels of the educational pyramid, especially the tertiary.

One point that needs to be stressed is that in many LICs, secondary schools do admit students from all regions of the state. It is conceivable, therefore, that students from geographical areas that are not well endowed with secondary school facilities can still utilize their social status to enjoy

---

[8] Philip Foster, *Education and Social Change in Ghana* (Chicago: University of Chicago Press, 1965); Philip Foster and Remi Clignet, *The Fortunate Few: A Study of Secondary Schools and Students in the Ivory Coast* (Evanston, Ill.: Northwestern University Press, 1966); and Paul P. W. Achola, "Differential Access to Education in Kenya: Some of Its Correlates" (unpublished paper, University of Iowa, May 1978).

[9] Stephen P. Heyneman, Joseph P. Farrell, and Manuel A. Sepulveda, "Textbooks and Achievement: What We Know," World Bank Staff Working Paper no. 298 (Washington, D.C.: World Bank, 1978).

educational advantage by attending secondary schools in regions of the country where superior educational resources do exist. Thus, sampling at the regional level in the LICs is fraught with difficulties. Cross-sectional surveys of a student population may result in two or three students from a given school being selected for inclusion in the sample. Although this procedure virtually assures that the heterogeneity of the total student population will be reflected in the sample, it does not allow for adequate measurement of the impact of "school effects," classroom environments, or community support (see the next section of this paper).

On the other hand, quota sampling only from a smaller number of randomly chosen schools is more susceptible to bias resulting from special recruitment characteristics or entry requirements unique to a specific school. For example, in Malaysia, a number of state secondary schools have been established regionally throughout the country that have a special curricular emphasis—mathematics or science, for example. Students are screened to attend these schools on the basis of their academic ability and financial need. Consequently, an achievement survey that uses random quota selection procedures might contain an unrepresentative number of high-ability students in science; subsequent interpretation might point to the efficacy of resource variables associated with that school. Falsely based, if not erroneous, conclusions might be drawn from the analysis. Conversely, if students representing the cream of the academic elite have been skimmed off the majority of regional schools and one or more of these institutions ends up as part of the sample in a study of achievement, it is quite apparent that the full value range of the dependent variable has been artificially constricted; a lower-end bias is likely. As the frequency of this type of error increases, the researcher's ability to make responsible, accurate statements about the determinants of achievement diminishes in direct proportion.

In short, the profile of academic performance at the national level may disguise considerable, albeit predictable, variations at the regional and local levels. Valid comparisons of educational effects must root out level-of-analysis errors and employ sound sampling and statistical procedures that allow the data to reflect anomalies in recruitment, resources, and restricted access relevant to the schooling process. The foregoing points also underscore the need to pay attention to the conjoint effect of region and ethnicity on academic achievement.

Perhaps because of social scientists' preoccupation with the relationship between race and academic achievement in a number of industrialized nations, less attention has been focused on the relationship between gender and academic performance. This shortcoming is especially apparent in reviewing cross-national comparisons of achievement involving the LICs.

Notwithstanding some contradictory evidence,[10] boys tend overall to obtain higher achievement scores than girls, especially in mathematics and science.[11] Findings of this sort are undoubtedly linked to gender-based social conditioning. The results of a study of academic achievement between boys and girls in GCE "ordinary" level exams support this.[12] The socialization of girls as intellectual inferiors of boys might be expected to be stronger in the LICs where women are still tacitly relegated to subordinate roles in the modern, institutional sectors of society. We suggest, then, that the relationship between gender and academic achievement is likely to be particularly marked for the LICs, especially those characterized by rigid sex-role differentiation.

Evidence is increasing that age may also be an important determinant of achievement. Studies of child development indicate that, at the elementary school level, a student's ability to master the learning process tends to be primarily the result of maturation rather than of cognitive ability per se.[13] One might therefore expect that, for elementary school students, the relationship between age and academic achievement will be positive.[14] At the secondary school level, however, there are indications that, at the same grade level, younger students register higher achievement scores than older pupils.[15] Some explanations for the negative relationship between age and academic achievement at the secondary school level include the possibility that early entry into school is a reflection of parental interest in schooling. Younger students at any grade level may be those who have avoided grade repetition because they are more intellectually able.[16] Moreover, older students are more likely than their younger classmates to diffuse their energies in such nonscholarly activities as work, extracurricular activities, and non-school-related leisure pursuits. Carefully stratified in-

[10] C. B. Chappell, III, "The Relationship between Socioeconomic Status, Sex, Self-Concept, and Course Selection of Urban Black Tenth-Grade Students" (Ed.D. diss., College of William and Mary, 1979).

[11] J. F. O. Carey, "The Relationship between Attitude toward School, Sex, Intelligence, and Academic Achievement" (Ed.D. diss., University of Rochester, 1978); and Alexander and Simmons, p. 40.

[12] Robert J. L. Murphy, "Sex Differences in Examination Performance: Do These Reflect Differences in Ability or Sex-Role Stereotypes?" Educational Review 30 (November 1978): 259–63.

[13] Jean Piaget, Science of Education and the Psychology of the Child (New York: Viking, 1971); Erik Erickson, Childhood and Society (New York: Norton, 1963); and John Lavach and Roger R. Ries, "Ages and Stages: Child Development Revisited," Social Education 42 (May 1978): 375–77.

[14] Elizabeth M. Hyde, "A Behavioral Study of Maturity in Children of Elementary-School Age," Elementary School Journal 77 (November 1976): 140–49; and Nicholas Bennett, "Primary Education in Rural Communities—an Investment in Ignorance?" Journal of Development Studies 6 (July 1970): 92–103.

[15] Margaret Peil, "Ghanaian University Students: Broadening Base," British Journal of Sociology 16 (1965): 19–28; H. C. A. Somerset, Home Structure, Parental Aspiration and Examination Success in Buganda (Nairobi: East African Institute of Social Research, 1965); and Bibby and Peil (n. 4 above), p. 413.

[16] Bibby and Peil (n. 4 above), p. 413.

tranational, not cross-national, studies are most likely to demonstrate the existence of these relationships.

Investigators have noted that, among grade levels in the LICs, there is greater age range than among grades in the industrialized nations. For instance, Bennett reported the age of first-grade students in Niger and Senegal to run between a minimum of 3 years and a maximum of 11 years; for Uganda, Heyneman's sample of seventh graders contained pupils aged between 10 and 18 years; Bibby and Peil's sample of twelfth graders in Ghana included students aged younger than 17 years and older than 22 years; Theisen and Hamburg's sample of Iranian secondary students contained an age range of 3 years for each grade.[17] Consequently, because of greater age variance among students in the same grade level in the LICs, the relationship between age and academic achievement (positive and negative) should be more pronounced than for the industrialized countries, thereby raising further doubt about the efficacy of such cross-national comparisons for planning purposes.

In addition to the foregoing variables, intervening attitudinal and process variables are little emphasized in cross-national achievement studies, but they may have an impact on students' academic scores. These are a function neither of SES nor school resources per se; rather, they are the product of the general aspirational and utilitarian milieu of a society. Outstanding among the attitudinal factors are parental aspirations for the educational attainment of their children, peer group expectations, and students' own self-concept and educational aspirations.

Of course, as noted earlier, most of these intervening variables are likely to be moderately to strongly correlated with socioeconomic status, ethnicity, region, and gender. However, the motivations to achieve highly or to encourage others to excel academically are as varied as the societies and social systems in which they are found. Thus, we have stressed in previous sections the need to take into account contextual effects when considering the possible impact of peer group expectations on students' academic performance.

School Resources

School resources can be defined more standardly than can family background variables, but their impact on achievement has been more difficult to isolate. Although Coleman and associates found that school resource indicators had little effect on achievement in the United States, the findings are mixed for the LICs. Heyneman, for example, has found that SES among the Karamojong in Uganda is negatively correlated with

---

[17] Gary L. Theisen and Edward Hamburg, "Non-Cognitive Outcomes of Schooling: Maturation or Socialization?" (paper delivered at the annual meeting of the Comparative and International Education Society, Ann Arbor, Mich., March 1979).

achievement, in contrast with its positive relationship in most countries. Heyneman and Jamison's research indicated that sharply defined regional variations in SES and access to schooling provide the setting for an exceptionally strong predisposition to succeed.[18] This is especially true among the underprivileged children who are fortunate enough to make it past the economic hardships presented by the first few years of formal schooling.

However, surveys reveal that not only do students have differential access to education but significant within-region variations in expenditures on schooling, teacher quality, and contact hours with students exist as well. Bloom's evaluation of the efficacy of the "master learning" concept has demonstrated, at least in the short run, the importance of the time spent on learning tasks to achievement in a given subject.[19] Comparative studies (especially within countries) have only recently begun to examine systematically the amount of time and emphasis actually placed on particular subjects during a typical school day.

As any observer of the educational process is well aware, the time prescribed by central educational authorities to be spent on a particular subject often bears little relationship to what actually goes on in the classroom. National systems vary in the amount of instructional time "lost" because of holidays, special national events, and other occasions. At the regional level, distance from the district education office may decrease adherence to Ministry guidelines as well as teacher expectations for the students' long-range educational achievement and attainment. It is conceivable that in some situations such freedom from bureaucratically prescribed strictures may have positive results! Within the school, the time devoted to record maintenance, discipline, and "secondary subjects" may vary as much as the enthusiasm of the classroom teachers, the leadership qualities of the administrators, and the motivation of the pupils. The length of the average instructional day (combined public instruction and private tutorial) and differences in absentee rates may further impinge on the students' ability to achieve in one or more subjects. Consequently, school-to-school variance in what is taught and how much it is taught is a crucial control of within-system as well as between-system differences in achievement. How well a subject is taught is a separate school resource issue.

Recent data from the United States indicate that time spent on tasks within subjects has been a neglected line of investigation. For example, although students in the United States devote a state-prescribed amount of time to studying English, a substantial amount of that allocation goes

[18] Stephen P. Heyneman and Dean T. Jamison, "Textbook Availability and Other Determinants of Student Learning in Uganda" (paper presented at the annual meeting of the Comparative and International Education Society, Ann Arbor, Mich., March 1979).

[19] Benjamin Bloom, *Human Characteristics and School Learning* (New York: McGraw-Hill, 1976).

to interpreting and critiquing literature. As a result, poor test scores in the areas of grammar and composition have been blamed on the lack of time devoted to these tasks in the schools.[20]

It is imperative, then, that achievement studies should focus not only on total time spent on instruction but must identify the specific task and time allocated to teaching it within the subject area that is under investigation. (Proposed and in-progress IEA studies such as SIMS do contain measures of this variable.) For example, meaningful comparison of Japanese and Swedish achievement rates in, say, mathematics must differentiate between components of overall mathematics performance, such as understanding of spatial relations, interpretive abilities, and the ability to classify and differentiate. It must also examine the students' understanding of relationships among the components and then control for the relevant time spent on each of these areas. But equally important is the necessity to be able to investigate localized variations in these achievement capacities and to apply controls in order to appreciate fully the attenuating effects of micro-level variables such as time-on-task on national-level data analysis.

Although national school systems differ widely in their total per capita resources such as books, supplies, and physical plants, these variations are, in most cases, better indicators of economic development than of educational thrust or enthusiasm. As indicated earlier in our discussion of background variables, more important than the amount of possessions or resources is *how* the equipment or money are used, if indeed they are applied to the instructional process at all. For example, research indicates that learning is severely hampered by an undersupply of basic texts. Put simply, students who do not have their own texts to study and to take home do not do as well as others who do have them.[21] But beyond this minimal distribution of materials, the relationship between the availability of books (and teaching aids and apparatus) and achievement is less clear. What may be more important than the amount of expenditure on books is the social qua community support behind the authorization to make the purchases in the first place. Anyone with a modicum of experience in education is aware of the phenomenon of the equipment-stuffed, locked closet that is opened only on visitors' day. But not all schools or educators contribute to this stereotype. For a variety of reasons, but one suspects primarily because of a desire to witness achievement in their students, certain communities are more supportive of the educational process than others are. Parents create a home climate that is usually embedded in a social environment that either fosters or discourages academic achievement by stressing certain standards of performance, social mobility, competition, cooperation, equality, and so forth.

[20] "School Scandal," *Wall Street Journal* (September 10, 1980), p. 26.
[21] Heyneman et al. (n. 9 above).

Performance in specific subjects may be emphasized by students because they can see that mastery leads to opportunities, either academic or occupational, at a later date. Achievement may be the result of a deliberate cost-benefit analysis of the functional outcomes of the effort that must be expended by the student. More will be said about this in a later section of this paper.

Classroom and School Environment

The growing body of research on classroom and school environment indicates that, even when social context and institutional resources are controlled, substantial variations exist in the organization and operation of schools as well as in the regulation of learning and behavior within classrooms. Investigators have found that the nature of the teacher's authority relationship with students, the openness of classroom decision making, the degree of formality, and the cohesiveness of students cause small but statistically significant differences in subject-specific achievement.[22]

Assessing the effect of classroom environment measures is a difficult theoretical and empirical task.[23] Measurement has been hampered by the somewhat arbitrarily defined, overlapping, classificatory categories used in assessments of classroom characters and by failure to distinguish between organizational properties of schools and the instructional processes that occur within them.[24] The logistical and methodological problems involved in collecting empirical data on classroom climate measures place further burden on financially and time-bounded research projects.

Because of these constraints, educators know very little about the impact of environmental measures on achievement, except to say that preliminary investigations indicate that effects exist. Observers of schooling in the LICs who have witnessed the spectacle of 65 students enclosed in a semipartitioned space that is open to the next class of similar size are painfully aware of the impact that spillover of noise and confusion can have on instruction. When differences in the physical characteristics of the facilities are placed alongside the variations in socially and culturally prescribed relationships between students and teachers, it is safe to conjecture that the wide-ranging configurations of environmental characteristics within schools may bear substantially on achievement. What has eluded us so far is exactly what to measure and how to measure it. It would

[22] Gary J. Anderson and Herbert J. Walberg, "Learning Environments," in *Evaluating Education Performance: A Source Book of Methods, Instruction and Examples*, ed. Herbert J. Walberg (Berkeley, Calif.: McCutchan, 1974); and R. O'Reilly, "Classroom Climate and Achievement in Secondary School Mathematics Classes," *Alberta Journal of Educational Research* 21 (December 1975): 241–48.

[23] Richard H. Pfau, "Sources of Invalidity When Comparing Classroom Behaviors across Cultures and Nations" (paper presented at the 25th annual meeting of the Comparative and International Education Society, Tallahassee, Fla., March 1981).

[24] Charles Bidwell and John Kasarda, "Conceptualizing and Measuring the Effects of Schools and Schooling," *American Journal of Education* 88 (August 1980): 401–30.

perhaps be surprising if we found that environmental measures had the same relationship to achievement in all societies. Since normative expectations of behavior differ, the response to environmental characteristics that impinge on behavior may also be expected to vary cross-culturally.

The IEA Classroom Environment Study headed by Doris Ryan of OISE and currently in progress should add considerably to our knowledge in this area.

Structural Classifications of Educational Systems

Comparative studies of academic achievement have employed conventional thinking in dichotomizing countries into developed and developing ones; yet only one very recent analysis of the IEA data has even bothered to adopt this admittedly oversimplistic form of stratification![25] Grouping countries according to the level of their technological development may be useful for some analytical purposes, but for explaining micro-level determinants of academic proficiency, such agglomerations disguise the heterogeneous characteristics of indigenous populations and the types of educational systems and practices that crosscut the developed versus developing countries typology.

Turner has classified educational systems by their function and selectivity, traits that seem more relevant to a discussion of types and levels of achievement than relative level of industrialization.[26] Turner posits that sponsored mobility systems are usually de facto elitist, with children of upper-class parents having greatest access to higher education. By contrast, in a contest mobility system a greater percentage of students retain high aspirations for advanced education since upper-level entry is easier to obtain and can be deferred for long periods; eventual access to higher education is as much a function of persistence and ambition as ability. Hence, completion of tertiary degrees is realizable for many individuals. At the upper educational levels, contest systems have a higher percentage of an age cohort enrolled. If we assume that ability is normally distributed among the members of the cohort, it is probable that, on average, achievement scores of these students will be lower than the average scores of pupils in a sponsored system. Because of the early selection process, only the most able students will be included in a national sample of "sponsored" secondary schools. Cross-national comparisons of aggregated test results from different systems can be very misleading.

Of course, most researchers attempt to incorporate an ability measure (as distinguished from one measuring achievement) to control for the

[25] Heyneman and Loxley (n. 3 above), pp. 13–21.
[26] Ralph Turner, "Sponsored and Contest Mobility and the School System," *American Sociological Review* 25, no. 5 (1960): 855–67.

selectivity of systems. There are several shortcomings to this approach. First, many ability measures suffer from both reliability and validity problems within national populations, especially in those characterized by high degrees of linguistic and cultural heterogeneity. Such measures suffer even more in their cross-national, cross-cultural comparability. Second, in a number of instances, ability data are not even available; the collection of any such information that could be used for labeling or stigmatizing students is banned by law. Denmark is a case in point.

But even if acceptable universal ability measures could be developed, it is conceivable that the "achievement ethos" found in an educational system is greater than the sum of individual student abilities. There is some evidence to indicate, for example, that, despite the many deleterious effects of academic tracking, high-ability students do seem to perform better in classes where they are in direct competition with their most able peers.[27] If this is true at the level of the instructional unit in contest systems, might not even a stronger case be made for the cumulative effects of peer-reinforced achievement in a system that is reward differentiated but is characterized by a cadre of homogeneously grouped, high-ability students? In short, different types of educational systems, each characterized by distinct patterns of selection and retention, have associated with them an achievement-related normative milieu that may influence a student's achievement and attainment expectations and that, at least in part, may affect national measures of academic performance independent of ability levels and previously mentioned resource and regional variables. Unfortunately, researchers have not yet capitalized on perceptions such as Turner's by examining the impact of national, regional, or local milieus on perceived communal and interpersonal expectations for academic success.[28] "Environmental press" in addition to individual abilities and aspirations is a component of the achievement process.

But not all educational systems conveniently fit into one of Turner's two ideal types. The educational systems in many Third World countries are difficult to classify since they display not only various shades of their mandarin, colonial origins but also adaptations created in response to the exigencies of political change. The class-conscious colonizing powers, interested as they were in serving their own bureaucratic and expropriative ends, introduced a type of education into their dependencies that, in many cases, was not only elitist but also conditioning and subjugative. In those contexts where the new dependency was itself characterized by fairly

[27] Karl Alexander and Edward McDill, "Selection and Allocation within Schools," *American Sociological Review* 41 (1976): 963–80, and James W. B. Douglas, *The Home and the School* (London: McGibbon & Kee, 1966).

[28] See also Francisco Ramirez and John Meyer, "Comparative Education: The Social Construction of the Modern World System," *Annual Review of Sociology* 6 (1980): 369–99.

rigid social strata even before the onset of colonization, access to education (and especially higher education) was limited to the socially privileged. A similar pattern can be observed in those dependencies where a European population reigned, not just as transient interlopers but as permanent settlers; many areas of Latin America serve as an illustration.

In many of these societies, the postindependence period brought a shift in political emphasis from one that stressed service to the colonial power to one that focused on the needs of the new society—that is, national development in its disparate forms. The availability of techno- logically oriented manpower as a prerequisite to national development has been a guiding assumption of specialists in capital formation. In consequence, the schools have been assigned the task of meeting manpower quotas as projected in national development plans. In those contexts where national policy proclaims the need for the preparation of more individuals with managerial and technical skills, academic emphasis may be relatively high on subjects such as business disciplines and law, which are linked to managerial and administrative training. A high probability of lucrative material rewards await those who successfully pass the tests and examinations that assure entry into these occupations. Motivation and effort to achieve may be disproportionately placed precisely on those subjects with the highest perceived payoff for the individual. The greater the rewards and inducements to achieve in a given discipline, the higher the resulting performance levels may be. National variations in subject proficiency may be explained, at least in part, by such macrostructural emphases.

The importance of environmental press—national, communal, and familial—should not be underestimated. Norms of achievement and at- tainment may have much to do with decisions to invest time and energy in the pursuit of high levels of academic performance. Additionally, the individuals' own perceptions of how achievement in a particular subject meshes with their educational and occupational plans may link motiva- tionally to the desire to achieve.

In the LICs, as the number of graduates increases, academic attainment discriminates less well among job hopefuls. Academic performance, as measured by standardized tests, receives increased weight in the mobility process. Consequently, tests of academic achievement increasingly tend to measure: (1) skills at taking examinations or tests; (2) the ability to reproduce factual knowledge; (3) the ability to marshal kinship resources to attend the best schools in the struggle for the top; and (4) the ability to secure supplementary educational assistance outside of and in addition to formal schooling.

A corollary to the foregoing points is that an educational system whose major objective is the production of predetermined labor quotas according to national, standardized evaluation techniques will tend to have a standardized, prepackaged curriculum. Hence, comparing academic achievement of students confronted by a rigidly set curriculum with that of students in an educational system characterized by a high degree of flexibility for disciplinary specialization is at best misleading. The danger of misinterpretation is of a qualitative, not a quantitative, nature. One system emphasizes measurement of ability to retain factual knowledge, skillfulness in the testing process, and the size of the student's fiscal resource arsenal; in the other case, the achievement measure may be reflecting more the student's self-selection into an area of high interest and, perhaps, ability.

Whether or not educational programs in ex-colonies are utilized as control or co-opting mechanisms or are used to "liberate" individuals and groups depends on the orientations of the political elites in power within each state.[29] There are countries among the ex-colonies that have reacted against not only the kind of class-based and educational inflation associated with manpower-oriented education but also the kind of cultural and educational legacy that survives political independence. Countries such as Guinea-Bissau, Tanzania, and North Korea have attempted to establish educational systems that place a premium on educating for equity and social transformation.

National systems of this sort emphasize four central points: ideologization, altruism, pragmatism, and analytical knowledge. From a centralized political body, information about the values and advantages of the systems are disseminated through a hierarchical network of party cadres and administrative organs. The schools are an essential part of this socialization process. Party loyalty, willingness to make sacrifices for the whole society, ability to make practical and productive use of one's academic knowledge, social equality, and service form the tenets on which educational instruction is based. Political leaders assiduously try to avoid creating a hierarchical society premised on educational and occupational credentials, while at the same time they struggle to reject foreign and capitalist rationalizations for educational expansion.[30]

Under education-for-liberation systems, achievement is measured according to four standards: (1) academic attainment, (2) party loyalty, (3) leadership/service qualities, and (4) attitudes toward work, especially productive physical labor. Thus the curricular emphasis is on socialization and vocational training, and performance is assessed by a spectrum of noncognitive, or at least nontraditionally cognitive, information and skills. On a comparative basis, then, academic performance (as measured by

[29] Robert E. Arnove, "Comparative Education and World Systems Analysis," *Comparative Education Review* 24 (1980): 48–62.

[30] Julius K. Nyerere, *The Arusha Declaration and TANU's Policy on Socialism and Self-Reliance* (Dar es Salaam: Publicity Section, Tanganiya African National Union, 1967).

conventional achievement measures) receives less social sanction in liberation social systems than in contest, sponsored, and manpower-oriented systems. We do not mean to imply that there is a total neglect of purely academic concerns in liberation systems; rather, curricular and motivational emphases are dispersed among a number of nonacademic educational objectives. The boundaries are certainly not clear; in some socialist countries, higher education may constitute a form of sponsorship for youth selected according to criteria of "ideological" correctness. In general, however, the environmental press generated by the liberationist social milieu offers less sanction for high achievement, as defined according to more traditional perspectives of schooling.

In short, education for liberation is flavored by a heavy seasoning of vocational training and antibourgeois socialization. Although the development of cognitive abilities is important, schooling primarily serves the practical needs of egalitarian social reform and collaborative social effort. The school is a microcosm of the larger society in which action, altruism, leadership, and equity are paramount virtues. Academic performance and credentialing occupy the backstage relative to their front and center status in sponsored, contest, and manpower-oriented systems. Even this generalization is overly simplistic, however. Ideological emphases and resulting educational practices may shift markedly over relatively short periods, as witnessed by events in the last 6 years in China.[31]

Conclusions and Recommendations

In summary, we suggest that there are a number of more meaningful ways of examining differences in achievement scores than by making comparisons, however complex, simply on the basis of national boundaries. Past methodological schemes may have been analytically convenient, but the results are hardly clear or convincing. Stratifying countries by stages of development is a more logical strategem, but even here the theoretical linkage between economic context and school performance is opaque. Even comparisons employing typologies such as contest, sponsored, and liberationist as control variables are flawed in their simplicity. But at least the data are placed into the sociopolitical context in which they were generated.[32]

In the past 15 years, significant advances have been made in the development of instrumentation to collect cross-culturally comparable data. Future efforts must be devoted to contextualizing the data we are

[31] Gary L. Theisen and Scott McNabb, "The Chinese Professorate during the Cultural Revolution: A View from Inside the Tower," *Asian Thought and Society*, in press.

[32] For an explication of hypothesized effects depending on contextual stratification, see Gary L. Theisen, Paul Achola, and Francis Musa Boakari, "Cross-national Achievement Studies: Shadow or Substance?" (paper presented at the annual meeting of the Comparative and International Education Society, Tallahassee, Fla., March 1981).

generating in a meaningful way. Theoretically there are any number of more policy-relevant ways this can be done; the empirical realization of this control will perhaps mark the next major breakthrough in cross-cultural educational research.

We have been rather critical of the lack of articulation between cross-national designs and their applications. Lest we be accused of "throwing the baby out with the bath water," we are quick to suggest that such studies do occupy an important place in educational research, but only if two conditions are met. First, control variables and sampling designs must be adequate to ensure true comparability of causal processes and resulting inferences. Second, the analysis must take place along the lines of clearly demarcated sociopolitical milieus that have a hypothesized bearing on the interaction of the determining variables.

Future cross-national studies of achievement will undoubtedly yield a bounty of data that will hold the attention of curriculum methodologists, policy planners, and social scientists for some years to come. Unfortunately, there is a tendency to regard standardized achievement tests not as measures of how much individual pupils know but as an index of how well schools (and worse yet, districts and national systems) are doing. The higher and more broad the level of aggregation of achievement scores, the less clearly defined the policy-relevant implications of those scores. As William Coffman, former director of the Iowa Testing Program, has observed, attention to the level of analysis is extremely important in interpreting achievement results and in targeting intervention strategies:

> National norms are developed by pooling the test scores from samples of pupils from schools all over the country—schools that teach subjects using different textbooks, different sequences, and different emphases. When patterns of growth for individual schools are charted, the patterns may be quite different from the one presented by the average. Spurts and slowdowns in the patterns appear, one school showing larger than typical changes from grade 5 to grade 6 while another school may show just the opposite. Generally, when teachers in school are asked to consider the patterns in relation to the content of the text and the characteristics of their curriculum, they can account for the departures from the norms. Sometimes, however, they can't, and it is in these cases that the test results may be most useful in directing attention to relationships between curricular patterns and test results.[33]

Although one may argue that curricular content in many IEA countries is considerably more standardized at the national level than it is in the United States, the fact remains that local educational contexts within all nations are tremendously varied. Educational strategies are unlikely to

---

[33] William E. Coffman, "Those Achievement Tests—How Useful?" *Executive Review* (University of Iowa) 1, no. 1 (1980): 2–3.

be very effective unless they take into account local objectives, methods, teaching and learning activities, and the specific social and economic contexts surrounding them. As far as the linkage between comparisons of national research efforts and policy is concerned, "there is no substitute for informed judgment based on accumulated experience in the local setting over a period of time. Unfortunately, there is a tendency to look for simple answers, and comparisons with national [and international] norms to provide such simple answers."[34] Thus, we return to Richard Wolf's plea, noted at the outset of this paper, for careful attention to well-articulated, stratified sampling procedures that call attention to, rather than suppress, regional and contextual variations in the educational process.

At the same time, a reexamination of the key social and contextual variables that may be operating at these levels is called for. Policy strategists may find that interpretation of national data is enhanced by considering such variables as: (1) occupational aspirations of student—both level and type; (2) general educational and occupational aspirational and expectational levels prevalent in the local environment; (3) job opportunities and economic payoffs in fields related to achievement in different disciplinary areas; (4) quantity and emphasis of instruction that occur within schools, especially in cases where samples stratified by regions, SES, and so forth are likely to produce sharp cross-sectional differences on these measures; (5) classroom environment measures such as the extent to which independence is fostered, authority is exhibited, encouragement is supplied, and so forth; (6) perceived importance of the subject by the students as assessed by (a) level of parental encouragement, (b) functional importance of achievement in subject area to the student's general status in society, and (c) functional relationship of achievement in the subject to educational and occupational goals; and (7) general structure of the educational system and the opportunity and values incumbent on it.

With the exception of the fifth and seventh set of variables—classroom environmental measures and structure of educational systems—questions soliciting information on the variables suggested above can be easily formatted and included in most questionnaires. Although researchers must always be conscious of the problem of overburdening respondents in the collection of data, the policy-related benefits would seem to outweigh by far the liabilities associated with expanding slightly the research agenda.

As indicated at the outset of this paper, national achievement studies are beset by a host of linguistic, logistical, and methodological problems. It is a tribute to past investigations that we have as much high-quality data as we now possess. However, with many nations of the world paying

[34] Ibid., p. 3 (our parenthetical comment).

increased attention not only to the provision of basic educational opportunities for their populations but also to improving the quality of the training that goes on within schools, the time is ripe to move from aggregate, descriptive studies of determinants of achievement to those that will be of use in vitalizing efforts to improve educational outcomes.

Ideology, Reproduction, and Educational Reform

MICHAEL W. APPLE

Introduction

Liberal educators have taken a rather optimistic posture on some aspects of the past 10–15 years of educational reform in the United States. This is particularly evident, perhaps, in those individuals and groups who are concerned primarily with curriculum, with the knowledge that gets into schools, and who have either witnessed or participated in the growth of discipline-centered curricula throughout the country. The position is often taken that school people, scholars, the business community, parents, and others, all somehow working together, have set in motion forces that have increased the stock of disciplinary knowledge that all students are to get. Supposedly, this process of increased distribution of knowledge has been enhanced by comparatively large amounts of funding on a national level for curriculum development, teacher training and retraining, and so on. Success may not have been total—after all, it almost never is—but better management and dissemination strategies can be generated to deal with these kinds of problems.

Given this posture, we have tended to forget that, often, what is not asked about such widespread efforts at "reform" may be more important than what we commonsensically like to ask. Who benefits from such reforms? What are their latent connections to the ways inequality may be maintained? Do the very ways we tend to look at schools and especially the knowledge and culture they overtly and covertly teach (even ways generated out of a fairly radical perspective) cover some of the interests that they embody? What frameworks have been and need to be developed to generate the evidence which answers to these kinds of questions require? In what follows, I shall outline some approaches for dealing with these issues, approaches which incorporate some of the current economic criticisms of schooling but which also respond to the complex functioning of schools that even some of the analysts of the political economy of education may tend to gloss over. Only when we can see this complex functioning, some of which embodies clear economic

The analysis on which this article is based is expanded in Michael W. Apple, *Ideology and Curriculum* (London: Routledge & Kegan Paul, in press).

Reprinted from *Comparative Education Review*, vol. 22, no. 3 (October 1978).

APPLE

and cultural contradictions, can we honestly judge the worth of many of
the recent curricular reform effects to change schools in various ways. In
order to do this, we shall have to focus more clearly on two things: (1) the
ideological as well as economic role of schooling in general and the
curriculum within it and (2) the ideological role of the models most
commonly used by educators and policy analysts to understand these
reforms.

Cultural and Economic Reproduction

Many economists and not a few sociologists and historians of education have a peculiar way of looking at schools. They envision the
institution of schooling as something like a black box. One measures
input before students enter schools and then measures output along the
way or when "adults" enter the labor force. What actually goes on within
the black box—what is taught, the concrete experience of children and
teachers—is less important in this view than the more global and
macroeconomic considerations of rate of return on investment or, more
radically, the reproduction of the division of labor. While these are
important considerations, perhaps especially that dealing with the role of
the school as a reproductive force in an unequal society, by the very
nature of a vision of school as black box they cannot demonstrate how
these effects are *built within* schools. Therefore, these individuals are less
precise than they could be in explaining part of the role of cultural
institutions in the reproduction they want to describe. Yet, as I shall
argue here, such cultural explanations need to be gotten at; but it
requires a different but often complementary orientation than the ones
these and other scholars employ.

There is a unique combination of elite and popular culture in schools.
As institutions, they provide exceptionally interesting, and politically and
economically potent, areas for the investigation of mechanisms of cultural distribution in a society. Thinking of schools as mechanisms of
cultural distribution is important since, as the late Italian Marxist Antonio
Gramsci noted, a critical element in enhancing the ideological dominance
of certain classes is the control of the knowledge preserving and producing institutions of a particular society.[1] Thus, the "reality" that schools
and other cultural institutions select, preserve, and distribute may need
to be particularized, in Mannheim's words,[2] so that it can be seen as a
particular "social construction" which may not serve the interests of every
individual and group in society.

[1] Thomas R. Bates, "Gramsci and the Theory of Hegemony," *Journal of the History of Ideas* 36
(April–June 1975): 36.
[2] Karl Mannheim, *Ideology and Utopia* (New York: Harcourt, Brace & World, 1936).

Now it has become something of a commonplace in recent sociological and educational literature to speak of reality as a social construction. By this, these scholars, especially those of a phenomenological bent, mean two things. (1) Becoming a person is a social act, a process of initiation in which the neophyte accepts a particular social reality as reality *tout court*, as the way life "really is." (2) On a larger scale, the social meanings which sustain and organize a collectivity are created by the continuing patterns of commonsense interaction of people as they go about their lives.[3] Now this insertion of the social element back into what has increasingly become a psychological problem in Anglo-Western society is certainly an improvement over the view of many educators who hold that the patterns of meanings which people use to organize their lives and attempt to transmit through their cultural institutions are independent of social or ideological influences. The notion that there is a "social construction of reality" is a bit too general, however, and not as helpful as we might think in understanding the relationships that exist between cultural institutions, particularly schools, and the framework and texture of social and economic forms in general. As Whitty succinctly puts it, "the overemphasis on the notion that reality is socially constructed seems to have led to a neglect of the consideration of how and why reality comes to be constructed in particular ways and how and why particular constructions of reality seem to have the power to resist subversion."[4] Thus, the general principle of the social construction of reality does not explain why certain social and cultural meanings and not others are distributed through schools, nor does it explain how the control of the knowledge preserving and producing institutions may be linked to the ideological dominance of powerful groups in a social collectivity.

The opposite principle, that knowledge is not related in any significant way to the organization and control of social and economic life, is also problematic, of course, though this may be a surprise to many curriculum theorists. This is best stated by Raymond Williams in his critical analysis of the social distribution of culture:

> The pattern of meanings and values through which people conduct their whole lives can be seen for a time as autonomous, and as evolving within its own terms, but it is quite unreal, ultimately, to separate this pattern from a precise political and economic system, which can extend its influence into the most unexpected regions of feeling and behavior. The common prescription of

[3] This is, of course, best laid out by Peter Berger and Thomas Luckmann, *The Social Construction of Reality* (New York: Doubleday, 1966). The most articulate challenge to the use of such "phenomenological" formulations in education is found in Rachel Sharp and Anthony Green, *Education and Social Control: A Study in Progressive Primary Education* (London: Routledge & Kegan Paul, 1975).

[4] Geoff Whitty, "Sociology and the Problem of Radical Educational Change," in *Educability, Schools and Ideology*, ed. Michael Flude and John Ahier (London: Halstead, 1974), p. 125.

education, as the key to change, ignores the fact that the form and content of education are affected, and in some cases determined, by the actual systems of [political] decision and [economic] maintenance.[5]

Both Whitty and Williams are raising quite difficult issues about what might be called the relationship between ideology and school knowledge, yet the context is generally British. It should not surprise us that there is a rather extensive history of dealing with issues concerning the connections between culture and control on the Continent and in England. For one thing, they have had a less hidden set of class antagonisms than the United States. That the tradition of ideological analysis is less visible in American educational and cultural scholarship speaks to two other concerns though: the ahistorical nature of most educational activity and the dominance of an ethic of amelioration through technical models in most curriculum discourse.[6] The ahistorical nature of the field of curriculum is rather interesting here. Anyone familiar with the intense argumentation both within and on the fringes of the Progressive Education Association during its history soon realizes that one of the major points of contention among progressive educators was the problem of indoctrination. Should schools, guided by a vision of a more just society, teach a particular set of social meanings to their students? Should they concern themselves only with progressive pedagogical techniques, rather than espouse a particular social and economic cause? Questions of this type "plagued" democratically minded educators in the past, and the controversy continues, though in a different vocabulary, to this day.

In fact, as Stanwood Cobb, one of the early organizers of the Progressive Education Association, stated in a recent interview, many progressive educators throughout the early decades of this century were quite cautious about even raising the question of what actual content should be taught and evaluated in schools. They often preferred to concern themselves primarily with teaching methods, in part because the determination of curriculum was perceived as inherently a political issue which could split the movement.[7] Cobb's estimation of the larger structural causes behind these educators' choice of arenas in which to act may or may not be historically accurate. The fact remains though that, at least phenomenologically, many educators recognized that the culture pre-

---

[5] Raymond Williams, *The Long Revolution* (London: Chatto & Windus, 1961), pp. 119–20.

[6] Herbert M. Kliebard, "Persistent Curriculum Issues in Historical Perspective," in *Curriculum Theorizing: The Reconceptualists*, ed. William Pinar (Berkeley: McCutchan, 1975), pp. 39–50.

[7] Taped interview given at the University of Wisconsin—Madison. The necessity for large-scale educational reform movements to have this cautious penumbra of vagueness is analyzed further in B. Paul Komisar and James McClellan, "The Logic of Slogans," in *Language and Concepts in Education*, ed. B. Othanel Smith and Robert Ennis (Chicago: Rand McNally, 1961), pp. 195–214.

served and distributed by schools as well as other institutions was not necessarily neutral. They perceived their own actions as often stemming from that recognition. Unfortunately, as I noted, these recurring historically significant issues have not informed current curriculum argumentation in the United States as much as they have in, say, England and France. Yet, there is a growing recognition that schools in advanced industrial societies like our own may serve certain social classes rather well and other classes not at all well. Thus, I can think of few areas of investigation more pressing than that which seeks to uncover the linkages between meaning and control in our cultural institutions.

While I cannot present a fully worked-out theory of culture and control at this time (though individuals such as Raymond Williams, Pierre Bourdieu, and Basil Bernstein have begun such a task),[8] I would like to do a number of things here. First, I will provide a discussion of the basic framework of assumptions under which the recent work on the relationship between ideology and school experience operates. This will be compared with the traditions which now predominate in curriculum research today. I will then take one aspect of the argument about the linkages between curriculum and ideological and economic structure and outline some general propositions about it. These propositions should be seen more as hypotheses than as final proof and will undoubtedly require historical, conceptual and empirical—to say nothing of comparative—investigations to demonstrate their fruitfulness. These hypotheses will concern the relationship between what curricular knowledge is accorded high status in our society and its economic and cultural effects. I shall argue that it is difficult to think through the past and present problems of the form and content of curriculum without attempting to uncover the complex nexus linking cultural and economic reproduction together. Let us begin by briefly examining the extant traditions—as ideal types—that tend to provide the assumptive background of a good deal of current curriculum work.

The Achievement and Socialization Traditions

A large proportion of educational and curriculum theories and scholarship today derive their programmatic impetus and their logical warrant from the various psychologies of learning now available. While Schwab and others have demonstrated that it is a logical error to attempt

---

[8] See, e.g., Raymond Williams, *The Country and the City* (New York: Oxford University Press, 1973); Pierre Bourdieu and Jean Claude Passeron, *Reproduction in Education, Society and Culture* (London: Sage Publications, 1977); and Basil Bernstein, *Class, Codes and Control*, vol. 3, *Towards a Theory of Educational Transmissions*, 2d ed. (London: Routledge & Kegan Paul, 1977).

to derive a theory of curriculum (or pedagogy) from a theory of learning[9]—something all too many curriculum theorists still do not seem to realize—there is another difficulty that is more germane to my own discussion here. The language of learning tends to be apolitical and ahistorical, thus hiding the complex nexus of political and economic power and resources that lies behind a considerable amount of curriculum organization and selection. In brief, it is not an adequate linguistic tool for dealing with what must be a prior set of curriculum questions about some of the possible ideological roots of school knowledge. In their simplest aspects, these questions can be reduced to the following issues: "What is actually taught in schools?" "What are the manifest and latent social functions of the knowledge that is taught in schools?" "How do the principles of selection and organization that are used to plan, order, and evaluate that knowledge function in the cultural and economic reproduction of class relations in an advanced industrial society like our own?"[10] These questions are not usually part of the language game of psychology. Let us examine the conceptual framework, the board, on which language games of this type are played just a bit further.

There seem to have been two rather distinct ways educators (and psychologists, sociologists, and economists) have investigated school knowledge. One has centered around the issue of academic achievement. The second has been concerned less with questions of achievement than with the role of schools as socialization mechanisms.[11]

In the academic achievement model, curricular knowledge itself is not made problematic; rather, the knowledge that finds its way into schools is usually accepted as given so that comparisons can be made among social groups, schools, children, etc. Thus, academic performance, differentiation, and stratification based on relatively unexamined presuppositions of what is to be construed as valuable knowledge are the guiding interests behind the research. The focus tends to be on determining the variables that have a major impact on an individual's or group's success or failure in school, such as the "adolescent subculture," the unequal distribution of educational resources, or, say, the social background of the students. The social goal is maximizing academic productivity.

[9] Joseph Schwab, *The Practical: A Language for Curriculum* (Washington, D.C.: National Education Association, 1970), and Dwayne Huebner, "Implications of Psychological Thought for the Curriculum," in *Influences in Curriculum Change*, ed. Glenys Unruh and Robert Leeper (Washington, D.C.: ASCD, 1968), pp. 28–37.

[10] I have discussed these issues further in Michael W. Apple and Nancy King, "What Do Schools Teach?" *Curriculum Inquiry* 6, no. 4 (1977): 341–58.

[11] I am drawing on the insightful exposition of these two research traditions in Philip Wexler, "Ideology and Utopia in American Sociology of Education" (unpublished paper, Department of Sociology, University of Wisconsin—Madison), pp. 20–21.

Unlike the academic achievement model, the socialization approach does not necessarily leave school knowledge unexamined. In fact, one of its primary interests is in exploring the social norms and values that are taught in school. However, because of this interest, it restricts itself to the study of what might be called "moral knowledge." It establishes as given *the* set of societal values and inquires into how the school as an agent of society socializes students into its "shared" set of normative rules and dispositions. Robert Dreeben's well-known little book, *On What Is Learned in Schools*, can provide an excellent example here.[12]

These approaches are not totally wrong, of course, and have in the past contributed to our understanding of schools as cultural and social mechanisms, though perhaps not always in the way the approaches intended. In fact, one advantage of the extended accounts of, say, socialization by Dreeben and others is that they enhance our ability to illuminate what is taken for granted as common sense, as given, for such an approach to actually be accepted as a cogent explanation at all.[13] As such, they point beyond themselves to the nature of meaning and control in schools.

What they tacitly accept and, hence, fail to question is important for, on closer inspection, each of these two research traditions is problematic in its own way. The academic achievement model, influenced more and more strongly by managerial concerns of technical control and efficiency, has begun to neglect the actual content of the knowledge itself, thus failing to take seriously the possible connection between economics and the structure of school knowledge other than to argue, say, the importance of the "production" of students with strong disciplinary affiliations if "democracy is to be kept strong," and so on. The socialization tradition, while insightful in its own way, focuses on social consensus and on the parallels that exist between the "given" values of a larger collectivity and educational institutions. It thus ignores to a very large extent the political and economic context in which such social values function and by which certain sets of social values become the (by whose definition?) dominant values.[14] Furthermore, both almost totally disregard some of the latent functions of the form and content of the school curriculum. And this is exactly what the tradition of what has come to be called the "sociology of school knowledge" wants to inquire into.[15]

[12] Robert Dreeben, *On What Is Learned in Schools* (Reading, Mass.: Addison-Wesley, 1968).

[13] Michael F. D. Young, "On the Politics of Educational Knowledge," in *Education in Great Britain and Ireland*, ed. R. Bell (Oxford: Oxford University Press, 1973), p. 201.

[14] Wexler, p. 21.

[15] For further examination of the roots of this tradition, see Michael W. Apple, "Power and School Knowledge," *Review of Education* 3 (January/February 1977): 26–49; and Michael W. Apple and Philip Wexler, "Cultural Capital and Educational Transmissions," *Educational Theory* 27 (Winter 1978): 34–43.

The Sociology and Economics of School Knowledge

A fundamental starting point in this third and more critical tradition is that articulated by Young in his argument that there is a "dialectical relationship between access to power and the opportunity to legitimize certain dominant categories, and the processes by which the availability of such categories to some groups enables them to assert power and control over others."[16] Thus, to put it another way, the problematic involves examining how a system of unequal power in society is maintained, and partly recreated, by means of the "transmission" of culture.[17] The school, as a rather significant agent of cultural and economic reproduction (after all, every child goes to it, and it has important effects as both a credentialing and socializing institution) becomes an important institution here, obviously.

Like the socialization tradition, the focus of these investigations has been on how a society stabilizes itself. What is the place of schools in maintaining the way economic and educational goods and services are controlled, produced, and distributed? However, these questions are guided by a more critical posture than, say, Dreeben, for much of these individuals' commitment to this particular kind of problem stems from an affiliation with socialist movements. They begin with something broadly like a Rawlsian theory of justice, that is, for a society to be truly just, it must maximize the advantage of the least advantaged.[18] Thus, any society which increases the relative gap between, say, rich and poor in the control of and access to cultural and economic "capital" (as recent economic reports show ours does, for instance) needs to be questioned. How is this inequality made legitimate? Why is it accepted? As Gramsci would put it, how is this hegemony maintained?

For many of these researchers, this seeming social and ideological stability is seen in part "as relying upon the deep and often unconscious internalization by the individual of the principles which govern the existing social order."[19] However, these principles are not perceived as being neutral. They are seen as intimately interconnected with economic and political stratification.

For example, in the American, British, and French analyses currently being done by Bowles and Gintis, myself, Bernstein, Young, and Bour-

[16] Michael F. D. Young, "Knowledge and Control," in *Knowledge and Control*, ed. Michael F. D. Young (London: Collier-Macmillan, 1971), p. 8.

[17] Bourdieu and Passeron, p. 5.

[18] I have analyzed the conceptual and political commitments further in Apple, "Power and School Knowledge."

[19] Madeleine MacDonald, *The Curriculum and Cultural Reproduction* (Milton Keynes, England: Open University Press, 1977), p. 60.

dieu, the individual's underlying perception of the social order of which he or she is a part provides the locus of understanding. Thus, for instance, a British commentator on Bowles and Gintis's interesting but too mechanistic book writes:[20] "In the work of Bowles and Gintis emphasis is given to the importance of schooling in forming the different personality types which correspond to the requirements of a system of work relations within an economic mode of production."[21] In this way, for Bowles and Gintis, not only does education allocate individuals to a relatively fixed set of positions in society—an allocation of positions determined by economic and political forces—but the process of education itself, the formal and hidden curriculum, socializes people to accept as legitimate the limited roles they ultimately fill in society.[22]

Other similarly oriented scholars take a comparable stance in examining the effect schools may have on the formation of the consciousness of individuals. Thus, for instance, Basil Bernstein and I have argued that, to a significant extent, "through education the individual's 'mental structures' (i.e., categories of thought, language, and behavior) are formed, and that these mental structures derive from the social division of labor." In France, the investigation of the relationship between cultural reproduction and economic reproduction is being carried out in a parallel vein by Bourdieu. He analyzes the cultural rules, what he calls the *habitus*, that link economic and cultural control and distribution together.[23]

Bourdieu focuses on the student's ability to cope with what might be called "middle-class culture." He argues that the cultural capital stored in schools acts as an effective filtering device in the reproduction of a hierarchical society. For example, schools partly recreate the social and economic hierarchies of the larger society through what is seemingly a neutral process of selection and instruction. They take the cultural capital, the *habitus*, of the middle class, as natural and employ it as if all children have had equal access to it. However, "by taking all children as equal, while implicitly favoring those who have already acquired the linguistic and social competencies to handle middle-class culture, schools take as natural what is essentially a social gift, i.e., cultural capital."[24] Bourdieu asks us, thus, to think of cultural capital as we would economic

[20] Samuel Bowles and Herbert Gintis, *Schooling in Capitalist America* (New York: Basic, 1975).

[21] MacDonald, p. 309. This piece also provides a number of interesting criticisms of Bowles and Gintis's reliance on a correspondence theory.

[22] John W. Meyer, "The Effects of Education as an Institution," *American Journal of Sociology* 53 (July 1977): 64.

[23] MacDonald, pp. 34–47; see also, Apple and King (n. 10 above); and Bourdieu and Passeron (n. 8 above).

[24] Roger Dale, Geoff Esland, and Madeleine MacDonald, eds., *Schooling and Capitalism: A Sociological Reader* (London: Routledge & Kegan Paul, 1976), p. 4.

capital. Just as our dominant economic institutions are structured so that those who inherit or already have economic capital do better, so too does cultural capital act in the same way. Cultural capital ("good taste," certain kinds of prior knowledge, abilities, and language forms) is unequally distributed throughout society, and this is dependent in large part on the division of labor and power in that society. "By selecting for such properties, schools serve to reproduce the distribution of power within the society."[25] For Bourdieu, to understand completely what schools do, who succeeds and who fails, one must not see culture as neutral, as necessarily contributing to social progress. Rather, one sees the culture tacitly preserved in and expected by schools as contributing to inequality outside of these institutions.

Behind these points, hence, is an argument which states that we shall have to recognize that, like poverty, poor achievement is not an aberration. Both poverty and curricular problems, such as low achievement, are integral *products* of the organization of economic, cultural, and social life as we know it.[26] (I shall have more to say about seeing many curricular problems, such as achievement, as "naturally produced" by our institutions shortly, when we consider further the formal corpus of school knowledge in the next section of this analysis.)

Given arguments of this type, then, what is it that this third tradition is basically saying?

> The assumption underlying most of the "reproduction" theories is that education plays a mediating role between the individual's consciousness and society at large. These theorists maintain that the rules which govern social behavior, attitudes, morals and beliefs are filtered down from the macro level of economic and political structures to the individual via work experience, education processes and family socialization. The individual acquires a particular awareness and perception of the society in which he lives. And it is this understanding and attitude towards the social order which [in large part] constitute his consciousness.[27]

Schools, therefore, "process" both knowledge and people. In essence, the formal and informal knowledge is used as a complex filter to process people, often by class; and, at the same time, different dispositions and values are taught to different school populations, again often by class (and sex and race). In effect, for this more critical tradition, schools latently recreate cultural and economic disparities, though this is certainly not what most school people intend at all.

---

[25] Ibid.

[26] R. W. Connell, *Ruling Class, Ruling Culture* (New York: Cambridge University Press, 1977), p. 219.

[27] MacDonald, p. 60.

Let me pause here to clarify one thing: This is not to maintain that either culture or consciousness is mechanistically determined (in the strong sense of that term) by economic structure. Rather, it seeks both to bring to a level of awareness and to make historically and empirically problematic the dialectical relationship between cultural control and distribution and economic and political stratification.[28] Our ordinary perceptions—ones taken from the achievement and socialization models—hence, are bracketed. The "cognitive interest" underlying the research program is to look relationally, if you will, to think about school knowledge as being generated out of ideological and economic conflicts "outside" as well as "inside" education. These conflicts and forces set limits on (not mechanistically determine) cultural responses. This requires subtlety, not appraisals which argue for a one-to-one correspondence between institutional life and cultural forms. Neither all curricula nor all culture are "mere products" of simple economic forces.[29]

In fact, I want to note a critical caveat at this point. There is an obvious danger here, one that should not go unrecognized. To make the actual "stuff" of curriculum problematic, to hold what currently counts as legitimate knowledge up to ideological scrutiny, can lead to a rather vulgar brand of relativism. That is, to see overt and hidden curricular knowledge as social and historical products ultimately tends to raise questions about the criteria of validity and truth we employ.[30] The epistemological issues that might be raised here are not uninteresting, to say the least. However, the point behind these investigations is not to relativize totally either our knowledge or our criteria for warranting its truth or falsity (though the Marxist tradition has a long history of just this debate, as the controversy between, say, Adorno and Popper documents; we have much to learn from the epistemological and political issues raised by this debate, by the way).[31] Rather, as I just mentioned, the methodological dictum is to think relationally or structurally. In clearer

---

[28] The two-way nature of this relationship—how culture and economics interpenetrate and act on each other in a dynamic fashion—is best examined in Raymond Williams, "Base and Superstructure in Marxist Cultural Theory," *New Left Review* 83 (November/December 1973): 3–16.

[29] Ibid.; see also the final chapter, "Aspects of the Relations between Education and Production," Bernstein (n. 8 above).

[30] Michael F. D. Young, "Taking Sides against the Probable," *Rationality, Education and the Social Organization of Knowledge*, ed. Chris Jenks (London: Routledge & Kegan Paul, 1977), pp. 86–96; and Michael W. Apple, "Curriculum as Ideological Selection," *Comparative Education Review* 20 (June 1976): 209–15.

[31] See, e.g., Albrecht Wellmer, *Critical Theory of Society* (New York: Herder & Herder, 1971), esp. chap. 1; see also the discussion of the position taken by the French Marxist philosopher of science, Louis Althusser, in Miriam Glucksmann, *Structuralist Analysis in Contemporary Social Thought* (London: Routledge & Kegan Paul, 1974). Though it may be difficult to deal with "proving" critically oriented social assertions using the positivist tradition, this does not mean that empirical documentaion of aspects of the problem is inconsequential. This is nicely argued in Connell (n. 26 above).

terms, one should look for the subtle connections between educational phenomena, such as curriculum, and the latent social and economic outcomes of the institution.

These points are obviously similar to those often associated with the critical theorists of the Frankfurt school, who have argued that the context in which we perceive social facts, the general way we conceptually organize our world, may hide the fact that these seemingly commonsensical appearances serve particular interests.[32] But these interests cannot merely be assumed; they need to be documented. In order to lay some of the foundation of this documentation, we shall need to turn to some of the hypotheses that I mentioned earlier, I would suggest. We shall need to explore how cultural distribution and economic power are intimately intertwined, not just in the teaching of "moral knowledge" as in some of the reproduction theorists, but in the formal corpus of school knowledge itself.

On the Problem of High-Status Knowledge

The discussion in the previous sections of this analysis centered on the general political, economic, and conceptual arguments that those people interested in the problem of ideology and curriculum have focused upon. It compared this critical tradition with the current achievement and socialization models predominant in the field. I should now like to take one aspect of the relationship between cultural distribution and economic power and explore it further. I want to employ this critical framework in order to engage in some speculations about how certain knowledge— particularly that knowledge which is considered to be most prestigious in schools—may, in fact, be linked to economic reproduction. In essence, I want to begin to think through some of the issues associated with the distribution of knowledge and the creation of inequality that people like Bourdieu, Bernstein, Young, and others have sought to raise. At the forefront of our minds, I think, should be Bourdieu's point that I noted in the last section. If you want to understand how cultural and economic/political forms work in tandem, then think of both as aspects of capital.

In order to delve into the connections between these forms, I shall be using the language of cultural "transmissions," in effect treating cultural artifacts and knowledge as if they were things. However, the notion of "as if" must be understood as exactly that, as a metaphor for dealing with a much more complex process in which, say, students do not merely take in

[32] Ian Hextall and Madan Sarup, "School Knowledge, Evaluation and Alienation," in *Society, State and Schooling*, ed. Michael Young and Geoff Whitty (London: Falmer, 1977), pp. 151–71.

information, cultural attributes, etc., but rather they also transform (and sometimes reject) these expected dispositions, propensities, skills, and facts into biographically significant meanings.[33] Thus, while the act of treating knowledge as a thing makes for ease of discussion, a methodological simplification if you will, it needs to be understood as just such a simplifying act. (The fact that it is usually considered a thing in our society does, of course, point to its reification as a commodity in advanced industrial societies.)[34]

Once again, one of Michael F. D. Young's arguments is helpful as a beginning here. He states that "those in positions of power will attempt to define what is taken as knowledge, how accessible to different groups any knowledge is, and what are accepted relationships between different knowledge areas and between those who have access to them and make them available."[35] Though this is not always or even necessarily a conscious process of manipulation and control, and hence may be a bit overstated, it does raise the issue of the relative status of knowledge and its accessibility. For within this statement is a proposition that might entail something like the following. The possession of high-status knowledge, knowledge that is considered of exceptional import and is connected to the structure of corporate economies, is related to and in fact seems to entail the nonpossession by others. In essence, high-status knowledge "is by definition scarce, and its scarcity is inextricably linked to its instrumentality."[36]

This is an exceptionally critical point and needs to be gone into a bit further. I have argued that schools do not merely "process" people but that they "process" knowledge as well. They enhance and give legitimacy to particular types of cultural resources which are related to unequal economic forms. In order to understand this, we want to think about the kinds of knowledge that schools take as the most important, that they want to maximize. I shall define this as technical knowledge, not to denigrate it, but to differentiate it from, say, aesthetics, physical grace, and so on. The conception of the maximization of technical knowledge is

[33] See the articles by Hugh Mehan and Robert MacKay in *Childhood and Socialization*, ed. Hans Peter Dreitzel (New York: Macmillan, 1973), and Linda M. McNeil, "Economic Dimensions of Social Studies Curricula: Curriculum as Institutionalized Knowledge" (doctoral thesis, University of Wisconsin—Madison, 1977).

[34] Whitty (n. 4 above).

[35] Michael F. D. Young, "An Approach to the Study of Curricula as Socially Organized Knowledge," in Young, *Knowledge and Control*. There are interesting parallels here between the work of Young and Huebner in their joint focus on curricular accessibility (cf. Dwayne Huebner, "Curriculum as the Accessibility of Knowledge," mimeographed [paper presented at the Curriculum Theory Study Group, Minneapolis, March 2, 1970]).

[36] Bernice Fischer, "Conceptual Masks: An Essay Review of Fred Inglis, *Ideology and the Imagination*," *Review of Education* 1 (November 1975): 526; see also Hextall and Sarup, pp. 151–71.

a useful principle, I think, in beginning to unpack some of the linkages
between cultural capital and economic capital.[37]

Our kind of economic system is organized in such a way that it can
create only a certain amount of jobs and still maintain high profit levels
for corporations. In essence, the economic apparatus is at its most
efficient when there is a (measured) unemployment rate of approximately 4%–6% (though we know that this is a notoriously inaccurate
measure to which must also be added both the issues of much higher
rates for blacks and of high levels of underemployment). To provide
useful work for these individuals would require cutting into acceptable
rates of return and would probably require at least the partial reorganization of so called "market mechanisms" which apportion jobs and resources. Because of this, it would not be a misplaced metaphor to describe
our economic system as *naturally generating* specifiable levels of under-
and unemployment.[38] We can think of this model as one which is
primarily concerned with the maximization of the production of profit
and only secondarily concerned with the distribution of resources and
employment.

Now a similar model seems to hold true when we think about
knowledge in its relationship to such an economy. A corporate economy
requires the production of high levels of technical knowledge to keep the
economic apparatus running effectively and to become more sophisticated in the maximization of opportunities for economic expansion.
Within certain limits, what is actually required is *not* the widespread
distribution of this high-status knowledge to the populace in general.
What is needed more is to maximize its production. As long as the
knowledge form is continually and efficiently produced, the school itself,
at least in this major aspect of its function, is efficient. Thus, certain low
levels of achievement on the part of "minority" group students, children
of the poor, and so on can be tolerated. It is less consequential to the
economy than is the generation of the knowledge itself. Once again,
production of a particular "commodity" (here, high-status knowledge) is
of more concern than the distribution of that particular commodity. To
the extent that it does not interfere with the production of technical

---

[37] The principle that schools serve to maximize the production of technical knowledge was first
noted by Walter Feinberg in his provocative chapter, "A Critical Analysis of the Social and Economic
Limits to the Humanizing of Education," in *Humanistic Education: Visions and Realities*, ed. Richard H.
Weller (Berkeley: McCutchan, 1977), pp. 249–69. My analysis here is indebted to his own.

[38] Andrew Hacker, "Cutting Classes," *New York Review of Books* 23 (May 1976): 15. Hacker notes
that at full employment our economy can usefully employ only about 43% of the work-age
population. It is not profitable to employ more than that. "Some of the unnecessary 57% become
housewives, college students, or retire on moderate pension. Others, however, must settle for a
lifetime of poverty because the economic system offers them no alternatives."

knowledge, then, concerns about distributing it more equitably can be tolerated as well.

Thus, just as in the "economic market place" where it is more efficient to have a relatively constant level of unemployment, to actually generate it really, so do cultural institutions "naturally" generate levels of poor achievement. The distribution or scarcity of certain forms of cultural capital is of less moment in this calculus of values than the maximization of the production of the particular knowledge itself.

This, I think, goes a long way in explaining the economic role of the debate on standards and open enrollment at universities. It also clarifies some of the reasons school and curricula seem to be organized toward university life in terms of the dominance of subject-centered curricula and the relative prestige given to differing curricular areas. This relationship between economic structure and high-status knowledge might also explain some of the large disparities we see in levels of funding for curricular innovations in technical areas and, say, the arts.

The structure-of-discipline movement provides an interesting example of a number of these points about power and culture. The discipline-centered approach was not a serious challenge to the traditional view of curriculum; rather, it was an argument that a particular commodity— here academic knowledge—by a particular community was not being effectively "marketed" in schools.[39] Even when it was accepted by most school people as the most important curricular knowledge and was given large doses of federal support to assist its adoption in schools, competing power claims were evident about what was to be high-status knowledge.

For instance, substantial funding was given to mathematics and science curriculum development while less was given to the arts and humanities. This occurred then and still occurs now for two possible reasons. First is the question of economic utility. The benefits of maximizing the production of scientific and technical knowledge are easily visible and, at least at the time, seemed relatively noncontroversial. Second, high-status knowledge appears to be discrete knowledge. It has a (supposedly) identifiable content and (again, supposedly) stable structure[40] that are both teachable and, what is critically important, testable. The arts and humanities have obviously been seen to be less amenable to such

---

[39] Geoff Whitty and Michael F. D. Young, "The Politics of School Knowledge," *Times Educational Supplement* (September 5, 1973), p. 20.

[40] This is an empirical claim, of course, and is falsifiable. There are a number of educators and scientists who would take issue with such a simplification of science and mathematics (see, e.g., Thomas Kuhn, *The Structure of Scientific Revolutions* [Chicago: University of Chicago Press, 1970]). What aspects of scientific "paradigms" are stable is being argued right now (see Imre Lakatos and Alan Musgrave, *Criticism and the Growth of Knowledge* [London: Cambridge University Press, 1970], and Stephen Toulmin, *Human Understanding* [Princeton, N.J.: Princeton University Press, 1972]).

criteria, supposedly because of the very nature of their subject matter. Thus, one has a twofold, nearly circular proposition working here. High-status knowledge is seen as macroeconomically beneficial in terms of long-run benefits to the most powerful classes in society; and the socially accepted definitions of high-status knowledge preclude consideration of nontechnical knowledge.

It is important to note the stress on macroeconomic considerations. Obviously, television repair is a subject which, if learned well, may provide economic benefits to its user. However, the economy itself will not be unduly impaired if this is not accorded prestige status. In fact, if Braverman's analysis is correct—that our economic structure requires the continual division and breaking down of complex skills into less complex and more standardized skills—economic control may be helped by the lack of prestige given to such craftsmanship. The same does not seem to hold true for technical knowledge.[41]

We have two levels working here again. The constitutive or underlying social and economic rules make it essential that subject-centered curricula be taught, that high status be given to technical knowledge. This is, in large part, due to the selection function of schooling. Though this is more complex than I can go into here, it is easier to stratify individuals according to "academic criteria" when technical knowledge is used. This stratification or gouping is important because not all individuals are seen as having the ability to contribute to the generation of the required knowledge form (as well as partly because of the structural requirements of the division of labor, of course). Thus, the cultural content (legitimate or high-status knowledge) is used as a device or filter for economic stratification,[42] thereby enhancing the continued expansion of technical knowledge in an economy like ours, as well. At the same time, however, one might expect that, within this constitutive framework, educators would be relatively free to respond (or not to respond) to more immediate economic pressures, such as career education and so forth.

In short, one major reason that subject-centered curricula dominate most schools, that integrated curricula are found in relatively few schools, is at least partly the result of the place of the school in maximizing the production of high-status knowledge. This is closely interrelated with the school's role in the selection of agents to fill economic and social positions in a relatively stratified society.

With Young, I have suggested here that some of the relations among

---

[41] Harry Braverman, *Labor and Monopoly Capital* (New York: Monthly Review Press, 1975).

[42] The close relationship between academic curricula, the distribution of scarce resources, and the labeling and tracking of high school students is documented in James E. Rosenbaum, *Making Inequality* (New York: Wiley, 1976).

who controls rewards and power in a society, the patterns of dominant values, and the organization of cultural capital can best be uncovered by focusing on the stratification of knowledge. It would not be illogical to claim that, based on what I have argued here, generally, any attempt to make substantive alterations in the relationship between high-status and low-status knowledge, by, say, making different knowledge areas equal, will tend to be resisted. This would also probably mean that attempts to use different criteria to judge the relative value of different curricular areas will be looked on as illegitimate incursions, as threats to that particular "order."[43]

Examples of this are not difficult to find in the area of evaluation. For instance, the usual way one evaluates the success of curricula is by employing a technical procedure, by comparing input with output. Were test scores raised? Did the students master the material? This is, of course, the achievement model I described earlier. When educators or policy analysts want to evaluate in another, less technical way, by looking at the "quality" of that curricular experience or by raising questions about the ethical nature of the relationships involved in the interaction, they can be rather easily dismissed. Scientific and technical talk in advanced industrial societies has more legitimacy (higher status) than ethical talk. Ethical talk cannot be easily operationalized within an input/output perspective. And, finally, "scientific" criteria of evaluation give "knowledge," while ethical criteria lead to purely "subjective" considerations.

A current example might be helpful here. After massive reanalysis of studies relating schooling to mobility, Jencks, in *Inequality*, concluded that it was quite difficult to generalize about the roles schools play in increasing one's chances at a better future. Thus, he notes, it might be wiser to focus less on mobility and achievement and more on the quality of a student's actual experience in classrooms, something with strangely (though pleasantly) Deweyan overtones. However, Jencks's argument that we must pay greater attention to the quality of life within our educational institutions had its roots in ethical and political considerations and was dismissed rather readily. His criteria for making that statement were perceived as being illegitimate. They had little validity within the particular set of language games of which evaluation partakes and, hence, are accorded little status.[44]

[43] Young, "An Approach to the Study of Curriculum," in Young, *Knowledge and Control*, p. 34.

[44] Habermas's analysis of how purposive/rational or instrumental forms of language and action have come to dominate our consciousness is illuminating here (see Jurgen Habermas, *Knowledge and Human Interests* [Boston: Beacon, 1971], and Michael W. Apple, "The Process and Ideology of Valuing in Educational Settings," in *Educational Evaluation: Analysis and Responsibility*, ed. Michael W. Apple, Michal Subkoviak, and Henry Lufler, Jr. [Berkeley: McCutchan, 1974]). We would want to trace the growth in status of purposive/rational forms of action within the concomitant growth of particular economic systems. Raymond Williams's corpus of work provides essential models for this kind of inquiry (see *The Long Revolution* [n. 5 above] and *The Country and the City* [n. 8 above]).

Notice something else about what this insistence on technical criteria does. It makes both the kinds of questions raised, and the answers given to them, the province of experts, those individuals who possess the knowledge already. In this way, the relative status of the knowledge is linked to the kinds of questions deemed acceptable, which in turn seems to be linked to its nonpossession by other individuals. The form of the questions becomes an aspect of cultural reproduction since these questions can only be answered by experts who already have had the technical knowledge distributed to them. The stratification of knowledge in this case again involves the stratification of people, though less on an economic level here.

Hegemony and Reproduction

All of this is quite involved, obviously, and rather difficult to untangle, I know. While our understanding of these knotty relationshps is still tentative, it does raise anew one of the questions to which I referred earlier. Given the subtle connections in this process of the generation of cultural as well as economic reproduction, how and why do people accept it? Hence, the question of hegemony, of ideological stability, that is raised by the reproduction theorists emerges once more.[45] For it is here that the research of Bowles and Gintis, Bernstein, Bourdieu, and others on the social reproduction of the values, norms, and dispositions transmitted by the cultural apparatus of a society offers part of an explanation. One form of reproduction (through "socialization" and what has been called the hidden curriculum) complements another (the formal corpus of school knowledge), each of which seems to have ties to economic inequality. It is in the *interplay* between curricular knowledge—the stuff we teach, the "legitimate culture"—and the social relations of classroom life that the reproduction theorists describe, that we can begin to see some of the real relations schools have to an unequal economic structure.

Again notice what I am saying, for it constitutes part of an argument against the conspiracy theories so popular in some revisionist critiques of schooling. This process of reproduction is not caused (in the strong sense of that concept) by an elite group of managers who sat, or now sit, around tables plotting ways to "do in" their workers at both the workplace and the school. While such an account may accurately describe some aspects of why schools do what they do,[46] it is not a sufficient explanation of the

[45] Reviews of some of the relevant research on the question of hegemony can be found in David W. Livingston, "On Hegemony in Corporate Capitalist States," *Sociological Inquiry* 46, nos. 3 and 4 (1976): 235–50, and Connell (n. 26 above), chap. 7–10.

[46] Barry Franklin and I have documented part of this in a recent paper which examines the historical linkages between social and economic ideologies and the dominant modes of curriculum organization and selection (see Michael W. Apple and Barry Franklin, "Curricular History and Social Control," in *Community Participation in Education*, ed. Carl Grant [Boston: Allyn & Bacon, 1978]).

nexus of forces that actually seem to exist. I am arguing, instead, that, given the extant economic and political forms which now provide the principles upon which so much of our everyday lives are organized, this reproductive process is a "logical necessity" for the continued maintenance of an unequal social order. The economic and cultural unbalance follows "naturally."[47]

This may make it hard for educators such as ourselves to deal with the problem. We may, in fact, have to take seriously the political and economic commitments that guide the reproduction theorists. Serious educational analysis may require a more coherent theory of the social and economic polity of which we are a part. While I have explored cultural mechanisms here, it is just as essential to remember Williams's points that neither culture nor education are free floating. To forget that is to neglect a primary arena for collective action and commitment.

Some of this economic concern is summarized by Henry Levin. In a review of the effects of large-scale educational interventions by the government to try to reduce economic inequality through reforms in curriculum and teaching, he concludes:

> Educational policies that are aimed at resolving social dilemmas that arise out of the basic malfunctioning of the economic, social and political institutions of the society are not amenable to solution through educational policy and reform. The leverage available to the most benevolent educational reformer and policy specialist is limited by the lack of a constituency for change and the overwhelming momentum of the educational process in the direction of social reproduction of the existing polity. And, there is a deleterious result in our efforts if educational attempts to change society tend to direct attention away from the locus of the problem by creating and legitimating the ideology that schools can be used to solve problems which did not originate in the educational sector.[48]

Yet once again, we must be cautious of this kind of approach, for it can lead us back to viewing schools as little black boxes. And that is what we rejected at the outset.

Some Concluding Questions

I want to stop here, knowing full well that much more could be and needs to be said about the topics I have raised. For example, in order to go further with the relationship between high-status knowledge and an "external" social order, one would have to inquire into the history of the concomitant rise of new classes of social personnel and the growth of new types of "legitimate" knowledge.[49] These issues obviously require

[47] Williams, *The Long Revolution* (n. 5), pp. 298–99.

[48] Henry M. Levin, "A Radical Critique of Educational Policy," Occasional Paper of the Stanford University Evaluation Consortium, March 1977, mimeographed (Stanford, Calif.).

[49] Basil Bernstein has made some intriguing inroads into this area in his "Aspects of the Relations between Education and Production" in Bernstein (n. 8) (see also, Nicos Poulantzas, *Classes in Contemporary Capitalism* [London: New Left Books, 1975]).

much more thought to be given to the conceptual problem of the dialectical relationship between cultural control and social and economic structure. How does each affect the other? What role does an educational system itself play in defining particular forms of knowledge as high status? What role does it play in helping to create a credentialing process based on the possession (and nonpossession) of this cultural capital, a credentialing system that provides numbers of agents roughly equivalent to the needs of the division of labor in society? These questions imply something important, I think, for this relationship is not a one-way street. Education is both a "cause" and an "effect" here. The school is not a passive mirror but an active force, one that also serves to give legitimacy to the economic and social forms and ideologies so intimately connected to it.[50] And it is just this action which needs to be unpacked. Rather than asking whether large-scale attempts at educational and curricular reform contribute to greater "success," it might be more appropriate to ask "success for whom?"[51] If certain kinds of cultural capital are seen as important, who actually benefits from its distribution, accumulation, production, and increased legitimacy? We may find that the institutional and curricular reforms in which educators place so much hope may be part of a subtle and interconnected set of structural relations that are aspects of economic and cultural reproduction. Because of this I have argued that a serious appraisal of educational reform needs to be grounded in an analysis of the complex relationships among knowledge, ideology, economics, and power. I have suggested a number of questions and hypotheses about these relationships, as well, especially those dealing with the connections between economic and cultural capital.

Questions of this type are not usually asked in curriculum, of course. However, we need to remember that these concerns are not something totally new to the discourse surrounding American education. In fact, we must not see this kind of sociologically and economically inclined curriculum scholarship as being an attempt to carry on any so-called "reconceptualization" of the curriculum field, though that name has been applied to some recent analysts of power and school knowledge.[52] Rather, the questions which guide this work need to be seen as having rather deep roots in the curriculum field, roots we may have unfortunately forgotten, given the ahistorical nature of education.

[50] See the interesting essay by John W. Meyer (n. 22 above). Randall Collins's attempt to articulate a theory of cultural markets ("Some Comparative Principles of Educational Stratification," *Harvard Educational Review* 47 [February 1977]: 1–27) is also of some assistance here. It is a bit conceptually confused, though (see my reply to him in *Harvard Educational Review* 47 [November 1977]: 601–2).

[51] See, e.g., Rolland G. Paulston, "Social and Educational Change: Conceptual Frameworks," *Comparative Education Review* 21 (June/October 1977): 285.

[52] William Pinar, ed., *Curriculum Theorizing: The Reconceptualists* (Berkeley: McCutchan, 1975).

We need only to recall what stimulated the early social reconstructionists in education (Counts; Smith, Stanley, and Shores; Brameld; and so on) to begin to realize that one of the guiding themes in past curriculum work has been the role schools fulfill in the reproduction of an unequal society. While these individuals may have been much too optimistic in viewing schools as powerful agencies in redressing this imbalance, and while a number of them ultimately backed away from large-scale structural alterations in our polity,[53] the principle of examining the linkages between cultural and economic institutions is a valued part of our past. It is time to make it our present and future as well.

[53] Walter Feinberg, *Reason and Rhetoric: The Intellectual Foundations of Twentieth Century Liberal Educational Policy* (New York: Wiley, 1975).

Education for Alternative Development

MARTIN CARNOY

A 20-year effort to expand schooling in the Third World has largely succeeded: in 1960 there were 144 million pupils in developing country (excluding the People's Republic of China and Korea) primary and secondary
schools, and in 1976, 335 million; university-level enrollment increased
from 2.6 million to 12.5 million in the same period.[1] Even in relative
terms, the figures are impressive: 46.8 percent of 6–11-year-olds in developing countries attended school in 1960 and 61.8 percent in 1975.[2] Yet schooling was supposed to do much more than expand. Twenty years ago, "experts" implied that educational growth not only would contribute
forcefully to economic development[3] but would also equalize opportunities between social classes and income distribution[4] and develop a more
employable labor force. It may be that additional schooling in labor force
did increase productivity—indeed there is some reason to believe that it
has.[5] But at the same time, the absolute number of illiterates in the Third
World has increased;[6] the poorest 50 percent of the population remained
essentially as poor as before; income distribution, if anything, became
more unequal;[7] and open unemployment increased.[8] Poverty has been
transferred more and more from rural to urban areas, while rural areas
have continued to remain desperately poor.

It is tempting to argue that the increased education brought to Third
World populations was not relevant to the development of their societies

---

[1] Unesco, *Statistical Yearbook* (Paris: Unesco, 1980), p. 59.

[2] Ibid., p. 89.

[3] See, e.g., T. W. Schultz, *The Economic Value of Education* (New York: Columbia University
Press, 1963); Simon Kuznets, "Quantitative Aspects of the Growth of Nations. IV. Distribution of
National Income by Factor Shares," *Economic Development and Cultural Change,* vol. 7, no. 3, pt. 2
(April 1959).

[4] Simon Kuznets, "Economic Growth and Inequality," *American Economic Review* 45 (May
1955): 1–28.

[5] There are very few data which actually show an increase in productivity related to education,
largely because the most important productivity differences associated with education (if they exist)
would be in different kinds of work. Hence the difficulty of comparison of physical output per worker.
Neoclassical economists generally assume that income differences among workers represent productivity differences; in that case, more education accounts for significant increases in productivity. Mark
Blaug, *Education and the Unemployment Problem in Developing Countries* (Geneva: ILO, 1973),
treats these issues in detail, and, although his case for education's influence on productivity is probably
too strong, I think a case can be made for a positive relationship. The reader can also refer to Alex
Inkeles and David Smith, *Becoming Modern* (Cambridge, Mass.: Harvard University Press, 1974), for a
different approach which comes to the same conclusion as Blaug.

[6] World Bank, *Education Sector Policy Paper* (Washington, D.C.: World Bank, 1980).

[7] Irma Adelman and Cynthia Taft Morris, *Economic Growth and Social Equity in Developing
Countries* (Stanford, Calif.: Stanford University Press, 1973).

[8] Martin Carnoy, *Education and Employment: A Critical Appraisal* (Paris: IIEP, 1978).

Reprinted from *Comparative Education Review,* vol. 26, no. 2 (June 1982).

CARNOY

and, for that reason, it did not fulfill the distribution and employment needs of those economies; that the curriculum or the organization of the school system has been "inefficient" or "traditional" so that the children are "incorrectly" pushed either out of school too early—not realizing their full potential—or channeled into training that is difficult to employ in a "modernizing" economy. This is a tempting explanation because there *are* obviously a lot of things wrong with education in most low-income countries. It *is* characterized by high dropout rates, poor overall student performance, lack of materials, an overproduction of humanities graduates and underproduction of engineers and doctors, poor research and development capability, lack of rural education, and so on.

Can we improve educational quality, reduce illiteracy, make education more relevant for the mass of children and adults who want schooling, and improve economic and social opportunity by simply correcting these problems? Can we correct these problems within the context of societies marked by sharp social-class distinctions? To what extent is formal schooling autonomous from the society in which it is situated?

There are two different analyses used to answer these questions, and each analysis comes, quite logically, to different conclusions. The first implies that capitalist development is not marked by *inherent* class divisions; that these class divisions are either a leftover from previous (feudalistic or traditional) development or an aberration/inefficiency of a present stage of capitalist development.[9] In this analysis, again by implication, the state represents the society as a whole (or is a neutral reflector of general interests in the society) and would like, if it could, to produce an equal and just society without social classes,[10] a society with equal opportunity for all those who want it. What stands in the way of achieving such a society is lack of know-how rather than bad intentions. Thus, the problems of education are largely technical and financial; that is, the principal difficulties in resolving educational quality and equal educational opportunity are a function of sufficient resources, good management, and access to better educational techniques. Further, this analysis suggests that if more resources, better technology, and better management were forthcoming, they would produce more equitable income distribution, higher employment, and more equitable economic/social opportunity.[11]

Third World educational policymakers and planners are therefore prompted to attempt to increase the efficiency of revenue allocation in

[9] These are, of course, similar arguments made to those about the imperfections of socialist development in Eastern Europe, where the previous stages of development are capitalist and feudal. This is not to say that socialist and capitalist development are the same; we shall mention some of the differences later in this paper.

[10] This does not mean a society without individual differences in any single generation. In a society without classes, these individual differences would be distributed randomly, i.e., would not persist from generation to generation in the same groups.

[11] World Bank (see n. 6).

education (better management techniques), to increase the quantity and quality of educational resources, to shift the distribution of educational expenditures to the disadvantaged (rural, marginal urban) groups in society, to orient students to more employable careers, and to limit themselves to such efficiency reforms not only in education but also in the nature of production. Their idea is to make education better and better distributed within the context of societies where social inequality and the organization of work are fundamentally unchanged. Through educational expansion and improvement and some social/economic reforms such as progressive taxes, the worst of a society's social and economic ills can be cured.

The second analysis starts from the premise that capitalist society itself is marked by inherent class divisions and that the capitalist state in any and all of its forms is fundamentally a class state, attempting to reproduce those class divisions within a context of class struggle. Thus, even though capitalist development is marked by class conflict, and therefore what the state does may be seriously contested and affected by subordinate groups, state bureaucracies must, ultimately, contribute to the accumulation of capital and reproduce capitalist relations in production and dominant (bourgeois) hegemony in order to survive as a state. In other words, the capitalist state (and its apparatuses) can only change into something else as part of an *overall change* in capitalist society. That change may be first manifested as a result of political conflict (in elections, e.g.), and therefore the state bureaucracy may, in some sense, be the lead sector of changing capitalist society into something else, but other institutions, particularly the production sector and the repressive apparatuses, must quickly follow as part of a general transformation of social relations in order for the change to be effective (Chile and Portugal are good examples of state-led radical reform failures).

In this analysis, the educational system (as part of the state) may have technical and financial problems, but these problems have to be viewed as largely inherent in the class state and its reproductive mandate. The observed inefficiencies and inequalities in education are the product of the capitalist organization of production and the social-class structure inherent in it, not of lack of financial resources or inefficiency per se. Putting more resources into education and managing it better may make the educational system a more pleasant place and may even increase "learning" (particularly by making it possible for children to stay in school more years) but will not solve social and economic inequality or unemployment—these are attributes of the development pattern itself. According to this analysis, it is difficult or even impossible to discuss serious changes in an inherently class-reproducing educational system—the manner in which education expands, which levels are favored for expansion, the nature of the curriculum, and the value attached to each level of schooling—without discussing an overall strategy for changing the class structure of society and the dominant capitalist relations of production. Thus, class conflict could be reflected in important changes in the educational system, but if those changes are not extended to structural reforms in the development pattern (relations in production and dominant class hegemony), they will have little or no impact on the society as a whole.

Which of these analyses is correct? The preceding description, while very brief, should make clear why almost no set of data can convince advocates of either position that they are wrong. Taking the capitalist state as a class state or not is largely a theoretical construct used to explain phenomena. What makes the case for either view particularly complex is that the first allows for gross inequalities as the result of inefficiencies in an inherently just social system, and the second allows for the state's giving in to the subordinate classes on a number of issues, including expanded education, in order to maintain legitimacy[12] or as part of class struggle in the superstructural apparatuses.[13]

Nevertheless, it is possible to bring some evidence to bear on these theoretical constructs which, in my view, makes the second analysis of education (as inherently class based) more plausible than the first. Further, this same evidence shows that changes in education occur without having significant impact on social structure, suggesting that the educational system, even reformed, is inherently class reproductive as well as class based.

1. Almost every study of education in the Third World shows that the children of rural parents (despite rapid urban growth, still more than two-thirds of Third World children come from rural areas)[14] average very low levels of schooling, much lower than urban children. With expanded schooling, poor urban children achieve higher levels of schooling than in the past, but with school system expansion, graduation from primary and secondary levels has become much less valuable in getting a job or a higher salary or both. When we sum these two groups (rural and new urban children) we are probably including more than 90 percent of the entire primary school age cohort in most Third World countries.

2. Not only do children from rural and poor urban backgrounds receive less education than the small minority from middle- and upper-middle-class backgrounds, social class has a significant effect on income and type of job even for those who finish the same level of schooling.[15] Thus, the

[12] Claus Offe, "Laws of Motion of Reformist State Policies," mimeographed (Bielefeld: University of Bielefeld, Department of Sociology, 1976).

[13] Nicos Poulantzas, *State, Power, Socialism* (London: New Left Books, 1978).

[14] United Nations, *Compendium of Social Statistics, 1977* (New York: UN Department of International Economic and Social Affairs, 1980), p. 51.

[15] Martin Carnoy, "Rates of Return to Schooling in Latin America," *Journal of Human Resources* 2 (Summer 1967): 359–74; Hans Thias and M. Carnoy, *Cost-Benefit Analysis in Education: A Case Study of Kenya* (Baltimore: John Hopkins University Press, 1972); Gerald W. Fry, "The Educational Correlates of Occupational Attainment: A Bangkok Case Study of Large-Scale Organizations" (Ph.D. diss., Stanford University, 1977); Jacques Velloso, "Training, Employment, and the Distribu-

combined educational system/labor market clearly persists in favoring a small group in society both by restricting access to highly valued levels of schooling largely to that group and by favoring it in the labor market in competition with those not from that group. The class-based nature of educational systems is particularly evident in those countries where state investment per year of schooling is from 20 to 60 times greater at the university level than at the primary level.[16] Since productivity and education have some relationship even in economies where technology is simpler than in a modern factory,[17] it is logical, in some sense, that those with more education receive somewhat higher pecuniary rewards than those with less. But in most Third World countries, these differences are tremendously accentuated by the fact that a small, dominant group not only owns the means of production but also dominates the higher echelons of the state apparatus, including the technocratic elite. This does not mean that only the children of the already rich get access to high incomes through the unequal educational system. In general, however, the dominant classes are surprisingly effective in using an allegedly meritocratic educational system to reproduce from generation to generation their highly overweighted representation in the most lucrative professions.

3. It is generally agreed among economists of education that overall employment (and unemployment) and the division of labor (including who is unemployed) are not a function of the *level* of education in the labor force but rather of economic and social factors. In other words, raising the level of education in the labor force will not be a particularly important factor in reducing the level of unemployment, even though it may increase the employability of labor when and if the economy develops. The level of employment depends more on the level of investment for production and on the kind of technology used—that is, the use of more labor-intensive or more capital-intensive technology to produce a certain set of products. The fact that there is unemployment may depend on a number of factors: according to some economists, unemployment occurs because of distortions in the labor market, such as minimum-wage legislation, labor unions, and government-imposed hiring-firing constraints. Others consider unemployment to be the result of development policies which concentrate on maximizing the return to capital rather than maximizing the employment of labor. Very few economists, however, consider

tion of Earnings in Brazil, 1970" (Ph.D. diss., Stanford University, 1975); Glaura Vasques de Miranda, "Education and Other Determinant Factors of Female Labor Force Participation in Brazil" (Ph.D. diss., Stanford University, 1979); Martin Carnoy, R. Sack, and H. Thias, "Determinants and Effects of School Performance: Secondary Education in Tunisia," mimeographed (Washington, D.C.: World Bank, 1977).

[16] Philip Coombs, *Future Critical World Issues in Education: A Provisional Report of Findings* (Essex, Conn.: International Council for Educational Development, 1981).

[17] We have reviewed some of this evidence in R. Sack, M. Carnoy, and C. Lecaros, *Education and Rural Development in Latin America* (Washington, D.C.: Interamerican Development Bank, 1978).

that a major cause of unemployment is the mismatch of skills produced by the educational system with the requirements of the labor market.[18]

4. Similarly, income distribution—even the distribution of the earnings from labor—is only weakly related to the level and distribution of education, and the two variables often work against each other.[19] Educational change does not seem to increase or reduce inequality of income. Income inequality is due in part to the type of technology used but, in addition, depends on conventions establishing who gets paid how much for what.[20]

[18] The "matching" problem—making education more efficient in matching training provided to jobs available—has relevance, it seems, only in the case of the more highly educated: since their unemployment appears to be associated with job search rather than the nature of the jobs they do, more "relevant" schooling would reduce job-search time and might reduce the possibility of having to take a job for which the graduate has been overeducated. However, for the bulk of school leavers, better matching as a way of reducing unemployment time is an irrelevant issue. Even studies of vocational training at the secondary level suggest that, although present returns (earning differences) to vocational education are significant, expanding such education beyond a select few would decrease those returns substantially (see J. Puryear, "On Vocational Training and Earnings," *Comparative Education Review* 23, no. 2 [June 1979]: 283–92).

[19] Martin Carnoy, José Lobo, Alejandro Toledo, and Jacques Velloso, *Can Educational Policy Equalize Income Distribution in Latin America?* (Geneva: ILO, 1979).

[20] There has been a prolonged discussion in the basic research on how labor markets actually function (see M. Carnoy, "Segmented Labor Markets," in M. Carnoy, H. M. Levin, and K. King, *Education, Work, and Employment,* vol. 2 [Paris: IIEP, 1980], for a review). This discussion has important implications for income distribution and the division of labor. On the one hand, one group of economists consider that different people in the society with equal amounts of education are treated equally in the labor market. The principal proponents of this view in its pure form are associated with the Chicago school—Gary Becker, *Human Capital* (New York: Columbia University Press, 1964), and Glen Cain, "The Challenge of Dual and Radical Theories of the Labor Market to Orthodox Theory," *American Economic Review* 65 (May 1975): 16–22. Besides assuming that there is equal treatment of individual characteristics, this view of the labor market also assumes that each individual operates with equal power in the market, given his or her characteristics. Thus, discrimination is a temporary distortion in the market rather than a permanent feature. That is, if rural children—with all the social characteristics of a rural environment—or lower-social-class children in urban areas—with all the social characteristics of a low-social-class environment—are given the same schooling (quantity and quality) as higher-social-class urban children, they will have access to the same kinds of jobs and the same level of wages. This implies that the main problem in increasing the employment and income possibilities of the poor is to raise their level of schooling, giving them more skills which are employable in the labor markets. On the other hand, another group of economists consider the labor market *segmented,* and people who work in the different segments of the market are treated differently, even if they have the *same* education levels. There are two versions of segmented-labor market theory. One argues that technology separates labor markets; i.e., firms with advanced technology require a different division of labor and promotion pattern than firms with labor-intensive technology (Peter Doeringer and M. Piore, *Internal Labor Markets and Manpower Training* [Lexington, Mass.: Heath, 1971]). The second version argues that segments derive from the class struggle; in order to more effectively extract surplus, employers, particularly in monopoly firms, create divisions of labor which are not technologically necessary but rather separate different groups of workers one from another (M. Reich, D. Gordon, and R. Edwards, "A Theory of Labor Market Segmentation," *American Economic Review* 63 [May 1973]: 359–65; Michael Carter and M. Carnoy, "Theories of Labor Markets and Income Distribution," mimeographed [Palo Alto, Calif., Center for Economic Studies, 1976]; Richard Edwards, *Contested Terrain* [New York: Basic, 1979]). Sex and race discrimination are part of this social division. The higher, or primary, segment is characterized by relatively stable employment and high pay. The lower, or secondary, segment is characterized by frequent unemployment and relatively low pay. Furthermore, workers from rural and lower-class urban social backgrounds—even if their formal schooling is increased substantially—are likely to end up in secondary jobs and thus be subject to frequent periods of unemployment and receive relatively low pay, even though they have higher education than before. The problem, as seen by these economists, is not so much increasing the education of the poor—although that may be important also—as in changing the *kinds* of jobs to which the poor have access; in other words, changing the nature of *employment* itself. And changing

5. Research shows that there has been a rapid increase in education in the labor force in most countries of the world and that this increase has certain characteristics: (a) On the average it has been more rapid than the expansion of skills required in the economy, so that in fact the rate of production of skills is catching up and sometimes overtaking—in general terms—the educational manpower requirements of the economy. (b) Because of the structure of wages in most countries, and because higher education is usually free, there has been an incentive for students to take as much education as possible, particularly to continue on from secondary school to university. In many countries this has produced a bulge of university graduates who are often overeducated for the jobs which they end up doing.[21] That is, they end up in work which is relatively simple or even requires skills that they learn primarily on the job, while the formal educational system served largely as a selection device. (c) The high level of unemployment and the unequal income distribution in countries have acted to increase the pressure on formal school expansion at the secondary and higher levels over what it would be with fuller employment.[22] High unemployment, especially among youth, decreases the opportunity cost of continuing school, since job alternatives are not available. This process tends to accentuate overeducation in the labor force at the higher levels of schooling and increases drastically the funds needed for schooling, far beyond what would be spent in a full-employment economy. Unemployment and income distribution therefore have more of an effect on schooling than schooling on unemployment and income distribution.[23]

6. It appears that the nature of unemployment is considerably different among the more highly schooled (higher social class) than among the less schooled (lower social class): the highly schooled, even when they cannot immediately find jobs on graduation or school leaving, are generally unemployed at the beginning of their careers, during the job search. Then they usually find stable and career-type jobs marked by relatively low levels of unemployment during their career.[24] The less schooled tend to have a greater probability of being unemployed often in their work lives. Thus, if we look at the unemployed as a group, we find that unemployment continues to be a serious problem for the less educated throughout their work

income distribution means changing the pay differentials between the kinds of work as well as the possibility of having people rotate through different types of jobs during their work lives, even from year to year or month to month. Further, for those who see segmentation as part of class struggle, the problem is intimately tied to class relations in capitalist society; hence these must be changed to change the class division of labor.

[21] B. Sanyal and E. S. A. Yacoub, *Higher Education and Employment in the Sudan* (Paris: IIEP, 1975).

[22] Mark Blaug, R. Layard, and M. Woodhall, *The Causes of·Graduate Unemployment in India* (Harmondsworth: Penguin, 1969).

[23] Martin Carnoy, *Education and Employment* (see n. 8 above); Martin Carnoy et al., *Can Educational Policy Equalize Income Distribution?*

[24] Mark Blaug, *Education* (see n. 5 above).

lives, while, for the more highly educated, it tends to be a problem only at the beginning of their careers. However, the results also show that the definition of "less" and "highly" educated changes over time in the same country.[25] The rapid expansion of education relative to jobs noted above tends to push the definition of higher educated upward: while 10 years ago, for example, workers entering the market with secondary school education may have been able to find stable, low-unemployment career jobs, now this possibility is gradually being restricted to those who have attended university, and those with secondary school education find themselves increasingly in jobs marked by unemployment throughout their career. The problem in these unemployment marked jobs is not education but rather the conditions surrounding those kinds of jobs.

7. The research results on nonformal education are not extensive, but those that have appeared indicate that graduates of nonformal education courses have a very different structure of employment and income opportunities than those who take formal education.[26] Thus, although nonformal education's principal appeal is its low cost and the relevance on the job market, the basic research indicates that nonformal and formal education are not interchangeable. In practice, this means that extracting the skills component from formal schooling and teaching basic skills to both young people and adults may, indeed, provide them with skills at much lower cost than does formal schooling, but it does not get them access to jobs needing those skills. Apparently, employers in Third World economies consider those with nonformal training less desirable (employable) than those with formal schooling. Since nonformal education is clearly aimed at those workers with rather low levels of schooling and hence tries to deal with the employment and productivity problems of workers who are largely in the low-paying, high-employment, secondary labor market, it is very likely that such training fortifies the class division of labor rather than promoting social mobility for lower-social-class groups.

8. The special cases of youth, women, and racial/tribal groups in the labor market—all, of course, intimately related to the role of education in the social division of labor—both confuse and strengthen the case for the reproduction of that division through education. The case is confused because these groups do not represent social classes (although in the racial/tribal case, a discriminated-against minority may represent a particular fraction of the subordinated class) and yet have lower income and less job opportunity than the dominant race/male/prime working age group. Thus, it can be argued that the primary divisions in the labor market are along age/sex/race lines and not class lines. The case is strengthened

[25] H. Braverman, *Labor and Monopoly Capital* (New York: Monthly Review Press, 1975); Russell Rumberger, "Overeducation in the U.S. Labor Market" (Ph.D. diss., Stanford University, 1978).

[26] George Papagiannis, "Non-Formal Education and National Development" (Ph.D. diss., Stanford University, 1977).

because (*a*) higher-social-class youth, even though paid less and more likely to be unemployed than the older members of their own social class, also have access to much better jobs and potentially higher incomes even as youth than older members of lower social classes; and (*b*) women are class divided as far as type of job is concerned, although highly educated women (even more likely to come from a high-social-class background than highly schooled men) generally have lower incomes than men coming from a lower class;[27] and (*c*) discriminated-against racial or tribal groups, it can be argued, are part and parcel of the class structure.[28]

When all is said and done, these special cases, particularly the women's issue, are problematic for the class-based, class-reproduction analysis—not because they support the alternative view of an aberrated but inherently perfectable capitalist development process, but rather because they introduce another level of dominant/subordinate relations in society, a level which is not necessarily confined to capitalism. Even if higher-family-income youth, women, and minority-group members are better off than those youth, women, and minorities from families with lower incomes, and even if race discrimination and class are closely intertwined in the division of labor, these categories represent power relationships which, at least in part, transcend class. Certainly, for women and racial/tribal minorities, formal education usually becomes an issue not in terms of class discrimination but in terms of social mobility and equal opportunity.

This, then, is some of the evidence suggesting that education is class based and class reproductive (with caveats for the race/sex cases) and tied to a social division of labor which is inherent to the capitalist development process. None of the literature which discusses *how* that reproduction takes place has been cited because that is not the point to be made here. We are simply suggesting that the analysis which argues that the problems of education in capitalist society are rooted in capitalist development itself are persuasive on the basis of the empirical research available. What makes the evidence particularly convincing is that the conditions we describe above are not limited to low-income countries but also generally characterize more advanced capitalist societies. Thus, even in efficient capitalist economies, the educational system is class based and class reproductive.

Yet, our discussion has focused largely on Third World societies (although the arguments are not limited to them). It is, therefore, important to introduce another dimension to the discussion before going on to consider what this more "correct" analysis of education might imply for educational reform. A large body of research exists which argues that the economies and societies of Third World countries (including their state apparatuses and educational systems) cannot be viewed simply as national

[27] G. Standing, *Labor Force Participation in Developing Countries* (Geneva: ILO, 1978).
[28] See Michael Reich, *Racial Inequality* (Princeton, N.J.: Princeton University Press, 1981), for an analysis of the race/labor market/education issue in the United States.

systems. Rather, this literature suggests that the present organization of production in Third World capitalist economies, especially the type of technology used in the modern sector and the type of goods being produced there, is intimately tied to a transnational development pattern, a pattern whose dynamic center and focus is in the highly industrialized countries.[29] The development pattern and hence the dominant values and norms (dominant hegemony) being infused into these Third World societies are therefore largely external to the society itself. First, such dependency on transnational technology and investment (as well as foreign markets) has important implications for the pattern of economic development and for the possible participation in that development by the mass of Third World people:

> . . . Higher average rates of economic growth and modernization than ever before have been achieved in most countries, but the peculiar nature of the highly dynamic technological innovation process which lies at the heart of the expansion of techno-industrial oligopoly capitalism has simultaneously had extremely negative consequences, *over and above* the characteristic unevenness of traditional capitalist development. In the underdeveloped countries, this new pattern of growth is highly dependent on the wholesale importation of consumption patterns, production processes, technology, institutions, material outputs and human resources, adding new *internal* economic, socio-cultural and political dimensions to the old patterns of external dependence, and aggravating the structural tendency toward increasing external imbalance. . . . Given a high and increasing capital intensity, a very unequal income distribution and a relative shortage of savings and markets, capital accumulation tends to become highly concentrated and wasteful in the production of new consumption goods and services, creating very little new employment, while preexisting activities are starved of capital and stagnate or are seriously disrupted. This contributes to massive displacement of labor . . . adding to the marginal and informal sectors, to unemployment, underemployment, poverty, and inequality. . . .[30]

Second, a dominant hegemony whose economic and social dynamic is external to the national economy lends a dimension to the class struggle which is absent in both the theory and practice of such struggles in dominant advanced capitalist societies. The conflict is not simply between the dominant and subordinate classes in a given country, but between subordinate classes (sometimes including fractions of the bourgeoisie and petty bourgeoisie whose interests are contrary to transnational development) and an alliance of local dominant groups with a transnational technocracy, whose power lies not only in its financial strength but also in the willingness of metropolitan governments to support its cause with mil-

[29] Fernando Enrique Cardoso and Enzo Faletto, *Dependence and Development in Latin America* (Berkeley: University of California Press, 1979).

[30] O. Sunkel and Edmundo Fuenzalida, "Transnationalization and Its National Consequences," in *Transnational Capitalism and National Development*, ed. José Villamil (Brighton: Harvester Press, 1979).

itary backing. The states of dependent Third World countries are therefore the sites of political struggle on a *world* scale. Whether Chile or El Salvador, for example, has a leftist or rightist government is in practice an international question, much more so than whether France does, even though the international economic and social implications of the French elections may be greater than those in Chile or El Salvador.

Third, a dominant hegemony which is entwined with economic and political crises in the advanced capitalist societies is subject to crises which are out of the control of the local dominant class. Since educational change is linked in some sense to both the development pattern and economic/hegemonic crisis[31]—both, in this case, have their dynamic outside the domestic society—educational conflict over the nature of Third World educational systems and changes in education are dependent on the course of transnational rather than national development.

All this does not mean that dependent educational systems cannot be made more efficient or that education cannot be made more equitably accessible. To the contrary, expansion and improvement may create the possibilities for some youth to do better. The point is, however, that in the type of development characteristic of dependent capitalist economies, the degree of improvement possible for education and for the employment and income distribution pattern is inherently limited by the social relations of dependent capitalist production. Economic growth (even rapid economic growth) can take place with such social relations, but we cannot expect that the mass of people in the society will share more than marginally in the fruits of that growth. Similarly, education can expand rapidly, but the nature of that expansion will continue to leave the rural and urban poor in a disadvantaged learning, social, and economic situation.

Education for Alternative Development

If this second construction of reality is correct—that is, if capitalist development is inherently inequitable and the bureaucracy of the capitalist state (including the educational bureaucracy) tends to reproduce the relations which are the basis for inequity—how can and should education be changed to make it more efficient and equitable, and how do such changes fit into a more general strategy for social change (if at all)?

In discussing strategy, we cannot avoid a fundamental relationship: the process of development itself is education, an education probably more important than, but certainly as important as, schooling. Both youth and adults learn to deal with each other more in the economic and social reality of a society than in either the family or the school; indeed, the family and schooling provided by the state cannot be separated from the educational

[31] Martin Carnoy and Henry Levin, "The Dialectic of Education and Work," mimeographed (Palo Alto, Calif.: Center for Economic Studies, 1981).

process resulting from economic and social development. What occurs in school not only corresponds to the organization of production and the needs of production (the types of goods produced and corresponding labor needs) as well as the promotion of the dominant ideology in the society; it also reflects the contradictions and conflicts in the development process. We have tried to analyze this process systematically elsewhere.[32] The essence of our argument is that the development process, the educational process, and the schooling process are part and parcel of the same whole, with certain degrees of autonomy in each—but each is also inseparable from the same surrounding forces which influence them and bind them together. In the case of Third World countries, the forces go beyond national borders to the advanced capitalist societies: their production organization, the goods their dominant classes produce and their labor needs, and their dominant ideology, as well as the conflicts and contradictions of those advanced societies and how they resolve them.

We have argued that the development process in Third World capitalist countries is inherently unequal, dependent, and restrictive, and that development is education; that the development process, the educational process, and the schooling process are intimately entwined. How can education contribute to fundamental, structured change when it is part of an overall restrictive development?

We suggest that, paradoxically, it can make this contribution because it is an organic part of the development process. Production is not the only place in society where class (racial and gender or group) struggle appears. Capitalists and the capitalist state, within this context of struggle, have developed institutions which are organized to mediate, or soften, conflict in production. This brings the struggle into these institutions as well. In a society where the class and group conflict is inherent in the social relations of production, we would expect to find such a conflict in all social institutions, and social institutions are intertwined. Thus the conflicts which characterize them are also intertwined and impact on each other.[33]

Bowles and Gintis[34] in the United States and Baudelot and Establet[35] in France have analyzed public education in this context. However, their analyses imply that struggles in the superstructure are second-order effects (for Baudelot and Establet, "resistance" is the best one can hope for in the schools), doomed to insignificance because of production's overwhelming influence in defining the class struggle and the nature of superstructural institutions. We contend that the very nature of the mediation process in which the superstructure is engaged creates contradictions in the super-

[32] Ibid.
[33] Poulantzas (see n. 13).
[34] S. Bowles and H. Gintis, *Schooling in Capitalist America* (New York: Basic, 1975).
[35] C. Baudelot and R. Establet, *L'Ecole capitaliste* (Paris: Maspero, 1971).

structure itself.[36] Struggle in the superstructure is part of a conflict which pervades all of capitalist society and feeds back on other conflicts. Moreover, the responses to conflicts in production and superstructure by dominant political/economic groups are also interrelated; efforts to suppress or co-opt worker demands in production are accompanied by efforts to reform (bring into correspondence) superstructure institutions like the schools. Once the schools, media, and other mediating institutions become important in maintaining dominant class hegemony through softening contradictions in production, contradictions in mediation (Antonio Gramsci calls this "crisis of hegemony") are also important and must be resolved by the dominant class.

The intimate relation between contradictions in the superstructure and contradictions in production implies that conducting the struggle in either base or education system (as well as in other areas of superstructure— the legal apparatus, religion, the media, the family and relations between sexes) is meaningful for social change. Unlike some international agencies who want to bring schooling into line with transnational production, or Bowles and Gintis, who argue for radical social change and imply the struggle for that change must be concentrated entirely in the workplace, our analysis contends that the struggle does and should take place in both production and the schools (and other superstructural institutions).[37]

Strategies for School Reform

What kind of action in schooling would contribute to or reinforce nonreformist reforms? On the one hand, a reform movement in the schools must develop resistance to policies which are intended to mediate more efficiently the contradictions in production. In more positive terms, school reformers should develop strategies which exacerbate contradictions created by the nature of the education/production relationship. Exacerbating contradictions in schooling will reduce the mediating effectiveness of schooling, contributing to crises in the dominant hegemony. On the other

[36] Carnoy and Levin.

[37] This does not mean that every strategy for altering production or education heads in the direction of fundamental political and economic change. Employers, school administrators, and international agencies also have concepts of change which reform production and education so that they can better function to reproduce the existing class hierarchies and rewards. André Gorz asks: "Is it possible *from within*—that is to say, without having previously destroyed capitalism—to impose anti-capitalist solutions which will not immediately be incorporated into and subordinated to the system?" (A. Gorz, *A Strategy for Labor* [Boston: Beacon, 1968]). That is, are there reforms which advance toward a radical transformation of society? He calls these "nonreformist reforms." ". . . a struggle for nonreformist reforms—for anti-capitalist reforms—is one which does not base its validity and its right to exist on capitalist needs, criteria and rationales. A nonreformist reform is determined not in terms of what can be, but what should be. And finally, it bases the possibility of attaining its objective on the implementation of fundamental political and economic changes. These changes can be sudden, just as they can be gradual. But in any case, they assume a modification of the relations of power; they assume that the workers will take over powers or assume a force (that is to say, a noninstitutionalized force) strong enough to establish, maintain, and expand those tendencies within the system which serve to weaken capitalism and to shake its joints. They assume structural reforms" (ibid., pp. 7–8).

hand, reformers should push for educational alternatives which would create attitudes and skills more useful in an endogenous, worker-controlled development than in capitalist wage production. The two strategies are not separate; rather, they are two aspects of developing a different work culture in the schools.

Exacerbating Contradictions

One of the principal functions of schooling in Third World countries is to substitute for political rights and for increased material consumption. Increased schooling mediates present injustices by inducing the poor to consume hope for the future—hope that their children will do better by going to school. But in a restricted, transnational development process, the "skills" learned in school cannot be absorbed at a level that matches the aspirations raised; the hope generated cannot be realized. At the same time, skills are learned, and the socialization process in schools separated from capitalist production does not match exactly the needs of capitalist reproduction.[38] Thus, expanded schooling could be a force for radical change, particularly if set in the context of political struggles elsewhere in society.

The argument for expanded schooling to exacerbate contradictions depends largely on how well schooling is able to fit youth into the injustices and inequalities of Third World capitalist development. Schooling may be an effective socializer as long as the economy is increasing consumption rapidly and is distributing that increase broadly through the population. Reality must sufficiently fit schooling's abstraction of that reality. It is not just that growth rates have to be high but also that participation in increased consumption is general and significant and that schooling actually helps youth to better their position relative to their parents'. Since, under capitalist development, material consumption is the measure of social success, legitimization of the capitalist state requires delivering the goods. On the other hand, if the economy does not perform well, how effective can school socialization be? Even if schooling tries to convince youth that failure is their fault, a more articulate, literate, disappointed working class will ultimately not accept this explanation.

Furthermore, mass school expansion puts a strain on the state's financial capability to increase production. And while the poor themselves bear much of the burden of their children's schooling, investment in primary schooling particularly redistributes income from middle- to low-income earners.[39] Thus, a strategy of pushing for expanded primary schooling reduces the capability of the state to subsidize production directly, may even shift indirect benefits from higher- to lower-income earners, and may

[38] Carnoy and Levin.

[39] J. P. Jallade, *Public Expenditures on Education and Income Distribution in Colombia* (Washington, D.C.: World Bank, 1974).

produce a literate mass which could be a source of demands for radical change if the already strained Third World economy cannot deliver increased consumption.

In addition to pushing for expanded schooling, nonreformist reformers should struggle for actual control of school decision making by parents, pupils, and teachers (students and teachers in secondary schools and universities). We have argued that one of the principal contradictions in public education is that the schools are supposed to be public; that is, the community and professionals are allegedly in charge of decision making about curriculum and process. At some level of reality, schools are not separated from capitalist production and the inherent conflicts in production; but at another level the legitimacy of capitalist education resides in its autonomy from production. Thus, although school bureaucracies and classrooms are certainly characterized by hierarchical relations, relations which correspond roughly to the relations of production,[40] the educational system is probably more open to participative decision making than the workplace for which it prepares youth. Teachers' and administrators' prerogatives are probably more limited than those of their counterparts in production. The basis, therefore, may exist for parents and students to demand and get increased control over educational processes.

Must such changes aim specifically and consciously toward a set of nonreformist goals? It is not clear that they have to. Even with nonradical community control reforms, if the community does really control a school and maximizes its children's possibilities, it will, in some sense, have to respond to students' demands as well, and students will create a much more favorable learning environment for themselves. Since it is the poor who now have least control over schooling, the relative increase of their control would tend to interfere with the reproduction of labor power; that is, with the allocation of labor to different kinds of jobs. For example, if poorer communities develop effective ways to increase secondary and university entrance for their youth, it will be more difficult to allocate those youth to menial jobs or unemployment.

Educational Alternatives

The only way for most Third World countries to increase *mass* standard of living significantly in the future is to concentrate on the employment of people in the rapidly increased production of basic necessities: food, shelter, health care, and the machinery and energy necessary to produce those necessities. The more that the types of goods produced and the way they are produced respond to the needs of the mass of people in the society, the more likely it will be that coercion will not be necessary to achieve desired development. So the elements here are self-sufficiency, in-

[40] Bowles and Gintis (see n. 34).

dependence, catering to mass needs, and full participation—a development which has the worker-participant rather than capital and property at the center of the production and development process.

An alternative education which fits into such an alternative development might still be organized on the basis of classroom for part of the time, but socialization and the process of skill acquisition, to be consistent with the alternative development we have described, would have to be much more cooperative and set in more cooperative and participative work forms than under the present system.

Since schooling is expensive, and technical/financial problems are real even when the social impediments to an innovative educational system have been removed, new organizations of the formal school system are necessary. First, every Third World country will have to face the issue of rural poverty. For some, like those in Central America (not even excepting Costa Rica), the Caribbean, and Africa, there is little question that rural education—an innovative rural education as part of an innovative, labor-intensive rural development—will have to be a principal focus of the new educational system. For, as we have argued, the most important education is the development process itself. How can we imagine the mobilization of the peasantry in those societies without making rural areas a lead development sector? Despite all the difficulties of overcoming colonization in many countries, the peasant and landless rural labor must be a focus and reaper of the new development. This implies that an alternative development must integrate agricultural and industrial production so that the integration is beneficial to both workers and peasants. Thus, the new school certainly must be in large part a rural school, a school which responds to the new dynamic of rural development (which would include rural industrialization related to agriculture production and rural consumption—even to the extent of producing agricultural machinery and certainly manufactured consumer goods). These schools would still face the problem of having well-trained teachers able to teach effectively; of having a well-developed curriculum designed to serve the needs of the new development, including cooperative, participative production; of having textbooks and supplies in every school, and school buildings; and of having an efficient administration.[41] But if all of these elements do not function in the context of reality where the rural sector is the lead sector, where the peasant and landless labor are the center of the development process, and where technology (knowledge) is organized around this mass of rural workers, rural education can be nothing more than a way out of rural areas. A way out

[41] For the problem inherent in achieving such rival schooling even in a country committed to agriculture as a lead sector, see M. Carnoy and J. Werthein, *Cuba: Desarrollo Economica y Reforma Educativa, 1955–78* (Mexico: Nueva Imagen, 1980); Susan Shirk, "Educational Reform and Political Backlash: Recent Changes in Chinese Education Policy," *Comparative Education Review* 23, no. 2 (June 1979): 183–217.

because the education provided by the development process itself—an education which reaches everyone, whether in school or not—makes clear to people where their work gets its highest reward, where the society is headed, who will do well and who will fall behind, and what kind of knowledge is worthwhile and what worthless.

The distribution of knowledge in an economy run by workers and farmers for workers and farmers has to be different than the present distribution. And it is only under such an alternative development that semiindustrialized economies can move away from the concentration of educational resources in the minds of a few technocrats and capitalists in the dynamic industrial sector. Once it is admitted that all industrial and agricultural workers have organizational and production-decision responsibilities, the formal educational system will have to respond accordingly.

But the most important educational process will be taking place—as it is now—outside of formal schooling. A development process which demands participation of the masses in a development which benefits them increases participation in the acquisition of knowledge, particularly in the possibility of acquiring knowledge. A society which is organized around mass-based and for-mass production is one which, of necessity, spreads knowledge most widely, both through on-the-job training and the formal system. It is to the advantage of such a society to make as much knowledge (technology) as possible available to as many people as desire it rather than keep all but the simplest forms of knowledge in the hands of a relatively few, and even that higher knowledge divided among the few. The process of mass-base development itself is the most pervasive form of mass education. It incorporates people into development rather than excluding them: incorporation is education just as exclusion is education. The process of incorporation and exclusion teaches each and every member of society who he or she is in that society. Formal schooling is only a systemized part of the exclusion-incorporation process which depends on development itself.

This brings us to a crucial point: alternative development and its corresponding alternative education can easily be dismissed as utopian. However, we observe that even where alternative development has run into important constraints, particularly with regard to financing hard-currency imports (such as fuel) and hence continuing to depend on exports of primary products and credits from advanced capitalist and socialist countries, the educational system reforms have indeed achieved many of the goals outlined above.[42] Cuba and China have made concerted efforts to bring education on a massive scale to rural areas and have made important advances in equalizing urban and rural educational opportunities, even

[42] We have discussed these in detail for Cuba in Carnoy and Werthein. For discussions of Chinese educational achievements, see Jan-Ingvar Löfstedt, *Chinese Educational Policy* (Atlantic Highlands, N.J.: Humanities, 1980); R. Gamberg, *Red and Expert* (New York: Schocken, 1977); T. Hsi-en Chen, *The Maoist Education Revolution* (New York: Praeger, 1974).

though a child from a rural area still does not have the same possibility of attaining higher education as an urban child in either Cuba or China (now that higher education is reopened), especially a child from a major city.[43] Now Nicaragua has embarked on bringing education to its rural areas, very much on the Cuban model, with, apparently, similar success.

The obstacles both to alternative development and alternative education are many (and too complex to discuss in a short paper), even when the will to make radical changes is there. The drawbacks of socialist bureaucracies, including persisting inequalities, sexism, and racism, are well known. But without the pursuit of a radical transformation in the relations of production and their underlying power relations, an alternative education—mass education and social inclusion—is essentially impossible to achieve. A crucial fact is that those countries which have attempted radical transformations have also come much closer to achieving mass education and the equalization of opportunity than those which have not. A fundamental implication of an analysis which sees capitalist development as inherently inequitable is that, to achieve a more equitable and inclusive development, radical transformations are necessary; what the shape of those transformations is depends largely on the nature of the struggle which produces them.

[43] At the same time, the difference in wages between a director of a factory or a doctor and an average worker is only about two to one in Cuba, while in a Third World capitalist country the ratio is approximately ten to one.

Comparative Educators and International Development Policy

MATHEW ZACHARIAH

I shall begin with the premise that it is unnecessary to traverse ground already covered many times by my distinguished American and European predecessors. There is little value in reviewing the origins of our field, the research alliances we may forge with disciplines in the humanities as well as the social sciences, and the institutionalized cooperation we must seek with other professionals in teacher education. There is nothing genuinely new I can say about the stages and processes of comparison or the pitfalls we must avoid when using the methods and techniques available to us. It is not necessary, again, to lament or legitimize the lack of consensus in theoretical focus in our research, teaching, or other practical activities. Finally, I find it difficult to sound alarmed about the future of our field, for reasons that should become evident later.

The topic I wish to address is international in the clearest sense of the word. Yet it has found little recognition in CIES presidential addresses although some of them do discuss the need for us to work with international organizations. The Society changed its name in 1969 to include the word "international"; I hope to incidentally show respect for that decision.

Some Guiding Axioms

Shall we agree on certain axioms? (1) Comparison, inherent in all generalizations, is an abstracting and reconstructing intellectual activity. As such, comparative studies are implicitly or explicitly purposeful and directed. (2) In the systematic study of similarities and differences, we must often go outside the schools to explore the reasons for many—not all—practices inside the school. (3) Rhetorical claims notwithstanding, institutionalized education plays only relatively minor roles in promoting social mobility as well as economic, political, and cultural development irrespective of a society's professed ideology. (4) However, contacts between individuals in school-like settings—that is, the educative

This is the revised and edited text of the address delivered at the 23d Conference of the Comparative and International Education Society. I thank Philip Altbach and John H. Van de Graaff for their helpful criticisms of an earlier draft.

Reprinted from *Comparative Education Review*, vol. 23, no. 3 (October 1979).

processes—can and occasionally do set in motion events that bring about significant societal change that may or may not be desirable. The apprehension that much of history is ultimately the product of human volition as well as action is what does not make "cowards of us all" and gives some of us in the field of education the disciplined hope to withstand unjustified and ill-informed criticism. These maxims have been very helpful to me in trying to understand the part education plays in the modernization of countries such as India and China.

The Metropolis-Hinterland Paradigm

Paraphrasing Michael Sadler I might say: "The things outside the Third World countries should matter more *to us* than the things inside if we are genuinely concerned about educational development in those countries." Despite your and my current preoccupations about the economic instability and political crises that characterize the rich world of which we are part, may I seek your patience in discussing this statement?

But three caveats are immediately in order. I do not claim that this statement represents the whole truth and nothing but the truth. As in other societies and times, the development of education in most Third World countries depends on the establishment of sensible and appropriate priorities and plans; the solution of problems such as access to remote parts of the country and changes in the attitude of sections of people toward the education of females; the resolution of issues concerning the languages, content, and methods of instruction and the role of private enterprise in education; and the establishment of accountable, effective administration. Furthermore, it is much less difficult to document the impact of the international maldistribution of wealth on, say, trade than on education. After acknowledging these complexities, I do claim that that the statement is an important part of the truth. Second, I explicitly reject the presumed or alleged implication in some dependency theories that the billions of people who live in the impoverished countries of Latin America, Africa, and Asia are powerless marionettes manipulated by the rich countries. Such power as they do possess is severely circumscribed. But the behavior of OPEC nations and recent events in Asia, Africa, and Latin America provide compelling evidence of the potential power of people in these countries to overthrow oppressive systems if assisted by dedicated and skilled leaders. Finally, the statement is not an attempt to whitewash the behaviors of leaders such as an Idi Amin or a Pol Pot at various levels in some of these countries.

I will not review here in detail the debates on educational development that have appeared in the October 1975 (vol. 19, no. 3) and June/October 1977 (vol. 21, nos. 2, 3) issues of *Comparative Education*

Review. Let me state my thesis starkly. Trade and tariff arrangements which, among other things, favor transnational corporations, the control of finance capital by institutions such as the International Monetary Fund (IMF) and the World Bank (IBRD), and the strategic cooperation by institutions such as the Organization for Economic Cooperation and Development (OECD) help perpetuate and extend the real control the economically rich world exerts over the economically poor world. (The adjective "economically" is there to call attention to the fact that economic might is not the only indicator of richness.) This control is most evident in a central fact: in the approximately 35 years since the Second World War, the rich countries have become richer and the poor countries have stayed poor. This is a bold statement that calls for several qualifications that I shall not discuss here.[1] It is beginning to be widely acknowledged that there has been in the past and there is now a parasitic relationship which contributes significantly to the richness of the wealthy world and the poverty of the rest of the world. I am not saying that the rich world is completely responsible for the problems of the poor world. But the neocolonial policies of the rich world constitute a continuation of policies pursued by the former imperial countries that underdeveloped most of Asia, Africa, and Latin America and made possible the development of Western Europe. The granting of formal political independence did not significantly reduce their dependency on Western nations.[2] A great many entrepreneurs and salaried professionals in many Third World countries serve the interests of the rich nations by facilitating the export by transnational corporations and others of primary commodities at generally deteriorating prices (except for oil, copper, and a few other items) and importing mainly the consumer products of Western transnational corporations. This arrangement drains their acutely scarce accumulated capital which, among other things, leaves them with much less money for educational development.

For succumbing to blandishments and bribes, for acting as conduits and facilitators, which result in the exploitation of the poor people in their regions, many of these local entrepreneurs and salaried professionals in Third World countries enjoy greater wealth and prestigious privileges than the poor in their own backyards. It is not my intention here to portray all of them as black-hearted villains. I know many of these individuals personally and can attest to their moral uprightness and

---

[1] See Mahbub Ul Haq, *The Poverty Curtain: Choices for the Third World* (New York: Columbia University Press, 1976), for a readable discussion of this fact.

[2] See Johan Galtung, "A Structural Theory of Imperialism," *Journal of Peace Research* 8, no. 2 (1971): 81–117; Klaus Jurgen Gantzel, "Dependency Structures as the Dominant Pattern in World Society," *Journal of Peace Research* 10, no. 3 (1973): 203–15. For a critique, see Karl W. Deutsch, "Imperialism and Neocolonialism," *Peace Science Society (International) Papers* 23 (1974): 1–25.

dedicated work to reduce the horrible poverty and a host of other problems (such as the pettiness of officials) with which they—unlike I—have to deal every day. My intention is, however, to point to the structurally unjust situation within which even well-intentioned individuals have to work. I do not propose, either, to gloss over the ultimate responsibility of poor people for allowing others to exploit them. When they take that responsibility as a consequence of the recognition of the deterioration of their social as well as material conditions and as a result of the help they receive from committed leaders, they will also take their first step toward emancipation. In Iran, in southern Africa, in Nicaragua we have been witnessing the taking of such responsibility. In stating this, I am not attempting to be insensitively sanguine about the suffering of people caught up in painful maelstroms. I am, however, trying to point to the underlying causes which breed such revolutionary turmoil—and thus to indicate the pivotal significance of conflict in societal development. One is compelled to ask: Is fundamental structural reform possible without violence? I cannot pause now to explore that question. My personal and perhaps irrational and illogical commitment is to genuine reform.

There are a number of questions we could explore in depth if we were to subject variants of dependency theory to rigorous examination. Some of them are: the enduring issues of determinism and freedom; the social-psychological process involved in the acquisition of knowledge and skills (see the third and fourth axioms mentioned earlier); the apparent location of exploitation in circulation (as in dependency theory) instead of in production (as in classical Marxist theory); and, ironically, the irrelevance of most scholastic discourses about capitalism versus communism for Third World development. I omit their consideration here.[3]

Reassessment of Certain Concepts Is Necessary

I accept the view that the metropolis-hinterland paradigm helps explain much more satisfactorily than some other perspectives significant aspects of the phenomenon of the development of underdevelopment in parts of the rich world and much of the poor world. This acceptance compels me to assess critically a number of our cherished orientations and concepts.

It is necessary to look again at the view that the poor nations of Asia, Africa, and Latin America remained traditional primarily because of

---

[3] I have discussed the metropolis-hinterland paradigm in my unpublished paper, "Models of Modernization in Conflict: Reflections on *Northern Frontier Northern Homeland* [*NFNH*]"; *NFNH* was the *Report of the Mackenzie Valley Pipeline Inquiry, Vol. 1*, written by Mr. Justice Thomas R. Berger (Ottawa: Ministry of Supply and Services, Canada, 1977).

their cultural systems and take seriously the view that the poor nations were undeveloped, but that the underdevelopment of a number of them was a product of Western colonial exploitation.

What should be our view of development, which is a normative concept par excellence? It is now widely acknowledged that what Tibor Mende has called "the photocopy approach" of trying to reach Western standards of living through duplicating Western development stages is fundamentally wrong, inappropriate, and unattainable.[4] Most Third World countries are compelled by their practical circumstances to define development in terms of their own culture and history and to set realistic self-sustaining goals based on resources within their grasp instead of relying on allegedly munificent Santa Clauses from the North. There is at least widespread verbal acknowledgment now that cardinal develop-ment measures must meet two linked criteria: real increases in empiri-cally observable gross domestic product as well as gross national product in a society, and the fair per capita distribution of this increase to the poorest people in that society.

There is an understandable and in many ways justifiable view among many development scholars that urbanization is an important indicator of modernization. Implicit in this view (commonly known as the dual society thesis) are two orientations: modern urban life means greater progress in contrast to traditional rural life, and Westernized urban life is the most visible evidence of modernization. Recent scholarship which has become more cognizant of the values of conserving the world's resources is more respectful of the wisdom of many rural traditions and attitudes that retain the human scale and is (albeit minimally and inadequately) self-sustaining. We must recognize that there are features of urban industrial and commercial life that depend on the unjust, class-based exploitation of rural hinterlands fueled, in part, by transnational corpo-rations. Such exploitation hinders genuine societal development even though we may be mistakenly dazzled by the glitter of sections of Westernized metropolises in some Third World countries.

Does the diffusion of any kind or type of knowledge, skills, or organizational forms and values from the rich countries promote the development of Third World nations? The spread of modern technology is not always or necessarily a good thing. The metropolis-hinterland perspective implies that there is technology that increases dependency and is antidevelopmental and technology that builds on and gradually transforms the existing material conditions without doing violence to the

---

[4] Tibor Mende, "The New International Economic Order: From Theory to Practice," *Coopera-tion Canada* 24 (1976): 3–10.

society's current "individual or communal agricultural and artisan technology."[5]

Always there are, of course, costs associated with the development of any poor nation. For instance, extreme regimentation to force the pace of development is often costly; so is unwillingness to tamper with extreme inequality in the name of evolutionary change. It is romantic nonsense to pretend that one can stop or turn back, in any absolute sense, social change. I am reminded here of the probably apocryphal story about a right-wing Indian opposition party politician in the fifties. At a local election rally he severely criticized India's brand of social democracy. He conceded that the new cooperative association for collecting and distributing milk in their district was beneficial in some ways. He complained, however, that the association had taken away the people's freedom to separate butter from milk in their own homes and that one was now forced always to drink butterless milk. He exclaimed with the evident approval of his audience that butterless milk was tasteless. The politician now warmed to his subject of the perfidious implications of modernization. He pointed out that a dam was being constructed nearby to store water and generate electricity from it. He then thunderingly asked: "Just as milk without butter is useless, what good is water if electricity has been removed from it?" It is not my intention here to be a Luddite, but I do believe that it is appropriate to investigate the question of which groups benefit the most and which ones suffer the most from the spread of modern technology. When one raises such questions one is led to examine the extent to which bureaucracies can be neutral instruments in light of the extreme disparateness in the distribution of economic as well as political power (which are almost identical in many parts of the Third World). One is also led to question the value of concepts like "balanced development."

Implications for Policy

If the metropolis-hinterland paradigm has analytical value, what are the implications for our direct (through consultancies and job assignments) and indirect (through teaching and research) participation in international development? Do we wish to promote development or increase dependence? We can confront the hard issues implied in these questions or take comfort in well-intentioned but vague slogans like: "Let us promote international understanding."[6]

[5] André Gunder Frank, *Sociology of Underdevelopment and Underdevelopment of Sociology* (London: Pluto, 1971), p. 33.
[6] See Mathew Zachariah, "Can the Rich and the Poor Nations Cooperate to Internationalize the Curriculum?" *Compare* 9, no. 1 (April 1979): 65–69.

An economist friend of mine who believes in the validity of the kind of analysis I have sketched here occasionally undertakes work for Western governments and foundations and international development agencies controlled by Western nations. Not too long ago I asked him whether he did not see a contradiction between his professional activities and his scholarly conclusions. He said: "Of course, I do, but it couldn't be very different from the contradictions you must be living with." He and I proceeded to have a very cathartic discussion about the personal conflicts of an Indian-born, middle-class academic with left-of-center orientations living in the richest province of Canada and being the president of an American scholarly society. I mention this incident not to exculpate myself but to convey my recognition of our existential dilemmas. In the balance of this paper I shall occasionally call attention to these dilemmas as a means of indicating that the person who creates and transmits knowledge is an important (even though often unacknowledged) part of the process of developing and spreading knowledge.

Let us recall that policies are choices we make based on our real (but not necessarily accurate or complete) knowledge of social systems to guide concrete operational decisions. They are like the headlights in a dark night which illuminate the 20 or so meters in front of us. Policies may or may not assist us to reach goals which we see, if at all, only as silhouettes in the distance. Goals, as it were, are things "we see through a glass, darkly." In this sense, development is a goal. But what policies will get us there? There are many answers to this questions which I cannot even begin to discuss here. The comparative educator, however, is a person who must understand and relate to the tense world of political leaders who articulate goals, administrators who implement or sabotage goals through policy formation and implementation, and clients who are affected by the policies. For a genuine scholar, then, truth's search for power and power's avoidance and neutralization of truth constitutes a complex, many-faced hide-and-seek game.[7] I don't pretend to understand it fully, but I have found a 1975 article by David K. Cohen and Michael S. Garet in *Harvard Education Review*[8] helpful and will use it as a basis for my comments.

But first, let me note that there is a tendency in this Society to see policy questions as limited to our relationship with organizations of teacher educators, our contributions to teacher education or school curricula in our countries, and our contacts with organizations which will

[7] The phrase is from Howard Waitzkin's essay, "Truth's Search for Power: The Dilemmas of the Social Sciences," *Social Problems* 15 (1967–68): 408–19.

[8] David K. Cohen and Michael S. Garet, "Reforming Educational Policy with Applied Research," *Harvard Educational Review* 45, no. 1 (February 1975): 17–43.

advance our or our graduate students' careers.[9] I have nothing directly useful to say about these important matters here.

On the other hand, if we conceive of our policy role as making our expertise available to serve within the predetermined international framework of government objectives in an ambassadorial sense, we have only three alternatives. We can agree or refuse to take part in activities — such as consulting and research — on the basis of our best understanding of whether they will contribute to or hinder the development of poor nations. I say this in the full recognition that we may not be asked since, according to Irving Horowitz, policymakers in national governments are "marked . . . by a positivistic and utilitarian view of research that amounts to a 'near-universal rejection of social science as a critical system or a critique of systems.' "[10] Or as individuals we can attempt — without any great hope of success — to strengthen or change government policies. We can work with others of similar persuasion and use our democratic rights to put pressure on governments everywhere to improve their development policies and actions and to rearrange their priorities, for instance, from destructive armament buildups to human services.

But I believe that our most important role will continue to be indirect. We could continue to learn, teach, and do research in our specialties; communicate our findings and conclusions in as direct and simple a language as the requirements of integrity, rigor, and completeness will allow.

In their essay, entitled "Reforming Educational Policy with Applied Research," Cohen and Garet persuasively questioned several key assumptions about the application of research to policy formation in the sense of providing workable guidelines for administrative conduct. They pointed out. that the problems which policymakers face make it difficult for anyone to claim that applied research can provide a basis for making administrative decisions. For instance, policy decisions are not discrete acts. They occur in a context of administrative continuity. It is presumptuous for applied researchers to believe that their once-in-a-while intervention can decisively influence policy decisions. The orientations researchers use are unsuitable bases from which to make workaday decisions. The data which researchers collect often appear irrelevant to decision makers. Applied research does not engender consensus about courses of action for several complicated reasons. Cohen and Garet affirmed my growing conviction that better social science theory and data

[9] Gordon C. Ruscoe, "The Academician and the Practitioner: Reconciliation in Comparative Education," *Notes and Abstracts in the Social Foundations of American and International Education*, no. 18 (Winter 1967), pp. 8–14.

[10] Interview with Irving Horowitz about his recently published book on policy research in *Behavior Today* 10, no. 2 (January 22, 1979): 6.

will not necessarily influence fundamental policy decisions if we continue to ignore or conceal the political and economic bases of these decisions.

The authors, however, pointed to another possibility after documenting that applied research does occasionally affect policy "in odd and unexpected ways": "The function of policy research is at least as much to describe and discuss the premises and objectives of policy as it is to predict policy effects. In this sense, applied research resembles a discourse about social reality—a debate about social problems and their solutions. Like intelligent discussion or debate, applied research does not necessarily reduce disagreement. Instead, it calls attention to the existence of conflicting positions, sometimes elaborates them and sometimes generates new issues altogether."[11]

I find this metaphor about policy research as disciplined discourse much more acceptable than the metaphor of social research endeavors as steps taken in a long journey to find laws similar to the ones discovered or discoverable in the physical sciences. At a time when some North American opinion makers are again proclaiming variants of "the end of ideology" in society, it is necessary to remind ourselves of the illusory nature of such proclamations and the value of genuine discourse. In some scholarly work, "the end of ideology" syndrome is most evident in the almost exclusive attention to analyzing individual idiosyncrasies or small group interactions without taking any account of the economic and political context in which they occur, even when such context is an essential component of the situation. Obviously, research as discourse must be subject to the tests of validity and credibility from relevant publics to which all scholarly work must submit.[12] Such tests—or, shall I say, contests—are the best means available to us to avoid the mistakes of unsupportable assumptions, inappropriate procedures, and unwarranted conclusions that all of us, being human, are likely to make. You may have read about the group of social scientists stranded on a desert island with a few unopened cans of food but no implement with which to open them. One of them apparently tried to solve the problem by saying, "Assume we have a can-opener . . . !" Surely unrealistic assumptions about resources or goodwill or political determination are not helpful.

An Agenda for Research

What research activities can we undertake to contribute to the discourse on international development policies? The suggestions I make

[11] Cohen and Garet, p. 42.
[12] See John J. Honigman, "The Personal Approach in Cultural Anthropological Research," *Current Anthropology* 17, no. 2 (June 1976): 243–50, and following comments, pp. 251–61.

are not new. I reiterate them only to make them available to a wider audience.

Comparative education as a field of study came into being in large part as a consequence of the development of national systems of education. This legacy continues to influence many of us in formulating comparative statements that, as it were, stop at the borders of a nation. The metropolis-hinterland paradigm with its emphasis on structured economic and cultural inequality at local, regional, national, and international levels can help us to break free of this legacy to the extent that such freedom is necessary to understand the world in the last 2 decades of this century.[13]

We can do comparative studies of the role formal education plays in promoting ideologies that maintain exploitive economic, political, and cultural relationships keeping in mind the fact that most ideological claims are not deliberate lies but true statements in perhaps unconsciously maintained limited or distorted perspectives.[14] The rationales offered for teaching metropolitan languages and what Altbach has called "the 'infrastructures' of intellectual life"—publishing houses, journals and information agencies—are two of the many topics that can be examined.[15] Sometimes high-sounding rationales for continuing metropolitan languages in schools are no more than smokescreens for maintaining the advantages elites already possess over others. The critical functions of intergovernmental and private foundations in formulating problems, prosecuting research strategies and influencing policies provide us with another challenging area for investigation.[16] Pierre Bourdieu's work on the manner in which cultural capital (which includes academic credentials) is produced, appropriated, reproduced, and consumed offers unexplored opportunities for cross-national study.[17] When

[13] I agree with Harold J. Noah's call in his 1974 presidential address for more cross-national comparison of subnational units on topics such as the school and the inner-city child, the recruitment of teachers for rural schools, and school provision for important minority groups. Where we might part company would be on the framework to be employed. See Harold J. Noah, "Fast-Fish and Loose-Fish in Comparative Education," *Comparative Education Review* 18, no. 3 (October 1974): 341–47.

[14] Karl Mannheim, *Ideology and Utopia* (New York: Harcourt, Brace & World, 1936).

[15] Philip G. Altbach, "Servitude of the Mind? Education, Dependency, and Neocolonialism," *Teachers College Record* 79, no. 2 (December 1977): 187–204. For single copies of *Education and Neocolonialism: A Bibliography*, compiled by Esha R. Chaudhuri, Anthony Layne, Ratna Ghosh, and Mathew Zachariah, readers may write to Department of Educational Foundations, University of Calgary, Calgary, Alberta, Canada T2N 1N4.

[16] See "Special Supplement: Modern China Studies," *Bulletin of Concerned Asian Scholars* 3, nos. 3 and 4 (Summer–Fall 1971): 91–168; Robert F. Arnove, "The Ford Foundation and 'Competence Building' Overseas: Assumptions, Approaches, and Outcomes," *Studies in Comparative International Development* 12 (Fall 1977): 100–126.

[17] Pierre Bourdieu, "Cultural Reproduction and Social Reproduction," in *Knowledge, Education and Culture*, ed. R. Brown (London: Tavistock, 1973), pp. 71–112; Pierre Bourdieu and Jean Claude Passeron, *Reproduction in Education, Society and Culture* (London: Sage, 1977).

doing this kind of research, it would be important to keep in mind the "principle of opposite effect," that is, every deliberate action to bring about social change produces at least one effect that is contrary to the original intention.

We now know that it is mechanistic to give undue emphasis to the correspondence between the implicit hidden agenda of the social relations of schooling and the relations of production in any society. The relationships of economy, polity, religion, education, and the family are mediated by much more complex transactions. Thanks mainly to the work of British and French sociologists we know more than we once did about the complexity of these transactions, but we need to learn more still, as Michael Apple has argued.[18] Because we are aware of this complexity, we should be less prone to identify particular features of schooling in our society as the direct result of our economic organization. Such cause-effect claims are vulnerable to devastatingly accurate charges such as these: Hierarchy in school relations is evident in different economic systems and therefore cannot be attributed to capitalism alone.[19] Whether particular features of a society are a reflection of "human nature" or the consequences of the mode of production is a question to which we do not have answers. Comparative studies of education in societies with different economic systems can help us to separate the morphological characteristics (such as the elementary, secondary, tertiary structure) and functional features (such as formal tests and examinations, the selection function, etc.) of all educational systems and the specific structures and functions that are the result of an educational system's relationship to the economy and polity. Only comparative investigations can provide us with worthwhile hypotheses about functional attributes of institutionalized education which result from intrainstitutional imperatives and thus can be distinguished from attributes which are the result of political economy imperatives.

We can also undertake more research into the linkages between privately controlled schools in Third World countries and the attainment of occupational success for their graduates in contrast to the graduates of government-run schools. Private schools flourish in many Third World countries, yet not much systematic research about their economic and political leverage has appeared in the literature with which I am familiar.[20]

---

[18] Michael Apple, "The New Sociology of Education: Analyzing Cultural and Economic Reproduction," *Harvard Education Review* 48, no. 4 (November 1978): 496. Also see Michael Apple, "Ideology and Educational Reform," *Comparative Education Review* 22, no. 3 (October 1978): 367–87.

[19] This question is briefly discussed in Noel F. McGinn's review of Martin Carnoy's *Education as Cultural Imperialism, Harvard Education Review* 45, no. 2 (May 1975): 245–50.

[20] See Charles Elliot, "Selection and Exclusion in the Hunt for a Job," *Patterns of Poverty in the Third World: A Study of Social and Economic Stratification* (New York: Praeger, 1975), pp. 265–77.

The analysis of textbooks offers interesting possibilities. Minority groups in our countries have been "conscienticized" in significant ways by the detection, measurement, and discussion of biases in textbooks.[21] May we not give much more attention to the way the Third World is depicted in our schoolbooks to help present a more accurate view of their current predicament? If we wish to be ambitious, with our more extensive facilities and manpower, we can even contribute to analyses of biases in the textbooks used in Third World countires.

There are many places in the Third World where the relationship of formal education to its local (i.e., rural as well as urban) and national environment is being painstakingly and successfully renegotiated after many false starts and defeats. Some of them provide salutary corrections to our view of the ignorance or helplessness of these peoples. "The schools to the countryside" experiment in Cuba is an example. We can study the effectiveness as well as the problems of these experiments from a genuinely objective (which I distinguish from a cynical) perspective. Some of these experiments—such as Paulo Friere's "conscienticization" programs in Brazil and Chile—were destroyed in short order by repressive military regimes.[22] An examination of the reasons that lead authoritarian regimes to perceive such programs as a threat should prove instructive to those who wish to learn more about the economic and political constraints that affect education's potential for liberation. The study of these experiments, I suspect, would also offer us new insights about the minimum needs of people that basic educational programs in Third World countries ought to provide which may or may not coincide with current notions of "standards" in the rich countries.

Part of the problem of relating formal education to the environment involves responsible and responsive communication with the people that researchers subject to investigation. Here, too, much fruitful comparative work is possible. Such work will become increasingly necessary as the development and control of highly sophisticated technology in the rich world subjects the poor world to deepening dependency.

There is a respectable research tradition in sociological studies that looks for the manifest and latent functions of institutions, the open and hidden curricula of educational agencies, and the contrast between appearance and reality. What I am suggesting is one way to work within this tradition by probing deeper into the persistence of educational problems that defy optimistic prescriptions for administrative solution.

---

[21] See David Pratt, *How to Find and Measure Bias in Textbooks* (Englewood Cliffs, N.J.: Educational Technology Publications, 1972). Of course, it is also true that conscienticization leads to critical analysis of textbooks.

[22] On military intervention in Brazil and on his work in Chile, see Paulo Friere, *Education: The Practice of Freedom* (London: Writers & Readers Publishing Cooperative, 1973).

For example, most educational systems in the Third World share one common characteristic: very high drop-out (wastage) and examination failure (stagnation) rates. Why do appallingly high wastage and stagnation rates persist? One very important reason is that the educational system functions primarily as a selecting agency for the dominant political and economic order instead of as a truly educative agency for the benefit of most children. The noticeable discrepancies in the provision as well as standards of educational institutions between urban centers and rural hinterlands can also be attributed to a considerable extent to the social class nature of the political economy.[23]

Studies which give due significance to the economic and political bases of educational problems do not have to become hopelessly deterministic statements about the human condition. They can help produce more accurate and dynamic statements about problems and possibilities.

The scholarly study of educational implications of the division of the world into the rich and the poor can be enriched by Marxist and neo-Marxist perspectives and analytical tools as well as by other perspectives and research traditions. We can make use of the rich resources available to us in the Marxist, neo-Marxist, and Weberian scholarly tradition only if we can overcome certain attitudes. One of them is that Marxist scholarship will somehow compel us to be advocates of particular variants of Communist ideology. True social science scholarship takes a critical stance toward all socioeconomic systems.[24] Another attitudinal problem is that we may be unjustly and inaccurately identified as agents of specific politicians. "Intestinal fortitude" is our only guard against such criticism! We can continually remind ourselves and others that we have no wish to rationalize or justify those documented, inhumane domestic or foreign excesses of bureaucratic state socialism; and that we do not have any sympathy with absurd reductionist arguments which dismiss constitutionally guaranteed freedoms and the independence of the judiciary as meaningless bourgeois rights. The articulation and legal enforcement of these rights and guarantees are among Western civilization's most valuable contributions to humanity. One does not have to experience the rigors of a Siberian labor camp, the ignominy of dismissal to a reeducation farm in China, or the tortures of the dreaded secret services in the Shah's Iran or Pinochet's Chile to appreciate these measures for the protection of persons. Indeed, may I venture to say that the preoccupa-

[23] Walter Feinberg, "Educational Equality under Two Conflicting Models of Educational Development," *Theory and Society* 2 (1975): 183–210. See also in this connection Mathew Zachariah, "Public Authority and Village Reconstruction: The Case of Basic Education in India," *Journal of Educational Thought* 4, no. 2 (August 1970): 94–106; and "The Durability of Academic Secondary Education in India," *Comparative Education Review* 14, no. 2 (June 1970): 152–61.

[24] See Mathew Zachariah, "The Intellectual in a Political Democracy," *Western Humanities Review* 22, no. 2 (Spring 1968): 93–100.

tion of enlightened scholarship in the coming decades should be to help construct a decent standard of living for people without, in the process, creating a monstrously powerful state or other juggernaut macroinstitutions. Obviously, such a standard should confront the problems of wasteful overdevelopment and debilitating underdevelopment.

Perhaps by now some of you are convinced that I appear to be driven by the "prophet motive." So be it. But I hope I have made a small contribution to comparative education's loss of epistemological innocence or willful ignorance. Perhaps, now that our careers are not so munificently supported by government largesse, we have the freedom and the opportunity to be more genuinely scholarly in pursuit of ethical values that will increase the autonomy of people and decrease their dependency.

We have objective class interests. Our motivations are many: to secure our and our children's future, to ensure our social status, to sustain personal and professional friendships. We are plagued by the besetting sin of thinking that discussions about a problem necessarily lead to overcoming it. Above all, we unconsciously wear academic blinkers that prevent us from seeing things the way others see them. These human qualities make it virtually impossible for us to respond to Dylan Thomas's call to "Rage, rage against the dying of the light." The best that some of us can do is to whimper, whimper against the dying of the light in the determined hope that time is our friend and not our enemy. But let us not scoff at small efforts. The noble Hindu concept of *dharma* is often thought of as doing one's caste duty in the manner prescribed by sacred texts or traditions. That is only one form of *dharma*, namely, *varna dharma*. This view of *dharma* often leads one to a resigned fatalism, a conclusion about one's insignificance. But *Sādharana dharma* (the duty of all human beings to the human race) makes it incumbent on us to do our best as small but significant beings in the universe.[25] Such a view permits us to do what we can against the dying of the light. Thereby we may—note the auxiliary, contingent verb—make a small contribution to the creation of a more humane world—a new international economic order—during this incarnation. (Who knows, in our next incarnation we may all be born as rabbits in Rwanda.) If we do manage to whimper against the dying of the light, we should expect from our most honest friends only the recognition that dawned on the Earl of Kent when he turned to William Shakespeare's King Lear and said about the jester: "This is not altogether fool, my lord."[26]

[25] For an excellent, readable discussion of different types of *dharma*, see Troy Wilson Organ, "The Way of Action," *The Hindu Quest for the Perfection of Man* (Athens: University of Ohio Press, 1970), esp. pp. 210–42.
[26] I shall leave it to the reader to determine the relevance of this incident involving Lear, Kent, and the fool to the subject of this paper.

Explaining the Origins and Expansion
of Mass Education

JOHN BOLI, FRANCISCO O. RAMIREZ, AND JOHN W. MEYER

The prevalence of mass education is a striking feature of the modern world. Education has spread rapidly in the last 2 centuries, becoming a compulsory, essentially universal institution. It has even expanded greatly in the poorest countries. Unesco estimates that about 75 percent of the children of primary school age in the world are enrolled in something called a school (1980 data).[1] For the developing countries, the mean figure reported is 68 percent. Although the richer countries have long since reached virtually universal enrollment, the fervor for education in the poor countries may be even stronger.[2] Mass education is clearly no longer the prerogative of boys: the World Bank reports that elementary enrollment ratios for girls are as high as those for boys in developed countries, and they are only slightly lower than the ratios for boys in developing countries.[3] In both rich and poor countries, secondary education has expanded to the point where it is obviously to be considered a mass form of education as well. The day is not far off when at least some type of secondary schooling will be widely available in countries where it was completely absent a few decades ago.

Another way to gauge the universality of education is by the fact that about 19 percent of the world's population are students, nearly all of them in mass educational institutions. For most people, education may be the most important element of their social status, and their educational background will have a greater direct impact on their overall life chances than any other element but nationality.

In the first part of this article, we consider a number of lines of explanation of the rise of mass education that have emerged over the past 2 decades. Two general sociological themes characterize these theories. First, there has been a tendency to see vertical or lateral social differentiation

Work on this paper was supported by the Stanford Center for the Study of Youth Development and funds from Father Flanagan's Boys' Home. We assume responsibility for the work, of course. Our thanks go to Aaron Benavot for his contributions to the ideas expressed here.

[1] Unesco, *Statistical Yearbook* (Louvain: Unesco, 1955–83).

[2] D. Hansen and A. Haller, "Status Attainment of Costa Rican Males: A Cross-cultural Test of a Model," *Rural Sociology* 38 (1973): 266–67; Stephen Heyneman, "Influences on Academic Achievement: A Comparison of Results from Uganda and More Industrialized Societies," *Sociology of Education* 49 (1976): 200–211.

[3] World Bank, *Education: Sector Policy Paper* (Washington, D.C.: IBRD, 1980).

Reprinted from *Comparative Education Review*, vol. 29, no. 2 (May 1985).

as the core feature of modern society. The relations of complex inter-dependence among social units, whether seen as reciprocal and mutually beneficial or as asymmetric and exploitative, are believed to be the root of all other features of modernity. Lines of reasoning employing this theme attempt to explain such modern rituals of mass solidarity as de-mocracy, universalistic cultural and religious movements, and mass ed-ucation. On the right, mass education is explained as a means of resolving the strains of differentiation, with emphasis on the lateral dimension, whereas on the left it is explained as a means of legitimating vertical differentiation.

Second, there has been a reductionist tendency that overemphasizes the importance of interest groups as central social actors. As particular groups or classes arise and gain power, they build institutions such as mass education for their own purposes. The expansion of education is therefore directly related to the strength of the dominant group vis-à-vis its competition and to the particular problems it must solve to control its local situation. Explaining the rise of mass education involves analyzing the power relations of interest groups in society.

We argue that these two themes generate misleading analyses of mass education and themselves face serious theoretical and empirical difficulties in dealing with the highly institutionalized and universalistic aspects of mass education. Viewing education as a creature of differentiation un-derstates its strong linkages with the integrating institutions of Western political and religious universalism and overlooks the importance and autonomy of these institutions as driving historical forces. At the same time, the reductionist stress on interest groups or classes as causal forces ignores the generality of the institutional level at which mass education developed. Education has been generated by worldwide social movements in modern history, and a satisfactory explanation of its origins must take into account the very broad ideological and institutional pressures that have been at work.

Our own analysis, developed in the second part of the article, stresses the modern reconstruction of the individual and the expanded linkages between the individual and newly emerging, more inclusive social units—the rationalized society and the rational state. We see mass education as an outcome of the religious, economic, and political processes that expand and secularize the organization and ideological rules of individual mem-bership in these larger units.

In the third part, we outline several lines of empirical research that derive from our analysis, with applications to both the formative period of mass education (the nineteenth century) and to the rapid expansion of education in the twentieth century. We develop a series of hypotheses specifying the particular aspects of modern political, economic, and religious mobilization that should be most strongly related to the formation and expansion of educational systems. We emphasize that our arguments are of very general applicability: we believe that they hold for Third World countries as much as for the developed West. Even though such countries are characterized by a good deal of traditional social organization, extreme social inequality, and relative lack of autonomy due to their subordination to the developed countries, they are nonetheless enthusiastically engaged in the same progress-oriented societal project as their richer counterparts. If anything, our arguments apply with even greater force to the Third World than to European countries in the eighteenth and nineteenth centuries, when they were at comparable levels of economic development, because education has become increasingly closely linked to the national project and is now a virtually indispensable element of national development.

Core Elements of Mass Education

The emphasis on social differentiation and inequality as determinants of mass education fails to appreciate some of the central features of mass education as an institution.[4] We distinguish three primary institutional features, which constitute an umbrella of claims under which all modern systems of mass education have emerged and expanded. As institutional claims, they are, of course, often at variance with what researchers studying particular schools or national systems actually observe; institutional ideology is never fully realized in practice. But the striking thing about modern mass education is that everywhere in the world the same interpretive scheme underlies the observed reality. Even in the most remote peasant villages, administrators, teachers, pupils, and parents invoke these institutional rules and struggle to construct schools that conform to them.

1. Mass education is institutionally chartered to be universal, standardized, and rationalized.[5] This element always characterizes educational ideology; in practice, it is a goal that is usually sought but not always obtained. Education is a mass institution in the sense that it incorporates everyone, cutting across such lines of differentiation as ethnicity, region, class, and gender. This characteristic is often taken for granted, because in many countries it is observable as empirical fact: all, or nearly all, children attend elementary schools that are supposed to be similar in

[4] Francisco O. Ramirez and John W. Meyer, "Comparative Education: Synthesis and Agenda," in *The State of Sociology: Problems and Prospects,* ed. James Short (Beverly Hills, Calif.: Sage, 1981); "Comparative Education: The Social Construction of the Modern World System," *Annual Review of Sociology* 6 (1980): 369–99.

[5] Francisco O. Ramirez and John Boli, "Global Patterns of Educational Institutionalization," in *Comparative Education,* ed. Philip Altbach, Robert Arnove, and Gail Kelly (New York: Macmillan, 1982).

cultural content, purposes, structure, funding, and general control.[6] In some countries, the same can be said of secondary schooling. Even where higher status people send their children to distinctive elementary schools, these schools differ from the mass institutions more in the resources they have available than in their general aspirations or curricula.

Explanations viewing mass education as the creation of interest groups or classes have difficulties with this general fact. They can readily account for a variety of uses of schooling but not so easily for the extraordinary standardization and universalism of the institution. Very elaborate but unconvincing arguments have been developed to explain why a standardized and homogeneous institution "really" (i.e., behind the scenes) arises to prop up a differentiated division of labor.[7] For some, the universalism of mass education is an obfuscating plot; for others, it is a response to "situational strain," a fuzzy concept indeed.

2. Mass education is very highly institutionalized at a very general collective level.[8] It is remarkably homogeneous in aspiration throughout the world, and this uniformity has led to increasingly homogeneous organizational forms as well. Note how easy it is for Unesco to assemble data on the prevalence of education, precisely because educational systems everywhere are built to conform at least nominally to world-institutionalized standard models. This sweepingly institutional, or ideological, element has characterized education for perhaps 2 centuries.[9] Mass education has arisen not as a practical device to deal with particular local problems or group conflicts but as a general system expressing principles of broad meaning and validity. It developed out of comprehensive religious structures, as well as broad national regulations and laws. It encompasses the most central aspects of human life: the nature of God and moral action, the laws of the natural world, and so on.

Many current theories about mass education also wrestle uneasily with this element. They could explain the emergence of school systems in limited areas designed to provide specific advantages for particular groups, but they have difficulty explaining the broad ideological mission of education. This mission deals with the most general aspects of social reality, especially when it is so similarly defined across localities, regions, and even countries that are so radically different from one another.

[6] Alex Inkeles and Larry Sirowy, "Convergent and Divergent Trends in National Educational Systems," *Social Forces* 62 (December 1983): 303–33.

[7] Joel Spring, *Education and the Rise of the Corporate State* (Boston: Beacon, 1972).

[8] John W. Meyer, "The Effects of Education as an Institution," *American Journal of Sociology* 83 (September 1977): 340–63.

[9] Yehudi Cohen, "The State System, Schooling, and Cognitive and Motivational Patterns," in *Social Forces and Schooling*, ed. N. Shimorhara and A. Scrupski (New York: McKay, 1979); and "Schools and Civilization States," in *The Social Sciences and the Comparative Study of Educational Systems*, ed. J. Fischer (Scranton, Pa.: International Textbook, 1970).

3. Mass education is institutionally chartered to conduct the socialization of the individual as the central social unit.[10] Although education is supposed to be homogeneous and standardized, the formal values and rituals it promotes celebrate the competence, capacities, and responsibility of the individual member of society. Even the most statist or collectivist modern systems have this individualist character in the sense that they also define the individual as the central unit of action, stress the importance of proper socialization, and view collective progress as the result of the competence and commitment of progressive individuals. More traditional educational forms aim less to socialize individuals as distinct social entities than to redefine their social identity through highly ritualized methods and rote instruction, which affect not the individual but his relationship to corporate social entities.

Given the diversity of modern political systems in so many respects, it is surprising how consistently educational systems attempt to build collective society by enhancing individual development. The individual is to know, to understand, to explain, to choose, and ultimately to become an effective person capable of making suitable choices and engaging in proper action. The rituals of mass education celebrate the reality of individual choice and responsibility, not the immersion of individuals in corporate groups such as castes, classes, extended families, and so on. Again, many theories cannot come to terms with this element. They can explain rituals of complete passivity for the masses, but they are mute with respect to the heavy stress on individual competence, initiative, and responsibility.[11]

Explanations of Mass Education

Any theory of the origins and expansion of mass education must deal with the core ideological elements of the institution: its highly institutionalized structure, its explicit incorporation of all members of society, its dramatic stress on individual action, and its homogeneous and universalized rationalistic frame. Seen in this light, mass education is clearly linked to a complex of other modern institutions that structure society as a rational project and extend its boundaries to include control of the individual's behavior and worldview. These include religious ideologies that emphasize the individual's relation to transcendental authority (God, history, the universe) as a matter of personal faith and action; political legitimations of authority relations that build on both the sovereignty of

---

[10] John Boli and Francisco O. Ramirez, "World Culture and the Institutional Development of Mass Education," in *Handbook of Theory and Research in the Sociology of Education*, ed. John G. Richardson (Westport, Conn.: Greenwood, 1984).

[11] See the critique of Bowles and Gintis (n. 17 below) in Christopher J. Hurn, *The Limits and Possibilities of Schooling* (Boston: Allyn & Bacon, 1978), pp. 76–80.

the individual actor (e.g., as voter) and on the rights and obligations of the individual (as subject or citizen); and economic market systems that make assumptions about individual capacities and motivations in both production and consumption. Contemporary polities systematically assume that social institutions have this general modern character, even though there is considerable variation in the specific types of institutions emphasized.

The argument we develop in the next section views mass education as a secular procedure for constructing the individual—the central actor of modern institutions of religious, political, and economic organization. We argue that mass education expands where institutional forms emphasizing the individual dominate. This type of causal link has often been discussed: with respect to mass education and the citizen-based nation-state, by Merriam and Bendix; with respect to religious and economic individualism, by Weber and McClelland.[12] But these discussions have tended to be cynical about the institution of individualism rather than analytical about its relation to inequality and differentiation. Disappointed theorists consider free democracy as sustaining inequality, the lawful bureaucratic state as oppressive, the free religion of disciplined Puritans as coercive, and the economy of free exchange as generating much inequality. This is all true, but it is a mistake to ignore the power of such structures as institutions that form the basis of modern society.

Perceiving a mismatch between individualist ideals and social practice, modern theories of the rise of mass education turn to the other main dimension of modernization, the increasingly differentiated division of labor. Rather than straightforwardly explain the rise of mass education as depending on the expansion of the universalistic institutions of individual membership in society, many theorists have tried to present these institutions (and, hence, education) as epiphenomenal reflections of social differentiation.

Education and Differentiation

Clearly, modern societies are highly differentiated. They are made up of many different, interdependent roles and groups. As organizational structures, they are differentiated even at the individual level, so that for better or worse every individual occupies a structurally unique position in society. The conception of society as a network of highly differentiated roles has so much power over modern social scientific imagination that any other conception of what is central in modern society seems idealistic and naive.

---

[12] C. Merriam, *The Making of Citizens* (Chicago: University of Chicago Press, 1931); Reinhard Bendix, *Nation-Building and Citizenship* (New York: Wiley, 1964); Max Weber, *The Protestant Ethic and the Spirit of Capitalism* (New York: Scribner's, 1958); David McClelland, "Does Education Accelerate Economic Growth?" *Economic Development and Cultural Change* 14 (1966): 257–78.

But how does differentiation explain the construction and expansion of homogeneous mass education? It is easy enough to explain how a sorting process in secondary schools or universities could arise to allocate individuals among stratified occupational positions. How does a long period of homogeneous mass education serve the same ends?

Several theoretical approaches address the problem; some make fairly direct links between social differentiation and mass education, and others specify more indirect links.[13] Both types start with a society composed of different roles and interests and try to account for the development of a combination of interests that will push society down the road toward mass education. Highly functionalistic, these explanations suppose that forces or interests located in differentiated society produce education to make society work better. In mainstream versions, society works better for the general good;[14] in more critical (leftist) versions, society works to sustain the position of dominant groups.[15] In either view, mass education somehow makes the differentiated role system work more smoothly. What is the connection?

In some theories, the proposed link is a direct connection between education and the cognitive or normative base "needed" for members of a complex society to play their different parts successfully. Individuals need to understand the diverse roles generated by an urbanized, industrialized society and the power relations among them, or they will not be able to fit into the structure. Hence, education is necessary to provide the cognitive skills required by the modern system. If individuals approve of the roles and power relations, "internalizing the values" of the differentiated society, their willing participation in the structure will be all the more certain.[16] Thus the imputed functional requirement of differentiated society for cognitive or moral competence creates a need for mass schooling to provide knowledge of the structure and adherence to the norms that support the structure. The connection between differentiation and education is generated by a need for a common cultural base in society.

More indirect links between differentiation and education are posited in social control theories. Here the strains engendered by social complexity threaten to fragment modern society, and social control becomes problematic. Mass education arises as a mechanism for legitimating the structure

[13] Spring; Remi Clignet, *Liberty and Equality in the Educational Process* (New York: Wiley, 1974).

[14] Émile Durkheim, *L'Evolution pédagogique en France* (Paris: Alcan, 1938), vol. 2; Talcott Parsons, "The School Class as a Social System," *Harvard Educational Review* 20, no. 4 (1957): 297–318; S. N. Eisenstadt, *From Generation to Generation* (Glencoe, Ill.: Free Press, 1956).

[15] Pierre Bourdieu and J. C. Passeron, *La Reproduction culturelle* (Paris: Editions de Minuit, 1970); Basil Bernstein, *Class, Codes, and Control*, 3 vols. (London: Routledge & Kegan Paul, 1971–75).

[16] Robert Dreeben, *On What Is Learned in School* (Reading, Mass.: Addison-Wesley, 1968); Alex Inkeles and David Smith, *Becoming Modern: Individual Change in Six Developing Countries* (Cambridge, Mass.: Harvard University Press, 1975); Gabriel Almond and Sidney Verba, *The Civic Culture* (Boston: Little, Brown, 1963).

of society; it becomes an essential device of social control, providing a normative base legitimating the differentiated system (mainstream version) or a mystification constructed by dominant elites to legitimize their power (critical version). Education props up the authority structure with theories of formal equality (political rights, universal suffrage, freedom of economic consumption, etc.) that are sustained by schools and a variety of other institutions. It emphasizes equality in a very unequal society either by providing "equality of opportunity" as the appropriate social response to inequality (mainstream version) or by maintaining the illusion of equality where true equality is impossible (critical version). It is generated not by a direct need for cognitive or moral integration but by a more indirect need for legitimation to support the differentiated order or the ruling elites.[17]

The heat of the political disputes between mainstream and critical theorists obscures the fact that, with regard to education, their arguments are virtually identical. In both lines of analysis, mass education helps meet the functional need for integration of the increasingly differentiated system, providing a unifying culture of universalistic equality.[18] There are differences in tone: the critical Left speaks more about vertical differentiation ("class structure") as a source of strain; the mainstream Right draws greater attention to the Durkheimian concern about education as a remedy for excessive lateral differentiation ("division of labor"). Similarly, the Left emphasizes the immediate group or personal interests of the elites advocating mass education, whereas the Right emphasizes more systemic purposes or problems. But the predictions of the two perspectives with respect to education are hard to distinguish.

Too many questions are raised by such theories, even apart from the obvious problems that plague all functionalist explanations, whether of the Left or the Right. If the elites have enough power to build a system of social control through mass education, why do they need the system? If they wish to generate a system that integrates society through obfuscation, why do they design it so to enhance the membership and institutional importance of the otherwise dispossessed? If the structural features of mass education are so epiphenomenal and illusory, why does the educational system operate so hegemonically? How can such massive false consciousness be maintained?

Many of these same questions are troublesome for another variety of explanation that at least has the virtue of avoiding a functionalist approach to the problem. In what has come to be known as "conflict" theory, the

[17] Samuel Bowles and Herbert Gintis, *Schooling in Capitalist America* (New York: Basic, 1976); Michael B. Katz, *Class, Bureaucracy, and Schools: The Illusion of Educational Change in America* (New York: Praeger, 1975); Spring (n. 7 above).
[18] For alternative critiques, see Randall Collins, "Functional and Conflict Theories of Educational Stratification," *American Sociological Review* 36 (1971): 1002–19; and Margaret S. Archer, "The Neglect of the Educational System by Bernstein and Bourdieu," *European Journal of Sociology* (in press).

central notion is that mass education arises as a result of competition among status groups for social dominance.[19] Education is the modern arena of two aspects of status group competition: in the first, groups compete for education because it facilitates occupational and social success; in the second, groups compete to use education for their own purposes, knowing that dominant groups can structure educational curricula to insure the hegemony of their own cultural values. In this perspective, then, social differentiation produces competing status groups that try to dominate education for their own purposes.

Like the other perspectives, conflict theory is unable to answer a number of crucial questions regarding the rise of mass education. Why does education become the arena of competition in the first place? Why do groups that are capable of controlling society and imposing their values on others bother with a set of institutional rules stressing universalistic equality and individual competence rather than straightforward dominance and hierarchy (as has usually been the case in the past)? All these theories have a peculiar and unspoken premise: dominant groups (or the differentiated order) cannot survive in the modern world without propagating a myth of equality; elites are just strong enough to keep it a myth but not strong enough to dispense with it. The theories also rely heavily on the supposition that false consciousness can be massively imposed and maintained, even in the face of very severe inequality.

In fact, all these theoretical lines beg the crucial questions surrounding mass education. Why is it so universalistic? Why does it so greatly emphasize the individual as the primary social construct and make of that individual the locus of social value and competence? Why does it stress equality in such unequal social structures?

Problems of Evidence

The most telling failure of the modern attempt to connect mass education with social differentiation is empirical, however, not theoretical. Certainly, mass education is the creature of a modern system of which urbanization, economic development, and industrialization—the organizational concomitants of differentiation—are central components. But just as certainly, differentiation as such is not closely associated empirically with the origins and expansion of mass education.

First, the evidence is consistently negative on the direct connection between differentiation and education. Mass education in Europe, Japan, and the United States commonly preceded industrialization and extensive urbanization.[20] Within Europe, the early industrializers were not the first

[19] Randall Collins, *The Credential Society: A Historical Sociology of Education and Stratification* (New York: Academic Press, 1979); Hurn.

[20] Bendix; Ronald Dore, *Education in Tokugawa Japan* (Berkeley: University of California Press, 1964); C. F. Kaestle and M. A. Vinovskis, *Education and Social Change: Nineteenth Century Massachusetts—*

to embrace the ideology of mass education and begin to construct universal school systems: Prussia, Austria, and Denmark were ahead of France and England,[21] and Scotland has had higher educational enrollment rates than England throughout the modern period.[22] Furthermore, regional analyses fail to show a connection between urbanization or industrialization and the expansion of enrollments.[23] Within the United States, the less industrialized western states moved more rapidly to create and expand mass education than had the eastern states,[24] and analyses of the nineteenth century find no effect of urbanization on educational enrollments.[25] In cross-national analyses of the contemporary world, industrialization is found to be poorly related to the growth of mass education as well.[26] Hence industrialization and urbanization are not central causal factors directly generating mass education at all.

Second, empirical analyses do not support the social control or status group conflict theories any better. Such theories predict greater educational expansion in cities, where the need for social control is stronger, but urbanization is not related to increasing enrollments. They also predict that immigration rates should be closely associated with the expansion of education because immigrants are prime targets of social control efforts. The evidence, however, is negative on this point for the United States; in cross-national studies, educational expansion has been shown to be unrelated to ethnic fragmentation.[27]

On reflection, the evidentiary failure of these theories makes a good deal of sense. If dominant groups, faced with social control problems, had the power to construct massive educational systems to legitimate themselves, why would they bother? Would not direct subordination of the unruly orders be a more probable and effective alternative? In fact, of course, social systems facing problems of disorder, labor unrest, or failure of social control mechanisms have not resorted to education. They have relied on straightforward repression. In extreme instances, this is obvious: in the American South, the education of slaves was strictly for-

---

Quantitative Studies, Final Research Report, Project no. 3-0825 (Washington, D.C.: National Institute of Education, 1976).

[21] Boli and Ramirez (n. 10 above).

[22] Peter Flora, *State, Economy, and Society in Western Europe: 1815–1975,* 2 vols. (Frankfurt: Campus Verlag, 1983).

[23] John Craig and Norman Spear, "The Diffusion of Schooling in Nineteenth-Century Europe: Toward a Model" (paper presented at the annual meeting of the Social Science History Association, Columbus, Ohio, 1978).

[24] John G. Richardson, "Historical Sequences and the Origins of Common Schooling in the American States," in Richardson, ed. (see n. 10 above).

[25] John W. Meyer, David Tyack, Joane P. Nagel, and Audri Gordon, "Public Education as Nation-Building in America," *American Journal of Sociology* 85 (1979): 591–613.

[26] John W. Meyer, Francisco O. Ramirez, Richard Rubinson, and John Boli-Bennett, "The World Educational Revolution, 1950–1970," *Sociology of Education* 50 (October 1977): 242–58.

[27] John Ralph and Richard Rubinson, "Immigration and the Expansion of Schooling in the United States: 1890–1970," *American Sociological Review* 45:943–55; Meyer et al. (n. 26 above).

bidden, not encouraged, and slaves were controlled through physical punishment. In less extreme examples, repression has still been the standard approach to social control.

For example, in most European countries, early urbanization generated a variety of labor control methods that were plainly repressive. Expanding the educational opportunities of the disorderly or potentially disorderly classes was unthinkable until late in the nineteenth century.[28] Even then, the educational improvement of the lower classes was not generally proposed when maintaining order was seen as most problematic. In times of internal disorder, repression was the usual response. Today, repression rather than rapid educational expansion remains the favored response to politically threatening situations, as in colonial societies or southern Africa. There are no empirical analyses showing that political instability results in educational expansion.

Theoretical Reconsideration

Before proceeding to our own argument, we present some general considerations. First, it makes sense to see the differentiating institutions of the Western system as dialectical counterparts of the integrating institutions.[29] The two sides of this dualism constitute a single cultural frame. The political, religious, and economic institutions that integrate the individual into society cannot simply be ignored or treated as epiphenomena; they are not just mystifications that hide the inequalities of the differentiated system. Since the twelfth century, the legal and ideological bases of Western political and economic differentiation have been rooted in integrative ideological soil, including a universalistic doctrine of the individual and a fundamental commitment to equality; empirically, educational ideology as expressed in official documents is still linked closely to doctrines of equality today.[30] One need not believe in equality as an established fact to see the profound effects of these doctrines on religion, law, the economy, and political structures.

Second, it is these institutions of integration that are especially relevant to the origins and expansion of mass education. Education flourishes where these institutions are strong. It is more weakly associated with differentiating social forces. Indeed, we argue below that organizational differentiation in and of itself may be negatively related to mass education, in that an institution such as education that enhances and equalizes the status of individuals is more difficult to establish in a highly differentiated

---

[28] See Donald K. Jones, *The Making of the Education System, 1851–81* (London: Routledge & Kegan Paul, 1977).

[29] See Perry Anderson, *Lineages of the Absolutist State* (London: Verso, 1974).

[30] Walter Ullmann, *The Individual and Society in the Middle Ages* (Baltimore: Johns Hopkins University Press, 1966); Colin Morris, *The Discovery of the Individual, 1050–1200* (London: SPCK, 1972).

system. The failure to find positive effects of differentiation in the postwar period suggests that this line of thinking may prove very fruitful.

Third, the package of institutional elements that constitute modern society contains somewhat varied contents in different societies; some dimensions of modernity vary more or less independently of other dimensions. For example, the purest examples of modern political egalitarianism and individualism are to be found in rural areas of the American North and West, not in areas of maximum industrial concentration. As we shall argue, mass education accompanies not differentiation per se but universalistic individualism. The nature of the process by which mass education develops is determined by the particular way in which the individual is bound to the social collectivity.

Creating Members of the Rational Society and Modern State

Instead of seeing differentiation as the crucial factor leading to mass education, it is more useful to look at the other central aspect of modern society: its structures of universalistic integration. Modernization involves the construction of rules of political and economic inequality, to be sure, but it also involves legal and cultural principles of equality—principles that are even more heavily emphasized, and in greater detail, in Third World countries than in European nations. There is considerable disagreement about which of these aspects is primary and about what are the consequences of each for long-term societal development. But the key point, often overlooked or denied by theorists for various ideological reasons, is that modern society contains both highly differentiated roles and binding common cultures, both highly fragmented images of action and sweeping assertions of common human identity.

In our view, mass education is produced by the social construction of the main institutions of the rationalized, universalistic worldview that developed in the modern period—the citizen-based nation and state, the new religious outlook, and the economic system rooted in individual action (originally in markets, now more commonly in organizations such as those found in contemporary socialist countries). Mass education arose primarily as a means of transforming individuals into members of these new institutional frames that emerged in Europe after the Middle Ages. The nature of society was redefined; society became a rational, purposive project devoted to achieving the new secular ends of progress and human equality.[31] The project was defined in the new institutional frames to include individual members of society as essential components—loci of sovereignty and loyalty, production and consumption, faith and obedience. Thus the individual

---

[31] See Robert Nisbet, *History of the Idea of Progress* (New York: Basic, 1980).

must be made rational, purposive, and empowered to act with autonomy and competence in the new universalistic system.[32]

In the emerging society built around individual membership, theories of socialization developed and became central.[33] In the new view, the unformed, the parochial, or even the morally defective child could be molded in desired ways if its environmental experiences were controlled in a rational and purposive manner. Such deliberate socialization was necessary, because all of the virtuous goals of society increasingly were seen as attainable only to the extent that individual members of society embodied the corresponding personal virtues. Because society was held to be essentially a collection of individuals, the success or failure of its effort to realize progress and justice was dependent on the nature of the socialization experiences encountered by the individual.[34]

Such a view—that mass education is part of the effort to construct the universalistic and rationalized society, incorporating individuals and their actions—fits well with the distinctive features of mass education we have noted above. Mass education is too all-encompassing and homogeneous to be explained by the division of labor. It is too highly institutionalized in political and religious collectivities of too broad a purview to be seen as a simple reflection of local interest relations. Finally, it focuses too much on the individual as chooser and actor to be conceived as a simple instrument of passivity and labor control in a differentiated society. This is true even in socialist and Third World countries, for their educational programs assume individual competence and responsibility as much as those of the developed West.

It is important to see that, in modern history, all this has been a highly institutional and ideological business. It is not simply an accidental by-product of social changes that happened to occur in one or another locality. Both the differentiating and the integrating aspects of the modern system were pursued as rationalizing projects by all sorts of elites mobilizing their societies for improvement. The political, economic, and cultural aspects of individualism were inherent in these projects and eagerly pursued by mobilizing elites, and it is individualism that gave rise to visions of the necessity of mass education. Of course, it is precisely this project-oriented, or ideological, character of the institutions of individualism that generates the great gulf between doctrine and reality. Just as the rules of the market

[32] John W. Meyer, John Boli, and George M. Thomas, "Rationalization and Ontology in the Evolving World System" (paper presented at the annual meeting of the Pacific Sociological Association, Portland, Oregon, March 1981).

[33] Philippe Ariès, *Centuries of Childhood* (New York: Vintage, 1962); Bernard Jolibert, *L'Enfance au XVIIe siècle* (Paris: Librairie Philosophique J. Vrin, 1981); John Sommerville, *The Rise and Fall of Childhood* (Beverly Hills, Calif.: Sage, 1982).

[34] Francisco O. Ramirez and John Boli, "The Political Construction of Mass Schooling: European Origins and Worldwide Institutionalization," mimeographed (Stanford, Calif.: Stanford University, Department of Sociology, 1984).

economy or democratic regime are rhetorically invoked most loudly where they are weakest,[35] the ideological bases of mass education are often most solemnly celebrated where they are least put into practice. Nonetheless, in the educational arena both the doctrines and organized school systems depicted in theory are coming to be universal.

Two Forms of Educational Construction of the Modern Individual

In the broadest sense, mass education arises as a purposive project to construct the modern polity, reconstructing individuals in accordance with collective religious, political, and economic goods and purposes. Because the modern polity takes different forms, the route to mass education involves somewhat different paths in different societies. One crucial distinction is whether the polity of progress-oriented individuals under construction is linked to the state apparatus or to less central societal structures.

Consider the case in which the effort to construct a rationalized society is grounded on a conception of individuals as members of networks of institutions and relations that together constitute the societal unit. There is no (or only a weak) formal central authority structure that is empowered to act on behalf of society as a whole. In this case, education is built around a model of *creating societal members*. Education is engendered by the effort to create properly socialized members of the rational society who have the capacity and disposition to join in the struggle for progress as workers, innovators, consumers, organizers, and committed members of the political community. Given the goals of progress and equality, this model depicts education as a process of mass mobilization linking individuals to a pervasive "civic culture" that has broad moral authority in the dispersed institutions of society. Social movements generated by this overarching institutional nexus create organizations to socialize children in a common experiential frame. The form and content of the educational system, although highly decentralized, varies little from region to region because the rational model of society is so thoroughly institutionalized in the civic culture.[36]

This is a fair and succinct description of the line of development followed in the United States. Education developed from movements motivated by religious, political, and economic visions of a progressive future, but these were not vested primarily in the state.[37] In fact, in this model of development, mass education generally precedes the adoption of formal state rules about education. The United States has long had the most expanded educational system in the world, but it still has no

---

[35] Jacques Ellul, *Propaganda* (New York: Knopf, 1965).

[36] John W. Meyer, "Myths of Socialization and Personality" (paper presented at the Conference on Reconstructing Individualism at the Center for the Humanities, Stanford University, February 1984).

[37] David Tyack, *The One Best System* (Cambridge, Mass.: Harvard University Press, 1974).

national rule of compulsory mass education; in this respect, it is almost unique.

The model of creating societal members has dominated educational development in only a few places; in most countries, modernization has centered less on society as the locus of the modern polity and more on the state organization itself. Here we have the model of education as *creating members of the nation-state*. The nation-state, along with the individual, has been a primary generator of social mobilization throughout modern history. It is now entirely dominant as an organizational form, having defeated or incorporated alternatives. Like the individual, the nation-state is seen in modern ideology as a rational, purposive actor, organizing society toward progress and competitive success in the larger interstate system. The state incorporates the individual through the institution of citizenship, which both grants participatory rights in political, economic, and cultural arenas and imposes strong obligations to participate in state-directed national development.[38]

In this model, education becomes the vehicle for creating citizens. It instills loyalty to the state and acceptance of the obligations to vote, go to war, pay taxes, and so on. It also equips citizens with the skills and worldview required for them to be able to contribute productively to national success. The state promotes a *mass* educational system in order to transform all individuals into members of the national polity, and it supports a *uniform* system to build devotion to a common set of purposes, symbols, and assumptions about proper conduct in the social arena.[39]

The dominant form of expansion of mass education in Western Europe took this route, the creation of nation-state members. To American eyes, this style of development looks "top-down" because the rules of mass education devolve from the organizational center of society represented by the state. In a broad sense, however, the "creation of societal members" model also involves top-down mobilization, because universalistic patterns that are institutionalized at a very general level are imposed on individuals. The latter model involves stronger assertions of individual sovereignty and autonomy, whereas the former locates authority in society more explicitly at the top, whence it is delegated downward to the individual. In this case, the individual's duties are as explicit and compelling as his or her rights, if not more so.

The contrast between the two models comes out most clearly if we see the construction of mass education as involving two distinct social processes. There is, of course, the expansion of schools as organizational

---

[38] T. H. Marshall, *Class, Citizenship, and Social Development* (New York: Doubleday, 1964); Bendix (see n. 12 above).

[39] Francisco O. Ramirez and Richard Rubinson, "Creating Members: The Political Incorporation and Expansion of Public Education," in *National Development and the World System,* ed. John W. Meyer and Michael T. Hannan (Chicago: University of Chicago Press, 1979).

entities. One can envision a rough scale with the establishment of nationwide networks of schools at the low end; universal enrollment and, later, universal attendance as intermediate steps; and universal attendance for a specified number of years at the high end. The other process involves not the organization of schools but the clarity and elaboration of the rules of mass education, which are given their fullest expression in the laws of the state. Here the scale has rules requiring the construction of schools and training of teachers at the low end; compulsory enrollment and attendance for all children as intermediate steps; and detailed rules specifying the levels, sequences, curricula, and administration of the educational enterprise at the top.

Our two models of educational construction differ in their implications for the organizational expansion of education as distinguished from the institutional rules and laws binding education into society. The model of creating members of the nation-state leads above all to the adoption of institutional rules of compulsory education; the system of schools and enforced attendance of students would expand later as a consequence. The model of creating members of the modern society (the "liberal democracy" model) entails the expansion of the system of schools and pupil attendance more than the creation of legal institutional rhetoric concerning mass education. Ultimately, either form of structural modernization leads to mass education, but the route traveled and the degree of state involvement and state adoption of formal rules varies considerably.

Let us flesh out this analysis with several examples before developing it as a set of research hypotheses. Although the United States represents the purest example of the model of creating societal members, this model also dominated in England. In these countries, educational enrollments expanded considerably ahead of the establishment of formal rules instituting compulsory primary education. Schools were established on a voluntary basis, often by religious organizations, and state support of education was limited and indirect until relatively late.[40]

By contrast, in countries such as Prussia and Denmark, the state took the leading role in establishing mass education; voluntary organizations played almost no role at all. In these countries, institutional commitments to compulsory education preceded the construction of school systems by well over a century, and it seems unlikely (though early statistics are not available) that primary enrollments in Prussia and Denmark encompassed as large a proportion of children as those in the United States until the late nineteenth century.[41]

[40] Meyer and Hannan, eds.
[41] Ramirez and Boli (n. 5 above); John Craig, "The Expansion of Education," *Review of Research in Education* 9 (1981): 151–210.

As these examples reveal, the adoption of institutional rules calling for compulsory mass education tends to be linked more with the location of social authority in the state, whereas the construction of a mass system of schools is linked more with the location of social authority in the individual. In any given country, of course, authority is divided between the state and the individual, and there is considerable variation in the nature of this division. Thus there is great variation in the date of adoption of compulsory education rules and in the rate of construction of mass schooling systems across countries. It is important to remember, however, that both forms of the new model of society devoted to the rationalized pursuit of progress lead to mass education. We can summarize this argument in three general propositions:

I. The penetration of society by any rational, purposive model of social organization leads to both the adoption of institutional rules of compulsory education and the construction of a mass system of schools to create members of the new model of society.

II. Social forces that incorporate the individual into the collectivity as a member of the rational society lead to the construction of mass systems of schools, but they have less impact on the adoption of central institutional (state) rules of compulsory mass schooling.

III. Social forces that incorporate the individual into the collectivity as a member of the nation-state lead to the adoption of national rules making education universal and compulsory, but they have less direct impact on the construction of mass systems of schools.

The first proposition implies that both the institutional rules and the organizational structures of mass education are generated by the expansion of the rationalized societal model. In other words, relative to other societal forms ("traditional," "primitive," "medieval" societies), the rationalized progress-oriented form of social organization is far more likely to generate mass education. The second and third propositions summarize the implications of the two models ("ideal types," in Weber's language) as different processes whereby educational development proceeds.

Research Agenda

Broadly comparative explanations of mass education often fail to specify the empirical implications of their central arguments and the research directions to be pursued in testing these hypotheses. The literature is replete with apologies for this shortcoming: lack of adequate data, problems of data comparability, lack of fit between variables and indicators, conceptual and methodological problems in sorting out the effects of intercorrelated independent variables, and so on. There are serious difficulties in all comparative investigations,[42] but the increasing availability of comparative historical data on mass education (including considerable information on non-European countries)[43] and the development of more powerful analytic models[44] make these problems more tractable. In the following subsections, we want to show how our theoretical argument can be evaluated with the resources currently available.

Our research agenda requires investigation of two dependent variables: (1) the establishment of national educational rules and agencies creating modern systems of mass schooling and (2) the organizational expansion of primary and secondary educational enrollments. The former can be measured by determining the date of *(a)* the adoption of compulsory primary education rules, *(b)* the establishment of national educational ministries or bureaus, and *(c)* national unification of primary and secondary school systems. Organizational expansion can be measured by computing the size of primary and secondary enrollments relative to the appropriate age groups. Information on institutional rules can be found in a number of comparative educational histories;[45] more systematic information on enrollments is reported by Flora, Mitchell, and Banks.[46] For the more recently independent nations, the same information is reported in the *World Survey of Education Handbook* and in the Unesco *Statistical Yearbook.*[47] The central research issue is determining how the independent variables indicated in our theoretical argument affect the likelihood of founding a national system of mass education and of expanding primary (and later, secondary) enrollment ratios.

Reorganization of a Society

Our three propositions identify the general conditions under which educational development occurs. From the first we derive three hypotheses:

i) *The institutionalization of the national exchange economy leads to the adoption of mass education rules and the expansion of mass educational enrollments.*—An exchange economy is institutionalized to the extent that production factors are unrestrained by traditional norms defining and regulating economic relations; where legal or religious structures sustain relative market freedom

---

[42] Morris Zelditch, Jr., "Intelligible Comparisons," in *Comparative Methods in Sociology,* ed. Ivan Villier (Berkeley: University of California Press, 1971).

[43] Flora (n. 22 above); B. R. Mitchell, *European Historical Statistics, 1750–1970* (New York: Columbia University Press, 1975); Arthur S. Banks, *Cross-national Time-Series Data Archive* (Binghamton: State University of New York at Binghamton, Center for Comparative Political Research, 1975).

[44] Nancy Brandon Tuma and Michael T. Hannan, *Social Dynamics: Models and Methods* (New York: Academic Press, 1984).

[45] See, e.g., Margaret S. Archer, *Social Origins of Educational Systems* (Beverly Hills, Calif.: Sage, 1979); Edward Reisner, *Nationalism and Education since 1789* (New York: Macmillan, 1922).

[46] Flora (n. 22 above); Mitchell, *European Historical Statistics, 1750–1970;* B. R. Mitchell, *International Historical Statistics,* 2 vols. (New York: Columbia University Press, 1983); Banks.

[47] Unesco, *World Survey of Education Handbook* (Geneva: United Nations, 1955–71), vols. 1–5; Unesco, *Statistical Yearbook* (n. 1 above).

in labor, land, commodities, and capital, mass education is more likely. Conversely, restrictions regarding the mobility of peasants, the sale of land, or the circulation of money should have negative effects on educational development. The pervasiveness of structures of economic individualism should be distinguished from other factors that have received more attention in studies of the impact of differentiation on education, particularly industrialization and urbanization. From our perspective, mass education is neither a functionalist mechanism of social integration nor a repressive social control apparatus generated by internal disorder and conflict. We therefore do not expect the more urbanized and industrialized societies to expand educational systems more rapidly than other societies when other factors are held constant.

The greater speed with which Scandinavian countries founded mass schooling in the nineteenth century illustrates the distinction between these two sets of economic factors: relatively greater market freedom in these countries contributed to their national commitment to mass education, even though they were less industrialized and urbanized than other European countries.[48] Today, strongly entrenched caste or tribalist principles, if restrictive of market freedom, can be expected to hinder the creation and growth of mass education, controlling for the level of urbanization or industrialization (see below).

ii) *The political rationalization of society leads to mass educational rules and enrollments.*—Political rationalization consists of both the expansion of state authority and power in society[49] and the expansion of citizenship links between the state and the individual.[50] Both state formation and nation building involve a sweeping reconstruction of the social order; collective and individual authority cease to be derived from nature or custom and instead become positive instruments in the quest for progress. The rights and powers of states and individuals cease to be mere immunities from traditional obligations and become action opportunities for attaining new goals and affirming new values.

Indicators of the expansion of state authority include constitutional powers,[51] fiscal powers,[52] size of the public bureaucracy,[53] and the presence

[48] Arnold Heidenheimer, "Education and Social Security Entitlements in Europe and America," in *The Development of Welfare States in Europe and America,* ed. Peter Flora and Arnold Heidenheimer (New Brunswick, N.J.: Transaction, 1981).

[49] Samuel Huntington, *Political Order in Changing Societies* (New Haven, Conn.: Yale University Press, 1968).

[50] Marshall (see n. 38 above); Bendix (see n. 12 above).

[51] John Boli-Bennett, "The Ideology of Expanding State Authority in National Constitutions, 1870–1970," in Meyer and Hannan, eds. (see n. 39 above).

[52] Flora (n. 22 above); Charles L. Taylor and M. C. Hudson, *World Handbook of Political and Social Indicators,* 2 vols. (Ann Arbor: University of Michigan, Interuniversity Consortium for Political Research, 1971).

[53] Flora (n. 22 above); Banks (see n. 43 above).

or absence of military conscription.[54] Indicators of citizenship rights include franchise rights,[55] civil liberties, and social welfare rights;[56] similar indicators are also available in Boli-Bennett's work.[57]

iii) *The institutionalization of individualist cultural ideology leads to mass educational rules and enrollments.*—The triumph of mass education presupposes cultural universalism, emphasizing the primacy of the individual and a strong link between individual growth and national development. Uniform socialization of the masses is in the national interest only if it is assumed that all properly socialized individuals will make positive contributions to national success. Since Weber, many have argued that there is a strong link between Protestantism and individualism; this argument squares with the common observation that mass education developed most rapidly in Protestant countries.[58] But religious individualism is more likely to become a national project to create a standardized "new man" if such religious sentiment is organizationally rooted in a national church. We thus expect that the establishment of a national church stressing the ultimate authority of the individual should make educational development proceed faster. (Data on the presence or absence of an individualistic national church can be obtained from such sources as the *World Christian Encyclopedia.*)[59]

These three hypotheses stress one common idea: the reorganization of society around a rational purposive model that emphasizes economic, political, and cultural individualism generates mass educational rules and enrollments. In this process, mass education is assigned a central role, linking beliefs in the efficacy of organized socialization and the importance of childhood learning experiences for adult capacities to the optimistic assumption that reconstituted individuals will further national development and progress.

Forces That Delegitimate or Inhibit

What we have said so far builds on the idea that newly legitimated structural and cultural elements promote mass education. Conversely, mass education is also boosted by forces that delegitimate prior structural arrangements and cultural recipes:

[54] Devi Prasad and Tony Smythe, *Conscription: A World Survey* (London: War Resisters' International, 1968).

[55] Tom Mackie and Richard Rose, *The International Almanac of Electoral History* (London: Macmillan, 1974).

[56] Flora (n. 22 above); Harold Wilensky, *The Welfare State and Equality* (Berkeley: University of California Press, 1975).

[57] John Boli-Bennett, "The Expansion of Nation-States, 1870–1970" (Ph.D. diss., Stanford University, 1976).

[58] William Boyd and Edmund J. King, *The History of Western Education*, 11th ed. (London: Black, 1975).

[59] David Barrett, *World Christian Encyclopedia* (Nairobi: Oxford University Press, 1982).

iv) *External challenges to the integrity of the national polity delegitimate older social institutions and create opportunities for new groups (often linked to the state) to promote efforts of national mobilization, thereby leading to mass educational rules and enrollments.*—External challenges often come in the form of national failure in the competitive interstate system, such as the military setbacks that stimulated mass education efforts in Prussia in 1807 and France in 1871; a systematic analysis of the effects of military victory or defeat on education can be undertaken using warfare data such as that compiled by Wright.[60] Similarly, a decline in the economic dominance of a given country in the world system may lead to a greater affirmation of the national commitment to education, as we have recently witnessed with the sober rhetoric of "a nation at risk" in the United States.[61] A corollary of this hypothesis is that more successful competitors are more likely to delay the adoption of educational ideologies and organizational forms. The relatively slow and incomplete adoption of national educational systems in England and the United States in the nineteenth century illustrates this aspect.

Our theoretical argument also suggests a number of factors that will inhibit both rules and enrollments. These factors represent alternative social organizational forms that are based on units other than the individual. Intermediate corporate groups are the fundamental social units and individual membership in society or the state is not at issue. We therefore hypothesize the following:

v) *Mass educational development is inhibited by plantation economic organization and industrial economic organization where the structure emphasizes intermediate groups rather than the individual; religious organizational forms that emphasize liturgical ritual and church mediation between the individual and God; and corporatist or feudal political organization, where intermediate groups (estates, syndicates, families) are considered primary elements of society.*—This set of hypotheses implies that Catholic countries, for example, will be slower than Protestant countries to develop mass education. It is important to remember, however, that Catholic countries today are nevertheless far more involved in mass education than any country in earlier times, before the rational, purposive model of societal development came to dominate social ideology. After the Counter-Reformation, the Enlightenment, and the French Revolution, Catholic polities increasingly took a modern rationalistic form, as in nineteenth-century Latin America. Similarly, modern polities that retain traditional elements in their authority structures (e.g., tribalism in African nations and other ethnic cleavages in a number of countries) are

---

[60] Quincy Wright, *The Study of War* (Chicago: University of Chicago Press, 1942).

[61] National Commission on Excellence in Education, *A Nation at Risk* (Washington, D.C.: Government Printing Office, 1983).

likely to have less expanded educational systems than more purely individualistic polities but much more expanded schooling than premodern polities.

This fifth set of hypotheses is central, for they distinguish our argument most clearly from the predictions of other lines of reasoning. Future research that supports or rejects them will be most telling for the perspective we have developed.

Promotion of a Nation

Our second and third propositions distinguish social forces that are especially likely to lead to the adoption of educational rules from those that more strongly affect educational enrollments. As specifications of the first of these propositions, we identify two sets of factors that promote nation building and the creation of members of the rational society but do not promote state formation and citizenship ideologies.

vi) *Market economy rules and political ideologies that delegitimate political collectivities above the level of the individual, or that legitimate only a universalist collectivity without a corresponding organizational structure, increase educational enrollments but delay the adoption of institutional rules.*—Examples relevant to this hypothesis include the rather pure forms of laissez-faire economic thinking that characterized Britain and the United States in the early nineteenth century[62] and the highly atomized view of the individual (now known as libertarianism) that was prevalent in the United States at the same time.[63] Where no national center is legitimated, membership in the state becomes meaningless and national compulsory education almost a heresy, although formal schooling is an eminently reasonable activity to prepare for participation in the rational society.

vii) *Individualistic religious movements not structured as national churches increase educational enrollments but hinder the adoption of national educational rules.*—Individualist Protestant sects emphasize the authority of individuals to work out their own salvation with God. Literacy becomes a broad requirement of Christians because each individual is to know the Word of God personally.[64] Movements reflecting such an orientation generate schools and pupils but not a centralized structure of rules and agencies. Social consensus on the value of mass education, rather than mandatory national law, is the goal and fulfillment of such movements. They flourish in "redeemer" nations such as the American Christian nation "under God," as distinct from models such as the Prussian or Scandinavian Lutheran nations that centralize authority.

[62] Karl Polanyi, *The Great Transformation* (Boston: Beacon, 1944).
[63] C. B. MacPherson, *Political Theory of Possessive Individualism* (New York: Oxford University Press, 1962).
[64] Carlo Cipolla, *Literacy and Development in the West* (Harmondsworth: Penguin, 1969).

Further Research Considerations

Two further research considerations are important. First, both forms of mass educational development are sensitive to forces that lie beyond the territorial boundaries of national markets, states, and cultures. Cohen's pioneering work is based on the premise that a civilizational network encompassing a number of national subunits is a prerequisite for the ideological success and organizational expansion of education.[65] As the system of national societies becomes more highly integrated, world standards of national development built on models of the mobilizing, progress-oriented society emerge. These standards strongly promote mass educational rules and enrollments. This line of analysis leads to two hypotheses:

viii) *Increasing integration of the world structure promotes educational development.*—A variety of forces internal to society, including the state itself, respond to world standards of appropriate nation-state structure,[66] individual citizenship rights,[67] and the need for mass education to link individuals to national purposes and goals.[68] The adoption of compulsory education itself becomes increasingly compulsory as the number of countries joining the ranks increases: the lag between date of independence and date of enactment of compulsory education laws or constitutional provisions has decreased dramatically over the last century.[69] The same type of thinking should apply to enrollments: enrollments in countries with given properties should increase more rapidly, the more expanded the educational systems in other countries are. This assertion can be tested by comparing educational enrollment growth rates at such historical periods as the end of the nineteenth century, the interwar period, and the postwar period. The extraordinary growth of enrollments in poor countries since the 1950s should turn out to be higher than growth rates for countries at comparable levels of development in earlier periods.[70]

ix) *Educational development is directly related to the degree of national linkage to the world system.*—Nations that are most strongly tied to the world system are subject to the greatest pressures to conform to world standards. They therefore are more likely to engage in educational expansion. Measures of linkage to the world system include such indicators as trade, treaties,

---

[65] Cohen, "The State System," and "Schools and Civilization States" (see n. 9 above).

[66] John W. Meyer, "The World Polity and the Authority of the Nation-State," in *Studies of the Modern World-System*, ed. Albert Bergesen (New York: Academic Press, 1980).

[67] John W. Meyer, Christopher Chase-Dunn, and John Boli-Bennett, "Convergence and Divergence in Development," *Annual Review of Sociology* 1 (1975): 223–46.

[68] John Boli-Bennett and John W. Meyer, "The Ideology of Childhood and the State: Rules Distinguishing Children in National Constitutions, 1870–1970," *American Sociological Review* 43 (December 1978): 797–812.

[69] Ramirez and Boli (see n. 5 above).

[70] Meyer et al. (n. 26 above).

diplomatic representation, and memberships in international organizations.[71]

Since 1900, there has been a great rise in the level of integration of the world system. Average national linkage to the world system has increased, and there has been a corresponding increase in the degree of world consensus regarding the necessity of mass education (see the "Educational Sector" reports of the World Bank).[72] We therefore expect that internal economic, political, and cultural factors are more weakly related to the adoption of compulsory education and the expansion of school enrollments recently than in earlier periods. Today, not even economic dependency can bar the growth of primary education; all nation-states seem to be marching to the beat of a common drummer.[73] Even the historically more libertarian states have moved toward a greater role for the state in education—however beleaguered, a Department of Education is still active in the United States, and in Great Britain the power of local educational authorities has declined relative to that of the national ministry.[74]

Relating the Dependent Variables

Finally, we should say a word about the relationship between mass education rules and educational enrollments, our two dependent variables of interest. We predict that rules have positive, but perhaps small, effects on enrollments. They signal a national commitment to building schools, and even though they do not guarantee that the requisite resources will be forthcoming, they probably increase the share of available resources allocated by the state to education. On the other hand, the expansion of enrollments may well inhibit the adoption of compulsory rules to some extent when such enrollments are grounded in a form of social organization that bypasses the national state (as in the United States). In brief, where the creation of members of the rational society is well advanced, it becomes more difficult for the state to create members of the national polity. Or,

x) *The adoption of national educational rules expands educational enrollments.*

xi) *The expansion of educational enrollments in the absence of national educational rules inhibits the adoption of such rules.*

Conclusion

Figure 1 summarizes the empirical implications of our central argument. Our theory of the rationalization of individual and collective authority,

[71] See David Snyder and Edward Kick, "Structural Position in the World System and Economic Growth, 1955–70: A Multiple-Network Analysis of Transactional Interactions," *American Journal of Sociology* 84 (1979): 1096–1126.

[72] World Bank (n. 3 above).

[73] Alan Sica and Harland Prechel, "National Political-Economic Dependency in the Global Economy and Educational Development," *Comparative Education Review* 25 (1981): 384–401.

[74] H. Perkin, "British Society and Higher Education," Yale Higher Education Research Group Working Paper no. 20 (New Haven, Conn.: Yale University, Institute for Sociological and Political Studies, 1977).

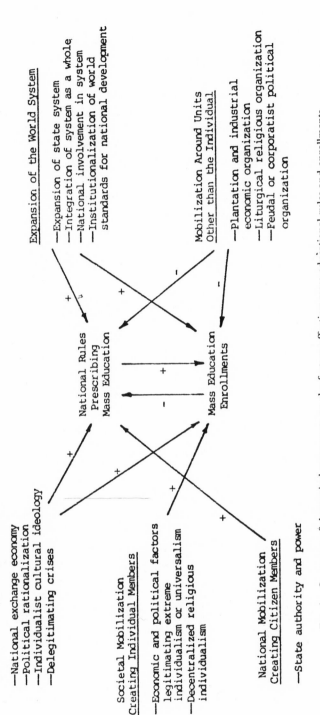

FIG. 1.—Summary of theoretical arguments on the factors affecting mass educational rules and enrollments

the incorporation of individuals, and the rise and expansion of mass education poses a clear alternative to other contemporary theories of education that emphasize processes of differentiation or the reproduction of inequalities. We have shown that these theories ignore the universal and institutional character of mass education and tend to take for granted what most needs to be explained, that is, the fact that everywhere individuals are being reconstituted as active, purposive members of the rational society or national state. Our theoretical framework opens the way to understanding why mass education has become a central project for achieving social progress and national success in the world of competing nation-states.

An Integrated Framework for Analysis of the Spread of Schooling in Less Developed Countries

MARY JEAN BOWMAN

The first and main task of this paper is the laying out of a framework in which microeconomic decision theory and elements of information and communication theory drawn from human geography and sociology are joined in an integrated approach to the analysis of the spread of schooling among the populations of less developed countries. Given the diversity of socioeconomic structures and cultures, this requires a framework that is at once of broad generality and yet sufficiently selective and precise to permit the specification of well-focused, testable hypotheses. The conceptual generality of the main features of the model serve, meanwhile, to sharpen the conceptualization of its components in terms of commonalities running through the differences among societies.

The second major part of this paper illustrates and tests the performance of the model in analyses of area variations in enrollments and school attainments in India, Brazil, and Mexico. Although some of this research has dealt with changes over time (for India, over a half-century), the comments here will refer only to analyses for single points in time. This makes it possible to compare some of the findings quite directly. It means, however, that longitudinal dimensions lying behind an essentially dynamic development process (and in some cases its stagnation) get less attention than they deserve.

The problem of moving between analysis focused on variations among individuals (using households as the units of observation) and variations among aggregated subpopulations (in the present case, using observations on populations classified by area of residence) is fully recognized. It is avoided here by careful specification and selection of variables, by the fact that our interest is in population aggregates, by the fact that observations are on fairly small area populations, and by the explicit adaptation of the model to such empirical treatment. Ideally, one would wish to work with data from individual households along with observations on entire sub-populations, but such matched data are rare, and for our purposes the

I am indebted to the Spencer Foundation for support of this work. My debts to Phyllis Goldblatt, David Plank, and Devindra Sharma will be apparent.

Reprinted from *Comparative Education Review*, vol. 28, no. 4 (November 1984).

area data (which internalize the effects of community on household decisions) are the more essential.

I. The Core Framework and Its Theoretical Foundations

The first analytical frameworks on which our more recent work at Chicago has drawn were laid out in three places in the late 1960s and the early 1970s: (1) in an article by Goldblatt,[1] which specified a framework used for analysis of the geographic spread of literacy among youth in rural and (separately) in urban communities in the states of Mexico in 1960; (2) in an article by Bowman[2] dealing with methodological approaches in the economics of education; and (3) in an unpublished 1966 study of migration in the Ivory Coast (also by Bowman), which has been used in teaching over the past 15 years. Most recently, those models have been tested out and modified with empirical applications in India, Brazil, and Mexico, and the development model laid out in the Ivory Coast study has been adapted in historical studies of the spread of schooling in now-developed countries.

Central to the analytical framework discussed here are two principal streams of thought. First is the development over the past two decades in the microeconomics of household behavior, led by Gary Becker. This work is easily enlarged conceptually to allow for variations in the values that people hold, even though values and preferences have usually been treated either as exogenously given or as fundamentally universal. Second, we are indebted to early work by Torsten Hägerstrand on the diffusion of innovations, which can be adapted in principle to the analysis of the spread of schooling.[3] His approach is important to us in two respects. *(a)* He looks at the behavior both of individuals (or households) and of collective agencies as adopters of innovations, but his interest is not in the behavior of particular units. Rather, he seeks to identify persistent patterns in the spread of activities or practices among subpopulations, whether defined in physical or in social space. While it is not possible to duplicate Hägerstrand's original methods here, his treatment of the individual and the aggregate is highly pertinent. *(b)* Hägerstrand has constructed an analytical model that has in principle two major components—what he called "information fields" and "resistances." To the latter, which is where the econ-

---

[1] Phyllis Goldblatt, "The Geography of Youth Employment and Enrollment Rates in Mexico," in *Schools in Transition*, ed. A. Kazamias and E. Epstein (Boston: Allyn & Bacon, 1968). Reprinted in *Education and Development: Latin America and the Carribean*, ed. T. LaBelle (Berkeley: University of California Press, 1972).

[2] Mary Jean Bowman, "The Economics of Education," *Methodology of Educational Research*, a special issue of the *Review of Educational Research* 39, no. 5 (December 1969): 641–70.

[3] Torsten Hägerstrand, *Innovation Diffusion as a Spatial Process*, trans. Allan Pred (Chicago: University of Chicago Press, 1968). See also his 1965 paper, "Quantitative Techniques for Analysis of the Spread of Information and Technology," in *Education and Economic Development*, ed. C. A. Anderson and M. J. Bowman (Chicago: Aldine, 1965).

omist's treatment of perceived benefit-cost balances belongs, he gives little attention, however. The richness of Hägerstrand's work is in his study of information fields. Drawing on his insights for our purposes, we introduce a slight modification, substituting the label "communication" for "information." The reason for this modification will become evident later. Finally, political science is brought into the analysis, albeit in a limited way, when we come to consideration of "supply-side" effects on enrollment rates and educational attainments of aggregated subpopulations defined by areas of residence.

The key sets of relationships are laid out in the simplest, most general outlines in figure 1. The solid arrows, whether heavy or light, all refer to schooling behavior as of a given date. They can be specified with reference to either individual households or aggregated population units. These solid arrows all lead directly or indirectly to the dependent variables: enrollments or school attainments. The dashed arrows pointing out from the central rectangle refer to effects of enrollment rates or school attainment at one date on the factors affecting the school attainments of later cohorts or generations. For example, increased schooling in the current cohorts of young people will contribute to their ability to pay for the schooling of the next generation. The factors transmitted today, indicated by the heavy arrows, are, of course, reflections in part of just such processes when today's adults were of school age.

The top three solid arrows refer to effects of current costs of schooling and the ability to defray them. Below these arrows on each side are arrows indicating the effect of perceived benefits of schooling on educational decisions and persistence in school. Centered at the bottom of the figure are "communication fields," which are most important in their effects on perceived present and future benefits, but which are linked also with collective decisions (the dashed, double-headed arrow) in the provision of school places and how those places are "priced."

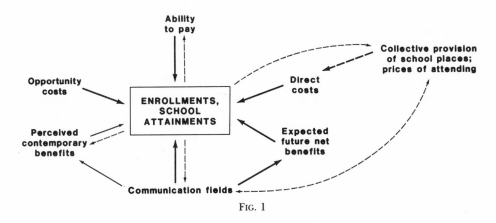

FIG. 1

Off to the far right, the "collective provision of school places" is shown here as affected by aggregate demands from households with school-age children along with the two-way relationships between such provision and the messages carried through communication networks. For the most part the direct monetary costs of schooling, especially at the primary level, are determined through the collective decisions, whereas "opportunity costs" are the cost values of children's time devoted to schooling.

Logic of the Allocation of Children's Time: Costs and Benefits

This allocation is at the very heart of decisions with respect to the schooling of children and youth. Time spent in school and in preparation for and travel to and from school cannot be spent in other activities. Even if there were no constraints in the various direct costs or in ability to pay those costs, there would be the ultimate time constraint. This is inevitable, whether schooling is seen primarily as an investment or primarily as a consumption activity.

Forgone opportunities in the use of time are of many kinds. We shall discuss them here under two subheadings—forgone current production activities and forgone learning—recognizing that these are not mutually exclusive uses of time. The other side of the picture is benefits expected from the allocation of children's time in schooling, whether in current enjoyment of schooling relative to other activities or in the nature of expected future options with and without the schooling. For the moment, we set aside the important question of what determines perceptions and expectations of relative benefits. This is to treat effects of messages carried through communication fields as already incorporated in the other elements of the analytical model and to ignore the direct effects of these messages on enrollments and on school attainments.

Forgone current production opportunities.—Most frequently cited in the economic literature is "forgone earnings," although economists do not define this as narrowly as it is commonly understood by noneconomists. Essentially, the economists' reference is to forgone contributions by children to the household economy, whether through monetary earnings or in other ways. Forgone current production opportunities may be classified in three main categories: (1) opportunities for nonfamilial employment, (2) opportunities for child contributions in market-oriented family enterprises, and (3) other productive services in the home.

The first of these is essentially an environment variable not ascertainable from household surveys unless those surveys are so organized that results can be aggregated to the community or local labor-market level. Notice that opportunities or demands for child labor outside of the family are not the same thing as actual employment of children in such situations, although the two will normally be positively associated in observations across small geographic units. This category of forgone production is most obviously a matter of "forgone earnings."

Category 2 depends in the first instance on the existence of family enterprises, whether viewed with respect to particular households or to aggregations of such households as proportions of the total local economy. Again, the opportunities for and the actual employment of children in family market-oriented enterprises are not the same thing; many such opportunities may be forgone in considerable part when the child spends time attending school. Category 2 may be included in census counts of "economically active" children, as is the case in Mexico when substantial amounts of a child's time are involved.

The third category of child production that competes for time of children in school (and in home study for school) is participation in contributions to the household economy that do not involve any market orientation, direct or indirect. The most obvious are assistance in child care, food preparation, and other domestic activities, but, in some families and some areas, the participation of children of both sexes in one or another aspect of subsistence agriculture may also be important. This sort of activity is rarely recognized in census documents but has been picked up in studies of family time budgets in several less developed countries. Because these activities rarely are counted, there is a major distortion in the reporting of production contributions of girls; for Mexico, we have found that economic activity of boys is the better predictor of school enrollments of the girls.

However they are measured, figures for child employment and for enrollment rates clearly are mutually interrelated, and their analysis calls for use of simultaneous equations wherever possible. The specification of variables suitable for analysis of forgone production opportunities requires a search into community traits that provide good proxies for demands, but there is a supply side also. The latter is associated with family size and with the economic status of the family and its need for the contributions of children. Ability to pay the costs of schooling includes not only defraying out-of-pocket expenses but also the ability to support the schoolchild and forgo contributions he or she might otherwise make to the current family economy.

Forgone learning.—All too often there has been a tendency to ignore the fact that time spent in out-of-school activities can entail learning that is valued by the decision-making household. Two distinct variants of forgone learning deserve particular attention: (1) forgone learning of productive skills through participation in family enterprises, and (2) forgone learning of traditional cultural values and behavior regarded as important by family and community.

The first of these is closely associated with occupational inheritance—most directly in agriculture or in traditional craft skills, although there are other examples as well. Where forgone learning of productive skills is important, that effect could show up in a narrowing of the expected net future benefits of advanced levels of schooling, but it is likely to be of little or no significance at lower schooling levels even in less developed countries. Data by individual households could be illuminating for analysis of forgone learning opportunities associated with family enterprises, although the general extent of such opportunities in a municipio, for example, can be estimated reasonably well on the basis of information concerning economic structures without data for individual families.

The second type of forgone learning, the learning of traditional values and behavior norms, is a quite different matter, since this may entail some direct conflicts with what is perceived to be the effects of schooling, whether in an individual family or through most of an entire community. The problem is likely to be greatest in this case with respect to the schooling of girls.

Perceived contemporary net benefits.—This refers to the current enjoyments or satisfactions associated with time spent in school relative to potential enjoyment of that time were it devoted to other activities. It is difficult to define this element of the model even conceptually in application to aggregated units of observation, and only in work on India has it received direct attention in empirical application of the analytical framework. For these reasons, only a thin arrow is drawn in the figure linking this heading with enrollment and school attainments. Contemporary greater enjoyment of school time could be quite important, however, in an analysis of differences in schooling among individuals. This is clearly the case when we consider, for example, likely effects of intelligence and home encouragement to academic performance on the enjoyment of schooling and hence on motivations to continue in school. It is at issue also in assessments of school effects on continuation or dropout rates.

Expected future net benefits.—In economic studies, the emphasis has been on monetary returns, which are the stream of incremental earnings over a working life attributable to the additional schooling—or to having schooling at all versus having none. Equally important, however, and widely recognized in the sociological literature, is the access schooling gives to occupations that may in themselves yield greater satisfactions and more prestige, whatever their income correlates. A third perceived or expected future benefit to the child currently in school may be future gains in consumer satisfactions and consumer efficiency. The allocation of a child's time to more schooling is largely an allocation of time to the acquisition of these future returns as they are perceived when the schooling decisions are made.

Ability to Pay and for What

We have alredy remarked that the ability to pay for children's schooling includes not only ability to meet out-of-pocket expenses but also the ability to support children in school, forgoing their contributions to the household economy. These elements in ability to pay have their aggregative analogues for entire communities, but the components of direct costs will look very different in the aggregative in contrast to the individual household perspective. This is primarily, though not solely, because of the interjection of public or other subsidies to the direct costs otherwise incurred privately; collective decisions are involved. Furthermore, direct costs are not just the costs of educational provision per se or, in the individual perspective, of tuition and fees charged. There are also costs of commuting greater or lesser distances, which entail differences among households in time costs even if there is full subsidization of direct costs of transportation to and from school. This can constitute an important item in differences across populations resident in places where settlement is thin rather than concentrated, and where terrain poses greater or lesser difficulties. There are also unsubsidized costs, such as the need for shoes among poor people who would otherwise not provide such footwear for their children; Gouveia has demonstrated that the need for shoes is an appreciable impediment to school attendance among poor families in São Paulo.[4] On the other hand, free or subsidized lunches may be provided in schools in some localities or countries; direct costs to individuals of attendance can become not only zero but negative in such cases.

While data on all these aspects of direct costs can be incorporated conceptually within the general model, whether by households or by area populations, in practice such matters as transportation costs and school lunches have been examined empirically only in special studies explicitly designed to identify effects of particular programs. The empirical work undertaken thus far in applications of our model has been limited to coarser indicators of costs and of ability to pay (whether by individuals or entire communities) along with indicators of provision of school places by nonlocal versus local agencies. This brings us to the treatment of "supplies of places."

Direct Costs and Supplies of School Places

With the partial exception of a few remarks in the immediately preceding paragraphs, the foregoing comments on the allocation of children's time have been focused on the demand side of the picture. But distributions of schooling among individuals and its spread across geographic areas and over time depend on supply-side factors as well. Furthermore, what

---

[4] Aparacieda Gouveia, "Youth Employment and Schooling in Brazil" (paper presented at the meeting of the Comparative and International Education Society, Atlanta, March 1983).

constitutes supply and the "price" of places depends on the perspective used in defining supply—supply to whom? Are we speaking of supply prices to individuals, to the aggregate of individual users in a locality, to the local area as a whole (users and nonusers alike), to the wider society? And are we including in the price of places the costs of commuting, of books and supplies used by individuals, and so on? Even at a less refined level, we still have to distinguish supply to whom.

The most extreme contrasts among both households and area populations in the direct private costs of schooling at any given level are undoubtedly those in the availability of schools within easy commuting distance, which will be shorter for primary than for secondary pupils. Although data on this point are not always available, there can be no doubt of the importance of the gap in an empirical study that ignores the question of local availability when there are, in fact, large locality differences in this respect. The question still arises, however, of why there is no provision in a local community—which brings us back to the costs of provision to the community as a whole and why demand has been insufficient to bring about local creation of places. Once that point is raised, the distinction between localities that do not have, let us say, at least upper grades in primary schools and localities that do have them begins to merge into larger questions of collective public action along with the summation of individual demands.

The direct costs of educational services must be specified in ways appropriate to the questions at issue and the ways in which provision is organized and supported. This may be best understood by specifying illustrative situations:

a) Suppose our interest to be in explaining differences among households in the schooling decisions they make, that tuition or fee charges (if any) are uniform, and that in the perspective of individual households there are always school places available at the existing charges or "price"—in technical language, the supply of places to households is perfectly elastic at that price. Under these circumstances, there is no variation of direct costs among households, even though the level of the uniform charges may affect rich and poor families differently, and even though the aggregate enrollment rates over an entire population will presumably tend to be lower the higher the price in tuition and fees.

b) Moving to a more aggregative focus, let us take the populations of municipios (analogous to counties in the United States) as the units of observation, posing as the central problem the explanation of differences among municipios in enrollment and school continuation rates. Assume further that all school places are provided by higher-level government agencies, that places are made available at the same price in all localities, and that the supply of places is perfectly elastic to the localities at the existing uniform price (which, again, could be but need not be zero). Here again the supply conditions do not differentiate among the populations of the various areas or municipios. Direct costs can be ignored with impunity so far as analyses of locality variations in enrollment rates, for example, are concerned. Nevertheless, a higher or lower uniform price to all localities would probably have some different effects on enrollment rates in predominantly poor than in predominantly affluent populations.

c) Let us suppose now that instead of being provided by outside agencies or governmental units the school places are provided entirely by the local people; they are thus endogenous in the perspective of an analysis of variations among districts in school enrollment rate. If we introduce along with this the assumption that real costs of school provision are the same across areas (teachers' salaries, supplies, and so on are obtained in essentially the same markets), we can again ignore direct costs in an analysis of the determinants of differences among areas in the enrollment rates of their children or youth. The situation is changed in a subtle way, however, by the removal of the exogeneity stipulation with respect to provision of places. Although the local provision of places is a reflection of community demand for those places, and at a given cost of provision to the community, the number of places made available is not merely an aggregation of demands of families for places for their own children. Some problems that should enlist the efforts of political scientists are now coming into play. Except as we may read them into the treatment of "communication fields," when seen at the community or municipo level these problems have not been incorporated in our analytical framework. Involved are questions of voting behavior, the altruistic as well as nonaltruistic interests of members of the community in the education of other people's children, and the qualities and traditions of local leadership and collective behavior.[5]

d) Finally, let us take the case in which there is a mixture of local and external support of education but with a greater external presence in some localities than in others. Where such differences are substantial, their representation in empirical analysis, however crude, can be of considerable importance for the understanding of variations among localities in the schooling of the younger generation. At the extreme, we come back to the presence or total absence of school places within commuting distance for a particular level of schooling, but now specified to consider the provision or nonprovision of places by external agencies. But are these "exogenous" differences among localities in fact fully exogenous— are they fully independent of local interest and effort and of the demands of local households for schooling for their children? Evidently here again

[5] On this, see Robert Jewell, "Household Demand for Public Education: A Study of Family Factors Related to Homeowner Willingness to Pay School Property Taxes" (Ph.D. diss., University of Chicago, 1969).

we are drawn into difficult and elusive questions with respect to leadership and political behavior but with an added dimension in factors that enhance or diminish the influence of local leadership in attracting support from distant centers of power. We are adding also questions relating to central policies toward the localities—policies that may be quite independent of, or even in contradiction to, the goals of local leaders. Steps have been taken toward the incorporation of such issues in Plank's empirical applications of our model to the study of school enrollment rates in Brazilian municipios, described briefly later on.[6]

Communication Fields

The conceptual starting points in our treatment of communication fields derive from the work of Torsten Hägerstrand, already mentioned. While he was not interested in the prediction of individual behavior as such, Hägerstrand started his analysis with the concept of a "private information field" defined as the entire pattern of person-to-person communications in which the individual participates. A "mean information field" is the sum of fields in which a group of closely associated persons participate: a mean field will have high-frequency common elements along with sparse frequencies at the fringes, where there is minimal mutual reinforcement of private fields.

Private information fields have three important attributes: (1) their structure is not random; (2) they are hierarchical; and (3) whether taken over wide geographic areas or across social classes or subcultures, they evince both patterns of strong overlap and "deficit troughs" across which person-to-person communications are sparse or nonexistent.

Goldblatt drew upon Hägerstrand's concept of information fields along with economic decision theory in her study of 1960 geographic variations in the literacy rates of Mexican children. She used states as the units of observation but separated her samples into the most rural populations (living in places of under 2,500 people) and all others (designated as urban). With so wide a range in the urban category, there is, of course, great variation in the characteristics of the urban places and in particular in the internal density of communications. Urban places range from those that are dominated economically and culturally by their rural surroundings to those that are lead centers from which new messages emanate. Goldblatt took a special interest in the effects of heavy rural-urban migration on the persistence of conspicuous lags in literacy and primary schooling in parts of the urban population.

The model as initially presented by Goldblatt has since been modified in several ways, including a shift of norms and values from the "resistance"

---

[6] David N. Plank, "The Determinants of School Enrollment Rates in Brazil, 1940–1980" (Ph.D. diss., University of Chicago, 1983).

side of the Hägerstrand construct to the "communication fields" of our present formulation—a considerable departure from Hägerstrand's initial construct.

Communications can be in varying degrees formal, as through the media, or informal, through direct personal interactions in the community and, at the extreme, within each family. The sorts of life cycle indicators that are pertinent refer to those characteristics of households and of greater or lesser proportions of a local population that can be safely presumed to entail participation in communication fields having a large "modern" or education-prone content on the one hand, and large "traditional" components on the other.

The pace and pattern of change of schooling in a community or area can be expected to reflect the pace of changes in the "true" options generally open to members of a population, the degree of homogeneity or heterogeneity in those options, and variations in perceptions of relevant options (whatever the objective situation) and in the speed or slowness with which perceptions respond to changing situations. Whatever a family may see or perceive of the benefits and costs of schooling for other people's children, there can be blockages in available options or in perceptions of them (or both) with respect, for example, to the postschool realization of educational benefits for their own children. The East London mother of a generation ago who said, in effect, "that's not for the likes of you," may be contrasted with the extraordinarily widespread belief in and the near reality of a class-free set of education-linked career potentials in Japan. The most severe blockages in some countries will be for women relative to men, whether linked to social class or not.

II. Illustrative Applications

Studies still under way or recently completed for India, Brazil, and Mexico have built on the foregoing model in analyses of the schooling of young children and of teenagers, in each case using geographic units of observation. In all three countries the research includes some attention to change over several decades—for India, over more than half a century. The illustrative applications in the following pages refer, however, to analyses using data for a single year. These single-year analyses lend themselves more readily to summarization, although even in such applications the theoretical formulation incorporates implicitly the developmental process of educational diffusion.

The single-dated cross-section analyses differ from one country to another primarily because of differences in the data available but also because some variables that might seem to be the same may, in fact, have quite different connotations in different settings. Indeed, this situation can arise even among regions of the same country, as separate analyses for major regions in Brazil and in Mexico have shown. Furthermore, contrasts in available data characterize the dependent as well as the independent variable specifications. For both India and Mexico there were satisfactory data on the economic activity of boys, whereas such data were not available for Brazil, where the predictor variables for child employment were also limited. For the 350 Indian districts and for Mexican municipios (which, like those in Brazil, are much smaller than the Indian districts), there is information on educational attainments, not merely the enrollment rates, of teenagers, whereas such information is not available on Brazilian municipios. On the other hand, supply-side data that were quite useful were available for municipios in Brazil but not in Mexico.

Diverse topics have been and are being pursued in these countries, but only three will be discussed here. The first is the performance of the model in demand-side explanations of enrollment rates at the younger and older ages in each of the countries. Second are the joint supply and demand factors as revealed in a two-stage least-squares analysis of variations in enrollment rates among Brazilian municipios. Finally, a summary of findings on progress through the schools in Mexico brings the development process into direct focus as it is reflected in data for a single year.

Demand-Side Analyses of Enrollment Rates of Young Children and of Teenagers in Three Countries

I shall follow the same order in presenting independent variables as was pursued in Part I except for the omission of direct costs. The opportunity costs of children's time are discussed first, then indicators of locally evident returns to schooling beyond mere literacy. These are the key elements in the economic-decision component of our framework. Ability to pay follows. Finally, attention is directed to formal and then to informal communication fields.

Opportunity costs of children's time.—In all three countries, we found the expected negative association between proportions of the population engaged in agriculture and enrollment rates of both younger and older children, but this variable is a proxy for many things other than demand or opportunities for child employment. It was the best available opportunity-cost proxy in the study for Brazil, however. For Mexico, we had several variables usable for predicting opportunities for child employment—the most important of which was the proportion of adults who were "family workers" in market-oriented enterprises, whether in agriculture or in other sectors.

The type of agriculture is important and can differ substantially both across nations and among regions within a large nation. The tidiest and most interesting specifications in this respect were in the study of India.[7] An equation taking child employment as the dependent variable carried strong positive coefficients on livestock and on the proportion of the rural population who were classified as "cultivators" (farm proprietors), but there were significant negative coefficients on *small* cultivators, reflecting primarily the fact that there was little that children could do to add to the output of tiny farms. (It must be remembered that even the average farms in India are extremely small seen on a world scale.) Children of landless laborers are the most likely to engage in work outside the home, in part no doubt reflecting their extreme poverty and the need for any increment to the family economy that they can scrape up.

Agriculture is not the only sphere in which children work, whether for the family or in other settings. Thus, in both India and Mexico, there was evidence of the importance of selling relative to white-collar employment in effects on the economic activity of children. For Mexico, however, this was important only for the subsample of municipios in which the largest place had over 10,000 people. Indicators of low income showed up in relation to demands for the employment of children in Mexico but not in India; this raises the question, just "how low is low?" To be relatively low in India will mean devastating poverty unmatched in Mexico, with associated effects on health and ability either to work or to attend school.

One way of treating forgone productive contributions of children who attend school was to use indicators of children's opportunities for productive activities, whether children were reported as in fact engaged in such activities or not. This was done for all three countries. For India and Mexico, however, we also ran regressions with observed rates of economic activity of boys aged 12 to 14. Two-stage least-squares analyses of proportions of boys working and proportions attending school gave striking results for India; coefficients on child (boys') labor were sharply reduced in the two-stage regressions. The Mexican data suggest that there also school decisions affect child labor more than vice versa.

Visibility of benefits.—The immediate visibility of benefits of schooling that can be observed in the local environment was estimated in the first instance for Brazil and Mexico from data on the occupational (and in some experiments the industrial) structure. Proportions in white-collar occupations—entered in equations with variables indicating low incomes, opportunities for child employment, proportions with radios (formal communications), and controls for size of largest place in a municipio—carried the expected significant positive signs on enrollment rates of teenagers

---

[7] These findings are in the draft of a study of area differences in educational attainments among children and teenagers in India, part of a doctoral dissertation at the University of Chicago by Devindra Sharma.

(12–14) for Brazilian municipios, especially in the southeastern states, but white-collar employment had much weaker effects on enrollment rates of teenagers in the northeast. Essentially similar results on proportions in white-collar occupations characterize the Mexican municipio analyses. District data for India do not provide information on proportions in white-collar occupations, the closest approximation being simply percentage of the population urban, which of course proxies many things, including supply-side conditions—especially for teenage enrollment rates and for attendance at secondary schools.

In working with Mexican data by states we used a finer specification of locally visible advantages of education: the percentage of white-collar workers who were earning relatively high incomes. Entered in an equation that included variables for two aspects of demand for child employment, a low-income variable, and indicators for both formal and informal communications, the proportions of white-collar workers with relatively high earnings had no effect on enrollment of either boys or girls aged 8; it came through, however, with strong positive coefficients (significant at .01 or better) for the enrollment of males aged 14 and for proportions of boys aged 15–19 who had completed at least the first year of secondary school. For girls, the coefficients on white-collar income were positive but were not significant even at a probability level of .10. The evidence is unambiguous in demonstrating the greater importance of local visibility of economic returns to schooling for teenagers and secondary-school attendance than for the attendance of younger children, and even among the teenagers for boys as compared with girls.

Available refinements in the analysis for India related again to specifications concerning agricultural structure. For both boys and girls in the rural places, the proportion of the adult population engaged in agriculture who were cultivators actually carried strong negative signs for primary schooling. By contrast, the "small" cultivators, who see no future for their sons in farming, looked upon schooling for boys with a more favorable view, for girls as definitely the route to a better life. Drawing on intimate knowledge of India, Sharma had predicted such results.

Ability to pay.—Specifications on ability to pay (including ability to forgo contributions of children to the family economy) were most satisfactory for Mexico, where proportions with low incomes carried highly significant negative signs for the 8-year-olds of both sexes and for the proportions of youth aged 15–19, again of each sex, who had completed at least some secondary schooling. Results for the teenage enrollment rates are ambiguous, however, because of the importance in some areas of overage proportions enrolled in the primary grades. The indirect poverty indicator for Brazil, proportion of households with no water in dwelling or courtyard, carried the expected negative signs throughout.

Formal communications.—Possession of radios is the simplest and most direct indicator of participation in formal communication networks, and even in Brazil and Mexico there were still, as of 1979, wide variations among municipios in the proportions of households having radios. Adding this variable to equations with indicators of opportunity costs of children's time, of locally visible advantages of schooling, and of ability to pay, improved substantially the explanatory power of equations on enrollment rates of young children (and also, in northeastern Brazil, of teenagers). For Mexican states, this variable was surprisingly strong also when the dependent variable was proportions of boys and of girls aged 15–19 with at least some secondary education.

Informal communications.—The Indian analysis turned up an extraordinarily powerful indicator of the importance of traditional communication fields for the discouragement or blockage of schooling among both boys and girls, especially girls. This is the proportion of child marriages arranged before a girl is 14 years of age.[8] These marriages will not be consummated for some years to come; the negative relationship to schooling of young teenage girls is not because they are already functioning as wives. What is involved is commitment to a very different sort of female training: the preparation of a girl to take her place as a properly oriented and well-qualified member of a traditional household toward which she is now specifically directed and to which her parents have committed her. No matter what the other variables in equations on the schooling of girls, this variable came through strong and clear. With it the coefficients of determination became higher for girls than for boys, whereas in the Mexican regressions we were able to account for a larger proportion of the variance in enrollment and attainment rates among males than among females.

Attempts to identify effects of proportions of a population belonging to distinctive ethnic groups in a Mexican municipio or an Indian district revealed no strong differences. In both cases, central efforts to neutralize negative effects may have been involved, but we have not been able to pin this down. It is clear enough, however, that, despite discrimination, the net benefits of schooling for members of the scheduled castes can be substantial even when their careers do not match those of men and women of the hereditary elites. There is nothing in our data to suggest myopia in the face of real options for members of this group.

What might be called the direct or imitative spread of schooling has two components: the transmission of relative school-attainment status of parents to their children and the effects of living in a community in which most rather than a few of a child's age mates are attending school. Both

[8] Ibid.

can be powerful influences on the way children's time is distributed among schooling and other activities, and both contribute to continuity over time in the ranking of communities on school attendance and attainment. The strength of these associations can and does vary substantially, however, both among countries and among major regions in a large country, even though everywhere the correlations between rankings in the parental cohorts and their children's cohorts are highly significant. The loosest linkages are in Brazil, where there have been large shifts of populations, including even changes in directions of flows with the opening of frontiers. The tightest intergeneration associations in educational attainments are in rural areas, especially for rural females in India. None of this should surprise us, for the face-to-face communications with respect to education must be dense indeed at the cores of both individual private and of "mean" private information fields, whatever Hägerstrand's "resistances" may be.

It would not be justified, however, to treat all observed associations between educational attainments in the older and the younger generations simply as a sort of benign contagion, important as that aspect of schooling decisions must be. For one thing, the very factors that might "rationally" explain local variations in schooling decisions for the younger generation could account statistically for a significant part of local variations in the schooling of adults. Parental schooling aside, these same factors will influence also the visible local evidence with respect to what schooling may mean for future opportunities and ways of life. In view of these considerations, we sought lower-bound estimates of effects of education in the parental generation by first explaining statistically the adult attainments and then taking the residuals from these equations as pared-down indicators of the most personal and informal component of communication fields. The coefficients on these adjusted measures of parental education remained powerful and highly significant in all tests applied to enrollment rates of young children in the municipios of both Mexico and Brazil and in equations on proportions of youth of both sexes who attained at least some secondary schooling in Mexico. Though positive, the coefficients were weaker for teenager enrollment rates in both countries. Zero-order relationships suggest a parallel pattern in India.

Supply and Demand in Enrollment Rates by Municipios in Brazil

David Plank[9] pursued the problem of supply-side effect on enrollment rates of "kids" and "teens" (children aged 7–11 and 12–14) in Brazil in 1970. His conceptual formulation included roles of voluntary agencies and community leaders, of entrepreneurs setting up local schools for profit, and of outside agencies (principally state governments) in the provision of school places. His model explicitly recognizes the likely im-

[9] Plank; see esp. chap. 6.

146

portance of interactions between the aggregate of demands for places by individual families and the provision of places by various agencies. It addresses also the question of the interest of local leaders in educational provision in their communities, these leaders' possible influence in attracting external support, and the priorities emanating from higher-level governments in educational policies.

Empirically, Plank's equations for supply of places (PLACES) were specified taking as the dependent variable the ratio of teachers in state-supported primary schools to children aged 7–14 in the municipio. (The proportion of all teachers who were externally supported varies substantially among Brazilian municipios.) The demand-side dependent variables are enrollment rates of "kids," labeled LKIDSIN (the L refers to the logit transform of the enrollment rate), and the enrollment rate of "teens," analogously labeled LTEENSIN.

A two-stage least-squares analysis requires, in the first step, the regression of each of the mutually dependent variables on a common step of independent variables. The values of the mutually dependent variables as predicted from these first-stage equations are then entered as regressors in a second pair of equations. To get unbiased estimates of the effects of the mutually dependent variables on one another, it is necessary to include in each of the second-stage equations a regressor presumed to affect one of the dependent variables but not the other. The formal communication measure RADIO was selected as the key variable in the demand equations on LKIDSIN and on LTEENSIN. The demand for educational facilities by groups other than parents as proxied by the proportions in white-collar occupations became the key variable in the equations on PLACES. The common independent variables included proportions in agriculture, the "no water" poverty indicator, an adjusted measure of educational attainments of adults, dummy variables for size of largest place (city, town), and dummy variables for the northeast and the southeast. The omitted dummies in these two sets were, respectively, villages and the western part of Brazil, including the state of Minas Gerais.

In the second-stage regressions on enrollment rates of "kids" (LKIDSIN) as the dependent variable, PLACES was totally insignificant, whereas RADIO, agricultural work, the poverty indicator, and the adult schooling measure all came in with high statistical significance. In the matched regression on PLACES, the enrollment rate for kids was marginally significant, with white collar carrying a highly significant positive sign and the northeast dummy variable strongly negative.

For the teenagers, on the other hand, the supply-side effect of PLACES on enrollment rates was significant at a .05 probability level, with agricultural work strongly negative and the adult schooling indicator strongly positive. The key variable RADIO came through with a probability level close to .01

but was much less powerful than in the regression on enrollment rates for kids. The equation on PLACES paired with LTEENSIN carried a marginally significant positive coefficient on proportions white collar (significant at the .05 level), with strong negative coefficients again on the northeast dummy.

Development Processes and Educational Attainments in the States of Mexico

Important as they may be as rough indicators of geographic variations in the spread of schooling within a country, the rates of enrollment at particular ages do not tell us directly how far these youngsters are, in fact, progressing through the school system or how regularly they attend. Neither can they reveal how much has been learned at any given level of attainment; this important question cannot be addressed with the data available in our studies. It is possible, however, to push the examination of educational progress considerably further by looking into the extent of overage enrollments at successive levels in the schools, the factors affecting overage rates, and how these relate to both enrollment rates and eventual school attainments. The importance of doing this showed up clearly in Plank's results on enrollments for northeastern in contrast to southeastern Brazil and in preliminary findings on Mexican municipios. It is not possible at present to report on a "progress through school" analysis for the Mexican municipios, although Goldblatt and Bowman have run some preliminary equations and hope to pursue this matter. Preliminary explorations for Mexican states have been completed, however, and it is to the design of that work that the immediately following remarks refer.

Mexican age-grade data by states are available for successive years, and several ways of working with these data could be enlightening. Thus far we have featured use of porportions of grade 1 pupils (by sex) who were substantially over age (age 10 or more) in 1970, treated as an intervening variable in a recursive regression model. Such a degree of delay or repetition (or both) is common in the least developed countries, where it may be as much a supply-side as a demand-side phenomenon.

The dependent variables, also specified in each case by sex, are: (1) UNDER 4: proportions of youth (aged 15–19) who had attained less than grade 4, including proportions with no schooling at all; (2) GRADE 6: proportions of youth who had completed primary school (grade 6) but no more; (3) GRADE 7Z: proportions of youth who had at least some secondary schooling (grade 7 or more). Enrollment rates at age 14 have also been analyzed as both final dependent variables and as intervening variables between OVERAGE and the above three attainment indicators.

Independent variables conform to the analytical framework presented in Part I of this essay. Particularly important have been adjustments of the formal communication and the informal communication indicators to exclude confounding effects of associations with other elements in the model. Thus RADIO has been adjusted to exclude effects of its association with income (and with proportions in white-collar occupations), and the educational attainments of the parental age cohort have been adjusted to exclude linear associations with all other independent variables. These adjustments provide both better empirical specifications matching our concepts and an escape from the problems of multicollinearity in aggregation to a state level. Two principal sets of equations have been used, one including proportions of boys economically active and the other substituting indicators of opportunities and demand for productive activities of children, whether or not the children were so employed. The former could be the most appropriate variable if the observed proportion of boys aged 12–14 who are economically active is regarded as a general indicator of the relative *un*importance attached to time spent in school and to regularity of school attendance. The latter is the more appropriate in an economic model of the opportunity cost of going to school. In any case, proportions of boys economically active display the stronger correlation with proportions of both boys and girls who were OVERAGE.

The most interesting of our findings in this preliminary investigation relate to the relatively great importance of indirect compared with direct effects on school attainments of rates of child employment and of proportions in the parental cohorts with given educational attainments (in both unadjusted and adjusted versions of those measures). Early perceptions about children's time and early delays and absenteeism can have long-lasting effects.

III. Some Concluding Observations

Several generalizations along with a few speculations emerge from the work done thus far and the relationships of findings to the analytical framework.

1. *Where the microeconomic decision model was most illuminating.*—The core of this model is in the comparisons that households make between what education costs (primarily forgone uses of children's time) and the perceived benefits of more schooling. Empirically we have found such considerations to be most important in the following cases: *(a)* explanations of enrollments in secondary schools and usually of enrollments of teenagers rather than of younger children; *(b)* even for teenagers, explanation of enrollment rates in relatively advanced, in contrast to generally backward, areas (The most dramatic illustration is in the contrast between northeastern and southeastern Brazil: in the northeast [as in many relatively backward parts of Mexico] 14-year-olds are often enrolled in grades far below a normal level for their age. In these situations, the coefficients on human capital, or investment, variables for attendance of teenagers may be no

stronger than the coefficients for attendance of younger children); and *(c)* in explanations of schooling of boys rather than of girls. This contrast shows up mainly with respect to schooling at secondary levels.

2. *The treatment of supply-side effects in analysis of area differences in enrollments and school attainments.*—It is shown that treatment of the availability of school places, or the supply side in the spread of schooling, must be very different when units of observation are area populations from the appropriate treatment when the data and the principal questions addressed refer to behavior of individual households. Where municipios or districts are the units of observation, as in the analyses for Brazil, Mexico, and India, political processes going beyond local communities must be brought into the conceptual framework.

Using two-stage least-squares regressions, Plank[10] demonstrated something of what could be learned about state policies in relation to local situations, and for which populations and schooling levels external provision or support had the greatest and the least effect on enrollments and school continuation rates.

Larger towns or cities generally have more complete school facilities in any country. It was found, nevertheless, that size of place had remarkably little explanatory power in either Brazil or Mexico when independent variables included indicators of incomes or of locally visible occupational benefits of schooling.

3. *Where "ability to pay" is most important.*—Indicators of ability to pay seem to carry generally stronger coefficients for girls than for boys at each age and school level in Mexico, and, especially, in India. (Data distinguishing by sex were not available for Brazil.) The sex differences observed for Mexico and India were to be expected.

4. *Where formal and informal communication networks are most important.*— Proportion of the population living in households possessing a radio was our formal communication indicator; this variable came through more strongly for young children than for teenagers in both Brazil and Mexico and especially among rural populations in Mexico and India, where separate regressions were run for the rural and urban populations. This performance persisted even when the coefficients on the radio variable were biased downward by adjustments to exclude its association with income.

Variables representing informal communications were measures of the educational attainments of adults, using a more stringent adjustment formula. Here again, the associations with schooling of children remained strong, especially in Mexico and India—most strikingly so in the intergenerational continuity of rates of primary school attendance among rural Indian girls.

[10] Ibid.

5. *Overage pupils and educational attainment.*—This exploration for Mexican states raises questions of quite general importance. Whether high overage proportions are a short-term catching-up phenomenon or a more persistent characteristic of the areas involved may depend on diffusion within as well as between area populations. Taken together with other evidence, the Mexican findings suggest, however, that a catching-up process must be viewed in more subtle ways than is usually recognized. It is relatively easy to see and imitate enrollment in schools, or to observe that those with more schooling generally have better future prospects. It is not nearly so easy for many people in particular cultural settings to understand that "getting an education" requires regular attendance, with priorities in the allocation of the time of schoolchildren that may not always coincide with traditional family claims.

In sum, each of the main components of the analytical framework is supported by the consistent signs on variables explaining enrollment and school-attainment levels. The relative strength of the microeconomic decision theory is greatest where investments in education as a route to higher future earning power would be expected to be most emphasized. The communication variables carry their greatest weight where the primary concerns may be in ability to deal with the written word in day-to-day matters.

The Use and Abuse of Comparative Education

HAROLD J. NOAH

My favorite anecdote in comparative study is from the field of comparative philology. One day, the story goes, a Spanish-speaking student of Russian language went to her professor and asked him: "Professor, do you have in Russian any equivalent of our Spanish word 'mañana'?" After brief reflection, the professor said to her: "Why, yes. In Russian we have 27 equivalents for 'mañana,' but none of them I think conveys the same sense of urgency!"

The more urgent and intractable our educational problems seem to be, the more tempting becomes the notion of a "quick fix." Reports of successes in foreign lands are all that is needed to release a flood of what I call "*My Fair Lady* prescriptions"—you remember:

> Why can't the English teach their children
> how to speak?
> Norwegians learn Norwegian, the Greeks are
> taught their Greek . . .
> Arabians learn Arabian with the speed of
> summer lightning,
> And the Hebrews learn it backward, which
> is absolutely frightening . . .

We have all surely noted the fanfare of attention given just at present to the (alleged) merits of the Japanese education system and the calls for us to learn from Japanese successes and to imitate what we can. A far cry indeed from the years of postwar occupation of Japan, when the shoe was precisely on the other foot! There may indeed be some truth to the adage that if you live long enough you will see everything at least twice, the second time the opposite of the first.

Recall, too, the exhibitions of intense interest in the Soviet school system after *Sputnik* was sent aloft. *What Ivan Knows That Johnny Doesn't* was the apt title that summed up the mood of the times.[1] Later in the 1960s the search for an educational model shifted to Britain and the well-publicized attractions of Open Education in the early school grades. Now it is Japan's turn. Perhaps we should be grateful for small mercies. After

---

This is a slightly altered version of the original paper, delivered as an inaugural lecture for the Gardner Cowles Chair, Teachers College, Columbia University, New York, on November 1, 1983.
[1] Arther S. Trace, *What Ivan Knows That Johnny Doesn't* (New York: Random, 1961).

Reprinted from *Comparative Education Review*, vol. 28, no. 4 (November 1984).

all, only a relatively small group here in the United States during China's Cultural Revolution urged us to follow that splendid example by sending our teachers out to the countryside for political reeducation, with specific attention to be paid to improvement of their latrine-cleaning skills.

So, there are clearly some problems, if not abuses, to contemplate in the comparative study of education—especially so when the object of the exercise is to find an easy solution abroad for complex problems at home. But comparative education does have its valued and legitimate uses, as well.

The Uses of Comparative Education

Properly done, comparative education can deepen understanding of our own education and society; it can be of assistance to policymakers and administrators; and it can form a most valuable part of the education of teachers.[2] Expressed another way, comparative education can help us understand better our own past, locate ourselves more exactly in the present, and discern a little more clearly what our educational future may be. These contributions can be made via work that is primarily descriptive as well as through work that seeks to be analytic or explanatory; through work that is limited to just one, or a very few, nations, as well as through work that embraces a wider scope; through work that relies on non-quantitative as well as quantitative data and methods; and through work that proceeds with explicitly formulated social science paradigms in mind as well as in a less formalized manner.

Description

Let us look first at the uses of description. Accurate description is a kind of "mapping" of what other countries are doing or not doing, planning, abandoning, or changing in their educational enterprises. A great deal of this used to go on in departments and ministries of education. Recall the work of the United States Bureau of Education under William Torrey Harris and of the Board of Education in England. Michael Sadler's series of Special Reports on foreign educational developments are a model of this genre. I have always been in special debt to one volume in the series, entitled simply *Education in Russia* and published in 1909, by one of His Majesty's Inspectors of Schools, Thomas Darlington. It is a work that reveals quite terrifying powers of observation, assimilation, and reporting.[3]

---

[2] I do not discuss the uses of comparative education in the education of schoolteachers in this paper. See Merle L. Borrowman, "Comparative Education in Teacher Education Programs," and three commentary papers by Andreas M. Kazamias, Harold J. Noah, and Cole Brembeck, in *Comparative Education Review*, vol. 19 (October 1975), for presentation of a variety of viewpoints.

[3] Board of Education, *Education in Russia*, Special Reports on Educational Subjects, vol. 23 (London: His Majesty's Stationery Office, 1909).

Help in Decision Making

It would be wrong to typify these efforts as "mere description." First of all, there is nothing "mere" about the tremendous amount of effort that has to be exerted simply to acquire systematic, parallel data on educational systems that differ in the particulars of their structure.

Second, accurate, reliable description will often show us that our own problems are not unique, and such knowledge can be most useful. It directs us to search out and try to understand forces and factors at work that transcend the boundaries of our own society. Exercises in mapping the experiences of other countries can feed directly into policymaking and decision taking. Indeed, as Edmund King has pointed out, comparative studies of education are legitimated and energized precisely to the extent that they originate from the need to make decisions about the conduct of education.[4]

Thus, we worry a great deal about youth unemployment, and we question whether our schools are preparing young people properly for the labor market. This is by no means a uniquely American concern; the British, for example, are struggling with similar problems, as are the French. In such cases, it is not only knowledge of parallel phenomena that is useful but also knowledge of other countries' attempted solutions and of the problems that those solutions are encountering.

These considerations are particularly to be borne in mind at present, as we try to deal with the flood of recent reports on the condition of American education and what we should be doing about it. If we have a tendency to flagellate ourselves for our shortcomings a little too enthusiastically, it may be because we do not recognize that other nations are also experiencing severe problems in defining what makes for an education of excellence in the modern world. From Britain to the Soviet Union to Australia and on around the globe, there are currently going on most vigorous discussions of proposals to change profoundly the content and structure of secondary education. Knowledge of what is being proposed and tried in cognate situations abroad is indispensable for reasoned judgment about what we need to do at home.

Comparative Standards

Another important use of descriptive studies lies in the opportunity they provide to estimate the standing of the United States relative to other countries along dimensions of education that are of interest. This was a major preoccupation in the early years of the nineteenth century; it remains a significant and viable contribution of comparative education. How do our arrangements for the education of the handicapped, the gifted, the

---

[4] Edmund J. King, *Comparative Studies and Educational Decision* (London: Methuen; Indianapolis: Bobbs-Merrill, 1967).

very young, and the not so young stack up against those of other countries that we consider our peers? The studies of the International Association for the Evaluation of Education Achievement (IEA) are built on a painstaking mapping of what schoolchildren in dozens of countries know in their own and foreign languages, mathematics, science, civics, and the like. Used properly (and, as we shall see, that is not always the case), the resultant intercountry rankings can be powerful pointers toward special problems and needed improvements.

Remedying Misperceptions

Even single-nation studies can be immensely useful, especially those dealing with countries that are important to us but to which access is difficult. The Soviet Union is a case in point. When I was working on aspects of the financing of Soviet education, the accepted view was that vocational education and higher education were the favored sectors of the Soviet system and that general secondary education took second place to other sectors that promised a more direct contribution to economic growth. My research led me to a quite opposite conclusion: as far as ruble allocations were concerned, the Soviet authorities had treated general secondary education far more generously than vocational and higher education.[5] Other single-nation studies in comparative education have shown equally unexpected results. Just one example is Foster's demonstration that Ghanaian vocational secondary schools did not so much provide the economy with a pool of young people ready to enter manual trades as serve as a vehicle for furthering the academic aspirations of Ghanaian youth.[6]

Education as Touchstone

Only cynics believe that nations get the governments they deserve, but it may well be that nations get the educational institutions they merit. As the recent report on secondary education from the Carnegie Foundation for the Advancement of Teaching put it: "A report card on public education is a report card on the nation. Schools can rise no higher than the communities that support them."[7] If this is true, then the state of the schools may be an indicator of more than just educational conditions. For example, indifference in the schools to the value of intellectual activity may betoken a more general anti-intellectualism in society; authoritarian classrooms may reflect authoritarian political arrangements; and inefficient use of resources devoted to education may simply be an extension of inability

[5] Harold J. Noah, *Financing Soviet Schools* (New York: Teachers College Press, 1966), pp. 109–13.

[6] Philip Foster, *Education and Social Change in Ghana* (Chicago: University of Chicago Press, 1965).

[7] Ernest L. Boyer for the Carnegie Foundation for the Advancement of Teaching, *High School: A Report on Secondary Education in America* (New York: Harper & Row, 1983), p. 6.

to use resources effectively in industry, agriculture, and commerce.[8] If these things are so, and there is a good deal of evidence that they are, comparative education can be a fruitful approach to understanding the values, culture, and achievements of other societies—certainly not in their entirety but, nonetheless, a significant portion of what we need to know about our neighbors on this globe.[9]

As I found when I was engaged in a study of school policies in Austria, the processes of educational policymaking told a good deal about Austrian society in general. I was a member of an international team reviewing Austrian education for the OECD. Two aspects impressed us deeply. One was the emphasis placed on what the Austrians termed *Betreuung,* which can be translated as "trust," or "stewardship." Teachers and school administrators, politicians and parents, employers and trade unionists all used the word, meaning by it their sense that the schools bore what I understand lawyers term "a duty of care" for the students. The second was the careful attention to collaborative decision making—joining government, employers, and trade unions—when figuring out arrangements for the final years of school and entry into the labor market. Both of these approaches were characteristic of contemporary Austrian attitudes in the wider arena. The concept of stewardship enuciated by Aquinas in medieval Catholic thought is alive and well today and living in Austria.[10]

Obviously, too, there are instances where the schools do *not* complement political aspirations or social processes of a given society. Take, say, the shah's Iran. Like so many of the oil-rich nations, it was a society with two distinct facets, the modern and the traditional. The shah's schools served the sectors of society that he most wished to develop: business, the army, the towns. But "modernized" schools flew in the face of the aspirations and world outlook of the more traditionally orientated segment of the nation. Hence, to look at the shah's schools was to have regard for official Iran only. Meanwhile, traditional Iran lived on, as strong as ever, and nursed its resentments to the point of revolution. Parallel disjunctions were evident in many of the colonial territories before independence as the schools and universities established by the colonizers produced an elite no longer subservient to imperial interests. Such disjunctions between school and society are keys to understanding the pressures that can build up toward sudden, and often discontinuous, political change.

[8] A. Harry Passow, Harold J. Noah, Max A. Eckstein, and John R. Mallea, *The National Case Study: An Empirical Comparative Study of Twenty-One Educational Systems* (New York: Wiley, 1976). See esp. chap. 3.

[9] Max A. Eckstein and Harold J. Noah, *Scientific Investigations in Comparative Education* (New York: Macmillan, 1969) presents many examples of the approach under discussion.

[10] Organization for Economic Cooperation and Development, *Reviews of National Policies for Education: Austria—School Policy* (Paris: OECD, 1979).

Origins and Influences

Although comparative education characteristically tends to emphasize differences, the basic similarities of formal education across countries are also of interest. With increasing speed, beginning about 1860, the nations of the world have made available the facilities for formal schooling to ever-larger fractions of their population. The institutional frameworks, the preparation of teachers, the equipment used, the systems of grading and examinations, the issuing of certificates and diplomas—all contribute to the basic commonality of school systems, wherever they are located. Two main factors have been at work to create this standardization: diffusion of educational practices across national boundaries, and ever-greater sharing of common objectives for expanding resources for formal education.[11]

Contemporary European practices in education cannot be understood without reference to models developed in the United States. For example, secondary education all over Europe has been powerfully influenced by the American model of the neighborhood comprehensive high school. Sweden was the leader in the European movement to establish secondary schools that were no longer differentiated according to the social class origins of their students. The Swedish planners and bureaucrats who effected the reform were well acquainted with the American experience and took it into account when formulating their plans (even though the American philosophy of decentralized control and predominantly local financing did not appeal to them at all).[12] From Sweden, the comprehensive school movement radiated to influence developments in England, France, the other Scandinavian countries, and recently even Spain and Portugal. In West Germany, some states (particularly those with Social Democratic governments) moved toward the comprehensive pattern (it is, e.g., the basic mode of secondary school provision in West Berlin), while the Christian Democratic Länder largely resisted what had become a European trend.[13] In each of these countries, there were local differences and adaptations, but the twin elements of comprehensive secondary education (massive expansion of enrollments and reduction in institutional differentiation)

[11] See particularly works published by Francisco O. Ramirez and John W. Meyer, e.g., "Comparative Education: The Social Construction of the Modern World System," *Annual Review of Sociology,* vol. 6 (1980).

[12] Rolland G. Paulston, *Educational Change in Sweden: Planning and Accepting the Comprehensive Reforms* (New York: Teachers College Press, 1968), pp. 30, 100–101, 109, 124, identifies individuals in Sweden who were influential in spreading the American comprehensive gospel. However, Paulston concludes that the U.S. experience was too remote for clear Swedish emulation and that probably the English progressives had a greater impact on Swedish developments. Of course, English educational reformers who were promoting comprehensive secondary schools between 1930 and 1950 were strongly influenced by American models. See W. H. G. Armytage, *The American Influence on British Education* (New York: Humanities, 1967), pp. 72–76.

[13] Max-Planck-Institut für Bildungsforschung, *Bildung in der Bundesrepublik Deutschland: Daten und Analysen,* 2 vols. (Stuttgart: Ernst Klett/Rowohlt, 1980), is an indispensable source for contemporary developments in West German education.

were everywhere in evidence, as they diffused either directly or indirectly from the American example.

Sometimes the diffusion was more forceful and took on the character of deliberate implantation or imposition. European and American colonial activities have spread a model of schooling that shows every sign of possessing tremendous survivability. For this reason, it is impossible to understand education in, say, contemporary Nigeria, Tunisia, or the Philippines without taking into account the models planted in those places by the British, the French, and the Americans, respectively.

Cross-cultural study of education, then, can identify the potentials and the limits of international borrowing and adaptation. Although nobody has yet tried to do a complete accounting, my impression is that international borrowing of educational ideas and practices has more failures to record than success. Transplantation is a difficult art, and those who wish to benefit from the experience of other nations will find in comparative studies a most useful set of cautions, as well as some modest encouragement.

From the Particular to the General

I now come to that use of comparative study which I believe to be its most exciting, though perhaps also its most difficult, that is, its potential for establishing the generalizability of what we think we know about education. Of course, results based on research conducted within a single country can be most valuable, and I am aware of the increasing trend among social scientists to emphasize the merits of particularist approaches and to express a distrust of generalization. This may simply be another swing of the pendulum of fashion in research, or it may have more substantial bases. But comparative education is caught inextricably in what Isaiah Berlin has described as the classic dilemma of those who wish to know about the world and to act on it.[14] Do we want to be "hedgehogs," who know one big thing, or do we want to be "foxes," who know many things—none of them presumably very big? Clifford Geertz, in his recent book *Local Knowledge*, wants us to settle for lots of little things; one big thing, he believes, is simply not attainable.[15] The debate will not be settled quickly—in comparative education or in any of our other intellectual enterprises. Those enterprises are characteristically partly a matter of science and partly a matter of art. Scientists take the very complex, even the mysterious, and by their work make it ordinary, lawlike, explicable. Artists take the ordinary and the humdrum and impart to it wider meaning, even mystery at times. In this manner, some in comparative study systematically try to move from the particular to the more general; others

[14] Isaiah Berlin, *The Hedgehog and the Fox: An Essay on Tolstoy's View of History* (New York: Simon & Schuster, 1953).

[15] Clifford Geertz, *Local Knowledge: Further Essays in Interpretive Anthropology* (New York: Basic, 1983).

are concerned with enriching our understanding of a greater number of particulars. While I enjoy the richness of the particular, I am committed to the enterprise of trying to make sense out of (which I take to mean "bring order to") the bewildering variety of educational phenomena we observe. One way that we do this is to take the propositions that arise out of the work done in single countries and test the extent to which they can be said to hold in other situations.

For example, research in the United States has shown that a child's family birth order has some relation (though not a large one) to the child's scholastic achievement. This finding lends support to theoretical models that emphasize the importance for children's school achievement of the time and other resources that parents spend on their children and the tendency for firstborn children to get more of their parents' (undivided) attention and purchasable resources than do subsequent children. Cross-national studies have shown, however, that the simple relation between birth order and school achievement does not always obtain, for example, in Scotland and France. Subsequent research has shown that, rather than birth order, it may be the spacing of births and family size that are of prime significance, and that the effect of birth order on achievement is mediated through family size and the birthrate.[16] In this way, cross-national work has not only pointed toward improved theoretical models but has also, in fact, prevented overgeneralization on the basis of results derived from a single country.

Let me take just one further example. What if we find that rates of return on investments in higher education are falling in the United States? The comparative approach primes us immediately to ask, Where else in the world is this happening? Are there countries that show rising rates of return? Which are they? What are the country characteristics that are related to declining or rising rates of return to education, respectively?[17] Is it true that rates of return to education are inversely related to rates of enrollment expansion in the recent past? Such a hypothesis is not unreasonable: as the number of young people graduated increases, we might expect a more abundant supply of labor to drive entry-level wages down and vice versa. If a relationship of this kind can be observed in a number of countries, we can be somewhat more confident that we are not observing just a chance phenomenon. There is also potential insight to be gained from examining more closely those countries where rates of return are not being driven down, despite a sizable increase in the number of young entrants into the labor market. We can try to answer the question, Under what conditions do rates of return to education hold up?

[16] R. B. Zajonc, "Family Configuration and Intelligence," *Science* 192 (April 16, 1976): 227–36.
[17] George Psacharopoulos, *Rates of Return: An International Comparison* (San Francisco: Jossey-Bass, 1973) examines 53 case studies in 32 countries to establish relationships between measured return to education and basic characteristics of the countries.

A comparative approach enlarges the framework within which we can view the results obtained in a single country: by providing counterinstances, it challenges us to refine our theories and test their validity against the reality of different societies; and, by providing parallel results, it can yield important confirmation of results obtained elsewhere.[18]

The Abuse of Comparative Education

After all this sweetness and light, let me now turn to the more problematic side—though I am happy that I can report much less in the way of abuse of comparative education than there seems to be legitimate use.

As I have pointed out, comparative education is an applied field of study that finds particular justification in the service of evaluation, management, administration, and policymaking. Like all applied fields, it is open to potential abuse by those who wish to use its results to support (or oppose) a specific program of change.

Making a Case

As I also noted when I began, we have special reason to be cautious in the United States when advocates of change rely heavily on reports of a successful program abroad. Diane Ravitch, in her recent book, *The Troubled Crusade,* provides a splendid recounting of the substantial misuse of reports of those English practices in infant education that became known as Open Education. She describes how Joseph Featherstone's original quite balanced account was soon superseded by exaggerated and distorted reports of what had been going on in a relatively few exemplary schools. American readers were given the impression that teachers in England had found a magic solution to the most fundamental problems of early education: sustaining the children's active interest in inquiry and learning while building a firm base for future scholastic progress.[19] Without a doubt there were some admirable aspects of some of the things some teachers in England were doing in some classrooms and schools. But of which nation is this not true? The Open Education message became the basis for an overenthusiastic movement, supported by considerable public funds and extending far beyond the early years of schooling (for which it was developed in England), even into the high school. Of such stuff are present fads and future disasters made. The authentic use of comparative study resides not in wholesale appropriation and propagation of foreign practices but in careful analysis of the conditions under which certain foreign

[18] The World Bank has an extensive program of inquiry concerning factors affecting rates of return to education around the world. For a description, see George Psacharopoulos, "Educational Research at the World Bank," *Research News* 4 (Spring 1983): 5–8.

[19] Diane Ravitch, *The Troubled Crusade: American Education, 1945–1980* (New York: Basic, 1983), pp. 239–51.

practices deliver desirable results, followed by consideration of ways to adapt those practices to conditions found at home.

A cautious approach to reports of foreign successes is particularly in order for the United States. Education in the United States is character-istically more open to experimentation and new ideas than is the case in most other countries—indeed, too open, in the opinion of many observers abroad. In such a climate, the job of the comparative educator often consists in tempering enthusiasm with a dash of realistic reporting. Not so in other, more conservative countries (e.g., the Federal Republic of Germany), where resistance to external ideas is much, much greater.

Misinterpreting Results

Scholars in general are used to seeing their results misinterpreted by reason of carelessness, ignorance, or intention. And scholars in comparative education are no exception. In the behavioral and social sciences and in historical and philosophical inquiry, responsible scholarship more often than not requires tentativeness in advancing conclusions. Explanatory models are not overly strong, data are often defective, and criteria for confidence in making inferences are subject to dispute. We do the best we can, and, when it comes time to announce our results, they are in effect offered up as hostages to those who can make use of them. Sometimes the use that is made surprises us.

A recent example of misinterpretation of results is probably known to many of my readers today, but let me cite it all the same. Barbara Lerner, in the fall 1982 issue of *Public Interest,* sought to answer the question, How are we doing in American schooling, and, in particular, how much have American youngsters achieved in the various school subjects, compared with their counterparts in other countries? Using data from the publications of the IEA, she concluded, "Relatively little."[20]

As my colleague Richard Wolf pointed out in an incisive critique of the various adjustments Lerner chose to make in the IEA data and the inferences she drew on the basis of those adjusted data, the original findings simply do not support her sweeping conclusion. The achievement picture is much more mixed than she would have us believe: relative to youngsters in other economically advanced countries, American school-children performed quite well in some school subjects at some age levels; they did only moderately well in others and really quite poorly in still other subjects.[21] All of us, no doubt, will agree with Lerner that there is room for substantial improvement in American school achievement levels:

[20] Barbara Lerner, "American Education: How Are We Doing?" *Public Interest* (Fall 1982), pp. 59–82.

[21] Richard M. Wolf, "American Education: The Record Is Mixed," *Public Interest* (Summer 1983), pp. 124–28.

we should not be satisfied with the pattern of results that was revealed (especially among blacks and students in the South). But the vital enterprise of raising school achievement levels in the United States is not assisted by misinterpretation of results of cross-national scholarship.

Ethnocentrism

One of the most difficult problems of the comparative method is ethnocentrism. This is the fault of looking at the world *primarily* from the point of view of the observer's own culture and values. Ethnocentrism has potential for bedeviling comparative education at every stage—from choice of topic to study, through choice of procedures to apply, to judgment concerning the meaning of the results of inquiry.

When we choose to define as a "problem" some phenomenon that is really a problem only from *our* point of view and given *our* set of values but is by no means a problem from the point of view of people in other societies, we have fallen into something of an ethnocentric trap. An oft-cited example of such inappropriate projection of problems has to do with the term "modernization." A great deal of work has been done in comparative education to trace the process and correlates of the so-called modernization process.[22] Special attention has been paid to the contribution that schooling has made to those changes that mark the transformation from a "traditional" to a "modernized" society. Patterns of change that describe well what happened to European and North American societies are assumed to be generalizable to other societies at a later date. Perhaps they are generalizable; perhaps they are not. Although this is a matter for empirical inquiry, the tendency has been to take their generalizability for granted and to go on from there. This lends a spurious color of definiteness to a process that may proceed very differently from one society to the next.

Projecting our own problems often entails exporting our own concepts and using them in situations where their fit with reality may not be very good. Thus, despite the efforts of scholars (notably among them, Lawrence Cremin) to broaden our view of education, it remains true that our concept of education is still typically limited to what goes on inside schools. If that broadened view is desirable in the United States, how much more necessary it is for work in societies that have not developed the elaborate systems of formal schooling that we have here.

Elsewhere, I have made this point in the following terms:

> ... modernization and education in India [are typically] examined on [some such] basis as the number of technical school places opened and filled. This

[22] See, e.g., Don Adams, *Education and Modernization in Asia* (Reading, Mass.: Addison-Wesley, 1970).

procedure simply reflects the role of formal technical education in Western societies. Yet the most important means of modernization in Indian society may be the increasing availability of automobiles, bicycles, water pumps, and so forth—all the Western-type machines that impose on their operators disciplines of use, maintenance, and repair. Insofar as the comparative educator is interested in examining the relationship between education and development, he would be utterly misled by giving attention just to the formal system of education and neglecting the informal educational effects of introducing Western machinery.[23]

Conclusion

Enough then of abuses, actual and potential. Let me conclude by underlining my belief that, with all its problems, comparative study is a most desirable way of approaching an understanding of education. The challenge is to do it in ways that are valid, persuasive, practically usable, and, above all, enlightening. But, beyond this, I assert that we need comparative scholarship in general, and comparative education in particular, for a reason that transcends workaday considerations of usefulness.

Our generation, and all those since August 6, 1945, live in a world fundamentally different from that which existed before the bombing of Hiroshima. Before that date man's inhumanity to man, most violently expressed in war, could be (and was) startling in its destructive effects; but the damage to people, institutions, and things was relatively localized, and recovery in at most a generation or two was the norm. Ours is a different prospect, so that unless we are exceedingly careful, lucky, and, above all, wise, we may be the last generation to inhabit a planet that we would recognize as our Earth.

The special wisdom that we and our heirs must cultivate is the wisdom to get along with our neighbors on this planet, in the company of weapons of overwhelming destructive capacity. However much we may wish that these weapons would simply go away, even the smallest dash of realism must tell us that this will not happen. In a sense that is profoundly Faustian, we have paid for our gifts of intelligence in the coin of permanent fear of global annihilation.

I am sufficiently Aristotelian to believe that knowledge is part of wisdom, though I am a long way from believing that it is the whole of that precious commodity. The knowledge we need more urgently than ever before is knowledge of our own society and of others'. And these two species of knowledge are separable only for purposes of cataloging them. For the fundamental assertion of comparative study is that we can truly comprehend ourselves only in the context of a secure knowledge of other societies: knowledge that is parochial is partial, in both senses of that word, and therefore potentially dangerous. It is knowledge without completeness,

[23] Harold J. Noah and Max A. Eckstein, *Toward a Science of Comparative Education* (New York: Macmillan, 1969), p. 116.

and it is knowledge without appreciation of the rest of the world's experience.

It may be that even our best efforts to negotiate the perils ahead will come to naught, and that humankind will indeed destroy itself in a tantrum of nationalistic and ideological rage. But, by cultivating throughout our society a tradition of rich understanding and knowledge of the other societies with which we share the planet, we shall at least have given the business of species survival our "best shot." Ultimately, I suppose, that is the real test of how well we have used the comparative approach.

The Comparative Mind

MAX A. ECKSTEIN

The thesis of this paper is based on three arguments: first, that comparative educators make extensive use of metaphors in their thinking and writing, and that while this has great strengths it also contains some real problems in the process of advancing knowledge; second, that comparing is inherent in human thinking as a developmental process; and third, that comparing through the use of metaphors is a fundamental and characteristic way by which researchers in all areas of knowledge seek to extend our understanding of the world around us. The metaphors we use presuppose or imply theories; the theories (or models) which purport to explain or account for phenomena contain specific metaphors, whether implicit or explicit. One of the more important themes of the paper is that the unexamined metaphor, like the unexamined life, may have limited value.

Metaphors in Comparative Education

There are three major ways in which we all approach the substance of our field: as teachers, as students and researchers, and as users of the knowledge accumulated to make, implement, and evaluate policy.[1] Most of what follows relates to the second approach, study and research, though it has implications of course for the other two. Furthermore, we should acknowledge that the ideology, values, and techniques of comparative education are not unique to our field but are common to philosophy and the social sciences. They are as helpful and as problematic for us as for our colleagues in other scholarly fields. Like them, we seek to establish transnational laws about social phenomena, specifically, generalizations about educations that are valid for different societies. Like them, too, we ponder whether this is at all possible, either because each society or culture is unique or because social science is an inappropriate or inadequate means to establish generalizations comparable to those of the physical or natural sciences. And like them, we often do ourselves a disservice, either by attending too closely to one nation or type of nation or by not being critical, self-conscious, and creative enough about the images, metaphors, and paradigms that we employ in our comparisons. On the one hand,

---

[1] Edmund J. King, "Students, Teachers and Researchers in Comparative Education," *Comparative Education Review* 2 (June 1958): 33–36; and Robert L. Koehl, "The Comparative Study of Education: Prescription and Practice," *Comparative Education Review* 21 (June/October 1977): 177–94.

Reprinted from *Comparative Education Review*, vol. 27, no. 3 (October 1983).

we may be too parochial or one-sided, and on the other, too many-sided in the attempt to make sense of the great unknowns that we study.

The first task, then, is to examine some of the basic metaphors current in the field, for it is through them that we communicate with one another.[2] Since metaphors are at the very least implicit comparisons, it is only to be expected that they will abound in our literature.

A quick dip into recent issues of the *Comparative Education Review* will net a rich catch of metaphors: Brown's reference to "Hard Core" ideology in Chinese educational policy, and Harrison and Glaubman's examination of "Open Education" (October 1982); Psacharopoulos's metaphor for higher education as "the top step of the learning ladder" and his use of the phrase "prescription for economic development" (June 1982); Masemann's use, in her review of various sociological and anthropological approaches to educational research, of familiar terms in reference to functionalist views, for example, "structures," "life process," etc. (she is to be complimented for being self-conscious and analytical about metaphors) (February 1982); Thomas La Belle's mention of "the national character" of nonformal education, Merritt and Leonardi's use of the terms "immobility and accommodation" when discussing responses to various secondary school reform efforts in Italy, Clignet's reference to the "Natural History of Educational Interactions," and Sica and Prechel's dwelling on "dependency" as a metaphor for educational relationships (October 1981); Eisemon's use of the idea of "center and periphery" in writing about science in universities, and Young's evocative and colorfully phrased description of the African university as "at once child of decolonization and intended parent of national development" (June 1981). This assortment of metaphors is random. At some other time we might join in the intriguing game of collecting them and pinning them down, like butterflies, in some order. But what follow are a few generic examples of metaphor, chosen to illustrate how they are used and the kinds of ideas they comprise.

The first example is quite simple and obvious but a pervasive and important use of metaphors to identify nations and cultures. Perhaps the best-known examples may be taken from Edmund King's *Other Schools and Ours*,[3] in which certain chapter titles serve primarily as powerful

---

[2] It may be helpful at this point to distinguish between metaphors and several other terms frequently used in this essay. "Metaphor" (deriving from a Greek root meaning "to transfer") is the figure of speech in which a name or a descriptive term is transferred to an object different from, but analogous to, the one to which it is properly applicable. A "paradigm" (also from a Greek root, connoting "to show side by side," i.e., to juxtapose) is a pattern or exemplar. A "theory" is, of course, a scheme or system of ideas held to explain or account for a set of facts or phenomena, or a statement of what are held to be general laws, principles, or causes. And "model" refers to a representation of a theory in some kind of structural form; here the phenomena are related to one another in terms of the set of ideas composing the theory. Any theory, model, or paradigm is likely to comprise a major metaphor (or set of metaphors); alternatively, any metaphor suggests or assumes a theory, model, or paradigm.

[3] Edmund J. King, *Other Schools and Ours*, 5th ed. (New York: Holt, Rinehart & Winston, 1979).

instructional devices:[4] "France—the Central Light of Reason," "The U.S.A.—a Nation on Wheels."

When proceeding from the individual case to the variety of cases under study, that is, the many nations of the world, we tend to group them into categories. We refer, for example, to developed and underdeveloped nations, selective and nonselective secondary school systems, centralized and decentralized administrations. Some nations are loosely called Third World countries in contrast to those of the First and Second Worlds, often without adequate identification of their common features. Such groupings of what, on the face of it, appear to be similar items are often no more than a preliminary sorting of the cards. We may not yet have seriously considered, let alone answered, the question, Similar with respect to what? We have not yet, in many instances, identified our rules of correspondence, and when we begin a closer examination we often find that the exceptions to the rule are more numerous than the items that conform. As we ponder the anomalies, the exceptions to the rule, and the possibilities of a new paradigm, the similarity of relations among the items is likely to change. Yet we stubbornly persist in retaining familiar categories, even when they force very dissimilar items into the same set and do not serve to explain what we seek to understand. And the reason for this persistence is quite simple: we are bound by the metaphors we create.

Both kinds of examples cited so far use metaphors to describe. They do not necessarily explain anything, even though they purport to do so. But the following examples do explicitly intend to explain: they propose connections and interactions, they suggest causes, and they even intimate the future.

The founding fathers of our field, working from a progress-oriented model, referred to the "warp and woof" of the social fabric into which schooling was woven; they noted the "forces" of society that shaped educational ideas and practices and the intellectual "currents" that moved not only school events but also the various configurations of political realities. Their paradigm included a number of significant assumptions: not only the sense that our subjects of study, nations or school systems, can be sorted into certain groups (e.g., developed and less developed, industrialized and unindustrialized), but that movement from one to the other is likely if not inevitable and represents some form of progress (by definition, in the conventional English usage, a Good Thing). In this same spirit of progress we have accepted the familiar analogy, influential in history and anthropology in particular, between changes in human societies

---

[4] Richard Boyd, "Metaphor and Theory Change: What Is 'Metaphor' a Metaphor For?" in *Metaphor and Thought*, ed. Andrew Ortony (Cambridge: Cambridge University Press, 1979). Boyd distinguishes between pedagogical metaphors (used for instructional purposes) and metaphors that function to cover gaps in knowledge.

and the development of the human individual: some societies are like human infants—simple and primitive; others are mature, complex, and sophisticated—like human adults. The metaphor of the growing human contains certain expectations and values, draws our attention to some similarities and differences rather than others, focuses on some research questions rather than others. The implicit value judgments are obvious.

A second general model, the so-called radical paradigm, as Kazamias and Messialas term it,[5] has enjoyed increasing attention over the past decade or so, though it, like the notion of progress, is rooted in nineteenth-century political thought. It has at its center the ideas of power and conflict and generates a number of evocative metaphors: reproduction, dependency, imperialism. Education thus becomes a means of exerting power, and elites use schooling as a mechanism for maintaining their hegemony over those with little or none. Unlike the first model, which is progress oriented and ecological and which conceives of education as the trigger or the yeast for general social growth and improvement, the second sees education as the tool or the conduit through which elite groups maintain their advantage over lesser groups.

To say that school developments are milestones on the road that leads inevitably to national improvement or are triggers for social progress does help to give us a perspective on a confusing and complex set of information. Such statements may even be true, but they are certainly inadequately founded either in theory or in fact and at best represent only possible parts of the picture. To say that the schools are instruments to maintain political power supplies a different and similarly limited perspective on complex events and phenomena. This view of the schools is familiar and simple, though not for that reason necessarily simpleminded, and also usefully illuminates otherwise hidden or disregarded aspects of our subject. To cite yet another metaphor, it is all well and good to liken the education system to a factory, whether in Lloyd Warner's sense of a social sorting machine[6] or in the more complex sense of a processor of human potential for the labor market (i.e., the production-function model), but this model, like the others, takes us only so far. Most of the metaphors we use to understand and to communicate with one another shed some new light on the subject. At the same time, they all leave too many questions unanswered and more unasked.

---

[5] Andreas Kazamias and Byron G. Messialas, "Comparative Education," in *Encyclopedia of Educational Research*, 5th ed. (New York: Macmillan, 1982), pp. 309–17. See also, e.g., Robert L. Koehl, "Cultural Imperialism as Education: An Indictment," *Comparative Education Review* 19 (June 1975): 276–85; Martin Carnoy, "Education as Cultural Imperialism: A Reply," *Comparative Education Review* 19 (June 1975): 286–89; Philip G. Altbach and Gail P. Kelly, *Education and Colonialism* (New York: Longmans, 1978); J. Karabel and A. H. Halsey, eds., *Power and Ideology in Education* (New York: Oxford University Press, 1977).

[6] W. Lloyd Warner et al., *Who Shall Be Educated?* (New York: Harper, 1944).

Ernest Nagel's comments on explanation in the social sciences appear especially appropriate here. He observes that a number of very different concepts (or variables) that cut across cultural differences have been used as the bases for transnational generalizations. But, he continues: "The social laws that have been perhaps most frequently proposed in terms of such concepts state orders of supposedly inevitable social changes, and maintain that societies or institutions succeeded one another in some fixed sequence of developmental stages. None of these attempts or proposals has been successful. . . ."[7] He goes on to suggest that what may be needed are more abstract conceptualizations, that is, metaphors more removed from the familiar notions used in the daily business of social life.

At the very least, our metaphors in comparative education help us to describe, and there is of course a limit to the extent that they explain. A powerful metaphor, however, both describes and explains and then goes even further:[8] it articulates new ideas, invites further exploration of similarities and differences, and generates new analogies which include features not yet fully understood and previously undiscovered. Our metaphors in comparative education are really quite simple, drawn from nature and from everyday life. They serve the purpose of bridging some of the known and the unknown. They cast the unknown into a shape that helps us grasp some of its elements. But so often they are used without consideration of what they really say or imply or of how far they can take us in exploring the territory. They must therefore be scrutinized critically lest they limit our thinking. And they must be challenged by new conceptualizations that have the potential of answering more questions and provoking yet new ones.

Comparison and the Development of Human Thought Processes

Needless to say, comparative education is not the only place where comparison goes on. Figurative thinking and comparing are, I believe, inherent in human thinking and in fact mark a fundamental step in the cognitive development of the young. This is indicated in developmental theory in general and particularly well illustrated in Piaget's formulation of stages of development. The general idea is that there is a set sequence, that under normal circumstances each stage follows the preceding one, and that each stage is a precondition for the next.

In describing intellectual development, Piaget identifies five characteristic stages: (1) sensorimotor thinking (the earliest, pre-speech); (2) emergence

[7] Ernest Nagel, *The Structure of Science: Problems in the Logic of Scientific Explanation* (New York: Harcourt Brace, 1961), p. 465.

[8] Zenon W. Pylyshyn, "Metaphorical Imprecision and the 'Top-Down' Research Strategy," in Ortony, ed., pp. 420–36.

and development of symbolic thought (approximately 1½–5 years); (3) articulated or intuitional representation (approximately 4–8 years); (4) concrete operations (9–12 years); and (5) formal operations. A word or two about stages 2 and 3 (i.e., those stages that coincide with the development of speech and are therefore the foundation of adult conceptualization) will suffice to make the initial point.

Stage 2 is associated with a dramatic increase in language use and indicates a fundamental development in mode of thinking that shapes an individual's life-long intellectual activity. Language begins to be used as a representation of action instead of being merely an accompaniment to it, as in the earlier infant stage. No longer just a part of the action, language evokes action.[9] This development marks a large spurt forward toward using language as a conceptual symbol system.

To narrow our focus momentarily, two key concepts that Piaget uses to describe thought processes at this stage recall theory and practice in comparative education as illuminated by Bereday some years ago: "juxtaposition" and "syncretism."[10] In Piaget, these terms refer to alternative modes of thinking by which children think, explain, and communicate at this crucial phase of intellectual development. To juxtapose simply means putting items together without relating them to one another, although some explanation (some nascent idea of cause and effect) is at least suggested or implied in the ways in which the parts or the details are placed next to one another. Syncretism, by contrast, is thinking about the whole without relating it to the parts (a sort of primitive Gestalt conceptualization).

All this mental activity is what Piaget calls "pre-conceptual thought," and it is clear that the subsequent stages of development rest upon this second stage and are shaped by it. But it may even be argued that juxtaposition and syncretism represent comparison in its simplest and least-developed form.

Piaget describes stage 3 as the threshold of operational thinking. Just as the preceding stage was marked by a rapid increase in speech, so this one is marked by increasing social involvement and sharing, as well as further language development. So far as thought processes of this stage are concerned, juxtaposition and syncretism begin to decline, and the details and the totality begin to be seen as a related whole.

This outline of Piaget's stages of mental development is sufficient for our purposes. At all stages, and with many examples drawn from his own careful observation of children, Piaget illustrates the growth of intellectual

[9] Jean Piaget, *Play, Dreams, and Imitation* (London: Routledge & Kegan Paul, 1967); P. G. Richmond, *An Introduction to Piaget* (New York: Basic, 1970); Ellen Winner et al., "First Metaphors," *New Directions for Child Development* 3 (1979): 29–41.

[10] George Z. F. Bereday, *Comparative Method in Education* (New York: Holt, Rinehart & Winston, 1964).

ability by drawing attention to how the young relate things: one thing to another, details to the whole, self to others, single items to classes of items (i.e., single facts to variables). Under normal circumstances, by the time adolescence is reached a "complete" system of thinking is available to the individual. It is a system independent of the context, an autonomous instrument that can be applied to all kinds of data. Propositional thinking and hypothesis-deductive reasoning are among the by-products. And all the way through, relating and comparing have been central.

The purpose of this brief disquisition on Piaget is to argue (if this is indeed at all necessary) that comparison is inherent in human thinking and that the development of this one faculty is in fact entwined in the development of all the human thinking processes. Cultivation of the one faculty is thus a particular form of advancing the total capacity to think, the capacity to draw meaning from things and experiences and to generate new ideas from them.

Metaphors and the Progress of Knowledge

The third leg of the argument addresses the question of how we think generally in advancing knowledge at a more sophisticated level: as students and as researchers seeking to expand our grasp of the world around us. We are here concerned with the ubiquitous use of metaphor as a tool for achieving knowledge, explaining parts of the unknown, and expanding understanding.

A familiar example of the role of metaphor in scientific discovery was dramatically presented in the television series and the book by Jonathan Miller entitled *The Body in Question*. It was not until the sixteenth century that William Harvey conceived of the way in which the heart functioned, as a pump for the circulatory system. This notion, with some elaborations, remains valid to this day. Harvey himself acquired no startling new evidence (the empirical evidence provided by Vesalius was certainly adequate, and what Galen knew in the first century, though incomplete, was not irrelevant). Why then, asks Miller, did it take so long—at least sixteen centuries—for understanding of the heart to develop to this point? Because satisfactory metaphors for thinking about what was seen were lacking: "In primitive societies, where technical images are few and far between and very simple at that, most explanatory metaphors are drawn from nature. . . . But the development of technology created a new stock of metaphors—not simply extra metaphors, but ones altogether different in their logical character."[11] Only after pumps and pumplike engines had become widely used in mining and civil engineering, and only when fountains and fire-fighting equipment had become familiar sights in the growing cities of preindustrial

---

[11] Jonathan Miller, *The Body in Question* (New York: Random House, 1978), p. 181.

Europe, was it possible for the pump to be thought of and accepted as a satisfactory metaphor for the working of the human heart.

Another example from human anatomy is even more familiar. More has been discovered about the workings of the brain in the past 2 decades than in several preceding centuries. Consider some of the terms widely used by cognitive psychologists and educators to describe various brain functions: thinking is "information processing"; learning to read, to comprehend, and to communicate consists of encoding and decoding symbols; consciousness is a feedback mechanism; memory is a matter of data storage and retrieval. The most illuminating contemporary metaphor for the brain is the computer. It is irresistible because it helps to fill in pieces of a model that purports to explain an unknown territory for whose description we lacked a language. In this way, it provides us with a theory of human functioning that explains large parts of what was previously a mystery to us.

In his analyses of the logic of scientific explanation, Ernest Nagel provides a host of examples from mathematics and physics to demonstrate how general analogies and particular metaphors serve to bridge the gap between familiar facts and new experiences and to articulate new theories.[12] In a similar vein, Thomas Kuhn, discussing the role of what he calls paradigms, cites examples from the physical sciences of new models or conceptualizations (he frequently uses the term "puzzle-solutions") facilitating giant steps forward from the known into the unknown regions of scientific knowledge.[13]

It is not in the physical and natural sciences alone that metaphor plays an important role in discovery. In the social sciences generally, and in history specifically, much of our knowledge is shaped by powerful metaphors. We use such terms as "the forces of history"; we refer to the youth, maturity, and decline of peoples or cultures, to the ebb and flow of social movements, to the rise and fall of nations. As Isaiah Berlin points out, this metaphorical language conveys the idea of an inexorable, fixed time order.[14] Such metaphors may be misleading, but they are pointers to categories which are helpful, if only to a limited degree. (It is worth noting that the metaphors that Berlin cites are all, to use Miller's phrase, "drawn from nature," simple and primitive.)

It is tempting to continue listing more of the metaphors we have lived by in expanding our grasp of the universe. But we must now pay some attention to examining the nature of the metaphor in our thinking, its

[12] See Nagel.

[13] Thomas S. Kuhn, *The Structure of Scientific Revolutions* (Chicago: University of Chicago Press, 1970).

[14] Isaiah Berlin, *Concepts and Categories* (New York: Viking, 1979); see esp. his chapters on "Logical Translation" and "The Concept of Scientific Inquiry."

function in helping us discover new knowledge, and some of the problems as well as advantages entailed in using it.

Common speech is full of expressions that were originally used figuratively but have now lost their original meaning and are used literally: the leg of a table, for example, or the head of a hammer. And it is probably impossible to compose more than a few sentences without having recourse to an explicit metaphor, since figurative speech is a common tendency in human communication. This tendency may not, for most people, be deliberate or conscious, though in the hands of a poet, scientist, or teacher the metaphor is likely to be thoughtfully and self-consciously used, but as Nagel observes, "the widespread use of metaphors . . . testifies to a pervasive human talent for finding resemblances between new experiences and familiar facts. . . ." "Analogies help to assimilate the new to the old, and prevent novel explanatory premises from being radically unfamiliar." And ". . . the desire to explain new domains of fact in terms of something already familiar" has controlled important developments in the history of scientific knowledge in all areas and disciplines.[15]

We must, however, draw attention to a number of caveats associated with how metaphors work. A metaphor or a model may be used to express a theoretical formulation, but it is not itself a theory. Correspondence must be demonstrated between the set of phenomena requiring explanation and the model itself, and, as Nagel argues, in attempts at scientific explanation there are certain rules of correspondence. A model may be an intellectual trap as well as a valuable tool if some inessential part is mistaken for a key feature of the theory it represents. The researcher will become distracted by spurious problems in his attempt to make the model fit the facts (or vice versa) and thus be led into unproductive efforts, all because of this basic error of confusing the model with the theory itself or, to put it in other words, of mistaking the vehicle for the journey itself.

As already indicated, figurative expressions are so fundamental to human thinking and communication processes that the use of a metaphor may not always be a deliberate or conscious act. If we do not pay attention to the limits of the resemblances between the reality and the metaphor or the familiar and the new (or between any of the sets of items we are comparing), we risk serious error. We may take a concept from a domain where its use is legitimate and use it in another where it is not. As Nagel points out, ". . . words like 'force,' 'law,' and 'cause' are occasionally still used with decided anthropomorphic overtones that are echoes of their origins." Nevertheless, a sense of even vague similarities between the old and new may be a starting point for an advance in knowledge, and "when reflection becomes critically self-conscious . . . [these vague similarities]

[15] Nagel, pp. 108, 46, 95–96.

may come to be developed into carefully formulated analogies and hypotheses that can serve as fruitful instruments of systematic research."[16] In another context, that of explanation in political science, Isaiah Berlin also acknowledges that metaphors may distort as well as explain. But in the end, he is not seriously concerned: ". . . the fact that many metaphors have proved fatal, or at least misleading, [does not] tend to show that all metaphors can or should be eliminated. . . ."[17]

The history of the development of human knowledge provides many examples of metaphors that failed to explain phenomena satisfactorily, leading researchers into unproductive directions and unsolvable puzzles. While it is in the nature of such conceptual models to serve the purposes of explanation for a period (perhaps a very long one), eventually they fail in the face of new and unanswered puzzles. Then the old metaphor, well established in the minds of experts in a field of study, serves as an obstruction to further solutions. This pattern of development is exactly what Kuhn argues in his disquisition on the role of paradigms in scientific revolutions. Explanatory models, he argues, have similar functions: "Among other things they supply the group with preferred or permissible analogies and metaphors. By doing so they help to determine what will be accepted as an explanation and as a puzzle-solution; conversely, they assist in the determination of the roster of unsolved puzzles, and in the evaluation of the importance of each."[18] But the "group," that is, a given scientific community, may be forced to confront what Kuhn terms an "anomaly" or a "violation of expectation." In the face of such a puzzle, a new paradigm is proposed, one that replaces the previous one that was inadequate to explain the unexpected phenomena. A paradigm is an entire set of beliefs, values, and techniques associated with a particular field of study, and it includes a set of concrete puzzle-solutions in the form of models or examples. A scientific revolution occurs when a general and widely held paradigm is replaced by another that is fundamentally different. The new paradigm marks a large advance in knowledge because it provides new models and metaphors for understanding. By the same token, the old metaphors are shown to have been incorrect, at least in part, or misleading and limiting in their explanatory power.

These observations on the role of metaphors in knowledge cannot be concluded without some reference to language and aesthetics. In the *Poetics*, Aristotle praises the metaphor: "The greatest thing by far is to have command of metaphor." But the argument made here goes beyond the traditional view of metaphor. It is not merely a decorative rhetorical

---

[16] Ibid., p. 108.
[17] Berlin, pp. 158–59.
[18] Kuhn, p. 184.

device, as Aristotle views it, but a characteristic form of human communication that is used, whether well or not, in teaching and in study. Metaphor is inherent in human thinking, and its main function is to help us bridge the known and the unknown, as children, as adults, and as researchers. The very nature of thinking, as I. A. Richards observes, is metaphoric and proceeds by comparison: "What is comparison? It may be several different things: it may be just a putting together of two things to let them work together; it may be a study of them both to see how they are like and how unlike one another; or it may be a process of calling attention to their likenesses or a method of drawing attention to certain aspects of the one through the co-presence of the other."[19]

Conclusion

To summarize my argument, metaphor is comparison. It is inherent in human thinking and communication, and it is central to furthering the progress of science, not just the physical and natural sciences, but all sectors of human knowledge. There are some real problems involved in using metaphors, for they may impede progress in discovery, but they serve as valuable tools when used consciously and with deliberation, even though they may, in the first instance, emerge in that flash of intuition and insight that characterizes great scientists and great poets. The metaphors that prevail in comparative education, as in the social sciences generally, need to be critically examined and new ones invented, since those we rely on are rather simple, overworked, derivative, and limiting. We need periodically to reexamine first principles and earlier practices. The very metaphors we use to represent our own field of study need scrutiny. For example, we might again consider the concept of comparative education as natural history, perhaps regenerating interest in comparative educational taxonomy; or we might conceive of our work as a geography of education and direct our creative energies toward developing original and visionary maps of the world educational scene with new and provocative projections. Metaphors, if they are to be illuminating and useful, must be scrutinized critically and new ones periodically considered.

What then, in conclusion, is the comparative mind? In the first place, like all other human mental activity it is inclined toward figurative thinking, using metaphors, models, and paradigms to explain the unknown in terms of the known. But the comparative mind is also like the minds of others

---

[19] I. A. Richards, *The Philosophy of Rhetoric* (London: Oxford University Press, 1938), p. 94; see esp. his chapter on "Metaphor." For further illumination of the function of metaphor as a cognitive instrument (in linguistics and philosophy), see also Boyd (n. 4 above); Max Black, "More about Metaphor," in Ortony, ed. (n. 4 above), pp. 19–43; Hugh G. Petrie, "Metaphor and Learning," in Ortony, ed.; George Lakoff and Mark Johnson, *Metaphors We Live By* (Chicago: University of Chicago Press, 1980).

engaged in the deliberate search to extend knowledge. It is curious, being especially drawn to puzzles concerning human behavior. It is creative and flexible, being capable of moving back and forth between the particular item and the whole pattern, between the facts and the variable, between data and theories, between contemplative study and other kinds of activity. In sum, the comparative mind is a particular case of the general human cognitive condition and an even more particular case of the inquiring mind, whether scientist, philosopher, or artist. And its most special attribute is that it is drawn to the fascinating game of solving complex puzzles and playing with ideas and facts through comparison—and the use of metaphors.

Paradigm Shifts in Comparative Education

BRIAN HOLMES

Paradigm shifts in the natural sciences occur infrequently, are partial, and are accepted reluctantly, and then not by all scientists. In physics, Galileo, Newton, and Einstein stand out as initiators of paradigm change; Lavoisier's theory of combustion eventually transformed the paradigm within which chemists work; and Darwin's theory of evolution represents an equally dramatic shift for biologists. Nevertheless, the theories and beliefs that predate major scientific revolutions in the natural sciences continue to be useful and to inform the work of practitioners in various parts of the world. We have among us flat earthers, Ptolemaic astronomers, astrologers, alchemists, phlogistonists, and Garden of Eden biologists. And why not, if the work they do is useful and satisfies them and their followers?

Since decisive tests in the social sciences are rare, paradigm shifts are even less dramatic, are rarely accepted by more than a few radical thinkers, and continue to be debated endlessly. Psychological, political, sociological, and epistemological theories never achieve the same status as Newton's laws of motion or Bohr's atomic model or, more recently DNA biological models. Paradigms created by Plato continue to inform the work of some social scientists, while others work within alternative paradigms based on the work of Marx. Indeed, from Plato to Marx, a host of theories, beliefs, models, and techniques have been established. Any of several paradigms are available to comparative educationists, many of whom, like Thomas Kuhn's commonsense scientists,[1] undertake substantive research without worrying overmuch about the theoretical assumptions on which it depends.

It is against this background that I have been examining, over the last 40 years, the theoretical assumptions on the basis of which the pioneers of comparative education founded the subject as a viable approach to the study of education in universities. In the process, I have rejected some of the beliefs about scientific method based on J. S. Mill's *System of Logic*,[2] into which I was socialized as an undergraduate student of physics during the early part of the Second World War. Then, after the war, I rejected my earlier views about scientific method while a student of Joseph Lauwerys,

[1] Thomas Kuhn, *The Structure of Scientific Revolutions*, 2d ed. (Chicago: University of Chicago, Press, 1969).
[2] J. S. Mill, *A System of Logic, Ratiocinative and Inductive*, 8th ed. (London: Longman, 1970); also, Morris R. Cohen and Ernest Nagel, *An Introduction to Logic and Scientific Method* (London: Routledge, 1934).

Reprinted from *Comparative Education Review*, vol. 28, no. 4 (November 1984).

who trained me as a potential teacher of science, and as a student of Nicholas Hans,[3] who introduced me to the study of comparative education.

Long before the notion of "paradigm shifts" became fashionable, I had begun to question some fundamental, but commonplace, beliefs about the nature of science. Today I assume that the constituents of a paradigm are the beliefs, values, theories, models, and techniques that are used by research workers to legitimize what they are doing or to give direction to their inquiries. I hold that the constituents of a paradigm may be held implicitly or proclaimed overtly; may be logically coherent and consistent or the reverse; and may be accepted by the majority, a few, or only one person associated with a field of inquiry. There are, in short, competing paradigms. Moreover, competing paradigms may include some but not all the same assumptions and theories, so that there are differences and similarities. Proposed paradigm shifts may be put forward piecemeal by an individual or by a group of like-minded pioneers. They rarely involve, in the first instance, a total rejection of an existing paradigm.

Thus, when writing about *my* paradigm, I am stressing the assumptions and beliefs that inform my research work. In restricting the term in this way, I wish to stress that I do not claim that my proposals have been accepted by a majority of comparative educationists, in spite of the fact that a great many doctoral students have stated explicitly that their research was informed by the "Holmes problem-solving approach."

The Constituents of a Paradigm for Comparative Educationists

The contexts in which I started to consider my position in 1945 were the vigorous debates taking place in England about the future of British society and, indeed, in other forums about the future of the world. Karl Popper's *Open Society and Its Enemies* persuaded me that the logical links between the theories of Plato, Marx, Hegel, and Mannheim and the practices we had learned to abhor made it impossible, if any of these theories were embraced wholeheartedly, to guarantee that Britain would remain democratic.[4]

Consequently, my acceptance of the beliefs and theories advanced by Popper in the *Open Society* was irrational, or at best based on logical arguments and not on decisive empirical evidence. Most of us make our choice of paradigm in the light of a mixture of emotions, political beliefs, and less than rational judgments.

What should be the constituents of a social scientific paradigm is neither agreed upon nor clear. Kuhn himself has been criticized for not

[3] Nicholas Hans, *Comparative Education: A Study of Educational Factors and Traditions*, 3d ed. (London: Routledge & Kegan Paul, 1958).

[4] Karl Mannheim, *Freedom, Power and Democratic Planning* (London: Routledge & Kegan Paul, 1965); Friedrich A. von Hayek, *The Road to Serfdom* (London: Routledge, 1944); Karl R. Popper, *The Open Society and Its Enemies,* 5th ed. (London: Routledge & Kegan Paul, 1966).

using any one of several descriptions of scientific paradigm systematically. Consequently, I suggest that in most paradigms within which social scientists work, I would expect to find some general philosophical theories, such as an ontology, or theory of reality; a taxonomy, or theory of classifying data; an aetiology, or theory of causation; an epistemology, or theory of the status of knowledge and how it can be acquired; an ethnology, or theory of the mental and physical differences between individuals; a psychological theory of learning; and political and sociological theories about the nature of society. Of these, epistemological and aetiological assumptions have a direct bearing on methods of inquiry, and political, sociological, and psychological theories inform the perspective from which we view societies, cultures, and individuals. In short, our paradigms influence the way in which we conduct our research, the data we collect and classify, and the models and techniques we adopt to facilitate comparison and analysis.

Central to the paradigm used by my mentor, Hans, was a theory of causation shared by pioneers such as Isaac Kandel and Friedrich Schneider.[5] The theory of factors (Hans), causes (Kandel), and *Triebkräfte* (Schneider) has its origins in Aristotle's theory of causation. For Schneider, Aristotle's "formal" and "final" causes, toward the realization of which educational systems were being drawn, were important and helped to explain differences between systems. Hans and Kandel emphasized the role of Aristotle's "efficient" and "material" causes, although the former took the view that "ideas," and the latter that "systems of administration," were the most important factors or causes behind the evolution of school systems and the differences between such systems. Adopting similar assumptions, Lauwerys used the term "determinants" of education to explain differences.

This theory of causation virtually reigned supreme until well into the 1950s,[6] and students of Kandel, Schneider, and Hans continued to accept it. It remains influential in the way comparative educationists speak and write, in spite of attempts made by Harold Noah to replace the term

[5] Issac L. Kandel, *Comparative Education* (Boston: Houghton Mifflin, 1933); Friedrich Schneider, *Triebkräfte der Pädagogik der Völker* (Salzburg: Muller, 1947), and *Vergleichende Erziehungswissenschaft* (Heidelberg: Quelle & Meyer, 1961); also, for a summary of several positions, see Philip E. Jones, *Comparative Education* (St. Lucia: University of Queensland Press, 1971); Franz Hilker, *Vergleichende Pädagogik* (Munich: Max Huebner, 1962); Vernon Mallinson, *An Introduction to the Study of Comparative Education*, 4th ed. (London: Heinemann, 1975); Angel Diego Marquez, *Educación comparada, teoria y metodogia* (Buenos Aires: El Atoneo, 1972); Alexandre Vexliard, *La Pédagogie comparée* (Paris: Presses Universitaires de France, 1967).

[6] For a discussion of many of the issues debated by social scientists, see Theodore W. Adorno et al., *The Positivist Dispute in German Sociology* (London: Heinemann, 1976); C. Arnold Anderson, "Methodology of Comparative Education," *International Review of Education* 7, no. 1 (1961): 1–23; Benjamin Barber, "Science, Salience and Comparative Education: Some Reflections in Social Scientific Enquiry," in *Relevant Methods in Comparative Education*, ed. Reginald Edwards et al. (Hamburg: Unesco Institute for Education, 1973); Alvin W. Gouldner, *The Coming Crisis of Western Sociology* (London: Heinemann, 1971); Harold J. Noah and Max A. Eckstein, *Toward a Science of Comparative Education* (London: Macmillan, 1969); Alan Ryan, *The Philosophy of the Social Sciences* (London: Macmillan, 1970).

"factors" by the word "variables" and to draw distinctions between cause-effect relationships and correlations. As I see his position, correlations are more immediately capable of study, but the establishment of causal relationships is the ultimate goal of inquiry.

The classical theory of causation, however, has deep roots, is not easy to dispel, and indeed was used by European comparative educators as the basis on which they classified data and the ground on which they justified reform proposals. Religious, linguistic, racial, political, and geographical factors were used by Hans and Schneider to collect and classify information about educational systems. Kandel polarized administrative systems into centralized and decentralized to compare school systems, explain their evolution, and contrast causally related characteristics. Thus Kandel favored the decentralization of education administration in postwar Japan to make that country democratic. Hans used to argue in favor of bilingual policies where linguistic diversity was found on the ground that such policies had been adopted in Belgium. A new generation of comparative educationists turned to social class, economic investment, and neo-colonialism as the "cause" of educational development or retardation. Their assumption about causation remain the same as the ones of those who accepted for so long the Kandel, Schneider, and Hans paradigm.

A second feature of this paradigm has its origins in positivism and induction. Implicit in the work of some comparative educationists is the view that universal panaceas can be induced from an objective study of educational "facts." Induction as a method of scientific research implies that the researcher should first observe, collect, and classify objective facts before inducing tentative causal hypotheses. Subsequently the observation of more confirming "facts" makes it possible for a hypothesis to be raised to the status of a universal, unconditionally valid law. This theory of inquiry is best outlined by George Bereday in his *Comparative Method in Education*[7] but is implicit in Kandel's generalizations about relationships between decentralized systems of educational administration and democracy and in Hans's statements about the provision of education in Roman Catholic countries.

Induction as an epistemological theory justifies an approach to comparative education research in which general laws are stressed at the expense of particular national circumstances. It cannot be reconciled with the epistemological assumptions of either John Dewey's reflective method of thinking[8] or Karl Popper's hypothetico-deductive method of scientific enquiry. From my perspective, a fundamental paradigm shift took place in my own thinking when I rejected the theories of causation and of

[7] George Z. F. Bereday, *Comparative Method in Education* (New York: Holt, Rinehart & Winston, 1964).
[8] John Dewey, *How We Think* (Boston: Heath, 1910).

knowledge which are constituents of the more general theory of induction. In doing so, I also rejected that part of the historical approach used by Hans and Kandel to discover the antecedent causes of national differences and took the view that historical data should be used pragmatically to illuminate present-day problems rather than to discover inevitable sequences of development.

The fundamental character of these changes cannot be overstressed. They involve accepting a new terminology, a forward- rather than a backward-looking perspective on events, the importance of particular national circumstances in evaluating policies, and a critical rejection of universal solutions to educational problems. Central to my new paradigm are the epistemological assumptions of Dewey and Popper.

Reflective Thinking and the Hypothetico-Deductive Method

The stages in Dewey's process of reflective thinking are well known. They include problem analysis, solution formulation, a description of the circumstances in which the problem is located and the solution is to be applied, the logical deduction of consequences under these circumstances were a solution to be accepted, and finally a comparison of predicted and observable events that either verifies or refutes the hypothetical solution. In spite of Popper's reservations about Dewey's instrumentalism, I can reconcile features of Dewey's reflective thinking and Popper's hypothetico-deductive method of enquiry insofar as in the latter scientists start from a problem, formulate hypothetical solutions, and test them by comparing logically predicted events with those that can be observed. A major difference between the two positions is that Dewey's interest lies in verifying solutions to problems; Popper's claim is that scientists are acting most responsibly when they attempt to refute hypothetical solutions. Central to my comparative education paradigm is the view that national or indeed international educational policies should be viewed as hypothetical solutions to societal problems that in the absence of experimental tests should be subjected to critical comparative scrutiny with the objective of eliminating those that are least likely to work, that is, achieve stated aims and resolve identified problems.

Models and techniques are needed to operationalize the various stages of reflective thinking and the hypothetico-deductive method of scientific inquiry. Having replaced induction in my paradigm, I made a search for theories and models that would enable me to operationalize the processes involved in problem solving through hypothesis testing.

Theories of Social Change

Problem analysis is based on the identification of sudden or unexpected societal change. Rather than assume a theory of social change, as many comparative educationists do, I make explicit the one on which I base my analysis of problems toward the solution of which educational policies are proposed. Contrary to early comparative educationists, I am prepared to accept, depending on my interest in a vaguely perceived problem, any one of several theories of social change[9] to make my research problem explicit. Failure to analyze a problem in any depth and in ways that cannot be readily followed or replicated by other researchers constitutes one of the most serious weaknesses in traditional comparative education research. Inequality in education and in access to education, economic growth, neo-colonialism, racism, and so on are terms all too frequently used to identify problems without making the constituents of these problems explicit. Gunnar Myrdal's analysis of *An American Dilemma*[10] remains for me a striking example of what can and needs to be done in terms of specific problem analysis.

Indeed, in Myrdal's assumption that individuals are likely at one and the same time to espouse very general and highly laudable views about equality and justice (what I have termed "higher valuations") while at the same time behaving in accordance with their own economic, social, and political self-interests (for me their "lower valuations") lies the source of many problems that may be analyzed in the first stage of comparative education research. In Myrdal's theory of social change, "higher valuations" change while "lower valuations" persist, giving rise to inconsistencies between what individuals say they believe and the way in which they behave. Generalized, new legislation or a new constitution may represent changed aspirations, aims, or "higher valuations." Relatively few individuals quickly learn how to behave in accordance with the new normative statements; a majority continue to be motivated by self-interest. Consequently, it is useful in comparative education to identify new educational legislation and to contrast its behavioral implications with the ways in which teachers, parents, students, politicians, churchmen, and members of other interested groups continue to behave in the light of their "lower valuations." In pluralist societies, of course, "higher valuations" may themselves be debated before and after legislation is passed, and behavior motivated by "lower valuations" may be condoned or go unpunished. Careful specification of the "higher" and "lower" valuations and by whom they are held is necessary if a "technical" problem is to be analyzed in general or in a particular national context.

The context in which many social philosophers put forward their theory of social change was created by processes of industrialization and

[9] Amitai Etzioni and Eva Etzioni, *Social Change: Sources, Patterns and Consequences* (New York: Basic, 1964).
[10] Gunnar Myrdal, *An American Dilemma: The Negro Problem and Modern Democracy* (New York: Harper, 1944).

urbanization during the nineteenth century. It must have been apparent to them that account had to be taken of the changes that were transforming economic life. Most theorists pointed to asynchronous social change, and suggested that technological innovations left individuals incapable immediately of coping with institutions and conditions of life with which neither they nor their ancestors were familiar. Accordingly, most theorists of social change established taxonomies within which they could identify technological and institutional "change" and "relative no change" in the deeply held beliefs or sentiments of individuals.

Comparative educationists interested in technological innovation have a choice of theories on which to base their problem analysis. William Ogburn described the material adaptive, the nonmaterial adaptive, and the nonmaterial nonadaptive aspects of society in order to identify the sources of social or cultural lag.[11] Parenthetically, Ogburn's theory enjoyed a vogue among professors of education at Teachers College such as Harold Rugg, who hoped that through education American society would be reconstructed.[12] Several other theorists pointed to the persistence of deeply held beliefs long after economic circumstances had changed, notably the followers of Marx in the Soviet Union who recognized that even after the economic and political foundations of capitalism had been destroyed in the Revolution, the "false consciousness" of capitalism would linger on in individuals, perhaps for several generations in the Soviet Union, thus giving rise to problems that would only be solved by creating a "New Soviet Man." Central to Soviet educational policy have been attempts to remove this form of cultural lag through appropriate curricula. To facilitate the analysis of a "technical" problem, I am happy to find a place in my paradigm for either a Marxian or Ogburn's theory of social change.

By the same token, there is room for dependency theories, which undoubtedly throw light on some of the issues arising from relationships between people in metropolitan or central nations and peripheral countries. In some cases the assertions made about penetration, distortion, and global concepts of center and periphery reduce the sophistication of any comparative analysis. Nevertheless, the theories of social change established to explain penetration and its consequences have a useful historical component. The value from some points of view of incorporating features of dependency theory in a working paradigm for comparative educationists should not be underrated.

A third type of theory that enables problems associated with change to be analyzed are those in which distinctions are drawn between simple

---

[11] William F. Ogburn, *On Culture and Social Change: Selected Papers* (Chicago: University of Chicago Press, 1964).

[12] Harold Rugg, *The Teacher of Teachers* (New York: Harper, 1952); see also William Graham Sumner, *Social Darwinism* (Englewood Cliffs, N.J.: Prentice-Hall, 1963).

communities or societies and complex ones and between rural communities and urban societies. Among the theories from which a choice may be made are those associated with the names of Ferdinand Tönnies, Max Weber, Émile Durkheim, Robert Redfield, and Talcott Parsons.[13] Each of them make it possible to compare the changes experienced by people who move from rural (within a country or from another country) to urban areas and thus to analyze the difficulties newcomers to the city are likely to face. Implicit or explicit in these theories is the view that rural and urban economic, political, and educational institutions differ. The internalized beliefs of people from rural areas are difficult to change, and consequently problems arise when urban institutions are run on the basis of "rural" values. This judgment points to another kind of social or cultural lag—the source of problems of interest to comparative educationists undertaking research into educational provision in urban areas and societies into which individuals from numerous cultural backgrounds have moved.

My own taxonomy in the light of which I classify relevant social and educational data offers the possibility of identifying various types of asynchronous change and of using any of the theories of social change referred to to sharpen the analysis of a "technical problem" as the starting point of research. I find few of the theories of social change logically incompatible with the assumptions built into my paradigm, in spite of the fact that the epistemologies associated with some of them, for example, that of Marx, are unacceptable. The possibilities of incorporating without distortion theories drawn from one paradigm into another paradigm should not be dismissed, and certainly I find value in using some constituents of a general position with which I am not in agreement. At the same time, social scientists from whose alternative paradigm I have "borrowed" theories may argue that I have misinterpreted them. What is important, however, is how they are used in research. For this reason, as stated earlier, some theories are so unacceptable to me that I would not include them in my paradigm, and others are so central to it that I would not be willing to abandon them in favor of any of several alternatives. One such theory is the basis of my societal taxonomy.

A System for Classifying Societal Data

The system of classification I have built into my paradigm is based on a distinction Popper drew in *The Open Society and Its Enemies* between "normative" and "sociological" laws. The former, he claimed, could be

---

[13] Ferdinand Tönnies, *Community and Association* (London: Routledge & Kegan Paul, 1955); Max Weber, *The Theory of Social and Economic Organisation* (New York: Free Press, 1964), and *The Protestant Ethic and the Spirit of Capitalism* (New York: Scribner's, 1958); Émile Durkheim, *Education and Sociology* (New York: Free Press, 1956); Robert Redfield, "The Folk Society," *American Journal of Sociology* 52 (January 1947): 293–310; Talcott Parsons, *The Structure of Social Action: A Study in Social Theory with Special Reference to a Group of Recent European Writers* (New York: Free Press, 1966).

formulated, accepted, or rejected at will in an open society. Sociological laws, however, are hypothetical statements from which may be logically deduced future outcomes or events. That sociological laws can be formulated implies that human action gives rise to a sequence of events over which we have little control. Much criticism has been leveled at my so-called determinism. While rejecting the charge, I maintain that the consequences of our actions cannot be willed away if they are either unexpected or unwanted.

From this basic distinction, described by Popper as "critical dualism" or "critical conventionalism," I concluded that selected normative statements debated or accepted by individuals in a particular nation could be brought together in a normative pattern. Selection of these statements can be based on theories about the nature of man, society, and knowledge. These theories take the form of what ought to be the case, although they are frequently stated as matters of fact. Such statements find expression in norms about economic man, society, and knowledge; political man, society, and knowledge; and educational man, society, and knowledge. Further differentiation of the normative pattern is possible to include religions, social class, artistic, and other aspects of society. In each of them man's "higher valuations" and metaphysical theories of man, society, and knowledge can be located.

The sources of these beliefs are many, and it would be unwise to assume consensus. Nevertheless, in all countries legislation implies that a measure of agreement has been reached on how the political, economic, religious, educational, defense, and social services affairs of a nation ought to be conducted. National constitutions and charters may provide a framework into which more specific recommendations must fit. As in the case of all normative laws, constitutional provisions and legislation may constantly be challenged in party political manifestos, in advisory committee recommendations, and by organized groups representing economic, religious, and educational opinion. Popper's criterion of "open societies" was that in them such challenges are freely permitted and dissent is not punished. It is consequently important to recognize that in classifying normative data, selection is inevitable, and a final national pattern, unless only national legislation is included, is an "ideal typical model" designed to clarify and simplify an enormous number of controversial data. In drawing up an ideal typical normative model it is important that the sources from which it is drawn are made public.

To establish an ideal typical institutional pattern is more difficult. The way in which I use the term "institution" implies that in the light of policy statements men and women create organizations and act through them, but in some sense these institutions exist independently of the people who run them. Institutions, however, have no life of their own, and cannot be motivated or seek to achieve aims or purposes. Only people have aims and purposes and seek to achieve them by establishing political, economic, religious, educational, and other types of institutions. Sociological laws describe hypothetical relationships between institutions and can be located in the institutional pattern. The assumption that sociological laws can be formulated implies that correlational statements can be made or causal relationships established about the consequences for ourselves and for other people of the way we behave in running institutions and organizations.

Many sociologists, political scientists, and economists of course claim that causal relationships exist between social class and access to education and between the provision of education and political stability and economic growth. My view is that only through examining the interaction of individuals in organizations can sociological laws (policy solutions) that link institutions in hypothetical relationships be studied and tested. I reject categorically the interpretation placed on my use of the term "sociological law" by my critics. The determinism associated with sociological laws comes from an aetiology (theory of causation) that I discarded long ago and finds no place in my paradigm. That is not to say, however, that I have worked out fully how sociological laws can be tested. They are, however, of fundamental importance to successful planning and to piecemeal social engineering. We use them all the time, without always making them explicit, when we anticipate the outcomes of our behavior. The possibility of formulating hypothetical, testable, and refutable sociological laws is central to my paradigm. This commitment does not make me a determinist, since sociological laws remain for me hypothetical, contingent, and refutable under given circumstances.

Thus insofar as institutional patterns describe institutions and the relationships between them (although mediated through human behavior), they are made up of statements about societal artifacts that exist even though we may not choose to describe them. They are components of our social world just as the terrain, geological resources, climate, and so on are constituents of our natural environment. Descriptions of features of the natural environment and relationship statements about them cohere as astronomy, physics, chemistry, botany, zoology, geology, and geography, that is, as the natural sciences. The natural environment and its descriptors is a third important part of my taxonomy, and consequently, unlike many social scientific paradigms, data from the natural sciences codified as theories and beliefs are included in my paradigm.

The fourth pattern is central to most sociological theory. It is made up of the mental states of individuals. They are more like Myrdal's "lower

valuations," Marx's "false consciousness," or Pareto's[14] "residues" than anything else. They are recognized not in what people say ought to be the
case, but in what they do. The need to distinguish them carefully from
the normative statements found in legislation is very important if "technical
problems" are to be identified and analyzed. To describe mental states is
difficult, and I have suggested that to do so, reference should be made
to historical philosophical positions from which beliefs and values have
historically been taken, disseminated, and internalized so as to become
the motivation of human behavior. For Europeans I have suggested that
Plato's views, expressed in *The Republic,* are a source from which can be
inferred important European mental states. These have been modified,
but not entirely eliminated, as a result of normative innovations that have
been internalized by some, but not all, Europeans. Pragmatic beliefs,
formulated in the late nineteenth century in the United States, now motivate
Americans, and Soviet leaders have worked since the Revolution to create
a New Soviet Man who would be motivated to act in accordance not with
Platonic or laissez-faire beliefs but in the light of Marxist-Leninism.

Beliefs about the nature of man, society, and knowledge are criteria
in the light of which "mental states" can be classified. They can be sub-
classified into mental states about economic, political, religious, and educational man and society and knowledge in the same way as normative
statements. They cannot, however, be accurately inferred from responses
to attitude tests or deduced from national legislation. Consequently, rather
arbitrarily, philosophical sources, both religious and secular, have to be
selected and used to prepare "ideal typical models" of a nation's mental
states. I have suggested Platonic and Christian sources for Europe as a
whole and the writings of Descartes and Locke for France and England,
respectively, but the beliefs and theories of other philosophers could
usefully be taken as sources of ideal typical national models.

In summary, then, within my paradigm I include normative, institutional, national environmental, and mental states patterns. Each is inevitably based on a selection from available data and must be considered
as providing extremely simplified ideal typical models that can be used
in problem analysis and in helping to predict the outcomes of policy
solutions. They should not, as I have repeatedly had to write, be used to
stereotype individuals or groups of individuals or to justify notions of
national character that lead to such stereotyping. Distinctions should be
made between normative laws, which can be accepted or rejected freely
in open societies; sociological laws, which can be refuted; the natural laws
of physics, chemistry, biology, and so on; and the internalized beliefs
about man, society, and knowledge that I describe as mental states and
that can best be inferred from a traditional philosophical position.

[14] Vilfredo Pareto, *Sociological Writings* (Oxford: Blackwell, 1976).

Policy Formulation, Adoption, and Implementation

Since natural scientists can test their hypotheses under controlled conditions, it is not particularly relevant to know how natural scientific hypotheses are formulated. Social scientific hypotheses cannot usually be tested experimentally, so that the participants in the processes of formulating policy solutions should be known if we are to anticipate whether or not they will be adopted and how they can be implemented. A further assumption I make is that individuals attempt to realize their aims by creating institutions and by working through them. The study of sociological laws can best be undertaken through analysis and description of the processes of policy implementation. Hence in order to investigate institutional relations expressed in sociological laws it is necessary to have models and techniques that are devoid of specific content.

For this purpose I habitually turn to an ideal typical formal organization model derived from Talcott Parsons.[15] I assume that in most democratic formal organizations some members form a public interest group intended to represent the wishes of an electorate. Parliaments, assemblies, local school boards, boards of directors, and so on constitute public interest groups in formal organizations in various spheres of life. A second group of members have managerial functions to perform; such individuals are usually appointed and interact not only with members of the public interest group but with members of the third group within a formal organization, namely, the technical personnel who deliver the service the organization is intended to provide. In the case of educational organizations, teachers are the technical personnel.

In the formulation of policy, I assume that interaction takes place between individuals in all three groups either informally or as a result of agreed-upon committee procedures and rules of office. The model is based on a rejection of the view that members of the public interest group formulate policy, managers adopt it, and technical personnel implement it. I also assume that in all three processes participants outside the formal organization have roles to play. Such participants may act through their own formal organizations designed to represent the wishes of politicians, employers, workers, parents, students, churchmen, and other pressure groups. Depending on the issue, such groups may participate in either the formulation, adoption, or implementation of policy. One thing is clear; the formal adoption of a policy does not ensure that it will be implemented unless individuals responsible for its implementation have incorporated appropriate beliefs into their mental states.

---

[15] Talcott Parsons, "Some Ingredients of a General Theory of Formal Education," in *Administrative Theory in Education,* ed. Andrew W. Halpin (Chicago: Midwest Administration Center, University of Chicago, 1958).

In most sovereign states, national formal organizations in the form of ministries of education have been established. In some countries, regional or provincial formal organizations are legally responsible for education. Again, in most countries, local formal organizations are responsible for some aspects of the educational system. Personnel in these organizations interact with each other in the formulation, adoption, and implementation of educational policy, and it is the task of the comparative education research worker to examine carefully the various forms of interaction.

These differ in accordance with the issue. On some questions of policy— for example, teachers' salaries—discussions may be restricted to the providers of the service—the teachers—and those responsible for paying for it—either, in publicly maintained schools, managers and public interest personnel, or in private schools, fee-paying parents. Questions of teachers' pay may be mediated by statutory regulations, national agreements, and national teacher association pressure if teachers are civil servants. If they are employed by the local school board, the politics may be similar, but localized, and property holders may have a much more decisive say in the outcome of negotiations than national income taxpayers have on the finalization of national teacher salary schedules. The final outcome of salary negotiations, whether conducted nationally or locally, should be viewed in the wider economic and political context, but my formal organization model makes it possible for the participants to be identified and their interaction analyzed.

Other educational issues are debated more widely by members of all kinds of social consensus groups. The aims or purposes of education are usually discussed informally by churchmen, politicians, industrialists, and teachers as well as by other members of society. Consensus may not be reached; some participants may wish to emphasize child-centered aims, while others may be in favor of aims related to the social benefits of education. The outcome of such debates may or may not be formulated in national legislation or the manifestos of political parties. In comparative perspective, the relative power of different groups to ensure that their educational aims are adopted varies considerably from country to country, but the range of persons involved is usually considerable.

A third type of issue is the concern of teachers. Of these issues, the content of education, methods of teaching, and examination techniques fall, regardless of systems of administration, within the province of teacher negotiations. Among the teachers involved are those teaching at all three levels of education. Debates about curricula may take place among primary school teachers or between them and secondary school teachers. At the third level, professors of education may disagree with professors of other subjects about the proper content of higher education. University traditions of academic freedom and the traditional influence academics have had

191

on school curricula legitimize the desire of teachers to restrict discussions about content and methods of teaching to members of the teaching profession.

Indeed, the formal organizations to which members of a profession belong are unique in that it is accepted that the public interest will be served by members of the profession regulating their activities in accordance with a code of ethics in which the public good is placed above the receipt of monetary reward. Medical doctors and lawyers even today regulate their own affairs by laying down training requirements and by controlling entry to the profession. Professions nevertheless have their own public interest group in the form of a general medical council or a law society that is responsible for the maintenance of ethical standards. The professions also have their administrators and general practitioners. Teachers aspire to become members of a profession, but the public service they are expected to perform is now disputed in many countries, teachers cannot agree among themselves what esoteric knowledge all teachers should possess, and national or local governments attempt to regulate the supply of teachers in the light of changing demands.

The fact that teachers meet some of the criteria for membership of a profession means that they are responsible for some aspects of policy and are almost exclusively responsible for what takes place in classroom and lecture hall. In order to analyze in more detail the role teachers play, and in order to describe school systems comprehensively, a taxonomy is required. The one I helped to work out in a meeting at the Hamburg Unesco Institute for Education in 1963[16] and subsequently developed for the International Bureau of Education in Geneva[17] serves me well and has an important place in my paradigm. It includes aims, administration, finance, structure and organization, curricula, and teacher education and training.

There is widespread agreement that education should be a human right provided for all regardless of age, gender, race, language spoken, religious belief, socioeconomic background, and place of domicile. Most educationists agree that schools should develop the all-round—intellectual, physical, aesthetic, and moral—potential of children. They also agree that education should benefit society by promoting economic growth, by sustaining democratic forms of government, and by helping to maintain peace. Appropriate knowledge and attitudes should be inculcated through the schools. In terms of emphasis, the aims of education may be child-, society-, or knowledge-centered. National differences can be detected in the balance between the three aims and in the attitudes and knowledge

[16] Brian Holmes and Saul B. Robinson, eds., *Relevant Data in Comparative Education: Report of an Expert Meeting, March 11–16, 1963* (Hamburg: Unesco Institute for Education, 1963).
[17] Brian Holmes, *International Guide to Educational Systems* (Paris: Unesco, 1979).

national educationists think important. In most ideal typical normative models, child-, society-, and knowledge-centered aims cohere.

As for the administration of education, there is a clearly identifiable trend toward decentralization as a way of increasing participation. In spite of this trend, in many countries personnel in the national ministry of education are very powerful and play a decisive role in the formulation, adoption, and, over some aspects of education, the implementation of policy. A major aim of policy today, however, is to equalize opportunity, access to, and the provision of education to meet general aims, and the achievement of this goal may imply increasing the power of the central agencies of administration.

Certainly to equalize provision throughout a nation involves providing financial support for the less wealthy communities at the expense of the more wealthy citizens. Consequently, the trend is that, while devolving power, central administrations are raising a higher proportion of the expenditure on education and have more responsibility for its distribution. Local communities differ greatly in their ability to raise money for schools. Methods of financing them are changing. Revenue for education consequently depends less on local property taxes and more on national income taxes than was previously the case.

As for the structure and organization of school systems, the trend is toward universalizing first-level education (where this has not been achieved), reorganizing second-level education along comprehensive lines, expanding third-level education, and introducing lifelong education by providing preschool facilities and improving adult and recurrent education. Debates turn on whether universal primary education should be provided in formal schools or through nonformal basic educational activities. Several models of comprehensive second-level schools exist from which a choice can be made—the Soviet, American, and British models are well-known examples. Third-level systems also vary. In the United States and Japan, at this level of education junior colleges and comprehensive universities offer opportunities for an extremely high proportion of young adults. Elsewhere, binary or tripartite systems of higher education include traditional universities, specialized technical universities, and pedagogical institutes. Many reforms have been initiated by party politicians whose views are left of center. Debates on all these issues involve teachers, although in the final analysis their views may not prevail. Frequently they ally themselves with party politicians.

As stated, teachers play a decisive role in the formulation, adoption, and implementation of curriculum policies. It is they who claim to know what knowledge is of most worth in the development of the potential of individuals, not only in their own interests but in the interest of society.

The politics of curriculum reform are restricted to teachers and their allies. Among these allies may be other members of educational formal organizations and groups of people, as mentioned, outside these organizations who have an interest in education.

Teachers are also very much concerned with teacher education policies, although they do not enjoy the power of medical doctors to regulate admission to training courses and the subsequent employment of their colleagues. To a large extent, however, teachers in third-level institutions determine the content of teacher education programs and are responsible for evaluating students as they pass through or leave the course of training. Frequently the recommendations of teacher educators are accepted by formal organizations such as a national ministry of education or a state board of education as the basis on which a certificate to teach is issued. Unlike medicine and the law, which are client-centered professions, attendance at school is now rarely a matter of choice. Compulsory attendance laws have been adopted by government, and consequently governments have a direct interest in the certification of teachers to ensure that schools are adequately staffed. Demand and supply problems have some bearing on how governments react to the training and certification of teachers. Consequently, teachers do not have the power to regulate entry to the profession in the way medical doctors and lawyers are able to regulate entry to their professions.

The content of teacher education, methods of training them, and examination procedures may be debated by teachers at different levels and within each level by teachers whose normative values differ, and indeed by teachers whose mental states differ. Professors of education are likely to advocate teacher training programs designed to ensure that teachers can realize child- or even society-centered aims. Their views may well be shared by first-level teachers and some second-level teachers. On the other hand, professors of other subjects and second-level teachers whose mental states are traditional may stress the importance of subject matter knowledge in the training of teachers. Only occasionally are persons from outside the teaching profession (widely conceived) brought into debates about the content of teacher education courses.

This taxonomy of educational aspects is useful in that it suggests the kind of sociological laws that might be established for institutions—relating, for example, structure and organization with curriculum, or administration with finance, or teacher education with finance. All these aspects of education have been institutionalized. Relationships between stated aims and institutionalized practices are deliberately excluded as falling within the category of sociological laws. What I am asserting, however, is that sociological laws that place the institutions in a causal relationship can best be tested by using formal organization models to examine the politics of policy formulation and adoption and to predict the possibilities of successful implementation.

Note should be taken of my reluctance to accept quantitative methods of comparative testing adopted by the sociologists of education and the economists of education because they do not take sufficiently into account the politics of implementing policies, which are in the form of hypothetical solutions based on relationship statements, under specific national circumstances. This is not, however, to deny the value of operationalizing statements on both sides of a sociological law. Social class position and access to education, amount of education provided, and political stability and investment in education and economic growth are useful hypothetical solutions to perceived problems, and each side of the equations can be operationalized. Tests designed to refute these statements under specified conditions should be carried out by analyzing the sources of political resistance to proposed policies.

Short- and Long-Term Planning

The difficulties of planning educational provision are manifold. Planning has been defined as a process of reaching decisions (or policies) that will, when put into practice, achieve stated objectives. In my paradigm, planning processes have a place. They include ways in which policies are formulated and adopted and an assessment of the possibilities of successful implementation. For me planning also involves discarding policies not likely to work in the light of predicted outcomes. Thus a paradigm shift involves replacing the assumption that planning is simply a matter of reaching decisions that will lead to success by assuming that a more important task for planners is that of discriminating between alternative policies with the intention of rejecting (or refuting) those that will not lead to desired outcomes.

Mathematical techniques, including linear programming and games theory, are being adapted by one of my colleagues, David Turner, to operationalize this feature of planning. Linear programming techniques and games theory make it possible to show how detailed national constraints (if normative and institutional constraints can be quantified) affect and limit realistic choice. It is very evident that linear programming techniques cannot be used except in highly specific circumstances, and consequently to employ them satisfactorily an intimate knowledge of norms, institutions, economic resources, political pressures, and mental states must be acquired. Some of this information may be available in international statistics, but if the techniques are to be used the comparative educationist must be in a position to collect national (or local) data relevant to the technical problem and the alternative policy solutions under consideration. The fact that the identification of a "technical problem" directs the attention of the researcher to some rather than all possible types of information makes data selection much more possible and effective. It is one of the major advantages of the "problem-solving" approach in comparative education.

Examples have been designed to illustrate how these techniques can be used to reduce the number of policy alternatives under a known set of circumstances. Turner is developing these further. As part of my paradigm, when refined through realistic examples, they will add greatly to the possibilities of planning educational provision more adequately. The value of a comparative approach lies in the possibility of learning from the experience of other countries what constraints should be taken into account and then quantifying them.

Linear programming techniques highlight some of the differences between piecemeal social engineering and holistic planning and between short- and long-term planning. They are designed to help comparative educationists advise on which given alternatives policy is not immediately capable of being realized in practice. Take, for example, the constraints in England associated with the desire on the part of government that more girls should study physics. A choice lies between developing coeducational or retaining single-sex schools. More parents may be encouraged to send their daughters to coeducational schools, and more teachers may be willing to teach in either single-sex or coeducational schools. Specifically, however, in England, with a sizeable Moslem population, account would have to be taken of hostile parental attitudes to coeducational schools for their daughters. Given the number of women qualified to teach physics, it would be necessary to know how many men could be persuaded to teach in girls' schools. To formulate additional policy options, it may be necessary if parental choice is to be increased to persuade some participants to act differently and to make more resources available.

The techniques demonstrate, if further demonstration is necessary, that panaceas to vaguely perceived problems are unlikely to work in the short term. Investment in education is one such panacea. The universalization of primary schooling is another. The reorganization of second-level schooling along comprehensive lines is yet another widely advocated panacea. They are, if anything, long-term aims and objectives, and insofar as they reflect highly desirable norms, cannot be refuted. Linear programming techniques are designed to demonstrate which policies, legitimized by high ideals, will not work in the short term under carefully stated conditions.

Theoretical and Practical Implications

My choice of paradigm has theoretical and practical implications. Theoretically it involves a rejection of positivism and induction as the method of science and the notion that absolute knowledge can be expressed in universal laws. It also involves a rejection of certain overt theories or covert assumptions accepted in the past by comparative educationists. My rejection of the assumption that the first stage of comparative education research should be the objective collection of "facts" constitutes a fundamental difference between my position and that of George Bereday. My acceptance of the view that a clearly articulated "technical problem" should be the starting point of enquiry differentiates my position from that of Harold Noah and Max Eckstein. The search for antecedent "causes" of social events advocated by Isaac Kandel, Friedreich Schneider, and Nicholas Hans is replaced in my paradigm by a forward-looking attempt to anticipate or predict the outcomes of policy. Correlation studies carried out by sociologists and economists of education are regarded by me as methodologically flawed because they pay too little attention to specific national conditions and assume too readily that functional relationships, represented in their simplest form by the equation $y = mx + c$, can be examined comparatively by operationalizing two variables in order to quantify and measure them in as many countries as possible so as to establish universal correlations.

In place of the methodological assumptions derived from positivism and induction, I have adopted aetologies, ontologies, and epistemologies based on John Dewey's method of reflective thinking and Karl Popper's hypothetico-deductive method. I prefer Popper's assertion that pure scientists should seek to refute tentative hypotheses to Dewey's insistence that problem solving involves verifying hypotheses. Both assume that the starting point of enquiry should be a problem. I consider that "technical problems" can be identified and studied in the light of a suitable theory of social change, many of which draw attention to changes in scientific knowledge and its technological applications. However, I am prepared to accept as a problem-creating change and the starting point of enquiry an innovation in one of my four societal patterns. In the absence of experimental testing procedures, which make it unnecessary for natural scientists to discuss how hypotheses are formulated, I assume comparative educationists need a model and techniques for examining in comparative perspective how policies are formulated and adopted and with what success they are likely to be implemented. For this purpose I have adapted a model from Talcott Parsons to analyze how members in various formal organizations and pressure groups outside them participate in the processes of policy formulation, adoption, and implementation.

Analyses of the difficulties of implementing adopted policies are based mainly on the assumption that, while the rhetoric or "higher valuations" of persons involved in a political process may be decisive in the formulation and adoption of policy, persisting "mental states," which may be very different, motivate behavior and hence influence significantly the ways in which policy is implemented.

Important in any prediction of how policy will be put into practice is a detailed knowledge of specific initial conditions that for most comparative educationists are national circumstances. Consequently, fundamental to my paradigm is a classificatory system that makes it possible for the research worker to describe accurately and weight the specific national circumstances within which a policy is to be implemented. The complexity of these circumstances and the distinction between our social, mental, and physical worlds draws attention to the need for simplified ideal typical models to describe our "real" worlds. In practice, before the success or failure of a policy can be predicted, knowledge of these worlds must be available. Normative statements about the nature of man, society, and knowledge can be inferred from constitutions, legislation, and psychological, socio-logical, and epistemological theories. General statements find specific expression in legislation dealing with political, economic, religious, ed-ucational, social welfare, and other societal activities. Legislation implies policies that are realized through the establishment of organizations and institutions. These can be described and the processes of implementing policies analyzed by using a formal organizational model derived from Parsons. Sociological laws can be established relating the operation of one institution with another. These relationships may be between either different educational institutions or an educational institution and a socioeconomic or political institution. Consequently, taxonomies of societal institutions and for educational institutions are needed in order to classify collected data. Tasks for the comparative educationist are to describe relevant in-stitutions and establish sociological laws that relate them together. An adequate description of institutions and mental states is necessary if testing under particular circumstances is to be carried out satisfactorily.

The "mental states" of people inform their behavior. Without knowledge of mental states it is impossible to predict human behavior. Consequently, some way of describing mental states is necessary. To do so requires the establishment of "ideal typical models" drawn not from attitude tests but from philosophical sources. Choice of source is somewhat arbitrary, but should clearly be based in part on historical judgments. For example, the writings of either Descartes or Condorcet may be selected as a source of an ideal typical model of French mental states. Similarly, either Locke, Burke, or Shakespeare may be selected as offering an ideal typical model for England. Choice from the alternatives is a matter of judgment. Once a choice has been made, a simplified ideal typical model can be established by selecting information about the chosen philosopher's views about man, society, and knowledge. Criteria for selecting data about man include concepts of equality, intelligence, kindness, aggression, and so on. Data about a philosopher's view of society include its economic, political, social class, religious, and educational aspects, while a broad distinction can be drawn between empirical, rational, and negotiated theories of knowledge. In establishing ideal typical models, it should be recognized that they are not intended accurately to describe reality but only to simplify an otherwise unmanageable number of data and to facilitate the analysis of problems and the testing of hypothetical solutions. Legislation, institutions, and mental states constitute man's social world.

The physical environment constitutes man's natural world. The presence of natural resources, climate, rainfall, fertility of the earth, and so on all influence the extent to which policies will achieve desired goals.

The practical implications for planners of my paradigm are significant. One implication is that we should not as comparative educationists seek educational panaceas and should be suspicious of those offered to us. Theories within the paradigm suggest that planners have two somewhat different tasks to perform. They may discriminate between policies in order to eliminate those least likely to work under particular circumstances. A second objective for which planning techniques are needed is to demonstrate how a policy that has been adopted can be made to work. Research workers should be able to show what consequential changes—in norms, institutions, and mental states—will be needed if the policy is to achieve stated goals or aims. Techniques are required to discriminate between policies and to demonstrate logically how policies can be implemented successfully. Some of these techniques in my paradigm are mathematical; others are based on systems analysis. Much more work has still to be done on this aspect of the problem-solving approach that can be used by comparative educationists as "pure" and applied social scientists. It is, in other words, a paradigm for comparative education as a generalizing science and as a set of assumptions for advisers and planners.

In this article it has not been possible to do more than mention some major features of the paradigm shifts I have proposed and to suggest theories, models, and techniques that could replace the assumptions of our earlier generation of comparative educationists. Since the changes are theoretically quite fundamental, I do not expect comparative educationists to accept them. Nor do I expect that their mental states will change to any great extent. Consequently, until Popper's assumptions about scientific method have been more fully internalized, I expect comparative educationists, in a commonsense sort of way, to conduct research in the light of assumptions and beliefs I reject. It is a fate most radicals should be prepared to accept.

The Necessity of Comparisons in the Study of Education: The Salience of Science and the Problem of Comparability

JOSEPH P. FARRELL

Traditionally, presidential addresses at CIES annual meetings have attempted to assess the "state of the art" of comparative and international education, typically suggesting that we are still far from God, if not close to the devil, and to offer some suggestions intended to increase our degree of saintliness. I am enough of a student of educational planning and educational reform efforts to realize that there are dangers attendant to breaking with tradition, and enough of an Ontario Tory to believe that some traditions are worth upholding. I do not promise to bring you any closer to God, though I do hope these next few minutes will not be a foretaste of purgatory.

In recent years society presidents have told us many times that our theoretical work must be more explicit and rigorous, and less embedded in traditional theoretical constructs, and have offered us a variety of specific problems, or classes of problems, upon which to focus our work.[1] We have in these last few years largely abandoned our concern with a set of "grand questions" which preoccupied members of the field in its early years. Is comparative education a discipline? With which other social sciences does it, or ought it to, have the closest links? How "quantitative" should comparative studies be? We have in a sense replaced these with a new set of "grand questions." What is the appropriate theoretical base for the field? To which key policy questions can we most fruitfully direct our attention? Debate on those earlier questions dwindled as we became convinced that there neither were, nor had to be, final universal answers to them. The latter set of questions likewise requires no definitive answers for our field to thrive. There is room for a variety of theoretical orientations; what is important is that the theoretical work be explicit and rigorous. There are a host of significant policy-related questions upon which we can usefully concentrate; the success of the enterprise will be

This paper (Presidential Address) was delivered to the annual meetings of the Comparative and International Education Society, Mexico City, March 1978.
[1] See, e.g., A. M. Kazamias, "Comparative Pedagogy: An Assignment for the 1970s," *Comparative Education Review* 16 (October 1972): 406–11; H. J. Noah, "Fast Fish and Loose Fish in Comparative Education," ibid., 18 (October 1974): 341–47; C. S. Brembeck, "The Future of Comparative Education," ibid., 19 (October 1975): 369–74; and R. G. Paulston, "Ethnicity and Educational Change: A Priority for Comparative Education," ibid., 20 (October 1976): 269–77.

Reprinted from *Comparative Education Review*, vol. 23, no. 1 (February 1979).

judged by the conceptual and methodological sophistication of the work and the salience and durability of the findings.

As I examine recent work in our field, and especially the material in the twentieth anniversary issue of the *Comparative Education Review*,[2] I conclude that we have made great strides in the past two decades. We have, in Noah's metaphor, collected many "fast fish."[3] However, we still have many problems, and, in good academic fashion, it is upon these that I would like to concentrate. (It should be noted that these problems are shared by social science generally; this should not be surprising, as we have always been shameless borrowers from the more established social science fields.)[4]

There is a lack of cumulation in our findings; we have many interesting bits and pieces of information, but they seldom seem to relate to one another. We have little in the way of useful and concise theory; what pass for theory ordinarily are abstracted rhetorical "world views"—for example, structural functionalism, a conflict or dependency orientation—unoperationalized and with little predictive power. Our research results are generally of little use to, and little used by, policymakers. These problems are interrelated. Without cumulated results it is difficult to build or test theory. Conversely, without well-defined theoretical premises it is difficult to cumulate results. And until we do have cumulated results, related to a growing body of theory, we will have little useful to say to policymakers. In summary, we have little impact upon policymaking not because we are focusing on the wrong questions, but because we have little to say about the questions we do address. And we will not find something useful to say simply by directing our efforts to studies of popular policy issues of the day—by being trendy. We will have something useful to say only when our observations regarding any particular policy problem are rooted in a more general understanding of how educational systems work, which is in turn based upon cumulated discoveries organized into and by theory. It is in understanding the role of comparative data in the building of theory about education that we can develop a central role for our field. Much of what I have to say about this role is not new. However, as with a good stew made from common ingredients, I hope the resultant mixture will be savory.

A basic assumption of my argument is that there is no such thing as comparative methodology. There are *comparative data*, to which a variety of analytical tools may be applied, the whole enterprise being constrained

---

[2] *Comparative Education Review* 21, nos. 2–3 (June–October 1977).

[3] Noah (n. 1 above).

[4] See, e.g., the 14 essays in the special issue on "The Future of Social Science" in *Society*, vol. 15 (March–April 1978).

by the requirements of the *scientific method*. Comparative education is one of several fields of enquiry which attempt to study a class of phenomena usually called "education," which seek, that is, to explain the complex web of interrelationships which can be observed within educational systems and between educational systems and other kinds of systems.

Comparative Education and the Scientific Study of Education

The question of whether comparative education, or the study of social behavior generally, is, can be, or should be "scientific" has been the subject of much debate over the years. The argument has until recently been mostly sterile, primarily because it has tended to center on a conception of the nature of science so pure and positivistic that it would likely horrify most working physical scientists—those who have been our unwitting role models. Scientific method is not a rigid set of prescriptions; it is a highly flexible and adaptable way to order our perceptions of the external world. I share the view of Silvert and Reissman, who described science as "a convention based on the belief that informed intellectual playfulness without fear of social sanction is 'good' for society, because it enlarges social understandings, broadens available alternatives, and enriches societies by making them more flexible, responsive, and able to take advantage of individual differences."[5] Contrary to the popular view, science is a fundamentally humanistic enterprise. However, as with any convention, science has its rules. I suggest, though, that there are only a few essential characteristics which distinguish scientific from nonscientific behavior. It is in understanding these characteristics that we may come to appreciate the special potential of comparative studies of education.

Science is, first of all, *systematic*. It is assumed that there exists a certain degree of order and uniformity in the world, that events are not random but are connected in a regular and constant way. As Einstein's famous aphorism put it, "the lord is subtle, but he isn't simply mean." In the specific field of human behavior it is assumed that there is regularity in the activities of human beings, and that some at least of these regularities hold across cultures. The extreme historicist position, that each cultural system can only be studied as a unique entity, is emphatically denied, as is the extreme phenomenological position that behavioral "facts" can have no meaning outside of their meaning for the person whose behavior is observed. Related to the above is the assumption that the order which exists in the world is discoverable by man, "that a communication tie,

[5] K. Silvert and L. Reissman, *Education, Class and Nation: The Experiences of Chile and Venezuela* (New York: American Elsevier, 1976), p. xi.

based upon sense impressions, exists between the scientist and 'external reality.'"[6]

Additionally, science is systematic in the way in which it tries to organize the knowledge of the external world which is acquired. The object is not simply to discover more and more "facts," but to organize and simplify such knowledge. It being obviously impossible to know everything, even in a fairly restricted field, in any useful sense, we try first to use what is discovered to establish generalizations which indicate the class of phenomena over which a given relationship holds. Second, we attempt to organize these generalizations into a hierarchy of increasingly abstract statements which are logically connected so that the more general can be said to explain the less general. In short, we attempt to build theory.

A second general characteristic of science is that it is *empirical*. Flowing from the assumption that it is possible to "know" the external world is the prescription that statements in science be tied implicitly or explicitly with a set of actual or potential sense experiences. This may be obvious, but as I read the debates in our field I note one point that is the source of some confusion. It is important to emphasize the presence in this prescription of the words "implicitly" and "potential." Education is one of a number of fields where the conceptual sophistication or technology are not yet sufficiently developed to permit one to observe directly many phenomena of interest. Likewise, in the social sciences there are many things we can never observe directly (attitudes, for example, or an entire economic system). These are not critical considerations.

The third, and for our purposes most important, general characteristic of science is that it is *comparative*. In a sense, of course, as Andreski has noted, "comparisons (verbal or numerical) enter into all induction. . . ."[7] Carrying this theme further, Reginald Edwards, in his presidential address to the 1970 annual meeting of CIES, dwelt at some length on the role of comparison in human thought processes.[8] The object of science is not simply to determine that relationships exist, but to determine the range over which they exist. It is simply not possible to conceive of a generalizing science which is not inherently comparative.

It is important to understand why this is so, as this shapes much of my view of what comparative education is about. Clearly the job of science is not simply to develop testable propositions about the relations between variables, which can then be built into theory, but to actually test them. I

[6] G. Sjoberg and R. Nett, *A Methodology for Social Research* (New York: Harper & Row, 1968), p. 23.

[7] S. Andreski, *The Uses of Comparative Sociology* (Berkeley: University of California Press, 1965), p. 66.

[8] R. Edwards, "The Dimensions of Comparison and of Comparative Education," *Comparative Education Review* 14 (October 1970): 239–54.

accept Popper's position that a single negative finding can serve to logically disprove a proposition (so long as it is deterministic, containing an implicit or explicit "always" statement). However, a single positive test cannot in the same logical sense "prove" a proposition; it only makes it more credible. But only slightly more credible, since it has been tested in only one setting at one point in time. One has no idea if the particular setting or time is typical or represents a special case. So one must proceed to test the proposition in other settings and time periods. Each additional test of the proposition adds to its credibility, if the relationship is in each case in the predicted direction. In short, comparative data are essential to establish the credibility of propositions.

What happens when one discovers that a proposition holds in some cases but not in others—a frequent case in studies of education? One is then led to ask what is peculiar about the settings where the relationship does not go in the predicted direction. This leads one to attempt to refine the proposition by introducing specifying variables, producing ever more complex understandings of how variables are interrelated. As Noah pointed out 4 years ago, it is only when educational research produces such carefully specified propositions that its results are likely to have an impact upon policymaking,[9] and comparative analysis is essential to develop such propositions.

Comparison, it should be noted, is particularly critical in the study of human behavior. First, the argument above has been phrased in terms of deterministic, or "always" propositions, which can be falsified by a single negative case. Most propositions regarding human behavior, however, are probabilistic, taking the form: "the greater A, the likelier B." Here the logical relation between the results of a single test and the status of the proposition is even less clear, and comparative data are even more necessary.

Second, the physical scientist is ordinarily working with relatively homogeneous material. A sample of, say, heavy water created in the United States is the same as one created in China, or wherever. Thus a "crucial experiment," wherever conducted, can provide definitive information regarding heavy water. It is assumed that the "special universe" being studied, the sample, is completely representative of the general universe, all heavy water. The role of comparison is not to compare different samples of heavy water, but to compare the effects of different variables and controls on its behavior, and to compare heavy water with the behavior of other (equally homogeneous) materials. In the study of human behavior one cannot make this assumption of complete identity between special and general universes. We know that people in different

[9] Noah (n. 1 above), p. 346.

cultures and nations behave quite differently in at least some respects. We do not know in what respects all of humanity, or certain segments of it, can be considered homogeneous. Hence the question of the representativeness of a particular sample becomes crucial, and the need to sample data from a wide variety of nations and cultures becomes paramount. Comparison enters into the study of *human* behavior at an earlier point.

From these two arguments flows a third. The need for comparative data applies even if one is testing a proposition through the use of controlled experimentation in a laboratory setting. Suppose, for example, that one is interested in the effect of various environmental factors upon the ways in which children perceive stimuli, as part of an effort to build a theory of learning. Even the most elegant experiment performed using white North American children will produce results that are credible only for white North American children. There is strong evidence that the perception of even such elemental features of the environment as noise levels and the color spectrum varies from culture to culture.[10] At a broader level, Hall has made the fundamental point that "people reared in different cultures *learn to learn* differently."[11] If one wishes to establish a proposition in this area which is credible for all children, or at least for children other than North American whites, one must perform the experiment with children from other, different cultures and compare the results. In short, until we do know the relationship between special and general universes, no single test of a proposition, however conducted, will suffice. There must always be comparative data. Comparison is not simply a substitute for controlled experimentation, as many have argued.

Much of the ground covered thus far has been trod before, although in different format and organization, especially in Noah and Eckstein's landmark book, and in Barber's excellent critique of methodologism masquerading as science.[12] However, Noah and Eckstein limited their argument in a significant way when they claimed that "not all propositions in education and society require cross-national treatment. . . ,"[13]

---

[10] See, e.g., the experiments conducted by Lenneberg and colleagues: R. W. Brown and E. H. Lenneberg, "A Study in Language and Cognition," *Journal of Abnormal Social Psychology* 49 (1954): 454–62; E. H. Lenneberg and J. M. Roberts, "The Language of Experience," *International Journal of American Linguistics*, vol. 22, suppl. (1956). More recently, see J. Gay and M. Cole, *The New Mathematics in an Old Culture: A Study of Learning among the Kpelle of Liberia* (New York: Holt, Rinehart & Winston, 1971).

[11] E. H. Hall, "The Vocabulary of Culture," in *Introduction to Education: A Comparative Analysis*, ed. D. K. Adams (Belmont, Calif.: Wadsworth, 1966), p. 62; see also M. Cole et al., *The Cultural Context of Learning and Thinking* (New York: Basic, 1971).

[12] H. J. Noah and M. A. Eckstein, *Toward a Science of Comparative Education* (London: Macmillan, 1969); B. R. Barber, "Science, Salience, and Comparative Education: Some Reflections on Social Scientific Inquiry," *Comparative Education Review* 16 (October 1972): 430.

[13] Noah and Eckstein, p. 118.

even though they went on to add that "even in single-country studies, the cross-national dimension can *enrich* explanation."[14] As may be obvious, I do not accept this limitation. My position is that *every* proposition regarding education (indeed, regarding human behavior generally) ultimately requires cross-national treatment.

Simply discovering that a given relationship holds in a particular society is of little use unless we understand *why* the relationship holds, unless, that is, we have an *explanation* for it. Any explanation contains a reference, whether implicit or explicit, to a theory. In an important sense one never explains an event or a relationship simply by referring to another event or phenomenon, past, present, or (in the case of functional analysis) future. A theory always intervenes, for it is the theory which explains why the cited cause is a cause of the observed relationship. As I have argued above, comparative data are essential to establishing the credibility of our theories, and hence of our explanations.[15]

Since we have little in the way of credible theory regarding education, most of our "explanations" are partial and unverified. Indeed, a great deal of educational research is devoted to attempts to provide explanations for already observed relationships, and thus hopefully to build the theory we need. But here too comparative data are essential. Let me use a simple example of a relationship found to exist in a particular society, Jencks's well-known proposition, following Coleman, that in the United States variations in school-related factors account for almost none of the variation in students' achievement independent of the effect of home-background factors.[16] The voluminous literature reacting to Coleman's and Jencks's work testifies to the difficulty scholars have had in explaining—or explaining away—this relationship. But we have in recent years discovered through comparative studies that the relationship among these variables is different in other, especially less developed, societies.[17] This, then, raises the question, Why is the relationship in the United States different than in, say, Chile or Uganda? I submit that if one

---

[14] Ibid., p. 119 (emphasis added).

[15] As Merrit and Coombs have recently noted, " . . . the explanation of why something happens in a given system requires the application of a theory. The development and testing of theory requires explicit comparison. Without the systematic cross-system comparisons, we won't develop the theories we need; without these theories we won't explain much of anything, even within a single system" ("Politics and Educational Reform," *Comparative Education Review* 21, nos. 2–3 [June–October 1977]: 252).

[16] C. Jencks et al., *Inequality: A Reassessment of the Effect of Family and Schooling in America* (New York: Basic, 1972).

[17] Heyneman has systematized the available data and arrived at the proposition that the more developed a nation is, the greater is the proportion of achievement variance accounted for by home-background factors and the smaller is the proportion accounted for by in-school factors (S. P. Heyneman, "Influences on Academic Achievement: A Comparison of Results from Uganda and More Industrialized Societies," *Sociology of Education,* vol. 49 [July 1976]).

cannot answer that question, one has not provided an adequate explanation of the relationship in the United States; indeed, without the comparative data one would not be asking the right questions about the relationship in the United States. In summary, comparative data do not simply enrich the explanation of single-country findings. Without them there cannot be adequate explanation.

As Silvert and Reissman so eloquently put the issue, a prime intellectual duty of a scholarly community is "to explore the full limits of the cultures within which social scientists work. Otherwise, we will be hampered in checking the ethnocentrism which affects us all, unable to carry out our responsibility for comprehending total situations and their alternatives. The comparative study of societies, then, is not merely a technically desirable 'control'; it is the only way to understand the categorical bounds of historical situations."[18] I am suggesting, then, that *there can be no generalizing scientific study of education which is not the comparative study of education.*

It is certainly not my view that, because all science is comparative, all work in comparative education is scientific. However, as conceived here, science is sufficiently general a mode of enquiry that there is very little in comparative education which could not be scientific. And it is definitely my view that it should be. In a world where resources are always scarce and problems endless, if the field of comparative education is going to have any solid justification for its existence it will be in the fact that members of our field are uniquely qualified, whether by training, experience, or inclination, to systematically apply data from a wide variety of societies, to test propositions regarding education, in order to build theory about education, and hence to better understand this complex and fundamental human institution.

But if individuals in our field are to take seriously the role I have delineated, we must ask why so much of the vast richness of comparative data already available has not been exploited by members of our field. We have much grist for our comparative mill. But we have few millers. There are undoubtedly many causes, but I would claim that a fundamental reason is a misunderstanding of the nature of data comparability which has led many of us to take an unnecessarily restricted view of the utility, or even the possibility, of using our own data. This misunderstanding has been around for a long time and is evident in the writings of many of the "masters" whose work has set much of the tone of the field.

The Question of Data Comparability

Many leading scholars have taken the position that it is neither desirable nor possible to bring systematically to bear on a problem

[18] Silvert and Reissman (n. 5 above), p. x.

evidence from a wide variety of educational systems. Foster, for example, suggested almost 20 years ago that the only meaningful comparisons are done between countries which are very similar, suggesting indeed that intracountry comparisons are more likely to be fruitful than intercountry comparisons.[19] A decade ago, Halls made much the same point, suggesting, as an instance, that comparisons of education of women in Moslem and Communist societies would be of little significance, for "the size of the cultural gap is too wide to be bridged by the comparison. No general conclusion would be possible. Comparisons can, in fact, only be made when the phenomena compared are as *similar* to each other as possible."[20] The issue remains with us. Two years ago Masemann noted: "Questions can be raised here about the comparability of data gathered by different researchers, using different techniques, at widely varying points in time."[21]

Very recently, in reviewing evidence regarding education and stratification in industrialized nations, Bereday observed that "the methodological doubts about comparability of the assembled bodies of empirical data continue to plague the researchers and to agitate the critics."[22]

If one adopts the position of such individuals as Foster and Halls, the approach to the comparative study of education advocated in these pages becomes almost an impossibility. Indeed, it is but a small step from a call for maximum similarity to the sort of historicism which would deny the possibility of a generalizing science of education.[23] Therefore, careful attention to various sources of confusion surrounding this issue is warranted.

Calls for maximum similarity reflect a fundamental misunderstanding of the relationship between an observer and external reality. There is implicit in such calls an assumption that there is a sense in which any two entities can be said to be naturally similar, that similarity is a sort of preordained or inherent characteristic, which is somehow obvious to the discerning observer. This is simply not true. Similarity is not something which inheres in the data. It is a characteristic of the relationship between the observer and the data, and depends upon the conceptual structures within the mind of the observer. Cases which are similar for the purposes

[19] P. Foster, "Comparative Methodology and the Study of African Education," *Comparative Education Review* 4 (1960): 110–17.

[20] W. D. Halls, "Comparative Education: Explorations," *Comparative Education* 3 (June 1967): 189.

[21] V. Masemann, "Anthropological Approaches to Comparative Education," *Comparative Education Review* 20 (October 1976): 370.

[22] G. Z. F. Bereday, "Social Stratification and Education in Industrial Countries," *Comparative Education Review* 21, nos. 2–3 (June–October 1977): 195.

[23] For a useful discussion of this same problem in sociology, see Sjoberg and Nett (n. 6 above), p. 265.

of one observer will not be similar (or will be similar in different respects) for another.[24]

Karl Popper provides one of the most compelling treatments of this issue, and he concludes his argument with this statement: "For any given finite group or set of things, however variously they may be chosen, we can, with a little ingenuity, find always points of view such that all the things belonging to that set are similar (or partially equal) if considered from one of these points of view; which means that anything can be said to be a 'repetition' of anything, if only we adopt the appropriate point of view. This shows how naive it is to look upon repetition as something ultimate or given."[25]

Confusion regarding this issue is strikingly evident in Bereday's work. For example, in discussing juxtaposition, the third of his four stages of comparative analysis, he states that it is designed "to determine whether comparison is possible at all. Juxtaposition is really intended to provide an answer to the question 'compare in terms of what?'"[26] But this is exactly the wrong way to proceed. One does not look at the data first, hoping that some basis for comparison will become evident. Rather, one goes to the data with a hypothesis, even if it is not well specified, which tells one what to look for and which features of the data to ignore. It is the hypothesis, not the data, which provides an answer to the question, Compare in terms of what?

There is a further source of confusion. This is the very identification of comparability with similarity. Regarding this several points can be made. First, the idea of the logical utility of comparing situations which are alike in all respects but one has been around for a long time, receiving one of its earliest formal statements in the work of John Stuart Mill. It appears to be forgotten by some modern proponents of this approach that Mill also proposed the comparison of two situations which differ in every respect but one. I am not suggesting that modern-day analysis is going to be much advanced by hearkening back to methodological principles advanced more than a century ago. Rather, even then it was recognized that comparison cannot fruitfully restrict its domain to maximally similar phenomena. As Andreski has stated: "As there is a great deal of confusion on this point, it must be emphasized that comparing does not amount to equating, and that there is no logical

[24] Doby has put the issue this way: "If one reacted to his visual environment with purely sense-data responses he would be judged to be out of his mind. The mind and the eye are related and the relationship between 'seeing' and the stock of knowledge one possesses is complex" (J. T. Doby, "Logic and Levels of Scientific Explanation," in *Sociological Methodology 1969*, ed. E. F. Borgatta [San Francisco: Jossy-Bass, 1969], p. 139).

[25] K. R. Popper, *The Logic of Scientific Discovery* (New York: Harper & Row 1959), p. 422.

[26] G. Z. F. Bereday, "Reflections on Comparative Methodology in Education, 1964–1966," *Comparative Education* 3 (June 1967): 174.

reason why a comparison should be focussed on resemblances rather than differences . . . it all depends on what kind of question we are trying to answer."[27]

Second, even to state that two things are dissimilar is to have compared them, to have jointly considered the two sets of data and to have made a statement about their relationship. Hence, the statement "X and Y are too dissimilar to be compared" is internally contradictory, and quite literally a non-sense statement.

However, people who make such a statement do not usually seem to be claiming that no comparison of any kind is possible. Rather, they seem to be referring, albeit obliquely, to either or both of two different problems.

The first of these is relatively straightforward; it is the problem of data equivalence. One encounters this problem, for example, in the use of enrollment ratios across nations which have not been adjusted to take account of the varying lengths of stages of schooling in different countries. At a more complex level, this is the problem of excessive "operationalism" which Barber discusses well.[28] This sense of the comparison problem is not a question of comparability at all; it is a question of the adequacy of measurement, or frequently a result of not undestanding the nature of measurement.

The other typical referent of statements that "X and Y are too different to be compared" is more difficult. It is the problem of having too many uncontrolled variables. Suppose one is interested in the relation between some structural feature of educational systems, X, and some characteristic of student behavior, Y. One collects data from two school systems and discovers what appears to be relationship between X and Y. However, we know that student behavior is affected by many other factors, and if the two systems in question also differ on a number of these, it will not be possible to sort out the specific effect of X on Y.

The problem of uncontrolled variables does not arise, however, because the societies in question are "too different to be compared." It arises from having data on too few societies. Given the existence of data from a fairly large number of societies, even if they all differ widely on the various factors of interest, one can in most cases use any of a wide array of currently available data-analysis tools to statistically control for a large number of factors. One cannot, however, use these tools when dealing with only two or three cases. The usual answer to this argument is that there are many aspects of educational systems which are not amenable to cross-national measurement. As there has been much

[27] Andreski (n. 7 above), p. 67.
[28] Barber (n. 12 above), p. 432.

nonsense written on this point, a great deal of it based upon a much too rigid notion of what measurement is, I wish to make my own view quite clear. Even simple dichotomizations, or categorizations, are statistically manipulable forms of measurement. If one cannot at least dichotomize a particular phenomenon (e.g., tell me if it exists or not in a particular time and place) or hopefully categorize it (however judgmental may be the categorization—that is a question of accuracy of measurement, not of measurability), then one can make no credible or understandable analytic statements, even in a nonstatistical comparative analysis. The essential problem then is that one is attempting to use the method of covariation with too few cases.

As an example of this problem, one can note the debate in the *Comparative Education Review* between Foster and Mass regarding influences on the development of education in the West African Ashanti and Buganda Kingdoms.[29] Both writers use the method of covariation with two cases but come to entirely different conclusions. Partly the disagreement stems from the use of different methodological-theoretical approaches (functionalism vs. historical-institutional causal imagery), and from divergent readings of the "facts" of the two cases (which is, of course, related to the differing theoretical perspectives). But the heart of the difficulty is the fact that there are a variety of differences between the two cases. Foster gives causal priority to one set of differences, Mass to a different set. The argument is not resolvable by considering only the two cases.

The discussion above leads me to a general conclusion regarding strategy in comparative studies. If one is going to use the method of covariation, one is not likely to get fruitful results by using only two or three cases, for one cannot ordinarily find two or three societies alike in all respects but one, and one cannot therefore control adequately all possible intervening variables. On the other hand, if the object of the comparison is to generalize a relationship discovered within one system to other systems, in order to further establish the credibility of a proposition and/or to discover factors which specify the relationship, then one or two additional cases can serve well (although obviously the more cases one has the more credible the proposition). And in this case, the best additional test of the proposition would be to use a society maximally different from that in which the first test was made.

There is one final source of confusion regarding the issue of comparability which needs to be considered here—the distinction between

[29] J. V. L. Mass, "Educational Change in Pre-colonial Societies: The Cases of Buganda and Ashanti," *Comparative Education Review* 14 (June 1970): 174–85; P. J. Foster, "A Comment on 'Educational Change in Pre-colonial Societies,'" and Mass, "A Reply to Professor Foster," *Comparative Education Review* 14 (October 1970): 377–80 and 381–84.

concepts and observables. Some terms in our academic vocabulary refer to observable phenomena (e.g., age, sex, normal schools, skin color), while others refer to constructs which are inherently unobservable (e.g., social status, influence, economic development, differentiation). The latter are abstracted properties of empirically observable phenomena and have meaning and utility solely in their embeddedness in a theoretical context. Such concepts, not terms about observables, are the proper realm of theory. One does not hypothesize about observables but about concepts. The statement, for example, that in a study one expects to find a strong relation between sex, color, and university attendance is not hypothesis. It is a prediction about certain observable regularities in the social world. However, if such a study suggested that it would discover a strong association between social status of children and their access to sources of potential social power and prestige, a hypothesis would have been formulated (assuming that it was related to some body of theory). In testing such a hypothesis one might take sex and skin color as indicators of social status and university attendance as an indicator of access to sources of potential social power and prestige. A large number of studies in comparative education work strictly at the level of observables (particularly historical and descriptive studies) and even more present a confusing combination of both.

The importance of this distinction has long been recognized, as has the argument that working with observables leads neither to theory building nor to cumulation of research results.[30] What is less generally recognized is the bearing of this distinction on the question of comparability. In the example given above, if one were studying comparatively the relationship between sex, color, and university attendance, one would be hard put to deal with societies wherein there are no color differences, or where there is no university.[31] However, if one were studying the conceptually phrased theory-based hypothesis, one could look for other indicators of social status and other sources of social power and prestige in societies where the observables color and university were not relevant.

[30] For a good discussion of this distinction, see D. Willer and M. Webster, Jr., "Theoretical Concepts and Observables," *American Sociological Review* 35 (August 1970): 748–57.

[31] Bereday worries over this problem at great length in his 1967 article. However, by not recognizing that the problem arises because he is talking about observables rather than concepts, he is forced to advocate what he himself recognizes to be an inferior sort of comparison, "illustrative comparison" (Bereday, "Reflections on Comparative Methodology in Education," pp. 177–79). As I have pointed out, such illustrative or "apt example" comparison is very likely to lead to false generalizations (J. P. Farrell, "Review of Education and Development in Latin America," *Comparative Education Review* 14 [June 1970]: 199–202). For good examples of how working at the level of concepts can overcome apparent problems of comparability, see R. Young, *Some Dimensions of Development: A Cross National Study* (Ithaca, N.Y.: Cornell University, Department of Rural Sociology, 1966), and M. Eckstein, "The Elitist and Popular Ideal: Prefects and Monitors in English and American Secondary Schools," *International Review of Education* 12 (1966): 185–95.

That is, when working with concepts, data comparability is not the apparent problem that it is when working with observables. One uses for the concepts whatever empirical indicators are relevant for each country or time period.

I conclude, then, that the problem of data comparability, as typically discussed in comparative education, is a non-issue, which has seemed relevant primarily because of the confusion surrounding the issues just discussed. That is, the comparability question does not present a serious obstacle to doing the sort of comparative education advocated here.

Toward a General Theory of Education

LÊ THÀNH KHÔI

To this date, there is no general theory of education; rather, there are many "partial" and "local" theories that purport to explain the relation of schools to society. In this article I will argue that comparative education is indispensable to the development of a theory of education that will be able to transcend the limitations of current theories that are derived from specific times and places. In the first part of this article I will show how current theories are partial and local and argue the need for a general theory of education. In the second part I will present a model of analysis that can be applied to different kinds of societies over time and that may guide comparative research and lead to the development of a truly general theory of education.

Theory and Comparison

There are two types of theories of education: normative theories and sociological theories. The first—normative theories—are generated by philosophers and educators. They are based on conceptions of what constitutes a good education and focus on how to implement these conceptions in terms of structures, contents, and methods. Sociological theories, on the other hand, analyze concrete situations and assess the changing meaning and role of education in the broader social context. The two types of theories are not mutually exclusive. In reality, normative theories can always be interpreted sociologically. The ideas of a theorist are never independent from space, time, and the environment in which they evolved. The degree to which such ideas are accepted is due to historical context. Plato's educational ideas, for example, envisioned in the *Republic* and the *Laws*, never became official state ideology during his lifetime, nor did those of Confucius or Marx. However, in the cases of Confucius and Marx, their educational ideals were successfully translated into school practice and became, albeit after their deaths, official state ideology. Their philosophical norms were accepted by the state because they corresponded to the interests of the class or union of classes that held power. My point here is that normative theories are translated into realities only when they bolster the interests of those who hold power and become instruments of social production and reproduction. Thus, a "theory of education" is

I would like to thank Gail Kelly, Cherif Sadki, and Leslie Limage for their effort to prepare the English language version of my paper.

Reprinted from *Comparative Education Review*, vol. 30, no. 1 (February 1986).

the attempt to define the meaning and role of education from empirical analysis, which is itself not the analysis of "neutral" data.

As yet, there is no "general" theory of education that is valid for all societies in space as well as in time. Existing theories are "partial" and "local." They are "partial" because they cover only one aspect of social reality; they are "local" because they are based on the experiences of one type of society, mainly Western industrial society, or, in many cases, of a single society.

Let us take as examples reproduction and dependency theories.

Reproduction theory rightly emphasizes the role of education in maintaining the existing social order through the unequal distribution of "cultural capital" between social classes. However, in any society, change is also necessary. Without change, human beings cannot improve their existence. Yet, change produces tension. The tensions between continuity and change vary in intensity in place and time. Industrialized societies encourage scientific and technical innovation to add to their wealth, to which their rise in living standards is linked. These material changes are accompanied by changes in values. On the other hand, in societies where human control over nature is weak and outside constraints are overwhelming, social cohesion is the key to survival. In the Sahel, the following tale is used to educate young people: "If a man sees from the shore a sinking boat that carries his wife, his child, and his mother-in-law, who should he save?" The mother-in-law represents the sacred; the child, the future; and the wife, the possibility of reproduction. Contrary to what one might expect, the response is not given for once and for all. African wisdom leaves the individual free to decide. One may ask how this individual freedom contributes to social cohesion. The fact is that freedom is not total. It takes place within the social framework.

Dependency theory, developed in Latin America to describe its economic situation, has been applied to education. Different authors have analyzed the mechanisms through which the cultural models exported from industrialized capitalist countries serve, with the consent of the local "elites," to insure the control of these countries over the "periphery." This domination is also one of the mind. Schools and the mass media spread values, knowledge, and attitudes that perpetuate the interests of the "Center." What is left unexplained by the theory is how Third World resistance to foreign control occurs: "The national liberation movements in Latin America, in Asia and in Africa, always had intellectuals and students in the first row of combatants, while they have been formed by the educational systems of the countries against which they revolted."[1] The fact that dependency

---

[1] Lê Thành Khôi, *L'éducation comparée* (Paris: Armand Colin, 1981), p. 127.

theory emerged in Latin America may explain this insufficiency. The "Creole" aristocracy led a war of independence to gain political and economic power, while retaining the European cultural model. They did not have any other model because they destroyed the Indian cultures. On the other hand, in Asia and in Africa, the struggle was also between cultures and represented affirmations of indigenous values and a search for new ways. The older the culture is and the longer the established state structures and written histories are, the more intense is the resistance to foreign rule and the stronger the people's capacity to envision their future.

The theories just mentioned are inspired partly by Marx, despite the fact that Marx himself did not develop a theory of education. Now his famous distinction between infrastructure and superstructure is not applicable to education. In effect, education is a means of training the labor force and so is an element of the infrastructure. But it also forms part of the superstructure in that it disseminates the dominant ideology.

The meaning of education is not less important than its roles. What are the aims that each society assigns to education? What are the factors that influence or determine them? When educational goals change, why and how do they change? In our era, the economy has become the dominant factor, and one can say that in capitalist countries, the school is also "capitalist" to the extent that it spreads the norms and the knowledge necessary to perpetuate this type of social and economic system. But the economy cannot explain everything: each capitalist country has values that derive from its own culture and its history that are distinct to that country. What is true in our time was not necessarily the case in other times. Were not the purposes of education in Hindu or ancient Moslem society mainly determined by religion rather than by the economy? However, here too the dominant factor does not explain everything. Every society must generate the conditions for its own existence, and formal and informal education supply this society with the necessary qualifications for its functioning.

A truly general theory of education would be based on an in-depth study of reciprocal relations between education and society in different types of historical civilizations. Such a study would entail the examination of all dimensions—intellectual, moral, physical, aesthetic, familial, religious, socioprofessional, formal, and informal—of society and economy, of ideas and values, of social and political structures, and of education. It would also include investigation of the influence of society on education and of education on society in its statics (at one point in time) and in its dynamics (over time). The goal of such an undertaking would be to arrive possibly at a formulation of *laws:* laws that would not have the validity of those generated in experimental sciences but that would express relatively constant relationships in space and time.

Comparative education is indispensable to developing such "laws." Comparative education is more than a discipline; it is a field of study that covers all the disciplines that serve to understand and explain education. These disciplines include biology and psychology, linguistics, economics and sociology, history and anthropology, and so on. Comparative education allows us to identify the similarities and differences between societies and to distinguish the meaning of phenomena that appear similar. This meaning may be different according to societal type, and a relation (a "law") valid in one setting need not be so elsewhere. Comparison permits us to classify and develop typologies and, under given conditions, to make "indirect experiments."

History is equally useful because it brings to comparison some essential ideas: those of persistence and evolution and of relativity and totality. Societies change and a relation valid at one time may not be at another. History allows us to determine long-term trends and to differentiate between what is structural and what is conjectural, to distinguish the universal from the particular.

A general theory of education should be based on periods of study of long duration, those during which a society and its economic structure, social hierarchy, institutions, and values remain relatively constant. This notion of "long duration" is particularly pertinent for education, which represents a more stable institution than does government. Thus, Greek education, once it had arrived at its maturity in the Hellenistic era, persisted, despite the rise of Christianity, without major changes throughout the Roman empire, Europe, and Byzantium for at least several centuries.

A general theory of education should seek to explain change as well as persistence. It should ask why education changes—under its own dynamics, because of external factors, or both? Within each society there are some factors that cause change that are more important than others; the importance of these factors varies over time. Each society is affected by forces external to it; the relative strength of these external forces also differs depending on the time period. Finally, each society, regardless of the traits it shares with others, has its unique characteristics and institutions.

Formal and Informal Education

A general theory of education should examine all dimensions of education, both in and out of school. Formal education has too often been studied to the exclusion of informal or nonformal education. It is very important to study informal education—the education that the individual gets through his or her daily life, family, workplace, and the mass media—not only because it is the major educational vehicle in oral cultures but also because even in societies where there is a strong written tradition and formal school system, informal education does not always conform to the formal sector. By studying the relation of formal to informal education, we will be able to grasp the contradictions and conflicts within the society and their significance.

Any society educates. How it does so is sometimes open; sometimes, hidden. Objects are always symbolic of their culture. They remind individuals of how society views life and organizes itself. Tales and legends, proverbs, plays, and art in all its forms assume educational functions. Folklore occupies a central place in the African universe. The folktale serves as a vehicle for expressing the group's norms and beliefs and reminds deviants of the punishment that they could receive from men or supernatural forces.

Play has been characterized as a free activity that the individual engages in for amusement and as a discrete activity that is accomplished within fixed limits of time and place. In every society there is play because play functions as a safety valve by giving freedom to the forces that are repressed (in psychoanalytic terms, play can be seen as a resolution of libidinal tensions). Play also performs an educative function and is tied closely to the economic and social environment. "In collective games," Jean Piaget wrote, "the child learns to locate himself in relation to others in the framework of defined and hierarchical structures. This discovery will make him behave as a member of the group and thus determine his personal status and perceive the group in relation to him and other groups. By bending to the obligatory rules of the game, the child internalizes the norms of his society."[2]

Likewise, art is a free activity only for certain people and in certain societies. Except for landscape painting, which has always been free, art in China became a relatively free activity only recently. For thousands of years, particularly for people without a writing system, art was the privileged means for transmitting knowledge to the entire population. The indigenous bark paintings from Australia, for example, recall the myths of the so-called "time of dreams."

What tells us most about a culture is the architecture of its monuments and its cities. In all times, the city has been the center of power, temporal or spiritual. Architecture symbolizes a conception of space, tied to its religious, social, and political concepts. The location of each monument indicates its relative importance. Where religion dominates, the center of the city is occupied by the cathedral or the grand Mosque. If money assumes importance in a civilization, there will be commercial complexes and buildings. Elsewhere, as in the ancient Chinese city, the dominant building is the sovereign's palace or that of his delegate. In the case of China, the city is square like the earth in the ancient Chinese conception, and so is the royal palace: on earth the monarch represents the heaven

[2] Unesco, *L'enfant et le jeu: Approches théoriques et applications pédagogiques* (Paris: Unesco, 1979).

from which he received his mandate to rule. The palace corresponds to the polar star from which the humans' world is regulated. That is why the Chinese city is oriented toward the south—the south-north axis is the one of the celestial meridian. In the traditional European city, authority is housed in high buildings; in China, authority is represented in buildings isolated behind forbidden enclosures. The view is successively interrupted by gates and other edifices, designed to inspire fear even before the visitor gets to the Imperial City.

Play, art, and architecture are all part of informal education. This informal education may not always be in agreement with education that is formally transmitted in school. The congruence between the two changes over space and time. In the contemporary world, technology and science develop faster than the knowledge that schools can possibly transmit: television, books, and the computer bring more recent knowledge to the child than he or she would find in textbooks. There could also be a disjuncture between schools and the family: schools can disseminate values in direct opposition to those taught by a child's family. In Africa, for example, the ideology transmitted through schools is of European origin. It is an individualistic ideology, whereas the values of most African societies are communal. The same is true in Europe and North America where immigrant children are divided between two cultures: that of their country of origin and that of the host country. These conflicts and others appear between informal and formal education.

In sum, a theory of education should consider all dimensions of education: intellectual, moral, religious, aesthetic, physical, political, military, and the like. It should also consider all educational forms and agencies and consider the possibility that contradictions could arise among the different dimensions, educational forms, and educational agencies. How can one explain these contradictions? What is the meaning and role of education in a given society? What factors affect changes in the meaning and role of education? Up until now, I have argued for the necessity of developing a general theory of education; in the pages that follow, I will suggest a model of analysis that can be applied to different types of societies and possibly allow us to develop a general theory of education.

A General Model of Analysis

The model that has been described in this article is a model of analysis. It is not a theoretical model. No theory is proposed at this stage. The first step would be to identify, from the "static" and "dynamic" points of view, the various reciprocal relationships between the components of the model. The more numerous and different (politically, socially, economically, culturally) are the societies from which experience is drawn, the more valid will be the theory, as was stated in the first part of this paper. The next step will be to apply the model to a representative sample of historical societies: communal (in Africa, Amerindia, Oceania); pre–Western-arrival Asian (contrasting China-Japan, India-Sri Lanka, and various Islamic states); ancient and medieval European; capitalist and socialist; and finally "developing" societies. What will the theoretical outcome of this comparison be? Regardless of the results, the exercise is worth undertaking.

Education is influenced by and influences, in turn, the following variables, in differing degrees depending on space and time: (1) peoples, ethnic groups, and languages; (2) natural environment; (3) mode(s) of production; (4) ideas and values; (5) sociopolitical structures; (6) outstanding individuals; and (7) international relations. Let us briefly examine each of these variables (see fig. 1).

1. Peoples, Ethnic Groups, and Languages

Peoples and ethnic groups constitute the fundamental reality of a country. By "people," I mean all those living in the country who share a number of traditions and institutions (this excludes foreigners). Ethnicity is characterized by culture and language. For many states, most of which are in Africa, one can ask if there is a "people" or if the state is only a collection of ethnic groups inherited from colonial history and artificial boundaries. One of the functions that the state assigns to education is to promote national integration. However, this is not a process that can occur overnight.

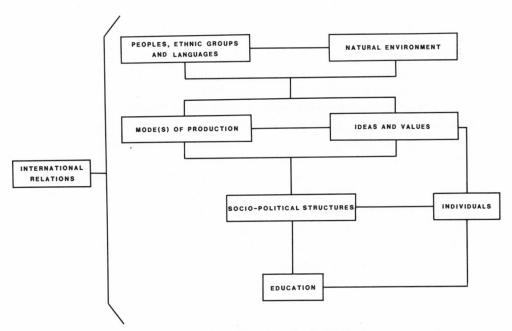

FIG. 1.—A general model of analysis of education

The notion of "national character" used by many in comparative education is open to criticism. There is no "national character" where there is no "nation" in the sense of a group of people who have unity of language, culture, and economic life and who are conscious of it and willing to live in common. The "state" represents the sovereign institutionalized power that is exercised on a population inside a defined territory. The state takes on different forms in all continents. "Nation" is a recent phenomenon that accompanied the rise of the bourgeoisie in Europe and that gave the state its contemporary form. Does "national character" even exist in Europe? This notion implies the existence not only of cultural specificity but also of a *group* of ways of feeling and acting that distinguishes one nation from another and that is relatively constant in history. Indeed, it is often said that French education is more "intellectualized" than British or American education. However, to say that this difference is explained by the "French national character" is to deny both its historical origins and the fact that this characteristic is not particular to France; it is found in other Latin countries, all influenced by the Greco-Roman tradition and Catholic theology. The notion of "national character" completely ignores the division of a "nation" into competing social classes. Finally, from a logical point of view, the concept of national character cannot account for change. The Chinese and the Vietnamese are different nations. Do the similarities of the transformations that have occurred in China and Viet Nam since the Communist revolution come from the similarity of their "national character," from the similarity of changes in this character, or from political changes that have nothing to do with national character?

This said, two important questions arise. The first concerns the distinction—fundamental for education—between written and oral cultures. Oral cultures possess a richness of interpersonal and social communication, but they permit neither the accumulation nor the rationalization of knowledge to the same extent as written cultures do. Is it by chance that sophisticated science appeared only with writing (a necessary condition, but not sufficient)? Science requires reasoning abilities, deduction, and induction, which cannot be exercised from memory. It also demands a precise conservation of knowledge that will allow the subsequent production of other knowledge. This possibility is not found in oral-based cultures. As an African philosopher, Hampate Ba said, "When an old person dies, it is a library that burns." On the other hand, oral-based communication is not an obstacle to the development of technology. We can compare the Indian civilizations of Central America and of the Andes. The Mayas reached an exceptional level of intellectual development in mathematics and astronomy; from the Incas we only know the *quipus* (a Quechua word meaning "knot"), a system made with a principal rope held horizontally on which little strings are tied with different kinds of knots. The color of the strings, their grouping, their number, and their relative position had specific significance, serving as a calendar, to transmit messages, and to enumerate men, animals, and things. But a truly sophisticated science could not be based on this precious statistical and administrative instrument as long as all knowledge was transmitted orally. On the other hand, the Incas mastered remarkable techniques for agricultural and public work. Without knowing the wheel, they built monuments that architects today admire. Generally, however, written communication encourages the elaboration of scientific knowledge, state organization, division of labor, and the diversification of education more than oral communication does. It also fosters the division of society into social classes and the domination and exploitation of man by man.

A second important issue that emerges concerns the relations between language and thought—between linguistic, cognitive, and affective structures. Whorf has shown that the Hopi language does not have the same notions of space and time as the French or English language does.[3] Galtung and Nishimura compare the role of language as a vehicle of "social cosmology" in the European, Chinese, and Japanese worlds along six dimensions: space, time, knowledge, person-nature, person-person, person-transpersonal.[4] Space and time are linear and endowed with structures that are relatively rigid and simple in the European languages but more flexible and ambiguous in Chinese and Japanese. European languages are made for atomistic reasoning—they are dichotomous and deductive; Chinese and Japanese allow for a more holistic and dialectical mode of thought.

We can find similar contrasts in how these languages express relationships between man and nature. In East Asia, there is no dichotomy between the soul and the body. In interpersonal relations, the expression is collective—centered on the in-group—rather than individualist (Chinese is somewhere between European languages and the Japanese language). Whereas the European languages do not make distinctions between the in-group and the out-group, Japanese is characterized by a strong hierarchical dimension.

These relations between grammatical categories and world vision allow us to speak of correlation but not of causation as Whorf did—for whom, "We view the world according to the lines drawn by our mother tongues." Whorf's linguistic determinism completely denies any influence of the society on the language. In reality there is a relation between language

---

[3] B.-L. Whorf, *Linguistique et anthropologie* (Paris: Denoël, 1959).
[4] J. Galtung and F. Nishimura, "Structure, Culture and Language: An Essay Comparing the Indo-European, Chinese and Japanese Languages," *Social Science Information* 22, no. 6 (1983): 895–926.

and society: language conditions thought, but language itself changes under the influence of social and cultural factors.

2. *Natural Environment*

The more elementary the techniques of resource utilization, the greater is the role of the natural environment in peoples' lives (and therefore in their education). The contrast between nomadic and sedentary cultures has formed the web of history in certain parts of the world for centuries. The development of knowledge permits us to master nature and diminish its influence on human civilization. The more human beings present, the less "natural" is the environment.

In *Childhood and Society,* Erik Erikson contrasts the education of two Native American peoples: the Dakota (or Sioux), who lived on the prairies from bison hunting, and the Yurek, fishermen who lived along a salmon river.[5] Their environments and the ways in which they earned their livelihoods determined their value systems, which were, in turn, embodied in the educations that they gave their young. For the Dakota, strength, courage and trickery—qualities necessary for hunting and fighting—were emphasized, as was generosity because the nomad needed only the minimum of domestic property and depended on gifts from the luckiest and most capable hunters. An education in these values started from early childhood. The baby was fed every time he or she asked for it and could even get milk from any woman because the milk that exceeds the immediate needs of one baby is common property. Later on, younger boys learned from older boys, who taught them the rules of hunting, aggressiveness, and solidarity. The emphasis placed on a boy's right to autonomy and on his obligations helped emancipate the boy progressively from his mother. During the highest ceremony, the Sun Dance, "war and hunting games glorified the competition between men, gifts and acts of fraternization glorified mutual dependency."[6] Men would place barbs in their chests and pull at them while dancing in order to join the spiritual elite.

Among the Yureks, the child was taught to be a fisherman. The Yureks emphasized autonomy at an earlier age than the Dakotas did. They encouraged the baby to leave the mother and her support as soon as possible. Starting on the twentieth day after birth, the grandmother would massage the baby's legs so that he or she would be able to crawl early. The Yurek learned to make good nets, to set them in the right place, and to cooperate with the other members of the tribe in jointly building a barrier each year to catch the salmon traveling up the river from the ocean. He prayed tearfully that his god would send him this food. The Yurek who was really capable was the one who would cry in the most touching, heartrending

---

[5] E. Erikson, *Enfance et société* (Neuchâtel: Delachaux et Niestlé, 1982).
[6] Ibid., p. 101.

way or who could bargain effectively in certain situations and be full of firmness in others. In other words, the Yurek's ego was strong enough to synthesize orality and "common sense."[7]

All societies teach their members to use natural resources to the advantage of the technology that they possess. When technology is simple, the dominant ideology is one of a harmonious relationship between humans and nature. In complex industrial society, the emphasis is on the exploitation of the globe, almost to excess. It has taken its toll today in pollution and destruction. Education for the environment, a new field, seeks to spread the conscience of this threat and the necessity of preserving the resources of the planet.

3. *Mode(s) of Production*

Marx's concept of "mode of production" can have different interpretations. I understand it as the articulation between productive forces and the relations of production. The productive forces consist of human's physical and intellectual work and the instruments of production. Relations of production are those between humans engaged in the process of production; these are not reduced to ownership of the means of production, even though ownership of the means represents the determining characteristic. Like other Marxist concepts, the concept of "mode of production" applies better to the capitalist society than to other types of societies. In fact, even if it is not totally economic (it is rather socioeconomic), the concept of "mode of production" implies a separation between productive activities and other activities. In many ancient societies (African, Indian, Chinese, etc.), all activities are tied. One cannot separate production from religion or from parental relations. Although this is the case, the concept is nonetheless heuristically useful in making sense of a complex reality. It also serves as a reminder to those who tend to forget that "the mode of production of material life conditions the process of social, political and intellectual life in general."[8] I prefer the "flexible" word "condition" to "determine" (which implies a relation of direct causality), which Marx uses in other parts of his writing. A look at universal history shows us that one mode of production can give rise to very different societies: for example, India and China were both based on what Marx called the "Asian" mode of production.

Three questions arise:

A. *What is the influence of the mode of production on culture and education?*— It could be direct or indirect. The mode of production acts directly when the child engages in adult productive activities and is educated by imitating adults. This type of learning occurs in industrialized and less industrialized

---

[7] Ibid., p. 122.
[8] Karl Marx, *A Contribution to the Critique of Political Economy* (1859), preface.

societies. The influence of the mode of production could also be indirect and transmitted through ideas and values that are associated with it. It could be hypothesized that each mode of production gives rise to one or more ideologies and that the dominant ideology strongly influences the goals, structures, contents, and methods of education and teaching. For example, in a communal society where land—the sole or almost sole means of production—belongs to the community and where there are no social classes, education will also try to spread communal values like solidarity, cohesion, cooperation, and so forth. Education will be collective, and the child will learn from all the members of the community and not only from the family or a specialized institution with professional teachers.

What are the limits of the economy's influence? Even if there are no social classes, there is a division of labor between male and female and hierarchies according to age, position, and so on. For example, the girl rarely receives the same education as the boy: beyond a certain level of education, there is differentiation. How can these differences be explained?

B. What is the influence of education on the mode of production?—In any society, education fulfills many functions: cultural (transmission and enrichment of the group's cultural heritage); social (socialization, differentiation, selection); and economic (training of the work force). These functions are intertwined, but the relative importance of each varies according to the type of society. The economic role becomes more important as the economy becomes more complex, and it comes to play a dominant role in society. There could be contradictions between the three functions of education: for example, the predominance of cultural and social functions in relation to economic ones in ancient China and India. Today economic efficiency is often obtained to the detriment of social equality because the "best" students, those who will get the best jobs, come from culturally and/or materially privileged families. Likewise, there may be contradictions between the economic and cultural dimensions. Teaching in a language of international communication gives direct access to the international scientific and technological literature, but it alienates the student from his own culture. And there are contradictions within the same role: education could be a factor in economic development but also an impediment to that development (bookish knowledge, inculcation of contempt for manual labor, excessive cost, etc.).

C. Is there a connection between economic changes and educational changes?—In contemporary society, changes in the economy occur more rapidly than changes in education, even in cases where a social revolution has drastically transformed the structures of production. What are the causes of this relative inertia of the educational system? It is necessary to study the educational system from the inside to see the change, or lack of change, in goals, structures, contents, methods, teachers' behaviors, learners' behaviors, and teacher/learner relations. By what means and on what terms do changes happen, when they happen?

4. *Ideas and Values*

Each mode of production does not "secrete" only one conception of nature and man. Rather, many conceptions arise that could be antagonistic: did not Marxism emerge from capitalism itself? Not all ideas have a material basis. They emerge from people's minds and travel from one part of the world to another.

Max Weber advances an extremely ingenious and plausible hypothesis about the relation between the conception of divinity and the mode of irrigation. The conception of an ethical God, who is both personal and transcendent, is found in West Asia; it is absent from India and China. In the deserts of Mesopotamia and Arabia, good crops are made possible through artificial irrigation, not from rain. From this stems the absolute power of the king: "It is from the (irrigation) that the king gets revenues in building canals—and cities along their banks—with slave labor." From this control probably came "the conception of a God creating the earth and men from 'nothing' (like the royal irrigation creating the harvest in the desert from 'nothing') and not only begetting them, as we believed generally elsewhere. The King created even the law through legislations and rational codes—something that the world has received here for the first time."[9]

In India and China, "the harvest depends on the rain that falls at the right time in sufficient but not excessive quantities." The king is the maker of rain; his administration's job is to build and watch dikes and canals, and he himself endeavors to propitiate (super)natural forces through sacrifices and virtuous conduct. In the Vedas or Chinese classics, there was no need for a personal and transcendent god. That god appears later in popular belief and in magical form.[10]

All ideas cannot be considered to have the same political significance and impact. Some overtake others; the dominant ideas in a given era are those of the dominant class. But I would not agree with Marx and Engels that "the class which has the dominant *material* power in the society *also* [emphasis added] has the dominant *spiritual* power."[11] If this assertion can be verified by looking at capitalist societies, it cannot in other types of societies where status and power are dissociated, even if there is an alliance between the two. In ancient India, the Brahmans were the dominant spiritual caste, and the Kshatriyas, the dominant material caste. Indeed, the Kshatriyas adopted the ideas of the Brahmans who served as their

[9] Max Weber, *Economie et société* (Paris: Plon, 1971), pp. 471–72.
[10] Ibid.
[11] Karl Marx and Friedrich Engels, *L'ideologie alle mande* (1846) (Paris: Editions sociales, 1977), p. 86.

advisers. But if there was alliance between the two, there was no fusion. There is, Louis Dumont writes, "absolute distinction between priesthood and royalty . . . In the absolute, the power is subordinated to the priesthood, while in fact the priesthood submits to the power. Status and power, and consequently spiritual authority and temporal authority, are absolutely distinct."[12]

Dominant ideas are transformed to collective values that directly influence culture and education. Alongside them are other ideas and values that originate from one class or another, from one group or another. Sometimes they are tolerated, sometimes repressed by the dominant class.

The ideology of a system of education reflects its economic basis: in one place, it teaches respect for private property; elsewhere, it teaches respect for collective means of production. Ideology can prevent neither challenges nor revolts: those of peasants in the past, those of youth today that burst out everywhere in the world and under different political regimes. A dominated class or people could use education to emancipate themselves to some extent from the control of a dominant class or state. History gives examples of religions or ideologies that went from being marginal to being state religions or doctrines: Confucianism, Buddhism, Christianity, Islam, and Marxism-Leninism. History also shows that the process occurs generally through the taking of political power. When this does not happen—or is in the process of happening—peasants' and workers' struggles include education to develop class consciousness and militancy.

5. *Sociopolitical Structures*

This term is deliberately general so as to include systems as different as caste, class, and kinship. The term, sociopolitical, accentuates the relationship between the social and the political because it is this relation that determines education rather than social or political structures taken individually. This assertion can be contested. What about education in the family as political? Education in the family is political in the sense that the family cannot exist by itself but rather is part of a larger social unit like class or caste.[13] Dominant class values affect those of the dominated classes. Even in communal society where there are no social classes, values have a political character because they serve to maintain and regulate the social system. In the family, the child starts to learn the language, its codes, and its modes. They are linked to the values and attitudes, traditions, and customs of a particular religion, class, or ethnicity and to certain skills and competencies that will serve later on in adult professional life.

[12] L. Dumont, *Homo hierarchicus: Le système des castes et ses implications* (Paris: Gallimard, 1979), p. 99.

[13] Lê Thành Khôi, *Jeunesse exploitée, jeunesse perdue?* (Paris: Presses Universitaires de France, 1978).

Today, the state is the major supplier of education. The ideological role that the state assigns education has been studied. Althusser designated school in capitalist societies as one of the "state ideological apparatus," which complements the repressive apparatus by ensuring the reproduction of the conditions of production. Althusser's conception excludes any possible contradiction between public and private education (which could include forces hostile to the state) as well as any contradiction within public education itself (all the teachers do not share the dominant ideology).[14] It does not explain how ideology can assure the reproduction of relations between exploiters and exploited. Applied to the Third World, the notion is even more questionable because here the opposition between public and private (esp. religious) education is often very strong. Public education seldom reaches all children, and the state does not always have a unified ideology; when it does, that ideology is often foreign.

What are the relations between the mode of production and sociopolitical structures? The idea that a given mode of production corresponds to a given social structure is valid for contemporary capitalist and socialist societies. In the Third World, capitalist penetration has given rise to the development of nuclei of social classes similar to those in Europe. However, tradition, religion, family ties, ethnicity, and region present many obstacles to the emergence of class consciousness and struggle. History shows us that the same mode of production could give rise to different types of social structure.

In any case, the dominant class eventually puts its imprint on education so that education will reflect its ideology and prepare officials and manpower that are necessary to maintain the existing system. However, education in its institutionalized form has for centuries, if not for millennia, been reserved for a very small minority, usually those who are destined to hold power. Others have been trained through family apprenticeships. The division of labor corresponds to social divisions even though there is always upward and downward social mobility. There is a variable relationship between dependence and independence, between knowledge distribution and competencies and the social hierarchy.

Political change can bring about ideological change without fundamentally changing the infrastructure. This was the case in Japan in the twelfth century when, following a long period of civil wars, the victorious military class took power from the imperial court and established a feudal regime that lasted seven centuries. At the same time Confucianism, which was then the dominant ideology in Japan, gave way to Zen Buddhism. It is somewhat astonishing that the samurai adopted such a contemplative

---

[14] In fact, the notion of "state ideological apparatus" elaborated by Althusser for capitalist countries applies best to the socialist states (Lê Thành Khôi [see n. 1 above], p. 119).

religion as quasi-official doctrine. In fact, there are some Zen characteristics that correspond to the samurai state of mind: Zen is not transmitted through the study of sacred books but through revelation. In Zen, the disciple should succeed by dint of his own efforts "by meditating on his own nature." Self-control is one of the warrior qualities, as is courage and the scorn of death.

6. *Individuals*

Aside from the role of social and political structures, there should be a place in a general theory for the influence of individuals. The individuals who influence education may include founders of religions, philosophers, educators, or politicians. Founders of religions who influenced education mainly include the Buddha, Jesus Christ, and Mohammed. A religion becomes a worldwide religion when it prescribes equality between people; this condition is fundamental. Philosophers encompass idealists or materialists, utopians or realists—the list of philosophers who influenced education is long, from Confucius to Marx. Educators who did not elaborate philosophical systems but brought pedagogical innovations—for example, Montessory, Freinet, Decroly—form a distinct group. Politicians who influenced education were pragmatic, such as Peter the Great and the Meiji emperor who both wanted to "modernize" their nations, or were ideologists, such as Lenin and Mao.

What is the role of individuals in relation to structures? Their role cannot be extrapolated from the times in which they lived, their country, or their social class. Individuals always act within historical contexts that exist independent of their free will. That context is derived from how productive forces are organized and from knowledge, ideas, beliefs, values, and social and political relations existent at that time. On the other hand, by their material and intellectual activities, men transform these conditions. Outstanding individuals accelerate the historical process or overthrow it radically.

The influence of individual action or ideas can be immediate or delayed. Some individuals are ahead of their time and have to wait decades, even centuries, before their ideas will be put into practice. For example, Komensky (Comenius, 1592–1670), at the time of the religious wars of the Counter-reformation, enunciated the principles of a "pan-Sophist" humanism based on peace that transcended nationality and religion while respecting cultural diversity. He argued that education is a continuous process from birth to death; in each stage of the life cycle, there must be appropriate content and methods for education. Education should be given in the mother tongue as well as in Latin (then the medium of international communication between European scholars). It should actively use the "living book of nature." Komensky insisted that elementary education be provided for everyone: boys and girls, rich and poor. It should not only teach reading and writing but also bring the knowledge of "all that which would help humans live in society." Yet Komensky remained a creature of his times. His pedagogical basis was religious and Aristotelian.

Individuals who were able to put their ideas into practice were those who held power. Mohammed can be distinguished from Buddha and Jesus Christ in this respect: he gave Islam its major characteristic—the fusion of the spiritual and the temporal. Power corrupts when it is exercised without limit. We have many examples of this in history; one of the most well known is that of Mao Zedong who, in his later days, "confused that which is just with that which is erroneous." His "cultural revolution," instigated to change peoples' world views, wrought economic chaos and cultural emptiness in spite of democratization of basic education.

7. *International Relations*

The last, but not the least important, of the variables that influence education and are influenced by it is represented by international relations. These reciprocal influences could be studied from four viewpoints: agents that implement them; means that are used; products that are exchanged; and type of transfer. The agents of international relations are states, firms, intergovernmental or nongovernmental organizations—including churches—and individuals (e.g., Marco Polo).

The means have been, in all times, commerce, wars, religion, politics, or simple individual curiosity. The different means often go hand in hand: commerce brings and follows war and is often associated with religion. The Silk Road was also the road that Buddhism used to enter China. Trade brought prosperity to the classical Islamic empire because of its geographic position between Europe, Africa, and Monsoon Asia. Catholicism played a major role in European expansion and colonization since the fifteenth century, bringing war with it. War destroys and creates. It has annihilated advanced civilizations, particularly in Indian America; yet, it also encouraged many scientific and technical discoveries and, consequently, advanced education.

The products that are exchanged include ideas, beliefs, values, equipment that incorporates a given technology, and consumer goods. These consumer goods are desired because of an acculturative education. Furthermore, they help to reinforce the economic and cultural model of the industrialized countries.

Transfers can be either imposed or invited. What has been imposed may later be accepted voluntarily for a number of reasons. The educational system introduced in Africa by colonization has been maintained without any fundamental changes in these countries after independence because it corresponds to the interests of the new ruling classes, which are themselves tied to international capitalism. Colonial school systems have also been retained because reforming methods, the linguistic medium, and content is slow and difficult, given the lack of qualified personnel and popular resistance to reform (many Africans believe that local languages do not serve as a means for occupational and social mobility). F. Schneider distinguishes between three modes of transfer: (1) mechanical acceptance or imitation; (2) selective transfer—after a critical evaluation based on national needs, one chooses elements that seem usable from among foreign models; and (3) productive transfer that stimulates the creativity of the receiving country.[15] These last two modes of transfer assume not only that the country is sovereign and makes its choices independently but also that it possesses necessary human and financial capacities.

From the point of view of universal history, the borrowings between cultures have been made in all times. At a certain time, some countries are more advanced than others; at other times, they are behind. Europe was behind China—between 1 to 15 centuries in inventions such as paper, printing, the clock, the compass, gunpowder, the eccentric, the connecting rod, the piston, the transmission belt, the harnessing collar for horses, and so on. When modern science emerged in Europe at the time of the Renaissance, it was due, in part, to accumulated knowledge from other civilizations: for example, the Indian numerals without which Galileo could not have built his work; the theory of perpetual movement also of Indian origin; algebra (*al-djabr*) from Islam; and the binary language of the *Yi-Ching,* the "Book of Changes."

With capitalism, the economy has become international. At this point in time, the North controls the flow of knowledge and innovations that go to the rest of the world. Dependency is a natural consequence of this situation. How to go from dependence to independence is one of the South's major problems. The process cannot happen overnight. The key is to prepare independence by developing the basis for revival, some of which can be found in the past. Let us conclude with this verse from a mystical Persian poet, Fariddudine Attar (1140–1230):

> The eminent men who lifted up their heads to the sky could only find their way with the light of knowledge.[16]

---

[15] Cited by W. Stephan, "The Concept of Educational Influence in Comparative Education and the Transfer of Ideas and Institutions" (communication to the 5th World Congress of Comparative Education, Paris, July 1984), p. 4.

[16] Fariddudine Attar, *Le livre divin* (Paris: Albin Michel, 1961).

Currents Left and Right:
Ideology in Comparative Education

ERWIN H. EPSTEIN

The thought that scholarship may not be wholly invulnerable to ideology profoundly disturbs the academic world. Science is supposed to discover truth—it seeks to scrape off the veneer of subjective judgment to achieve wisdom, insight, and understanding. Systematic methods are painstakingly devised to serve this goal. Entire tomes are devoted solely to advancing objectivity in procedure and to avoiding ideological deception. Such fear of ideology is well justified, for a science contaminated by partisan belief diminishes intellectual activity.

We in comparative education should be particularly concerned about entanglements with ideology. Comparative fields are peculiarly vulnerable, being exposed to varying national orientations and incompatible world views. Moreover, education is society's most enduring mechanism for inculcating belief systems. Yet we have rarely openly acknowledged the existence of ideology in our activities, however much we wrestle over competing methodologies. Whether out of a sense of academic etiquette or due to simple obliviousness, scholars in the field have generally failed to identify explicitly the ideological roots of rival orientation. Unless we boldly confront the issue of ideology it will obscure insight and erode the value of our work.

I shall argue that what matters about an educational theory—especially one devoted to politics of human action—is not only what the theory explicitly says but what it omits to say or what it contains that is difficult to acknowledge. I shall argue also that what matters about methodology in comparative education is not only the procedure employed in the investigation of a problem but the value judgments that inform that procedure. Finally, I intend to demonstrate that the leading model that has been used to explain the development of comparative education has been inadequate, and that we need more competently to account for the ideologies that have influenced the field's development.

"Progress" in the Development of Comparative Education

It has become conventional in our field to view the development of comparative education as having progressed in stages. Noah and Eckstein—

I gratefully acknowledge the helpful comments of C. Arnold Anderson, Sandra Ben-Zeev, John Craig, Gail Kelly, and the students and staff in the Spring 1982 Comparative Education Seminar at the University of Chicago.

Reprinted from *Comparative Education Review*, vol. 27, no. 1 (February 1983).

the title of whose influential book, *Toward a Science of Comparative Education*, is redolent with the notion of progression—identify three broad methodological stages: stage 1 is characterized as a data-gathering enterprise of an encyclopedic and somewhat indiscriminate order; stage 2, ushered in by Michael Sadler and advanced most notably by Nicholas Hans and Isaac Kandel, stressed explanation rather than description and sought that explanation in a study of the historical context and the influence of cultural forces; and stage 3, now considered mainstream methodology, consists of the application of empirical social science methods and a self-consciousness about procedures.[1] Kazamias, although differing somewhat from the way Noah and Eckstein view the field's development, nevertheless distinguishes between "old" and "new" approaches to methodology in comparative education. The old approaches, Kazamias claims, were descriptive and *prescriptive* and indiscriminately blended "what is" in education with "what ought to be." By contrast, the new methods—which Kazamias refers to as the philosophical, functional, and problem approaches—tend to be microcosmic, more analytic, and more "scientific."[2] More recently, Kelly and Altbach, after acknowledging the past approaches cited by others, report the rise of what now have become the "new" methodological perspectives in comparative education—ethnographic approaches and frameworks that utilize concepts such as neocolonialism, world-system analysis, and dependency theory to argue that educational systems are directly affected by international currents and that national school systems and the relations between school and the nation are no longer worthy subjects of analysis.[3] However much these descriptions of the field vary, they all maintain the notion of progress.

However convenient it has been to view the development of comparative education as evolving in stages, this perspective has created confusion over the relative utility and value of alternative approaches. With the maturing of comparative education we should be able to see how each successive stage has represented an increment of greater objectivity and clarity in the study of education. Instead we find the contemporary literature in disarray over the question of what is appropriate methodology in comparative education. Is the student of comparative education in the 1980s more likely to feel secure in the appropriateness or objectivity of a chosen methodology than was the student of the 1950s? I know that I, as a product of the 1960s, felt far more certain about what was "good" methodology

[1] Harold J. Noah and Max A. Eckstein, *Toward a Science of Comparative Education* (New York: Macmillan, 1969), p. 65.

[2] Andreas M. Kazamias, "Some Old and New Approaches to Methodology in Comparative Education," *Comparative Education Review* 5 (October 1961): 90–96.

[3] Gail P. Kelly and Philip G. Altbach, "Comparative Education: A Field in Transition," in *International Bibliography of Comparative Education*, ed. Philip G. Altbach, Gail P. Kelly, and David H. Kelly (New York: Praeger, 1981), pp. 12–15.

in those formative years than I do now. Methodologists continue to claim steady progress for our field as measured by the replacement of "old," ideologically biased approaches by "new," increasingly objective methods. I contend that such claims are groundless. However much we may have improved our application of technological and quantitative tools to the analysis of educational problems, we have progressed nary a step in becoming disinterested, ideologically unbiased observers of school-society relations.

The ideological roots of educational research have been identified before, most notably by Paulston, who views ideological tendencies that characterize major theoretical approaches as being not necessarily incompatible.[4] He even suggests that comparative research might draw critically from these countervailing orientations. Although Paulston's description of comparative research is unique in its acknowledgment of ideology and in its avoidance of the idea of progressive development, he underestimates the irreconcilability of competing ideologies and identifies only two paradigms—the equilibrium and conflict perspectives—as bases for more specific conceptual models. I believe, however, that if we view ideology as the framework of political consciousness, as the set of ideas around which a group of people organize themselves for political action,[5] the notion of achieving synthesis by drawing selectively from different paradigms having competing ideological roots is dubious. Furthermore, Paulston fails to identify a third major theoretical perspective—the "problem" approach—which differs substantially from the equilibrium and conflict paradigms.

To show how irreconcilable these paradigms are, infused as they are by rival ideologies, I shall examine two debates. The first was between Philip Foster on the one side and Martin Carnoy and others. The second was between Margaret Archer and Edmund King. These debates represent, in my judgment, the most acerbic, but possibly the most significant, exchanges ever to grace the literature in comparative education. At the risk of oversimplification, I will label the competing frameworks in these debates "neopositivist," "neo-Marxist," and "neorelativist." Neopositivists tend to connect deductive-nomological analysis, aimed at making lawlike generalizations using multiple nation or societal data, to functional explanation, in contrast to "orthodox" positivists who are concerned only with establishing

---

[4] Rolland G. Paulston, "Social and Educational Change: Conceptual Frameworks," *Comparative Education Review* 21 (June/October 1977): 370–95.

[5] See H. Mark Roelofs, *Ideology and Myth in American Politics: A Critique of a National Political Mind* (Boston: Little, Brown, 1976), p. 4. I prefer Roelof's definition to others that make little distinction between ideology and epistemology or cultural expression, because my purpose is to show that an intrinsic bias exists in prevailing comparative approaches. For example, Wuthnow's definition— as "any subset of symbolic constructions which, in fact, serves as a vehicle for the expression and transmission of collectively shared meanings"—would not serve my purpose (see Robert Wuthnow, "Comparative Ideology," *International Journal of Comparative Sociology* 22 [1981]: 121–40, at 121).

universal laws. This is not to say that in all cases positivists use multinational or multicultural data; they may focus on a particular society using a framework that calls for replication in other societies. Neo-Marxists view ideology as pervasive in all theoretical frameworks, unlike "orthodox" Marxists who see only theories that support capitalism as being ideologically infused. And in contrast to "orthodox" relativists, who focus on "verisimilitude" (rather than truth) in science, neorelativists are also preoccupied with the practical application of "critical rationalism" in particular situations. The fine distinctions between orthodox and neo-orientations are important to show the derivations of contemporary theories; my main concern, however, is with the overall contrasts between the positivist, Marxist, and relativist frameworks. These contrasts should become clear in my discussion of the debates.

First, however, it will be important to recognize that comparative education invites ideology insofar as that field has practical utility in the reform of schooling. If comparative education were no more than an academic exercise, it would furnish no motive for the development of political consciousness. Yet we display almost an obsession over the need to achieve some practical benefit from comparative study. Rarely have we viewed as a primary benefit knowledge for its own sake or the quest of knowledge to strengthen the mind or to gain personal mastery over the environment. Such benefits are apparently too elusive, too impervious to empirical demonstration to justify investment of our time, let alone of our research institutions' resources. The preoccupation over appropriate policy and the infusion of ideology which informs policy research should become evident in my review of the debates.

The Foster-Carnoy et al. Debate

This exchange focused on educational policy for developing countries. Foster's main argument was that in these countries "no type of educational planning will succeed unless it is based upon the aspirations and expectations of the majority of the population or provides incentive structures that will allow these aspirations to be modified to accord with national goals." Furthermore, although "the demands placed upon the central polity for equity, welfare and development far exceed the system's capacity to respond, [the] answer to this problem is *less*, not *more* concentration of authority."[6]

It would be difficult to find a statement manifestly more given to democratic action in education than Foster's. But this seemingly democratic statement is informed by functional thought and positivist methodology, which are not ideologically neutral. Although the neo-Marxist literature

---

[6] Philip Foster, "Dilemmas of Educational Development: What We Might Learn from the Past," *Comparative Education Review* 19 (October 1975): 375–92, quote on 393.

on the disabilities of functionalism is familiar to most of us, the critique of Foster's view by Carnoy and by Devon is worth examining.

Carnoy begins his analysis by showing that Foster's position is Schumpeterian; that is, it views the market system as comparatively just and fair and as most conducive to economic development. Interference by the state into the workings of the market erodes the inherent equitability and efficiency of that system and is therefore usually unwarranted. Carnoy contends, however, that the Schumpeterian model is naive, that the state in nonsocialist developing countries is controlled not by disinterested parties but by the local bourgeoisie and by foreign, ex-colonial groups who seek economic stability in their own interest rather than genuine reform and democratic, decentralized decision making.

According to Carnoy, the colonial "state of mind" that Foster attributes to antiquated interference with "natural" market forces is not an ephemeral characteristic of developing states but is the product of a firmly grounded economic system and social structure "essential to the functioning of dependent capitalism and the relatively small elite that profits from it." The state, for Carnoy, is not a frivolous manipulator of the market but a principal mechanism through which the mass of people is systematically controlled during the development process. Schools serve as an important part of the state's repressive apparatus by socializing and cognitively preparing labor for the capitalist production of goods. The idea that the state can simply refrain from interfering with the market is fatuous if not malicious, because it ignores the vested interests of elites and plays into their hands by making it appear that the state can be a just and politically neutral actor.[7] Devon further attacks Foster for his self-proclaimed neutrality as a social scientist. "How can his extensive defense of a *laissez-faire* economy with a decentralized *political* system be viewed as politically neutral? At one point, Foster explicitly admonishes what 'the state must *not* do' on a particular policy issue, and it is nowhere clear that he is offering any alternatives. Indeed, to a curious extent Foster reduces education to economics and economics to politics. For, having declined to discuss the important political and social functions of education, his contextual discussion of economics is primarily in terms of political prescriptions."[8]

Foster's response to his critics is classic positivism and can be summed up by his remark, "It has been suggested that I take refuge behind the data; I take this as a compliment and find it a vastly preferable alternative to taking refuge behind rhetoric."[9] To Foster, neo-Marxist analyses of

[7] Martin Carnoy, "The Role of Education in a Strategy for Social Change," *Comparative Education Review* 19 (October 1975): 393–402.

[8] Richard F. Devon, "Foster's Paradigm-Surrogate and the Wealth of Underdeveloped Nations," *Comparative Education Review* 19 (October 1975): 403–13, quote on 406.

[9] Philip Foster, "Commentary on the Commentaries," *Comparative Education Review* 14 (October 1975): 423–33, quote on 424. That the arguments of radical scholars are no more than empty

educational structures are elaborate and tortured excursions into a reality that exists only in the minds of neo-Marxists. His critics rely not on careful methods for testing assumptions but on predigested ideas of the "world order." For them the future is known, and revolutionary transformation is inevitable. Such thinking gives rise to a sense of resignation over the capabilities of education to influence the social order, and therefore "attempts at social engineering are doomed to failure and amount to nothing more than meaningless tinkering with an already 'doomed' social system."[10]

Thus Foster admonishes the neo-Marxists for their disdain of empirical validation to understand reality. Devon contends that Foster's claim of empirical objectivity is hypocritical in view of his inclination to prescribe policy, and Carnoy protests Foster's functionalism, which evaluates a system in terms of its capacity to meet the exigencies needed for survival in the face of change-threatening forces. It is worth noting that each side accuses the other of promoting passivity and obstructing genuine development. Foster claims that the neo-Marxists' preinterpreted reality gives rise to a sense of dealing with already doomed social systems, and the neo-Marxists contend that Foster's idea of self-regulated, functionally integrated systems resists change. Moreover, the real differences between the neo-Marxist and neopositivist orientations in comparative education have been not so much in terms of the latter's greater propensity to use empirical data but of these groups' tendency to apply knowledge—even identical data—for different ends. To the positivists, Marxists use information to bear out their predetermined views of social change. To the Marxists, the positivist facade of objectivity in empirical data collection obscures their support for the prevailing socioeconomic structure.

It is remarkable that two positions so vastly contrary could both dominate so much thought in comparative education. It is also noteworthy that so little effort has been made to examine the divergent points of departure upon which these positions, and so much of our literature, rest. I wish at least to begin such an examination, first with a brief review of the methodological assumptions of Anderson and Foster, who in separate pieces in the early 1960s established neopositivism as the mainstream paradigm for comparative education.

Positivism in Comparative Education

Anderson claims that the purpose of comparative education is "to deal with complex systems of correlations among educational characteristics

---

rhetoric is a theme to which Foster has returned recurrently. In his 1971 presidential address, Foster claimed that radicals are "trapped at a level of rhetoric which makes it difficult for them to think through the full implications of their arguments" (Philip Foster, "Presidential Address: The Revolt against the Schools," *Comparative Education Review* 15 [October 1971]: 268).

[10] Foster, "Commentary of the Commentaries," p. 423.

and between these and traits of social structure, with little reference to the individuality of the society from which our data were derived. By convention . . . comparative study involves correlation across the boundaries of societies—whether these societies represent different centuries in one area or spatially distinct societies and sub-societies."[11] With careful attention to categorizing empirical observations, correlating precisely delineated variables, and systematically testing experientially derived propositions, Anderson believes that the comparative method can reveal ordered and repetitive patterns of social change. Both he and Foster equate comparison with Nadel's description of covariation, which treats social situations as consisting not of random items but of facts that hang together by some "meaningful nexus or intrinsic fitness."[12] Schools function only partially autonomously within a matrix containing other social institutions; the comparative method regards education as a specific variable and attempts to control its association with other social variables to ascertain invariant relationships. In this way comparison is used "to throw light on processes abstracted from time and even apart from conceptions of [evolutionary] stages."[13] Anderson and Foster display their affinity to positivism by eschewing inquiry into the uniqueness and ultimate origins of discrete social phenomena—so characteristic of extreme historicism—in favor of bringing clarity to propositions about education and society.[14]

Anderson identifies three types of correlations necessary for the development of the field. These are (1) patterns of relationships among various aspects of educational systems; (2) a typology of educational systems that compresses many patterns of data into simplified constructions, thus allowing for a higher level of abstraction; and (3) relationships between various educational characteristics and associated sociological, economic, or other noneducational features. It is interesting, however, that in the 20 years or so that a positivist position has been established in comparative education, scholars working in this tradition have made only marginal progress in identifying appropriate patterns of relationships and in establishing a typology of educational systems, although studies by Hopper, by Archer, and by Anderson may be exceptions.[15] Almost no hologeistic

[11] C. Arnold Anderson, "Methodology of Comparative Education," *International Review of Education* 7 (1961): 24–43, quote on 29.

[12] Ibid., and Philip Foster, "Comparative Methodology and the Study of African Education," *Comparative Education Review*, vol. 4 (October 1960). See also S. F. Nadel, *Foundations of Social Anthropology* (Glenco, Ill.: Free Press, 1951), p. 224.

[13] Anderson, "Methodology of Comparative Education," p. 28.

[14] Modern positivism reached its zenith under the guidance of Rudolf Carnap in the 1930s at the University of Chicago, where Anderson and Foster wrote their seminal works on comparative methodology (see Rudolf Carnap, "Testability and Meaning," *Philosophy of Science*, vols. 3–4 [1936–37]).

[15] Earl I. Hopper, "A Typology for the Classification of Educational Systems," *Sociology* 2 (1968): 29–46; Margaret Archer, *Social Origins of Educational Systems* (Beverly Hills, Calif.: Sage, 1979); C. Arnold Anderson, "Social Selection in Education and Economic Development," mimeographed (Education Department of the World Bank, February 1982).

studies, which measure theoretical variables in large, worldwide samples of human cultures and test relationships among them, of the sort proposed by Anderson, are to be found in the literature on education,[16] and challenges to positivism have emerged that are serious enough to threaten its established place in the field.

There have been three notable obstacles to the advancement of a positivist tradition in comparative education. The first is a tacit but pervasive skepticism over what Kaplan refers to as the "myth of methodology"— the idea that it does not much matter what we do if only we do it right— that tends to be associated with positivism.[17] Self-consciousness about methodology might be a sign of a field's maturity, but if excessive it can have a repressive effect on the conduct of inquiry. Practitioners have often been reluctant to abandon descriptive, even impressionistic, approaches that are convenient to apply to practical problems in favor of methodological purity.

The second obstacle is a tendency to rely indiscriminately on nations rather than on more discrete entities such as tribal or ethnic groups as units of analysis. The analytic comparability of nations is highly problematic, as is the feasibility of reliable sampling when the number of units available for comparison is so small. Yet Noah and Eckstein, in the most comprehensive work to have advanced the positivist orientation since Anderson's and Foster's early pieces,[18] do not even consider hologeistic research, however much that approach may be the most logical extension of positivism. Indeed, it is not surprising that Noah, in his presidential address in 1974 (a few years after his and Eckstein's book, *Toward a Science of Comparative Education*, appeared), conceded the limitations of cross-national studies. What *is* surprising is his advancement of *micro* studies and a focus on "cases that may lie well off the regression plane" to fill gaps in understanding created by the small within-country and cross-country variances researchers were finding to explain such variables as achievement.[19] Rather than

[16] Anderson specifically mentions Murdoch's study of kinship and Udy's study of economic organization—both displaying hologeistic methods—as models for comparative analysis (Anderson, "Methodology of Comparative Education," p. 30). See G. P. Murdock, *Social Structure* (New York: Macmillan, 1949); and Stanley Udy, *Organization of Work* (New Haven, Conn.: HRAF Press, 1959). Perhaps the only examples of hologeistic research to be found in the literature on education are Erwin H. Epstein, "Cross-cultural Sampling and a Conceptualization of 'Professional' Instruction," *Journal of Experimental Education* 33 (Summer 1965): 395–401; and John D. Herzog, "Deliberate Instruction and Household Structure: A Cross-cultural Study," *Harvard Educational Review* 32 (1962): 310–42. For a description of the early development of the hologeistic approach, see John W. M. Whiting, "The Cross-cultural Method," in *Handbook of Social Psychology*, ed. Gardner Lindsey, 2 vols. (Cambridge, Mass.: Addison-Wesley, 1954), 1:523–31.

[17] Abraham Kaplan, "Positivism," in *International Encyclopedia of the Social Sciences*, ed. David L. Sills (New York: Macmillan, 1968), 12:394.

[18] Noah and Eckstein (n. 1 above).

[19] Harold J. Noah, "Fast-Fish and Loose-Fish in Comparative Education," *Comparative Education Review* 18 (October 1974): 341–47. In discussing the limitations of macro studies, Noah referred

suggesting the importance of refining units of analysis to advance the "science" of comparative education, Noah came close to saying that the field's scientific foundation—the systematic search for generalizations and repetitive patterns in social phenomena—was about as advanced as it could be.

The third obstacle is the most important and the one on which I wish to focus most attention. I refer here to the ideological component in the positivist orientation. Ironically, positivism—or scientific empiricism as it is sometimes called—emerged as a reaction against religious, metaphysical, and political explanation. Yet we find the positivist impulse under increasingly strident attack because of its ideological bias. To be sure, classical positivism is open to criticism because the degree of clarity it can bring to propositions is necessarily limited; criteria for confirmation or disconfirmation of propositions must be liberal enough to allow for statements containing theoretical terms, whose verification must remain remote and indirect and therefore susceptible to ideologies, myths, and even metaphysics. On this point Max Weber has given eloquent testimony, and I need do no more than refer you to his work.[20] But most of those who have advocated more precise measurement of variables and greater clarity in propositions about education have deliberately gone beyond the search for lawlike regularities. Anderson, for example, contended 2 decades ago that the great "missing link" in comparative education is "the almost total absence of information about the outcomes or products of educational systems."[21] Unlike the classical positivists, who were content with finding "logical" connections among statements capable of verification, leading ultimately to a comprehensive synthesis of such knowledge, Anderson and most other neopositivists in comparative education are preoccupied with *causal* connections. They are concerned not merely with how education covaries with other variables but with the consequences of education as an independent variable, especially as it has affected the development, or "modernization," of nations. It is in this regard that they have opened themselves up to the most serious criticism of all—that of ideological bias.

"Development" is not a value-free concept. It is infused with normative meaning, and, indeed, its content has changed, as have the end states with which it has been associated. Packenham has contended, for example, that as prevailing political values in the United States were revised during the post–World War II period, so was the conception of development. Originally, development was viewed in terms of economic growth and

---

largely to the research on international achievement in mathematics (see Torsten Husen, ed., *International Study of Achievement in Mathematics: A Comparison between Twelve Countries* [New York: Wiley, 1967], vols. 1–2).

[20] Max Weber, *Methodology of the Social Sciences*, trans. and ed. Edward A. Shils and Henry A. Finch (Glencoe, Ill.: Free Press, 1949), pp. 49–112. See also Kaplan, p. 390.

[21] Anderson, "Methodology of Comparative Education," p. 30.

was translated into policy by the Marshall Plan and Point Four Legislation. Shortly afterward, as reflected in the Mutual Security Act, development became associated in part with military security. Later still, goals of political participation and the building of democratic institutions, as embodied, for example, in Title IX of the Foreign Assistance Act of 1966, became equal with economic growth in defining development.[22] Most recently, the reduction of inequality has joined the set of propositional components of which "development" consists.[23] In short, the meanings ascribed to development have been determined by the range of values used to define desirable end states.

Notwithstanding the unquestioned acceptance of development as a universally desirable goal by comparativists in the neopositivist tradition, development can never be wholly based on objective, rationalistic, and indisputable premises. Indeed, scholars are increasingly observing "over-development" in some societies: a condition in which the intangible components of human existence decline as the tangible indices of development improve.[24] The benefits of development, including the outcomes and products of education, must remain open to question if social pathologies are a by-product of expanded material wealth and political equality. Neo-Marxists may be faulted for their relative inattentiveness to empirical validation, but they have a strong case in attributing ideological bias to the work of neopositivists such as Foster and Anderson. All scholars as members of society are part of the studied reality, and their beliefs, which are prior to their scholarship, are influenced by the historical reality in which they participate.[25] However much positivists may avow the probity of personal dissociation in the diagnosis of a subject, the process of investigation itself transforms social reality. Consider that a generalization regarding social reality is a statement about "typical"—or "regularities" in—behavior; a scientifically described mechanism of behavior is not simply an empirical fact descriptive of a sample of observations but a model of conformity for the entire universe of individuals to whom the statement

[22] R. A. Packenham, *Liberal America and the Third World* (Princeton, N.J.: Princeton University Press, 1973).

[23] See, e.g., Irma Adelman and C. T. Morris, *Economic Growth and Social Equity in Developing Countries* (Stanford, Calif.: Stanford University Press, 1973); and Dudley Seers, "The Meaning of Development," in *The Political Economy of Development and Underdevelopment*, ed. C. K. Wilber (New York: Random House, 1973).

[24] Robert N. Bellah, *Beyond Belief* (New York: Harper & Row, 1970); Dean C. Tibbs, "Modernization Theory and the Study of National Societies: A Critical Perspective," *Comparative Studies in Society and History* 15 (1973): 199–226; S. Chodak, *Societal Development* (New York: Oxford University Press, 1973); C. H. Anderson, *The Sociology of Survival* (Homewood, Ill.: Dorsey, 1976); and Daniel Chirot, "Changing Fashions in the Study of the Social Causes of Economic and Political Change," in *The State of Sociology: Problems and Prospects*, ed. James F. Short, Jr. (Beverly Hills, Calif.: Sage, 1981), pp. 259–82.

[25] See Jerzy J. Wiatr, "Sociology-Marxism-Reality," in *Marxism and Sociology: Views from Eastern Europe*, ed. Peter L. Berger (New York: Appleton-Century-Crofts, 1969), pp. 18–36.

applies. Typical behavior is normative behavior. To make known what is typical is often to make it more typical. To show that engineering students get higher-paying jobs is not simply a neutral finding; it may have the effect of producing more engineers. Merton recognized this when he wrote about "self-fulfilling" prophecies—forecasts that influence their own realization.[26]

The Archer-King Debate

I wish now to turn to the second pivotal debate in comparative education—that between Archer and King—in which positivism is challenged on another side, by exponents of the problem approach, whom I refer to as neorelativists. However radical the neo-Marxists are in comparison to the neopositivists, the neorelativists are conservative.

The debate between Archer and King was precipitated by King's criticisms of Archer's recent book, *Social Origins of Educational Systems*, in a review published in *Comparative Education*, of which King is editor.[27] Briefly, King views Archer's work as "so much quasi-theology about 'thinking and theorising about educational systems,' 'universal characteristics of structural elaboration,' and so forth—all linked with repetitious 'identification' of phenomena, sequences, 'causation,' 'determinants,' 'laws,' 'relevant empirical generalizations, the composition laws, which would then enable one to compute complex situations,' 'macro-sociological laws,' and the rest of the long-discredited apparatus of attempting to force educational and other systems into the typologies beloved of some seminar rooms."[28] In fact, Archer's book is an example of orthodox positivism, and it should be clear from my previous remarks that King's characterization of the volume as "so much quasi-theology" is not simply a criticism of the book but of the orientation that it represents.

Social Origins is a work of great subtlety and complexity, and represents the most ambitious attempt thus far to achieve the kind of comprehensive synthesis of propositions about education that positivists crave. It is about the mechanisms through which pressures for educational change or stability are transformed into policy. But what is noteworthy here is that synthesis is not gained by the use of macro samples of many societies. Instead, Archer emphasizes historical specificity and limits her analysis to educational policy in only four countries: Denmark, England, France, and Russia. By examining the contexts in which change occurs, Archer reveals the structural forces that encourage the survival of distinctive types of educational systems

---

[26] Robert K. Merton, *Social Theory and Social Structure* (New York: Free Press, 1957).

[27] Archer, *Social Origins of Educational Systems*; King's review is in *Comparative Education* 15 (October 1979): 350–52.

[28] Edmund King, "Prescription or Partnership in Comparative Studies of Education?" *Comparative Education* 16 (June 1980): 185–95, quote on 186.

and the nature of their adaptation to changing environments. In other words, what Archer does not achieve in terms of representative-sample reliability she attempts to make up for by being exhaustive in her analysis of factors and forces within particular societies. Despite her careful attention to contextual specificity, she avoids the kind of extreme historicism to which Anderson objects. She remains true to the positivist tradition by observing regularities and drawing overarching generalizations—albeit extremely cautiously—from data on educational centralization and control, interest groups, political elites, and economic resources. In a reaction to her book, Craig comments that "one is tempted to conclude that we now know everything we could ever want to know about the origins and development of educational systems."[29]

King's criticism of *Social Origins* provides insight into the field's third major theoretical orientation and its attendant ideological impulse. The neorelativists—proponents of the "problem" approach—and the neo-Marxists may hold mutually incongruous views, but they share a skepticism of positivist thought and methods. King's view is simply that propositions generalized cross-nationally are invalid, that all theoretical statements regarding education must be made entirely within particular contexts, and that the principal purpose of comparison is not explanation but the improvement of education, that is, within the context of specific situations. However attentive Archer is to contextual detail, it is not enough to satisfy King, in view of her tendency to use stereotypes such as "*the* impenetrable polity" and "*the* centralized system" as "constructs into which real-life phenomena can be thrust not merely from country to country and context to context but from age to age, and from one stage of development to quite different circumstances."[30] For King, Archer's macrosociological "message" is no more than a "latterday successor to theological orthodoxy."[31]

Archer's reaction to King's criticism is of equal interest not only for what it shows about her view toward relativism but what it reflects about her positivist orientation. In her rejection of the prescriptive value of comparison she reveals herself to be a more orthodox positivist than Anderson or Foster, who are concerned with the educational policy implications of development as well as with explanation and generalization. Archer's remarks are illuminating:

> Why then is the comparative method found so wanting by King? The answer lies deep at the heart of the "reformative" purpose of comparative education. It is because the comparative method can never tell us what *ought* to be done. To King the ultimate test of a theoretical framework is quite simply whether it can

[29] John E. Craig, "On the Development of Educational Systems," *American Journal of Education* 89 (February 1981): 189–211, quote on 201.
[30] King, p. 187.
[31] Ibid., p. 195.

"aid policy development." Hence his blurring of validity with utility parallels the earlier elision between facts and values and between explanation and prescription . . . . The instrumental criterion of validity has all the defects . . . for instrumentalism in general, notably that practical utility need have nothing to do with verisimilitude, least of all, one would add, in the field of political policy. Moreover policy formation is quintessentially a political process, in which the Comparative Educationalist can only be pushed around as a pawn rather than playing at being King. Any such educationalist would do much better by retreating to his seminar room and trying to understand this process, with the aid of the comparative method, than by naively joining one of the "policy-shaping comparative 'workshops' " . . . which King says have so "greatly strengthened Comparative Education since the later 1960s . . . ."[32]

The Ideological Bias of Neopositivism

The theoretical assumptions of the positivist orientation in comparative education should by now be clear, as should the objections to positivism of the neo-Marxists and the neorelativists. The positivists believe that ordered and repetitive patterns of social processes relating to education can be abstracted from time and space by systematically testing experientially derived propositions. And most of the positivists, and here I refer to the neopositivists, have attempted to apply systematic empirical methods to observations about the role of education in national development. It is in this regard that the neo-Marxists and the neorelativists have been most convincing. By showing that "development" is hardly a universally accepted, value-free objective, they have demonstrated the ideological bias of the neopositivists. I contend, however, that the neo-Marxists and neorelativists are themselves guilty of bias; their assumptions, too, are informed by ideology.

The Ideological Bias of Neo-Marxism

Marxists and relativists deny the validity of abstracting man's nature independent of particular sociohistorical conditions. Marxists in particular believe that an individual's character is always dynamic and that human existence is a process of becoming. For Marx, "right can never be higher than the economic structure of the society and the cultural development thereby determined."[33] For him, ideology applies to theories that universalize historical moments by projecting their characteristics beyond historical time as immutable traits of human nature. Orthodox Marxists equate ideology with the writings of intellectuals who, by claiming objective, universal validity for propositions about social reality, which is to ascribe permanence and stability to social relations, help to preserve the capitalist

[32] Margaret Archer, "Sociology and Comparative Education: A Reply to Edmund King," *Comparative Education* 16 (June 1980): 179–85, quote on 184.

[33] Karl Marx, *A Critique of the Gotha Program* (New York: International Publishers, 1938), and *The Poverty of Philosophy* (Moscow: Foreign Languages Publishing House, n.d.).

order.[34] Ideology invariably gives rise to false consciousness, a characteristic unique to intellectuals and capitalists.

Neo-Marxists, however, and particularly Gramsci, make a distinction between false consciousness and ideology. For them false consciousness — being oblivious to the social relations of production that prevail in society — is not limited to intellectuals and capitalists; the working class in capitalist societies is also prey to false consciousness. Yet working-class false consciousness is not illusory in the same sense as that of the bourgeoisie; the delusion of the former is not total because being oppressed means *feeling* oppression and being forced to deal with it. False consciousness becomes the normal way of perceiving and acting within capitalist society, but tendencies within the basic economic process of capitalist accumulation prevent such false consciousness from remaining permanent and secure among workers. Unlike Marx, the neo-Marxists admit to an ideological impulse; for them the development of revolutionary class consciousness is an ideological process of drawing and building on workers' fragmentary insight. Marxist ideology is thus offered as a counter to burgeois ideology.[35]

The role of education in neo-Marxism is obviously important. The school is a two-edged sword; it represents the repressive social conditions of capitalist society but potentially also the instrument for the dissipation of false consciousness. Education in capitalist liberal democracies promotes social class cleavages by transmitting to each successive generation a structured misrepresentation of reality. Rather than seeking "truth," capitalist schools impose an ideology that dupes the proletariat into contributing their labor in the production process, benefiting only the ruling class. They do this by teaching a positivistic world view that emphasizes discovery through experience and sense impressions. As Freud has shown, however, sense impressions are deceptive; individuals tend to select particular "facts" out of an infinite multitude of possibilities and further order and categorize their observations according to how well they fall into their particular matrix. We all fall prey to delusions, distortive defense mechanisms, prejudices, group pressures, and mental sets that twist our perceptions of reality. However, positivists, who rely on sensory experience to obtain data and whose view of reality is therefore shaped by the fallible senses, are particularly susceptible to such distortions. Instead of objective knowledge, their reliance on sense perceptions yields a misrepresentation of reality. Rather than promote the individual as the source of knowledge, positivist ideology, by viewing knowledge as something to be experienced,

[34] See Koula Mellos, "The Concept of Ideology in Marx," *Social Praxis* 7 (1980): 5–19.

[35] Antonio Gramsci, *Selections from the Prison Notebooks* (London: Lawrence & Wishart, 1971). See also Georg Lukacs, *History and Class Consciousness* (Cambridge, Mass.: MIT Press, 1972); J. Femia, "Hegemony and Consciousness in the Thought of Antonio Gramsci," *Political Studies* 23 (1975): 29–48; and Ron Eyerman, "False Consciousness and Ideology in Marxist Theory," *Acta Sociologica* 24 (1981): 43–56.

transforms the individual into a mere agent in knowledge production. Education in capitalist society, therefore, may be viewed metaphorically as a factory, with knowledge as the product emitted by, but existing apart from and outside the control of, the individual who labors to produce it.[36] World-system analysts such as Arnove have extended this critique to the international arena in an attempt to show that schools contribute to the emergence and consolidation of a world economic system in the grip of capitalism.[37]

Neo-Marxists, while not denying that they, like the neopositivists, have an ideology, believe that their Marxist ideology is superior. Harris has gone so far as to propose a test to judge the veracity of the Marxist perspective of reality against the positivist, liberal democratic view. The test's sole criterion is the degree to which the ideology serves all social, economic, and political interests equally. Not surprisingly, Harris concludes that positivism, in marked contrast to Marxism, fails the test by serving disproportionately the interests of the bourgeousie. Education under capitalism, for example, teaches working-class children to accept their ascribed place in society while legitimating the elevated position of the wealthy. It does this effectively by emphasizing the self-professed trappings of liberal democracy—the openness of society, universal political suffrage, and opportunities for upward social mobility by means of individual effort—while ignoring the results: relatively little real social mobility and an enduring inequity in the distribution of wealth and resources. The working-class child thus learns undeservedly to blame himself for his inferior position, because he is unable to advance socioeconomically amidst a supposed multitude of opportunities, and the middle- or upper-class child learns similarly to justify his position vis-à-vis those who are purportedly not smart or diligent enough to do better. In this way the school teaches a false consciousness at all social levels, one that plays into the hands of the rich, even as they too believe the myth of open opportunities.[38]

Unfortunately, the neo-Marxists are as given to exaggerated claims in defending their position as are the positivists in defending theirs. Whereas the positivists' denial of ideological bias is unsupportable, the neo-Marxists are on equally unsure grounds in contending the superiority of their ideology. Consider that for all of their mistrust of empiricism, the neo-

[36] The neo-Marxist literature relating to education has become extensive in recent years. For a description of some of its more influential currents, see Vandra Lea Masemann, "Critical Perspectives on Issues in Comparative Education" (paper presented at the Comparative and International Education Society meeting, Vancouver, Canada, March 1980); and Pierre Bourdieu and Jean-Claude Passeron, *Reproduction in Education, Society and Culture* (Beverly Hills, Calif.: Sage, 1977).

[37] Robert F. Arnove, "Comparative Education and World-System Analysis," *Comparative Education Review* 24 (February 1980): 48–62; see also Martin Carnoy, *Education as Cultural Imperialism* (New York: McKay, 1974).

[38] Kevin Harris, *Education and Knowledge: The Structured Misrepresentation of Reality* (London: Routledge & Kegan Paul, 1979).

Marxists depend on the validity of certain empirical claims for the efficacy of their position. Harris, for example, relies on the findings of Bowles and Gintis[39] to show that economic success under capitalism is a function of the economic system and tends to run in families almost independently of intelligence (as measured by IQ tests); the rich stay rich and the poor stay poor regardless of intellectual ability. The Bowles and Gintis data refute the arguments of geneticists and psychologists, principally Jensen and Herrnstein,[40] that socioeconomic stratification can be best explained by the "fact" that intelligence, "known" to be highly inheritable, is passed on within economic groups to such an extent that education simply cannot compensate for genetic differences. Those arguments, Harris believes, by focusing on the individual rather than on social relations as the source of economic differences, are rooted in class-serving, self-interest-serving ideology; their data tend to justify the perpetuation of class-based economic inequalities as deriving from real genetic variations in individuals. By contrast, Bowles and Gintis's findings, in purportedly showing that economic inequality is rooted in this very structure of society and cannot be explained by the intellectual and genetic superiority of the dominant class, are free of ideological distortion.

Harris's position, however, is dubious at best. Both the Bowles-Gintis findings and the Jensen-Herrnstein data purport to measure the influence of genetically inheritable intelligence on economic productivity and status attainment. The fact remains, however, that they have worked with different data sets, which, although susceptible to empirical evaluation, have yet to be systematically compared, and Harris's "test" cannot yield definitive results given gaps in the current state of knowledge. Bowles and Gintis, as have many others,[41] persuasively demonstrate the inadequacies of the Jensen-Herrnstein position; but, then again, Bowles and Gintis's data, purportedly showing that schools serve primarily to develop noncognitive characteristics necessary to the reproduction of the social relations of production in a capitalist economy, have been found to be largely unsupported by Olneck and Bills.[42]

Moreover, much of Harris's thesis rests on the supposed failure of compensatory education programs introduced in the United States in the

[39] Samuel Bowles and Herbert Gintis, *Schooling in Capitalist America: Educational Reform and the Contradictions of Economic Life* (New York: Basic, 1976).

[40] Arthur R. Jensen, "How Much Can We Boost IQ and Scholastic Achievement?" *Harvard Educational Review* 39 (1969): 1–123; Richard J. Herrnstein, "I.Q." *Atlantic Monthly* 228 (December 1971): 43–58.

[41] See L. J. Kamin, *The Science and Politics of I.Q.* (New York: Wiley, 1974); N. J. Block and G. Dworkin, eds., *The I.Q. Controversy* (New York: Pantheon, 1976); Stephen Jay Gould, "Jensen's Last Stand," *New York Review of Books* 27 (May 1, 1980): 38–44; and Sandra Scarr, *Race, Social Class and Individual Differences in I.Q.* (Hillsdale, N.J.: Erlbaum, 1981).

[42] Michael R. Olneck and David B. Bills, "What Makes Sammy Run? An Empirical Assessment of the Bowles-Gintis Correspondence Theory," *American Journal of Education* 89 (November 1980): 27–61.

1960s to equalize economic opportunities between rich and poor. These programs, Harris suggests, were mere disguises used to deceive people into believing the liberal democratic rhetoric about the value of schools to promote social mobility. Yet recent studies indicate not only that compensatory education programs may have had more of an impact than early investigations, such as those of Coleman et al. and of Jencks et al.,[43] had claimed,[44] but that school characteristics can powerfully affect student outcomes and that schools might be able to break the link between class, race, and academic achievement after all.[45] For our purposes, the most important findings are by Heyneman and Loxley, who, in an examination of various influences on academic achievement in Africa, Asia, Latin America, and the Middle East, show that the power of socioeconomic status to determine achievement is substantially less in lower-income countries, and the lower the income of the country the greater is the power of the school to determine directly students' performance.[46] These findings challenge the contention of Marxist world-system analysts that schools, if anything, do even more to perpetuate social class differences by influencing noncognitive outcomes in the Third World than in technologically advanced countries.[47]

Ultimately, however, Harris's position fails at the point where neo-Marxism is most vulnerable: its view of false consciousness and the question of how to deal with it. If the proletariat in capitalist societies is susceptible to distortions of social reality, and schools serve dominant-class interests by perpetuating false consciousness, how can growth in revolutionary consciousness be achieved? Many neo-Marxists, such as Lukacs, have taken a Leninist view that the vanguard party rather than the proletariat "is the historical embodiment and the active incarnation of class consciousness" and must therefore guide the transition to socialism. By virtue of being submerged in the travails of economic necessity, the proletariat is unable to raise itself as a class to a state of revolutionary awareness. The party, on the other hand, by maintaining a creative distance between itself and

[43] James Coleman, E. Campbell, C. Hobson, et al., *Equality of Educational Opportunity* (Washington, D.C.: Government Printing Office, 1966); Christopher Jencks, M. Smith, H. Arland, et al., *Inequality: A Reassessment of the Effect of Family and Schooling in America* (New York: Basic, 1972).

[44] Irving Lazar and Richard Darlington, *Lasting Effects after Preschool* (ERIC/ECE, 1979).

[45] Diane Ravitch, *The Revisionists Revised: A Critique of the Radical Attack on the Schools* (New York: Basic, 1978); Wilbur Brookover, Charles Beady, Patricia Flood, et al., *School Social Systems and Student Achievement: Schools Can Make a Difference* (New York: Praeger, 1979); G. Madaus, T. Kellaghan, E. Rakow, and D. King, "The Sensitivity of Measures of School Effectiveness," *Harvard Educational Review* 49 (1979): 207–30; and M. Rutter, B. Maughan, P. Mortimore, and J. Ouston, with A. Smith, *Fifteen Thousand Hours* (Cambridge, Mass.: Harvard University Press, 1979).

[46] S. Heyneman and W. Loxley, "The Impact of Primary School Quality on Academic Achievement across Twenty-Nine High and Low Income Countries" (paper presented to the American Sociological Association Meeting, Toronto, August 1981).

[47] Marxist world-system theorists link educational events to the workings of an international economic order to explain why the expansion and reform of schooling often help to perpetuate

the ideologically imprisoned masses, is capable of constructing a politically coherent world view from the inchoate sentiments that struggle for expression within the proletariat. The party actually becomes the "objectification" of the proletariat's own will, however much the workers are unable to recognize it. From this reasoning it is a short step to the conclusion that the very existence of the party is tangible proof of its infallibility.[48]

Understandably, neo-Marxists such as Harris, who focus on the role of education, tend to avoid discussions of how to achieve revolutionary consciousness under capitalism when institutions such as the school control knowledge. They seem to be tacitly sensitive to what Berger calls "epistemological arrogance" to describe any process by which some individuals, by virtue of their putative higher consciousness, help redeem the masses from capitalist domination.[49] Yet neo-Marxists are unable to reconcile the condition of domination with a reality that precludes "demystification" by those who are dominated.[50] Without such a reconciliation the neo-Marxist position will remain hopelessly impositional; by implication it is the neo-Marxists who see themselves as the vanguard to guide the masses to a new level of consciousness.

There is a final way to test the relative virtue of competing ideologies using Harris's criterion of serving all social, economic, and political interests equally. That is to examine the results not only in capitalist societies but in socialist societies as well, something which Harris neglects to do. In view of the available evidence, it would appear that schools in state socialist countries have fared no better, and perhaps have done worse, than they have done in state capitalist countries in meeting the test. That significant inequalities exist in state socialist countries has been well documented. Several studies have shown that informal pay bonuses, special rations,

---

existing stratification systems. However, recent analyses have seriously questioned the assumptions and historical reasoning that have given rise to Marxist world-system theory (see, e.g., Chirot [n. 24 above]). Cardoso and Faletto even claim that dependency theory, a Marxist corollary to world-system theory, is dead (see F. H. Cardoso and E. Faletto, *Dependency and Development in Latin America* [Berkeley: University of California Press, 1979]; see also Mary Jean Bowman, review of Martin Carnoy, *Education as Cultural Imperialism*, *Economic Development and Cultural Change* 24 [July 1976]: 833–40). Yet not all world-system analyses are Marxist. In particular, the findings of Meyer, Ramirez, Rubinson, and Boli-Bennett oppose the Marxist contention that educational expansion has helped to maintain the existing status hierarchy as well as the functionalist use of modernization to explain educational growth (John W. Meyer, Francisco O. Ramirez, Richard Rubinson, and John Boli-Bennett, "The World Educational Revolution, 1950–1970," *Sociology of Education* 50 [Fall 1977]: 242–58; see also John W. Meyer and Michael T. Hannan, eds., *National Development and the World System* [Chicago: University of Chicago Press, 1979]; and Francisco O. Ramirez and John Boli-Bennett, "Global Patterns of Educational Institutionalization," in *Comparative Education*, ed. Philip G. Altbach, Robert F. Arnove, and Gail P. Kelly [New York: Macmillan, 1982], pp. 15–38).

[48] Lukacs, pp. 42 and 327; see also Frank Parkin, *Marxism and Class Theory: A Bourgeois Critique* (New York: Columbia University Press, 1979), pp. 145–55.

[49] Peter L. Berger, *Pyramids of Sacrifice: Political Ethics and Social Change* (New York: Basic, 1974), pp. 19 and 114.

[50] For a discussion of this point, see Erwin H. Epstein, "The Social Control Thesis and Educational Reform in Dependent Nations," *Theory and Society* 5 (1978): 255–76.

privileged access to stores selling scarce goods at lower prices, the provision of country houses, exclusive access to vacation resorts and superior hospitals and medical care, and rights to better housing and travel abroad have created noticeable socioeconomic disparities between the privileged and the masses in such societies.[51] Parkin has observed that as Eastern European countries have responded to economic inefficiencies by adopting incentive strategies, they have experienced a clearly discernible pattern of increasing inequality. Moreover, the record of Communist regimes in protecting the interests of all groups during the transformation of the reward structure of former capitalist economies has been poor. Wherever Communist parties have come to power they have established a unitary political system in which the former bourgeoisie has been denied rights to oppose social change, and citizens have been subjected to gross abuses of constitutional rights.[52] Schools, of course, have not been exempt from displays of inequities; investigations have confirmed that children born into the upper socio-economic strata are more likely than others to attain high levels of education.[53] Moreover, Jews and certain other minorities in the Soviet Union have been deprived of an equal opportunity for advanced schooling, and religious instruction has been suppressed.[54] Until Harris and other neo-Marxist scholars can show that their test for the virtue of a theoretical framework is not one-sided, their critical view of positivism and education in liberal democracies will appear unreasonable.

We see, in short, that whereas neopositivism seeks to be value free *and* objective, neo-Marxism purports only to be objective.[55] In other words, neo-Marxism admits to an absence of detachment in its perspective but contends that its view of social reality is objective insofar as objectivity reflects relative truth. Neorelativism, however—the assumptions of which I now examine—purports only to be value free. It professes detachment, and claims that no particular view of reality is any more or less true than any other.

---

[51] David Lane, *The End of Inequality? Stratification under State Socialism* (Baltimore: Penguin, 1971); Mervin Matthews, *Class and Society in Soviet Russia* (New York: Walker, 1972); Seymour Martin Lipset and Richard B. Dobson, "Social Stratification and Sociology in the Soviet Union," *Survey*, no. 19 (Summer 1973), pp. 114–85; Murray Yanowitch, *Social and Economic Inequality in the Soviet Union: Six Studies* (White Plains, N.Y.: Sharpe, 1977); and Walter D. Connor, *Socialism, Politics, and Equality: Hierarchy and Change in Eastern Europe and the U.S.S.R.* (New York: Columbia University Press, 1979).

[52] Frank Parkin, *Class Inequality and Political Order* (New York: Praeger, 1971).

[53] Murray Yanowitch and Norton Dodge, "Social Class and Education: Soviet Findings and Reactions," *Comparative Education Review* 12 (October 1968): 248–67; Richard B. Dobson, "Mobility and Stratification in the Soviet Union," *Annual Review of Sociology* 3 (1977): 297–329; and Richard B. Dobson and Michael Swafford, "The Educational Attainment Process in the Soviet Union: A Case Study," *Comparative Education Review* 24 (June 1980): 252–69.

[54] Erwin H. Epstein, "Ideological Factors in Soviet Educational Policy toward Jews," *Education and Urban Society* 10 (February 1978): 223–54.

[55] See Michael Harrington, *The Twilight of Capitalism* (New York: Simon & Schuster, 1976).

The Ideological Bias of Neorelativism

Along with King, Brian Holmes is undoubtedly the best-known neo-relativist in comparative education.[56] Holmes's "problem" approach is prompted by the rise of relativity in the natural sciences, which challenges the concept of absolute measurement and the unconditional validity of general laws. Holmes contends that social scientists have been slow in recognizing the cogent meaning of relativity for social theory and research and for the need of a paradigmatic revolution. Just as relativity gave reason for questioning the logical validity of the absolutist traditional concepts of mass, force, and the like in the physical world, so should it challenge the idea that fundamental eternal laws underlie all behavior and social development, an idea that forms the basis for most contemporary social research. Rather than eternal or infallible laws, social theory should be informed by a search for contextual generalizations in which behavior is seen as governed by specific spatiotemporal, linguistic, and sociopsychological conditions within varying circumstances. Since the pursuit of absolute laws is fruitless, "pure" research is unwarranted and represents a waste of time and resources. Instead, the social sciences, and comparative education in particular, should be responsive to practical problems and the need for application. Piecemeal social engineering oriented to policy and emphasizing modest objectives within the context of specific initial conditions and unique national circumstances should guide comparative research. Investigation should begin not with the collection of data but from a careful identification and analysis of a discrete practical problem.[57]

Holmes's method represents a refutation of the positivist view that if all factors giving rise to a particular social behavior were known, then a multivariate statement would explain that behavior wherever and whenever it occurs. But it is also a repudiation of Marxian determinism, the belief that certain economic forces inexorably shape history. Rather than a search for universal regularities in nature and history, Holmes believes that comparative social research should be guided by a desire to discover the uniqueness of nations and societies, and he proposes adoption of the Weberian notion of ideal-typical normative constructs as models with which to examine particular structures and social relationships. Such constructs, insofar as they give coherence to the multiplicity of beliefs that exist in society and provide clues to collective mental states and social action, are appropriate starting points for investigation. The proposed

[56] However much King and Holmes bicker about their mutual epistemological differences, they both were students of Karl Popper and are very much in the Popperian neorelativist tradition (see Brian Holmes, *Problems in Education: A Comparative Approach* [London: Routledge & Kegan Paul, 1965], p. 53; Edmund J. King, *Comparative Studies and Educational Decision* [New York: Bobbs-Merrill, 1968], pp. 53–54; Brian Holmes, *Comparative Education: Some Considerations of Method* [London: Allen & Unwin, 1981], pp. 70–71, and "Models in Comparative Education," *Compare* 11 [1981]: 155–61).

[57] Holmes, *Comparative Education: Some Considerations of Method.*

use of ideal-typical normative models is not an abrupt departure from earlier theory in comparative education; analogues may be found in the ideas of classical relativists such as Michael Sadler and Vernon Mallinson, who thought, respectively, that a nation embodied a "living spirit" or a national character. Ideal-typical models focus more, however, on general aims and theories regarding man, society, and knowledge than on intangible, immanent forces. Holmes contends that aims, theories, and mental states are relevant constituents of the initial specific conditions associated with the "problem" to which the attention of the researcher is to be directed.

Various neorelativists have attempted to show that educational strategies lack universal viability. They occasionally follow Piaget in emphasizing the distinct perspective of each individual organism and its differential adaptation to the environment. Some have been inspired by ethnomethodological, phenomenological, or symbolic interactionist models, with their stress on the social construction of reality and the development of meaning through interaction. Clignet, for example, has suggested that what happens in schools is a product of the use that teachers and students make of distinctive and conflicting adaptive mechanisms; each individual's adaptation varies with the normative and sociopsychological profile of each classroom situation.[58] Hence no scientific law that purports to explain interpersonal interactions can validly apply to educational practice. Schrag contends that the contributions of psychology to science and epistemology have little practical utility in educational reform and policymaking, and that even our commonsense, pretheoretical understanding of human behavior is a better guide to practice than psychological theory.[59] Popper put it succinctly when he said, "What we should do, I suggest, is to give up the idea of ultimate sources of knowledge, and admit that all knowledge is human; that it is mixed with our errors, our prejudices, our dreams, our hopes; that all we can do is to grope for truth even though it be beyond our reach. We may admit that our groping is often inspired, but we must be on our guard against the belief, however deeply felt, that our inspiration carries any authority."[60]

Of the three main currents in comparative education, neorelativism seems on the surface to be the least given to ideology. It contends, after all, that *all* sources of knowledge—whether embodied in Marxist determinism or in the palpable regularities sought by positivists—are without authority. Yet both Marxists and positivists would be correct in arguing

[58] Remi Clignet, "The Double Natural History of Educational Interactions: Implications for Educational Reforms," *Comparative Education Review* 25 (October 1981): 330–52; see also M. Mulkay, *Science and the Sociology of Knowledge* (London: Allen & Unwin, 1979).

[59] Francis Schrag, "Knowing and Doing," *American Journal of Education* 89 (May 1981): 253–82; see also D. C. Phillips, "Toward an Evaluation of the Experiment in Educational Contexts," *Educational Researcher* 10 (June/July 1981): 13–20.

[60] Karl Popper, *Conjectures and Refutations* (New York: Harper Torchbooks, 1968), pp. 29–30.

that however much relativism may appear to be unbiased and free of partisan values, its effects are assuredly ideological. This is most apparent from a Marxist viewpoint, since any position that professes that no position has moral authority will tend to leave unchallenged the dominant ideology, which often, of course, happens to be capitalism.

More problematic but perhaps more cogent, however, is the positivist critique, consisting of two components. The first applies to the relativists' method of imaginative sympathy, that is, the method of understanding behavior by identifying with others' motives and points of view. Here there is a fallacy in that an understanding of behavior gained through the use of such a method can never be used to explain that behavior; identification with others' motives and views does not constitute valid evidence of an explanation, since it cannot be corroborated. For one thing, when we think we have identified ourselves with others, we may only have imposed our own feelings on them, however much we may think we grasp the relevant psychosocial contextual circumstances. For another thing, even if we somehow succeeded in projecting ourselves into the minds of others, to see things exactly as they do is to share their self-deceptions. As Frankel put it, "if we really believed that we can only prove the truth of a theory about human behavior by taking the attitude of the human beings we are talking about, we would ask paranoids to verify our theories about paranoia."[61]

The second component of the positivist critique focuses on the existence of certain permanent demands of human nature and certain unchanging necessities in human society that govern the effects that an idea has in history. There seems to be an intangible, universal need to believe that what one does is part of an eternal design, that one's accomplishments and hopes are not all bound to be swallowed up by time.[62] Human needs and demands give rise to fundamentally similar responses. We see, therefore, that classes of nations display common syndromes of historical, cultural, and social characteristics that cannot be explained by unique psychosocial contexts or by shared ideal-typical normative patterns. Modern nation-states manifest considerable institutional commonalities; they have legislatures, public administrative systems, armies, and interest groups. Structurally similar institutional arrangements suggest that certain functional linkages commonly exist, linkages that cannot properly be tested if each society is examined as a unique entity. The kind of ideographic research advanced by the neorelativists may be of value in producing insights about the nature of education under given circumstances and can inform policy, but it can hardly be effective in systematically disentangling the relevant

---

[61] Charles Frankel, *The Case for Modern Man* (Boston: Beacon, 1956), p. 130.
[62] See Jacques Maritain, *Scholasticism and Politics*, trans. M. J. Adler (London: Bles, 1940).

factors associated with education in a specified cultural situation from the irrelevant factors.

The most disturbing aspect of relativism, however, is that it too is not free of ideology. To suggest that every human event must be judged from the unique perspective of the participants is ultimately not an unbiased ideal. Consider Frankel's cogent analysis:

> In the end, indeed, there is an embracing paradox about the idea that all ideas about human affairs are true only from the point of view of a particular culture or social class. This statement is itself an idea about human affairs. If, like all other such ideas, it is a doctrine which is true for some people but false for others, there is no reason why people who hold a different point of view should pay any attention to it. If, on the other hand, it is not limited in its validity, then it is an exception to the very generalization it utters. It is one example of an idea whose truth transcends the historical circumstances in which it is uttered. And if there is one such idea, it seems arbitrary to suggest that there can be no others.[63]

If, indeed, the concept of relativity is not limited in its validity, and its truth transcends the historical circumstances in which it is uttered, then it seems logical that certain individuals—those trained to evaluate events in terms of their unique psychosocial circumstances, namely, the relativists—must be the ones called upon to expose systematically the partiality of all ideas. Such a formulation is Platonic in its implications; it invites the establishment of an oligarchy of intellectuals to be the guardians if not of "truth" then of the norms of correct procedure.[64]

Conclusion

Now that I have gored everybody's ox, where do I go from here? One thing I shall not do is to suggest the absolute superiority or inferiority of one or another of the three major currents in comparative education, for that would be contrary to my purpose. What I have attempted to do in the main is to show how inextricably ideological each current is, and I wish to argue for a fundamental change in the way we conceptualize the development of our field.

The conventional view of our field's development was established most firmly by Noah and Eckstein, who identify five evolutionary stages: (1) traveler's tales, (2) educational borrowing, (3) international educational cooperation, (4) identification of the forces and factors shaping national educational systems, and (5) social science explanation. Although Noah and Eckstein admit that these stages are far from being discrete in time,

---

[63] Frankel, pp. 135–36.

[64] This is essentially what Mannheim proposed (see Karl Mannheim, *Ideology and Utopia* [New York: Harcourt, Brace, 1951]).

their model is clearly evolutionary and as such is unsupportable and misleading. By virtue of their use of the word "period" to describe stages, their frequent allusion to historical circumstances associated with particular methods, and their emphasis on purposeful development, it is clear that they see each stage as a distinct occurrence in a larger evolutionary progression toward gaining clarity in understanding school-society relationships. Consider first their purpose: to reveal "the gradual, unsteady emergence of an empirically based, social scientific approach in comparative education, the history of which begins with simple narrative sometimes naive, but often astute, and ends, for the present with the application of the sophisticated methods now being employed in the social sciences." And, second, consider their claim that their evolutionary model, "loose though it is, provides a convenient, unforced framework within which to review the development of the field."[65] I contend, however, that evolutionary development may be ascribed to discrete epistemological currents, but not to comparative education overall, and that the evolutionary model is hardly an unforced framework within which to view the field's development.

The evolutionary model is inadequate because it violates three principles of theory construction: internal consistency, mutual exclusivity, and inclusiveness.[66] Let us consider first the related principles of internal consistency and mutual exclusivity.

A given theoretical model rests on the stability of its categories, which, in the case of Noah and Eckstein's model, are stages of development. For a category to be stable it must contain properties that in their internal consistency are reasonably distinguishable from properties of other categories. In Noah and Eckstein's evolutionary model, the properties of any given developmental stage, except for time itself, are virtually indistinguishable from any other. For instance, Noah and Eckstein characterize the early nineteenth-century writings of Marc-Antoine Jullien as "the prime example" of work done during the stage of educational borrowing. Yet their description of Jullien's contribution makes it clear that he had

[65] Noah and Eckstein (n. 1 above), p. 4.

[66] These principles correspond roughly to particular criteria for assessing theories in the philosophy-of-science literature. Internal consistency and mutual exclusivity are analogues of *logical consistency*, and inclusiveness is similar to the scope of a theory (see Philipp G. Frank, *The Validation of Scientific Theories* [Boston: Beacon, 1956], pp. 3–36; and Jack Gibbs, *Sociological Theory Construction* [Hinsdale, Ill.: Dryden, 1972], pp. 58–70). For an explanation of how the criterion of logical consistency can apply to dealing a "death blow" to a theory, see James D. Carney and Richard K. Scheer, *Fundamentals of Logic* (New York: Macmillan, 1964), pp. 367–68. A variety of disciplines have violated the principle of inclusiveness. The early years of American sociology, for example, were marked by narrow ideological boundaries that restricted reasonable considerations of Marxian thought (see Duskey Lee Smith, "Sociology and the Rise of Corporate Capitalism," in *The Sociology of Sociology*, ed. Larry Reynolds and Janice Reynolds [New York: McKay, 1970], pp. 68–81; Herman Schwendinger and Julia Schwendinger, *The Sociologists of the Chair* [New York: Basic, 1974]; and Patrick J. Gurney, "Historical Origins of Ideological Denial: The Case of Marx in American Sociology," *American Sociologist* 16 [August 1981]: 196–201).

little in common with the most prominent of his contemporaries. Indeed, Jullien was interested in observing regularities in educational practice through the collection of cross-national data, an activity that identifies him far more accurately as a positivist than as an educational borrower. It is interesting that Noah and Eckstein display their ideological bias as positivists by describing Jullien's work not as the precursor of a particular stream, that of positivism, within comparative education, but as the beginning of modern comparative education as a field overall, which it is not. By contrast, they describe the "borrowing" of Jullien's fellow countryman and contemporary, Victor Cousin, in less favorable terms as oriented to the strength of French culture and "the indestructible unity of our national character," thus revealing Cousin's decidedly relativistic tendencies.[67] To place two individuals like Jullien and Cousin, who were so mutually opposed epistemologically and ideologically, in the same category, as do Noah and Eckstein, violates the principle of internal consistency and stretches the imagination beyond reason. Noah and Eckstein then proceed to describe Michael Sadler's work at the turn of the twentieth century as bridging the stage of data collecting "of an encyclopedic and somewhat indiscriminate order" with the forces and factors period.[68] In reality, Sadler's preoccupation with education as "an expression of national life and character," despite his rather advanced scientific methods for the period, reveals his affinity to Cousin rather than to Jullien, and to relativists both before and after his time. By ignoring Sadler's negligible influence on nonrelativists and glorifying his contributions to the field overall, Noah and Eckstein and other comparative educationists persistently violate the principle of mutual exclusivity. Kazamias and Massialas, in a fit of hyperbole, go so far as to argue that "Sadlerian principles have become the cornerstones of the theoretical orientation of twentieth century comparative education."[69] Finally, Noah and Eckstein's violation of the principle of inclusiveness is displayed by their framework's complete neglect of Marxism. Nowhere do they have room in their analysis for Marxism or the radical critique in comparative education as part of any stage in the field's development.

Another test for judging the adequacy of a framework to grasp a field's development lies in its ability to discern the field's cumulative life. As I have shown, the evolutionary model fails in the last analysis because it attempts to view the major currents in comparative education within the same universe of discourse, when in fact these orientations proceed from incompatible philosophical theories of truth and irreconcilable ideologies that keep each of them in a closed niche. Yet, however much we

[67] Noah and Eckstein (n. 1 above), pp. 14–33.
[68] Ibid., pp. 40–57 and 65.
[69] Andreas M. Kazamias and Byron G. Massialas, *Tradition and Change in Education: A Comparative Study* (Englewood Cliffs, N.J.: Prentice-Hall, 1965), p. 3.

might lament the self-righteous superiority that each of these currents proclaims against the others, and what this may imply in regard to achieving unity for our field, each of them displays a strong cumulative life of its own and a proven ability to attract disciples who keep the faith. The field as a whole cannot claim to be as successful. The fact that exponents of each current are reluctant to accept the methods and findings of the others signifies that knowledge accumulation is not so much within the generalized field as it is partitioned selectively according to ideological affinity. Neo-Marxists have very little to say to neopositivists and neorelativists, and the latter have very little to say to the former and to each other. That the field is able to survive at all is due more to the pragmatic expediency of association—a group marriage of convenience, if you will—when numbers are small and resources to support meetings and journals are scant, and to a common interest in comparison, however variously defined, than to common epistemological assumptions and a shared universe of discourse about education.

Comparative education has not evolved as a unitary field but as a loose unity of separate though thriving currents. It is strange that despite the adherence of scholars to one or another of these incompatible currents, very few analysts have discerned their ideological incongruities. A notable exception is Paulston, who advances a paradigmatic model of the field's development. Unfortunately, although Paulston satisfies the principles of internal consistency and mutual exclusivity, and therefore posits a framework that is a considerable improvement over the evolutionary model, he violates the principle of inclusiveness by completely ignoring the relativist tradition. More important, although he pays lip service to the role of ideology in paradigm construction, Paulston vitiates its meaning by calling for a common framework that would specify "testable generalizations about necessary and sufficient conditions for large-scale structural and normative change efforts," and that would be "locked into neither functionalist nor conflict theory but [would draw] selectively and critically on each orientation."[70] Regrettably, ideologies are less amenable to such accommodating impulses than Paulston would have us believe.

The danger that ideology poses to our field is not so much in terms of its simple existence as it is in terms of our tendency to avoid its recognition. If, indeed, ideology is an inescapable part of whatever epistemology we subscribe to, we can learn to live with it only by admitting to its existence in our own scholarship. This act of admission and the application of our energies to dealing with ideology in our own work would serve two vital purposes: (1) it would make us more self-conscious about the bias and

[70] Paulston (n. 4 above), p. 395. Paulston's framework includes the equilibrium paradigm, which shares assumptions in common with neopositivism, and the conflict paradigm, whose most prominent analogue is neo-Marxism.

values that infuse our own methods, and thereby contribute to a more informed scholarship; and (2) it would make us less self-righteous about the scholarship of others with different epistemologies, and thereby help to avoid internecine quarrels that could tear apart our field. Because comparison involves interaction among cultures and polities and their varying sensibilities, and education concentrates on the most impressionable segment of society, the nature of comparative education is particularly delicate and vulnerable to devastating cleavages. It is not enough to be able to rely on the commonalities of nonacademic activities—the preparation of meetings, the printing of journals, the publication of newsletters, the establishment of communication networks, etc.—to help us overcome our philosophical differences and keep our field alive. We must also work conscientiously to understand those differences and to respect, however critical we may be of them, the fundamental assumptions and beliefs of others. Until the day we discover a one best method of scholarship, this is the most we can hope to do. On this note I am reminded of the words of George Orwell, who wrote, "I know it is the fashion to say that most of recorded history is lies anyway. I am willing to believe that history is for the most part inaccurate and biased, but what is peculiar to our own age is the abandonment of the idea that history can be truthfully written."[71] What Orwell said of history may yet apply to comparative education. If we are to avoid that danger we must do better in the future than we have done in the past. I trust that with sensitivity toward others' presuppositions, a forbearance of dissensus, and a healthy recognition of ideology that informs our own thought, we shall do better. However much we may disagree over methods and however contervailing are our epistemological assumptions, we must guard against the exercise of our respective beliefs in such a way as to narrow the scope of inquiry for others. Our vigilance will reap ample rewards in the new paths to be paved and in the maturity that is sure to follow from mutual understanding.

[71] George Orwell, *Such, Such Were the Joys* (New York: Harcourt, Brace, 1953), p. 141.

What Is Comparison? Methodological and Philosophical Considerations

REIJO RAIVOLA

The investigation of problems associated with research into comparative education dates back over 150 years to M.-A. Jullien's work. The field of study was widened by Sadler, who demanded that research into social phenomena take into account the fact that they are bound up with the ecological context and tradition. Educational problems have to be examined in the light of culturally determined needs, objectives, and conditions. To fully understand this culture dependency, it is necessary to compare cultures. Indeed, during this century the term "comparative" has been coupled with "education" whenever school conditions in other countries have been the object of study. But what is meant by "comparative"? The term has sometimes been used without its meaning having been methodologically established, and the concept of comparison has rarely been analyzed by educational theorists.

Two unfortunate misconceptions become apparent when reading the literature on comparative education. The methodological concept "comparison/comparative" is confused with the concept in psychometrics of "comparability," which Good, for example, defines as follows: "the condition existing when two measures are expressed in the same units thus making possible direct comparison."[1] Some theorists, meanwhile, have made the mistake of regarding comparison as an end in itself instead of a method and a logical tool in the solution of research problems. This article sets out from the assumption that the concept of comparison has been insufficiently investigated and seeks to point to ways in which it can be methodologically approached.

As recently as 1963, Pedro Rossello pointed out that although comparative education is often defined as the application of comparative techniques to specific educational problems, many studies do not in fact make any comparison at all. Many simply present a particular country's education system or educational problem and leave the reader to make the comparison. It is assumed that a comparison is made between the situation described and the reader's own educational context. According to Rossello, even the practice in area studies of juxtaposing various systems of education or educational solutions leaves the reader with the task of discovering correspondences and differences.[2]

---

[1] C. V. Good, ed., *Dictionary of Education* (New York: McGraw-Hill, 1959), p. 114.
[2] P. Rossello, "Concerning the Structure of Comparative Education," *Comparative Education Review* 7, no. 1 (1963): 103–12.

Reprinted from *Comparative Education Review*, vol. 29, no. 3 (August 1985).

Only with Bereday can the methodological problem of comparison be said to have been taken seriously, for he proposes a clear model for carrying out a comparison. But even Bereday does not consider in more depth what comparison is, what possible dimensions are involved, or what kind of mental operation it is. In general, comparative education theorists have assumed that the concept of comparison needs no definition. It is sufficient that the essential condition for comparison is fulfilled: a point of reference is established, a *tertium comparationis*, so that all the units to be compared can be examined in the light of a common variable, the meaning of which is constant for all units under comparison. This basis of comparison forms a kind of third dimension on which the units to be compared can be unambiguously projected.[3]

Comparing Comparisons

Comparison is not always used for the purpose of constructing an explanatory theory. Often it is used in creating a frame of reference to which varying observations can be related. The units being compared can be powerfully described by means of comparison variables, which according to Nurmi form equivalence criteria for the classification of phenomena.[4] Such equivalence classes created for descriptive purposes make a preliminary comparison possible and form the first step in constructing a theory. Thus the purpose of descriptive comparison is to construct concepts according to which phenomena can be classified and arranged. When speaking of comparison as a methodological problem, it is necessary, therefore, to distinguish between descriptive and propositional purpose: Is the aim to distinguish interesting idiographic phenomena or to establish nomothetic generalizations?[5]

Not all comparative research, then, seeks general explanations, but all research that seeks to offer general explanations must be comparative. Comparison is always involved in inductive reasoning. Research workers cannot be content with ascertaining the existence of a dependency relationship; they must also define the extent and conditions of its occurrence. Scientists have to refine their hypotheses about a relationship by testing it over and over with new variables. Generalization also always involves

[3] See, e.g., R. Edwards, "The Dimensions of Comparison, and of Comparative Education," *Comparative Education Review* 14, no. 3 (1970): 239–54; and H.-H. Groothoff and M. Stallmann, eds., *Neues pädagogische Lexikon* (Berlin: Kreutz Verlag, 1971).
[4] H. Nurmi, "Vertailevan politiikan tutkimuksen metodologisista linnoista," *Politiikka* 14, no. 1 (1972): 3–32.
[5] A. Alanen, "Kansainvälinen vertailu aikuiskasvatuksen tutkimus alueena," in *Vapaan sivistystyön XXii vuosikirja* (Porvoo, Finland:WSOY, 1978).

conceptualizing phenomena, and stating the relationship between them means theorizing this relationship.

Warwick and Osherson list a set of requirements that a theory must fulfill, in which task comparison can be helpful: (1) A theory has to be built on clearly defined concepts. This, however, is a question of isolating logical rather than empirical universals. (2) The theory has to cover the whole of the area of reality to be explained. (3) All claims included in the theory must be general. (4) The theory must be economical: it should be as comprehensive as possible using a minimum of concepts.[6]

How, then, can we work toward such goals by cross-cultural comparison? Between theoretical concepts and their operational counterparts, culture-specific values have to be recognized. This calls for analyzing individual communities' value systems, which in turn demands that a theoretical concept be expressible by a different operational counterpart, with its culture-specific features, for each culture under comparison. No trust should be placed in such face validity of measurement as when the same terms or the same method of quantification are used. Care must be taken to keep concept equivalents and identical indicators apart.[7]

Joseph Farrell, in his opening address as president of the Comparative and International Education Society, Mexico City, 1978, gave a wide-ranging analysis of the concept of comparability and comparative research method. He also drew attention to the problems caused by the confusion of comparability with sameness. J. S. Mill, for example, posited the processes of convergence and divergence as a necessary condition for the establishment of a causal relationship. But the phenomena under comparison may be alike in all properties except one, and they may also be different in all but one of their properties. There is no logical reason why comparison should be based only on the principle of convergence.[8]

Cross-cultural comparison may reveal institutions and their functions that are nonexistent within some other culture. In explaining cross-cultural relationships, Marton has adopted the term "functional equivalence": Event A does not have the effect B (as in the observer's own culture) but effect C, which is related to B insofar as it fulfills the same function as B. But as Köbber points out, it is insufficient to recognize the relationships of A to B and A to C; a comprehensive theory should also explain the relationship between A and C.[9] For example, in one country an increase in the number

[6] D. Warwick and S. Osherson, "Comparative Analysis in the Social Sciences," in *Comparative Research Methods*, ed. Warwick and Osherson (Englewood Cliffs, N.J.: Prentice-Hall, 1973).

[7] See M. Zelditch, Jr., "Intelligible Comparisons," in *Comparative Methods in Sociology*, ed. I. Vallier (Berkeley: University of California Press, 1971).

[8] J. Farrell, "The Necessity of Comparison in the Study of Education: The Salience of Science and the Problem of Comparability," *Comparative Education Review* 23, no. 1 (1979): 3–16.

[9] A. Köbber, "The Logic of Cross-cultural Analysis: Why Expectations," in *Comparative Research across Cultures and Nations*, ed. S. Rokkan (Paris: Mouton, 1968).

of places in higher education may cause a great demand for education; in another, the result might be a surprising drop in demand. In one case, the return on investment in higher education is seen as higher than that on rival investments (e.g., in vocational training at the level of further education); in the other case, lower.

The generality of a theory may be tested by elaborating relationships postulated by means of cultural variables. This calls for the replication of cultural research, to which educational research belongs, in different communities in order to reveal the possible conditional nature of relationships.[10] The human capital theory, for example, should take into account the initial circumstances of peoples at different levels of development, the attitudes of different communities to performance motivation, and the kind of income structure and policy practiced, including its historical development. There are in fact so many variables to be controlled for that the straightforward relationship "education $\rightarrow$ economic growth" put forward in the 1960s has been thrown into question.

Farrell observes that each hypothesis concerning education calls for cross-cultural treatment. Demonstrating that a claimed relationship holds true in a given community is not particularly useful unless the nature of that relationship is understood. For this, a theory is always needed, and the credibility of a theory in turn always increases with the presentation of comparative evidence. Comparative research is thus not only a tool of technical elaboration and control but also the only way of demonstrating the ethnocentric nature of many generalizations. Farrell in fact concludes with the assertion that there can be no scientific theory of education at all without comparative research.[11]

As to the demand that a theory should be economical, cross-cultural research provides help of a heuristic kind. It enables terms to be more precisely formulated, helps in the classification of phenomena, and points to testable hypotheses. The formation of equivalence classes makes it possible to treat the many variables as parameters in turn. There is a danger, however, that the aim of establishing a small number of comprehensive classes may cause unique culture-specific phenomena to be overlooked. Here, indeed, the structural conflict within comparative research is evident: How can a *tertium comparationis* be found to serve as a basis for the comparison of cultures, such that it would combat relativism and historicism but would nevertheless gradually cover the particular sociocultural properties of each object of comparison? Smelser indeed points out that it is often more reasonable to seek relationships between categories of phenomena within one culture than to examine the same class of

---

[10] S. Nowak, "The Strategy of Cross-national Survey Research for the Development of Social Theory," in *Cross-national Comparative Survey Research,* ed. Szalai et al. (Oxford: Pergamon, 1977).
[11] See Farrell.

categories across cultures. He illustrates this point with reference to the student riots of the late 1960s, which seemed more often than not to have no connection with the study program or other organizational matters. The decisive factor appeared to be the culture-specific way in which graduates are allocated their position as full citizens in society. In South America, this process usually happened quite smoothly, and there was hardly any student unrest, whereas in the United States and in Europe there were a "forced continuation of puberty" and a prolonged process of allocation, and student unrest became violent.[12]

International Concerns

International comparison makes the research worker very effectively aware of the danger that one's assumptions, system of values, and prejudices could lead to a cultural bias in the gathering and interpretation of data. By the same token, it can be difficult without comparison to learn to see and appreciate the special characteristics of one's own culture, simply because one is accustomed to react automatically to them.[13]

Five Types of Relation

In trying to define a common element, a basis for the comparison of phenomena, it is easy to make the common mistake in comparative educational research of seeing comparability as a unidimensional property, as a kind of degree of similarity. Nowak, however, distinguished the following five types of relation in theoretical research, which rely on the concept of equivalence, or correspondence.[14]

Phenomena are observed or judged in the same way in different cultures (cultural equivalence).—Väänänen analyzes this assumption of convergence as the starting point of comparative political sciences.[15] In the social sciences, the process of convergence means movement toward a stable condition, a dominant system, or an ideal. It is thus a question of uniformity. A comparative analysis should focus attention on the isomorphism of the elements of the systems, which can be evidenced (*a*) as based on experience (analogy), (*b*) as based on generally valid normative rules (homology), or (*c*) by setting out the specific conditions and prerequisites of uniformity (explanation). The assumption of convergence is a description of the process leading to isomorphy. The rate of change varies among systems or among different elements of the same system, but the direction, according

---

[12] N. Smelser, "The Methodology of Comparative Analysis," in Warwick and Osherson, eds.

[13] L. Honko, "Kulttuuri-identiteetin tutkimuksesta," in *Valtion humanistisen toimikunnan kulttuuritutkimuksen metodiseminaari* (Helsinki: Suomen Akatemia, 1976).

[14] Comparison cannot be based on the concept of absolute similarity or identicality, because culture-bound phenomena cannot be quantitatively or qualitatively absolute. See also Nowak.

[15] P. Väänänen, "Konvergenssioletus vertailevan politiikan tutkimuksen lähtökohtana," *Politiikka* 14, no. 1 (1972): 51–60.

to this assumption, is always the same. By means of the assumption of convergence, it is possible to compensate for the inability of ex post facto research to manipulate events and arrange them in time. It enables the time dimension to be replaced by selecting systems in different stages of development as objects of comparison. The process of change in systems could thus be studied through a diachronic cross section.

Cultural anthropologists speak of parallelism, according to which all forms of culture have the same evolutionary development curve, which emerges when they are compared side by side. This concept rests on the inherent unity of the human psyche. Its obverse is the theory of cultural diffusion. This explains similarities between cultures by means of contact and external factors, one of which is conscious borrowing. Clearly, one's paradigm of comparative education and the research models derived from it will have a completely different character according to whether one adopts the convergence/evolutionist view or the diffusionist view of the origins and development of systems of education. Associated with this (when operating with statistical data) is what is known as Galton's problem—whether cross-sectional correlations should be interpreted as nomothetic or idiographic. Because aspects of culture often do spread by means of diffusion (migration, common history, conscious borrowing), how is it possible to tell from correlations based on a single measurement whether the relationship observed is functional? (One measure of diffusion to have been used is the coefficient of correlation between property X measured in one country and the average $\bar{X}$ for the corresponding variable in neighboring countries.)

The objects of comparison (people or institutions) are part of a higher level of systems that have earlier been defined as equivalents (contextual equivalence).— For example, if the compulsory schools in two countries are defined as equivalent in structure and function, can the position of the teachers in these schools also be regarded as equivalent? Or should the variables and units of comparison be carefully delineated in order to find components that correspond to each other? Should the teacher's activity therefore be interpreted on the basis of institutional tasks or logical and strategic (i.e., pedagogic-didactic) tasks? Evidently the correspondence of the subcomponents of the systems cannot be assumed. The equivalence of objects of comparison has to be defined at the same level of the system (or concept).[16]

The objects have the same role in the functioning of the system (functional equivalence).[17]—This aspect of comparability has already been mentioned. It has often been overlooked in comparative education, however, in the search for structural or contextual equivalence. Different institutions may

---

[16] See Zelditch (n. 7 above).
[17] See also S. Verba, "Cross-national Survey Research: The Problem of Credibility," in Vallier, ed. (see n. 7 above).

be responsible for the same functions, and similarly structured institutions may carry out different tasks. For instance, the expansion of education (in South America) and restriction of civil rights (in Poland) may both be seen as institutional responses to political pressure. Not even on the individual level do reactions reveal what function is being fulfilled. If an Arab boy enters a mosque in his sandals or a Finnish girl the primary school classroom in her rubber boots, the teachers will immediately instruct the offenders to take them off. The students have offended against norms of two completely different kinds, however, and the measures taken by the teachers after their initial reactions may differ from each other considerably.

Phenomena correlate empirically in the same way with the criterion variable (correlative equivalence).—The absolute value of the correlation coefficient is taken as a measure of equivalence. The type of equivalence that Nowak proposes represents a different level from previous proposals. It is an operational method of showing equivalence. It is on the calculation of correlation that the reliability and validity values of empirical research are based, but classical test theory has shown that to establish reliability does not yet mean that validity is established. Predictive validity is only one type of validity. The existence of a correlation is a necessary but not a sufficient condition for the establishment of a causal relationship.

The phenomena under comparison derive from the same source, namely, the same conceptual class (genetic equivalence).—Education throughout Europe, for example, has a common heritage of a classical and Christian tradition, but this does not mean that education worldwide could be examined using equivalence classes formed on this basis.

The Question of Comparability

Because the concept of comparison has many dimensions, it is clear that theoretical research comparing different cultures will have many problems to solve. The central problem, however, always boils down to the same question: Is it at all possible to compare different social and/or cultural systems and units scientifically? Warwick and Osherson divide the question into three parts.[18]

First, do the concepts under comparison correspond?—(*a*) Are they similarly situated on the general-specific continuum? What is meant by formal education in different cultures? How vocational (particularistic) is the professional training given by the formal education system in different countries? At which point on the compulsory-voluntary dimension is each "compulsory" school situated? (*b*) Do the definitions given to concepts correspond? Or is it the case that although the definitions are identical, their meanings are construed differently in different contexts? In the field

[18] Warwick and Osherson (n. 6 above).

of education, the content of a definition depends on the definer's view of human nature, education, and knowledge.[19] (c) How easy are the concepts to identify? Though a concept may be theoretically perfectly clear, its operational and linguistic formulation may present great difficulty. *Kasvatus, uppfostran,* "education," *Erziehung,* and *éducation,* for example, largely but still only partly cover the same area of reference. It can even be said that attempts to standardize educational terminology, such as the Unesco ISCED (International Standard Classification of Education) project, may do as much harm as good by lulling researchers and planners into a false sense of security.

Second, how is the correspondence of measurements to be assessed?—How are valid indicators for concepts to be found, especially when there are often different indicators for the same concept depending on the particular bond with culture? Even the interpretation of supposedly objective demographic statistics proves problematic. Should age, for example, be regarded purely as a chronological or also as a socially normative factor? A 2-year age difference between two preschoolers means something quite different from a 2-year age difference between two adult students. Similarly, it is unreasonable to consider the internal rate of return on education when deciding whether 60 is the appropriate age of retirement in both Finland and India. The Unesco *Statistical Yearbook* is a superb information bank for education planners and administrators. The research worker has to treat this body of statistics with care, however, because it has been put together precisely for purposes of administration, not research.

Third, can the problem of how concepts are linguistically expressed be resolved?— Different cultures verbalize different aspects of the same concepts. There is considerable semantic fuzziness among representatives of the same culture, let alone between cultures. Often the problem is confronted for the first time when the compiler of an international questionnaire attempts to translate the form into different languages. It has become customary to use bilingual or multilingual experts and repeated translation back and forth until unclear points are eliminated.

Truth and Meaning

The conceptual and operational difficulties outlined above have led many researchers to suggest that only very similar phenomena and structures can be compared. If the cultural gap between the objects of comparison is too great, it cannot be bridged by any common dimension of comparison. Not only the research community's scientific orientation (i.e., its paradigm) but also the habits of thought built up by the national culture generate in the researcher many untested assumptions that affect his or her values,

[19] See Groothoff and Stallmann, eds. (n. 3 above).

motivation, selection of facts, and interpretation of them. The essence of cultural bias is precisely this: The way individuals represent the world to themselves and their concept of knowledge and truth are such an organic part of their culture-bound thinking that they cannot recognize a different world or a different truth. Truth and the meaning of concepts are relative. The ethnomethodological view, of course, is that truth amounts to the subject's interpretation of a problem he or she is faced with solving.[20]

Thus the problem of comparative research could be said to be how to find a body of material suitable for comparison that is independent of the collector and interpreter.[21] This prescription, however, involves a peculiar view of the nature of a corpus, for it assumes that objective data for comparison are somewhere in existence just waiting to be gathered. Such a view evidently confuses concepts with empirical phenomena that are directly observable and with variables derived from them. But concepts are generalizations and abstractions from what is empirically observed, and these have meaning only in the context of a theory.

The mere collection of experimental data does not lead to an advance in our knowledge, nor to the formation of a theory. Hypotheses are formed not by relating facts but by relating concepts. Depending on the culture, the same concepts can be operationalized by different combinations of facts; in this case, the same relationship of concepts can be found in different cultures even though not a single identical indicator of the concepts is used in the statistical testing of the hypothesis. The claim has been made that comparison is the measuring, weighing, and evaluating of phenomena themselves in order to find their common denominator.[22] Hilker similarly wishes to exclude comparison from theoretical consideration. In his view, comparison can only be applied to concrete empirical observations or, as he puts it, "the realization of theories, philosophies or individual historical occurrences." It is this unfortunately widespread view that gives rise to the whole controversy about the possibility of comparison.

The formation of concepts (and even comparison, too) is a process of reasoning, the processing of information to create knowledge.[23] Comparison is not, therefore, the reception, or perception, of information. This being the case, it cannot be simply linked to the properties of the stimulus. Edwards refers to an early twentieth-century psychologist, George Stout, who writes, "To compare deliberately is always to compare in some

[20] See also W. Harris, *Comparative Adult Education* (London: Longman, 1980).

[22] See, e.g., M. Eckstein, "The State of the Field," in *Review of Research in Education*, ed. F. Kerlinger (Itasca, Ill.: Peacock, 1975).

[22] F. Hilker, "What Can the Comparative Method Contribute to Education?" *Comparative Education Review* 7, no. 1 (1964): 223–25.

[23] By this I mean deductive reasoning. In deductive logic, comparison can be defined, e.g., as follows: after generating all possible conclusions from the premises, the reasoner processes them all and chooses one that best matches the meaning of composite premises.

special respect. Some theoretical or practical end is to be subserved by the comparison. The difference or agreement to be discovered is not any difference or agreement, but one which has significance for the guidance of conduct or for the solution of a theoretical difficulty. Thus comparison takes place only in regard to the characteristics which happen to be interesting at the moment, other characteristics being discarded or set aside as unimportant."[24]

It has been said that the basic human mental operations are recognition, comparison, and classification.[25] But the precise formulation of definitions and the conceptualization of phenomena come after, not before, classification. The researcher thus cannot set out to look for similar or different phenomena in different cultures, for similarity is not something that is an inherently inseparable part of an empirical observation. Indeed, as Farrell points out, similarity is a relationship between the observer and the data, one that depends on the observer's system of concepts.[26] If comparison is understood in the way presented above, the researcher cannot set about collecting a body of material in the hope that some comparison dimension will automatically emerge from it inductively. A working hypothesis to tell one what to look for is necessary. Robinsohn, in the tradition of hermeneutics, speaks of a level of preunderstanding, which springs from knowledge of the structures of a system and its past history.[27] Preunderstanding generates assumptions and suppositions that form research hypotheses. Theory and hypotheses are what form the comparison dimension in comparative research, not the raw material itself, as Bereday, for example, claims.

It is, of course, understandable that similarity/difference has been seen as an intrinsic property of observations, because this view has a long tradition in behavioral sciences. The perception of similarities and differences has been one of the cornerstones of Binetian intelligence tests. The later use of analogies and functional relationships in test items is based on the same inadequate view of the way in which the world can be unambiguously and objectively dissected without taking account of the uniqueness of the observer's situation and experience. The similarity or difference of the stimuli has been decided in advance by another on a priori principles. The tester has stripped the testee of the opportunity to give a divergent definition of similarity; the relationship between the tester and the stimulus is imposed as normative. For over 20 years there has been talk of the cultural distortion in intelligence testing. The foregoing

[24] See Edwards (see n. 3 above).

[25] P. Foskett, "Recent Comparative and International Studies in Non-Library Fields," in *Comparative and International Library Science*, ed. J. Harvey (Metuchen, N.J.: Scarecrow, 1977).

[26] Farrell (n. 8 above).

[27] S. Robinsohn, "Erziehungswissenschaft: Vergleichende Erziehungswissenschaft," in *Handbuch pädagogischer Grundbegriffe* (München: Kösel Verlag, 1970).

is intended to show that it is not just a question of different living conditions in different cultures but of a fundamental misconception of the relationship between the observer and the stimulus. Although this view has receded and is receding further in psychology, it nevertheless still holds sway in the manner in which knowledge is understood in comparative research.

One of the central insights of ethnomethodology is that research workers are like the rest of their contemporaries in that they, too, are governed in their actions by "common sense" and also in that they, too, make decisions on the basis of a minimum of information that seems reliable. The problem for research workers is precisely that they need to be able to detach themselves from the normal way of thinking in order to be able to examine it from the outside, which in turn is essential to the understanding of another person's behavior. The biggest difficulty here is one of language: words the researcher uses as labels for concepts have their own accepted meanings in normal usage. Terms that are invented or stipulative, based on agreement within the research community, are not helpful because they do not communicate efficiently. Language regulates itself on its own terms.

Particularly interesting is one of the definitions given to the word "difference" in *The Oxford English Dictionary:* "a discrimination or distinction viewed as conceived by the subject rather than as existing in the objects. Now only in phr. 'to make a difference'." This definition accords precisely with the view of the concept of comparison adopted in this article. But the dictionary informs us that this is an outdated use. Could it be that everyday language has come to reflect a change in thought during the great upsurge of the natural sciences and the period of domination of the positivist scientific paradigm? That sameness/difference has come to be regarded as a property that can be numerically measured and no longer as an indicator of the observer's/interpreter's system of concepts?

Eckstein adds an interesting psycholinguistic perspective to the consideration of the concept of comparison. Both in everyday communication and in research we use a great number of figures of speech. Articles dealing with comparative education abound with them (the "hard core" of ideology, the educational "ladder," the "open university," the "Third" World, the national "character," etc.). A metaphor always involves a comparison, but rules of correspondence are not defined in our everyday thought. But we persist in using categories labeled by familiar metaphors, because our thinking is bound by the conceptual categories we create. Metaphors are at their most useful (as are analogies generally) when they relate familiar experience and new observations. Eckstein illustrates this point with reference to the great advances made in the 1960s and 1970s in neurophysiology and cognitive psychology. Concepts created in other connections were transferred as metaphors to this field of research, thus providing the necessary conceptual terminology to guide our thinking and communication about it (e.g., coding, information processing, memory store, and the entire computer analogy). For Eckstein, metaphor is not simply a feature of decorative language but a central factor in human thinking. A set of metaphors guiding thought is to him what the paradigm is to Kuhn.[28]

Educational systems process people through the agency of other people. Understanding the other person is radically different from understanding objects or phenomena, because it involves a personal relationship between two information-processing systems, a relationship mediated to an important extent by language. The philosophy of psychology has sought in its argument of analogy to show that classical empiricism is wrong in assuming that we learn to know the other person via external and ascertainable properties. When in seeking to be objective we make the judgment from the outside that some other is the same as ourself, we passivize the object of comparison so that he or she becomes an analogical object. This does not admit any personal relationship with or interpretation of the analogy in question.[29]

Conclusion

It would be impossible to form empirically testable hypotheses about the actual process of education. It remains possible to test hypotheses concerning organization, aims, resources, roles, and other such "external" relationships because the tester is able to make empirical observations without getting involved in a person-to-person relationship. But no dimension of comparison can be created solely by the researcher's conceptual apparatus for the teaching-learning process itself, because this is an interactive process that cannot be understood as an aggregate of observable reactions. It is, in any case, out of the question for a researcher from a foreign culture to penetrate this relationship using only statistical methods.[30] But if complete understanding is impossible to achieve, some degree is attainable. Hamlyn sees this as possible by using the following procedure:

a) we have to acquire inductively derived knowledge of human beings and their environment;

b) we have to think of ourselves in the position of those we are studying (cf. Sadler's call for empathetic observation);

---

[28] M. Eckstein, "The Comparative Mind," *Comparative Education Review* 27, no. 3 (1983): 311–22.

[29] See D. Hamlyn, "Person-Perception and Our Understanding of Others," in *Understanding Other Persons,* ed. T. Mischel (Oxford: Blackwell, 1974).

[30] In fact, the ethnomethodological or symbolic interactionist view rules out the possibility of one-to-one correspondence even in communication between representatives of the same culture. Communication conducted on the basis of common sense and untested assumptions proceeds smoothly only until something unexpected causes a breach.

c) we have to make observations of external properties and attempt to discover subjectively what significance they have for those under study;

d) we have to apply general (theoretical) knowledge objectively to the observations we have made.[31]

The logical conclusion of a process of comparison is always a classification that is not based on the concepts of identity and incompatibility but on a definition of equivalence, the conditions for which are determined by the observer. In his or her conclusion, the observer either accepts or rejects a hypothesis of correspondence between the phenomena under comparison. Sameness and difference are thus relative concepts. In principle, there are no phenomena too different to be compared, because the presentation of such a claim implies that some dimension of comparison has already been tried.

Finally, I can say, along with Eckstein, that comparison is born in the "comparative mind" of the researcher:

> What then . . . is the comparative mind? In the first place, like all other human mental activity it is inclined toward figurative thinking, using metaphors, models, and paradigms to explain the unknown in terms of the known. But the comparative mind is also like the minds of others engaged in the deliberate search to extend knowledge. It is curious, being especially drawn to puzzles concerning human behavior. It is creative and flexible, being capable of moving back and forth between the particular item and the whole pattern, between the facts and the variable, between data and theories, between contemplative study and other kinds of activity. In sum, the comparative mind is a particular case of the general human cognitive condition and an even more particular case of the inquiring mind, whether scientist, philosopher, or artist. And its most special attribute is that it is drawn to the fascinating game of solving complex puzzles and playing with ideas and facts through comparison—and the use of metaphors.[32]

[31] See Hamlyn.
[32] Eckstein, "The Comparative Mind."

Comparing Educational Policies: Theory, Units of Analysis, and Research Strategies

FREDERICK M. WIRT

This article explores some of the conceptual and strategic problems of research which is truly comparative. Until recently, comparative studies of education have been marked by the single scholar studying a single nation's education system. He or she is usually a specialist in education, less often in sociology, but only occasionally in political science. Each transfers his disciplinary training to a foreign shore, conducts the requisite fieldwork in interviews or documents, and analyzes the meaning of such data for that nation and sometimes for social theroy.

However, there is increasingly a call for comparison of national units and their education systems, policies, and results within a consistent theory. Why the comparative method is significant in terms of producing knowledge that is more valid and generalizable has been recently well argued.[1] It is not my intention to redefend that position. Rather, the purpose here is to extend this emphasis on comparative methodology by developing one of its major elements—the meaning of "unit of analysis"—and by analyzing the alternative strategies by which scholarship may be organized. By "strategies" I mean the different mixes of personnel, time, and funds which must be thought out in research planning.

This paper proceeds within a theoretical framework, as must all comparative research. Merritt and Coombs recently put concisely the interactive nature of theory and the comparative method: " . . . the explanation of why something happens in a given system requires the application of a theory. The development and testing of theory requires explicit comparison. Without the systematic cross-system comparisons, we won't develop the theories we need; without these theories we won't explain much of anything, even within a single system."[2] In order that what follows is not received as a "how to" chart divorced from theory, it will help to set out such theory drawn from my current research. For it will be theory which directs us to the appropriate units of analysis requiring comparison and,

---

[1] C. Arnold Anderson, "Methodology of Comparative Education," *International Review of Education* 7 (1961): 5; Max A. Eckstein and Harold J. Noah, *Scientific Investigations in Comparative Education* (London: Macmillan, 1969); and Joseph P. Farrell, "The Necessity of Comparison in the Study of Education: The Salience of Science and the Problem of Comparability," *Comparative Education Review* 23 (1979): 3–16, and the recent sources cited there at p. 3, n. 1.

[2] Richard Merritt and Fred Coombs, "Politics and Educational Reform," *Comparative Education Review* 21 (1977): 252.

Reprinted from *Comparative Education Review*, vol. 24, no. 2 (June 1980).

from that, to the questions of how scholarship may be mobilized for such study.

The Uses of Theory

Two current research projects may be sketched here for their theoretical focus. One examines the role of educational professionals in the making of school policy in the United States and Australia.[3] The other centers on the group interactions which arise when ethnic minorities enter national schools that reflect dominant group values.[4]

Evolving State Education Policy among Federal Systems

The study of federal theory deals with the distribution of power among local, state or provincial, and national levels of government. Empirical theory of federalism explores the forces underlying shifting patterns of intergovernmental power, while normative theory of federalism deals with the value of such arrangements.[5] Both objects of knowledge interweave, of course, in prescriptive propositions about how such interactions should be structured in order to achieve certain benefits for groups or the nation.

In Australia and the United States recently, the state level has been subject to new pressures demanding new responsibilities in schooling. The usually weak states of the United States (traditionally reflected in the aphorism, "Education is a state responsibility locally administered") have quite recently taken a much firmer grasp on local schooling. They have mandated new minimums of services, special programs, financing schemes, accountability methods, and so on.[6] Where once "local control" was extensive, now the state is the active organ of power, despite considerable variations among states.[7]

[3] This U.S.-Australian Education Policy Project is jointly financed by the Center for Educational Research at Stanford (under Ford Foundation and National Institute of Education grants) and the government of Australia; the specific study is jointly directed by Grant Harman, University of Melbourne, and the author.

[4] A first statement of this process is found in Frederick M. Wirt, "The Stranger within My Gate: Ethnic Minorities and School Policy in Europe," *Comparative Education Review* 23 (1979): 17–40.

[5] Major works dealing with both would include Kenneth G. Wheare, *Federal Government*, 4th ed. (New York: Oxford University Press, 1963); and S. Rufus Davis, *The Federal Principle* (Berkeley: University of California Press, 1978). Excellent introductions to the subject in the two relevant nations are Daniel J. Elazar, *American Federalism*, 2d ed. (New York: Crowell, 1972); and Jean Holmes and Campbell Sharman, *The Australian Federal System* (Boston: Allen & Unwin, 1977).

[6] Ellis Katz, *Education Policymaking 1977–1978* (Washington, D.C.: Institute for Educational Leadership, 1978); Michael W. Kirst, *The State Role in Regulation of Local School Districts* (New York: Academy of Political Science, in press), and "The New Politics of State Education Finance," *Phi Delta Kappan* (February 1979), pp. 427–32. For a comprehensive review of the state in school policy, see Frederick M. Wirt, "Education Politics and Policy," in *Politics in the American States: A Comparative Analysis*, ed. Herbert Jacob and Kenneth Vines (Boston: Little, Brown, 1976), chap. 8.

[7] For this variation, see Frederick M. Wirt, "School Policy Culture and State Decentralization," in *The Politics of Education 1977*, ed. Jay Scribner (Chicago: National Society for the Study of Education, 1978), pp. 164–87, "Does Control Follow the Dollar? State Centralism and School Policy," *Publius: Journal of Federalism* (May 1980), and "The Allocation of Values in State Education Policy" (paper presented to the American Educational Research Association, San Francisco, 1979).

If political pressure moves more power to the American state, pressure also works in Australia to check what was once the enormous power of the state minister, and particularly the permanent bureaucrat, the Director-General of Education (DGE). A recent brief review of these state school-policy systems reports pressures from below—teachers unions, some parent groups—and from above—the national government's recent special programs of education.[8] Still wielding impressive powers, however, the DGE symbolizes a state government significantly more powerful than his American counterpart.

A comparison of these two nations' educational policymaking systems must proceed within a theory which enables us to select the units of analysis to test the theory. In this case the process may be conceptualized as one of professional versus lay conflict over policymaking. The conflict marks all professions, not merely schooling. But at its heart it is a conflict over the definition of the volume and quality of services delivered to clients by professionals. Such definitions include: Who should define these matters, how should personnel be trained and socialized, and how should the service that is delivered be evaluated? These are matters in contention, over time, between the professionals (in this case, teacher, administrator, and other educational specialists, with their bureacratic cohorts in the government) and the laity (those who receive the service and the governmental cohorts responsive to their service needs).

The conflict may be theorized to occur in a linear fashion; at each stage, termination is possible, depending on the balance of forces. For analytical purpose we begin with the stage of quiescence, in which the professionals are triumphant and unchallenged by the laity. Most of the latter are satisfied with services and primarily support the professionals.

Then, at the issue-emergence stage,[9] dissatisfaction from the laity arises over service levels and quality, which professionals ignore as being uninformed, until the discontent becomes so widespread it enters the societal agenda (what everyone is discussing) and eventually the governmental agenda (what policymaking agencies decide to discuss). If the process continues, there ensue authoritative formulation and decision on new policy. Here there is politicizing of the professionals, that is, reaction to its challenge to professionals having public effects; mobilizing the laity to put demands on government to redefine these policy definitional matters; and eventually a policy decision (statute, regulation, resolution, etc.) incorporating some or all of the laity's demands.

[8] See Jerome T. Murphy, *Schoolmen in the Squeeze: A Look at Australian and American Education* (Stanford, Calif.: U.S.-Australia Education Policy Project, Center for Educational Research at Stanford, 1979), a version of which was presented at the International Political Science Association Congress, Moscow, 1979.

[9] A little-studied theoretical phase; but see Roger Cobb and Charles Elder, *Participation in American Politics: The Dynamics of Agenda Building* (Baltimore: Johns Hopkins University Press, 1972), chap. 5.

Thereafter, a closure stage takes place. This begins with implementation of the new policy definitions, their incorporation over time into the training of new professionals and their subsequent service delivery techniques, and laity mobilization greatly reduced to a cadre, which oversees the service reforms won.

This brief sketch of a theoretical paradigm is developed further elsewhere.[10] But here it can serve to show how it directs our attention to units of analysis. For in comparing two or more national units in federal systems, we see that we must (1) examine all three levels of government for evidence of this conflict, in particular, their policymaking processes; (2) review the professional and lay groups that get involved; and (3) set out the professional policies over which there is satisfaction as well as discontent.

We could test the theory for its utility in California or Victoria, Mississippi or Queensland—or Bavaria, Berne, Guadalajara, or Alberta for that matter. But when we compare, our attention must be directed to the same level of government, the same processes by which state education policy is made, and the same professional and lay groups. Furthermore, we must concentrate on the same set of education policies (e.g., financing schemes, evaluation/assessment, curriculum development) to determine whether this theory of conflict may take different courses when the policy or the government is held constant. Between the theory and the data, however, there must be hypotheses which will test the conflict theory, but that element is ignored for the purpose of this article. The point to be made is that theory guides us to the units of analysis—governmental bodies and processes, pressure groups, and policies—which must be compared to test that theory.

Majority-Minority Conflict and Ethnic Policy in National Schools

There may be no nation in the world without an ethnic minority, excluding tiny enclaves like Liechtenstein. But the phenomenon is seldom studied comparatively.[11] The ubiquity of ethnicity rests on diverse bases—language, religion, territory, culture, and so on. But in each nation, the school system must confront such differences and relate them to the dominant group's values.

Such a policy program, in turn, stems from how the minority is regarded by the dominant group.[12] This regard is a function of the size of

[10] Frederick M. Wirt, *Diversity and Turbulence in American State Education Policy: E Pluribus without Unum* (Stanford, Calif.: U.S.-Australia Education Policy Project, Center for Educational Research at Stanford, 1979), and "Politics and Political Conflict: A Research Paradigm" (paper read at American Political Science Association convention, September 1980.

[11] For an authoritative call for such research, see Harold J. Noah, "Fast-Fish and Loose-Fish in Comparative Education," *Comparative Education Review* 18 (1974): 345. A seminal work is R. A. Schermerhorn, *Comparative Ethnic Relations: A Framework for Theory and Research* (New York: Random House, 1970).

[12] What follows is more fully developed in Wirt, "The Stranger within My Gate."

the disparity between the values of the two groups. The closest of value ties produces policies we can term "assimilation"; over time, as with the Saxons in the United Kingdom or the Pomeranians in Germany, the ethnic minority in effect disappears. Here the minority comes to accept totally the dominant values and is thus incorporated invisibly into the society's structures of power—government, church, business, university, and so forth. School policy in this case does not distinguish between the two groups because they assume a unitary value system.

Second, if the gap between the two groups' values is moderate but there are some value bases that both share, the ethnic group may be incorporated into some of the structures of power. But political power may be blocked from fears of the dominant group of the potency of this power in all social matters. Here school policy will more likely emphasize some of these cultural differences in at least the curriculum, stressing the value of such differences and the rightness of their maintenance by the ethnic group. Such elements exist in what we term "cultural pluralism" policy systems, prototypically found among the Swiss.

Third, another possibility—socialized isolation—arises when ethnic members are socialized to accept the dominant values but are little incorporated into power structures because of their special difference on one value. Thus American blacks accepted a wide range of religious, economic, and cultural values after the Civil War but were fenced off from making decisions in such institutions which affected them. The isolating factor was race, with its attendant status and sexual fears. A parallel case has been made for the United Kingdom's "coloured immigrants" after World War II.[13] Such is the case with "native" cultures in many places (the Japanese Ainu, American Indian, Australian aborigine, Scandanavian Lapp). Here the isolating factor is a perceived cultural alienation that cannot be bridged. Under this condition, school policy ignores the contribution of the ethnic group to the total society. It rejects its compatibility if the question is raised and creates separate schools for that group, schools which are sometimes obligatory for their members.

Fourth, when the two groups differ across all ranges of values, a pattern we can term "colonialism" exists. The minority rejects the dominant values across the board, and the dominant group isolates the minority from all power structures. Wide differences may be permitted in some values—religion or language—but there is total exclusion from political, economic, status, or other social institutions. The British or Roman strategy of their "indirect rule" of subject tribes and nations illustrates the practice in earlier and modern periods. Under this condition, schooling may be either greatly reduced (education carries the potential of chal-

[13] Ira Katznelson, *Black Men, White Cities* (New York: Oxford University Press, 1973).

lenging that which must never be challenged) or it may ignore the ethnic group's values—usually both.

Yet these four stages on the continuum of majority-minority ethnic conflict and school policy cannot be tested without comparison. The pivotal influence of the gap between these two groups' values may be mediated by other cultural factors that need explanation. How is movement along this dimension—and subsequent school policy—affected by such factors as the kind of political system? Does federal versus unitary or democratic versus totalitarian systems have characteristic stages? Do the stages of economic development? Does the capitalist versus socialist system make a difference, or simple versus advanced industrialism? Is the size of the ethnic minority a factor? Is the minority more accommodated when its size is nearly equal to the majority—as with the Catholics and Protestants in the Netherlands[14]—or when it is so tiny that it represents no threat?[15]

Pulling back from the increasing complexity of these comparisons, note that, as with the study of federal school policymaking, the units of analysis are still the same. That is, one is comparing governments and their processes, pressure groups, and public policies. Other foci of research may be called for, such as the role of history, the influence of ideology, or the mix of demography. While not dropping them in any study, note that each has its putative influence already built into the three units of analysis. Saying we will focus on the government and its characteristic processes, on the groups interacting in the distribution of resources and values, and on the policy and its results means that we must necessarily look at the influence of history, ideology, and population on these units of analysis. In short, these units do not exist independently of prior influences, for such influence is not a given but, rather, an empirical proposition to be investigated. These may be seen as mediating variables, which may shape, or be shaped by, the three units of analysis themselves. But only comparative methodology will enable us to test for the causation implied here.

Mixes of Units of Analysis

The mix of units to be compared is fortunately not endless. Whatever the theory examined or the derived hypotheses tested, there is, surprisingly, a small set of combinations of governments, groups, and policies. In table 1 these are set out logically.

The kinds of hypotheses generated by one's theory must lead to one of these sets. Suppose we wish to hold constant the level of government,

[14] Arend Lijphart, *The Politics of Accommodation: Pluralism and Democracy in Divided Societies*, 2d ed. (Berkeley: University of California Press, 1975).

[15] For an inventory of hypotheses on these intervening variables, see Herbert M. Blalock, Jr., *Toward a Theory of Minority-Group Relations* (New York: Wiley, 1967).

TABLE 1

LOGICAL SETS OF UNITS OF ANALYSIS FOR COMPARISON

Unit of Analysis	Sets							
	1	2	3	4	5	6	7	8
Government	Like	Like	Like	Unlike	Like	Unlike	Unlike	Unlike
Group	Like	Like	Unlike	Unlike	Unlike	Like	Unlike	Like
Policy	Like	Unlike	Unlike	Unlike	Like	Unlike	Like	Like

the ethnic group, and the policy in order to determine whether under these conditions results are obtained which our theory predicts. That is found in set 1 in table 1. For example, if the theory of professional versus lay conflict is correct, then among the Australian states (purportedly very similar governments), lay interest groups seeking to alter curricula they find objectionable should be successful depending on the degree to which they mobilize to modify professional decisions. But holding the group and policy the same, while varying the government's susceptibility to pressure politics of this kind, should result in greater success for the laity (see table 1, set 8).

Set 8 raises an old question in political science about the impact of forms of government. In the context of this article, do differing constitutional structures dealing with the same educational problem (say, academic deficiencies) of the same ethnic group make a difference in schooling results? That is, are policy results differentiated by, for example, unitary versus federal systems, centralized versus decentralized systems, parliamentary versus presidential forms, or democratic versus authoritarian politics?

Alternatively, in working out the ethnic conflict theory, across different governments and policies, is the same ethnic group treated differently, for example, the gypsies of Europe, Cornish-Bretons of the United Kingdom and France, Turkish immigrants moved across Common Market nations, or the Finns or Lapps across Scandinavia? Or, if parents in both the United States and Australia seek more "accountability" of educators for their children's learning, but there are differences in the relative power of the states in the two, do the results of this conflict favor the professionals over the laity? In both cases, the relevant unit of analysis is set 6 in table 1.

Again, with unlike national governments and unlike ethnic groups but the same policy (set 7), are school policy and results the same for all groups? For example, what difference does it make to immigrants if they may participate in local school policymaking, as with their right to vote in Sweden or the United Kingdom, but may not elsewhere in Europe? Or if the immigrant groups seek school training in both their native and the local language? In the case of the two state systems, can the same educational policy be produced, or the same academic results achieved, if the states are unlike and the relative power of professionals and laity is different? That seemingly illogical outcome can possibly be accounted for by professional networks across nations which generate acceptable norms of service which are then adopted in differing governmental and power contexts.

Similarly, take set 4, where all units of analysis are different. This could be the case in the role of international organizations (a special level of governance) among unlike governments, ethnic groups, and national school policies. Thus the Council of Europe and the International Labor Office have had continuing concerns about educational problems of immigrant workers' children. And bilateral commissions of European nations have sought to oversee the education of these children in their host nations. The presence of such bodies might well moderate national policies which otherwise would tend to emphasize the gap between dominant and minority groups.

Or, in a comparative federal study where states, groups, and policies are different, historical studies could explore the role of emerging professions in imposing private norms of educational services. Thus the authority of Australian DGEs and American top state school officials at an earlier period (T_1) seem quite different. But the latter should expand their power as laity seek educational improvements which professionals incorporate at a later period (T_2). For the U.S. state school officials will be given responsibility for such new programs, causing them to look more like the Australians over time (T_3). Similarly, as the federal government and private interest groups, like teachers unions, seek to redefine the DGE's power, over time he can look more like his American counterpart —two figures at the end of a continuum, moving toward one another from T_1 to T_3.

We need not illustrate the other sets of table 1 to make the point. That is, what we select as units of analysis depends on the theory and the hypotheses derived from it. But, for comparative purposes, these units factor out into a limited number of combinations, no matter what the theory, hypothesis, or policy matter.

The degree of unlikeness of units may be minor but still have major discriminating effects, for example, the policy role of American courts. Also, the degree of unlikeness may be vast and still permit exploration of an encompassing theory. As Farrell has recently stressed, "Similarity is not something inherent in the data. It is a characteristic of the relationship between the observer and the data and depends on the conceptual structures within the mind of the observer."[16] Readers of science fiction

[16] Farrell, p. 11.

about "alien" cultures know that "some things are like other things," even when separated by parsecs of space or millenia of time.[17] Indeed, the greater the range of experience encompassed, the greater the robustness of the theory. The absence of the latter is the crucial weakness of the case study which has dominated so much "comparative" education studies of the past.

Strategies for Mobilizing Scholarship

Scholarship is a resource, mixing not only interest and intellect but qualities of time, control, finances, and strategies (the organization of resources for fixed purposes). So often the choice of the units of analysis discussed above is predicated on only one of these resources, such as a scholar's interest or available funding. Properly conceived, however, the mobilization of scholarship is not merely an integration of numerous resources but an essential consequence of the guiding theory, on the basis of which directed hypotheses and the units of analysis are selected.

The choice of strategies, involving estimates of different costs, regularly—not occasionally—shapes our theoretical and conceptual structure and affects the units of analysis selected. All research is a compromise with one or more of the ideal mix of scholarly resources. Equally important, compromises like this interact to alter the theory and concept. If one has money and time to study only one country, the result will be restricted in validity and generalizability. Unfortunately, there is rarely the chance to study intimately all units of analysis relevant to a research field—Third World nations, socialist countries, the 50 American states, and so on. Quantitative studies may cover the full set, but always by limited criteria which seem theoretically relevant.

That consideration of theory does not exhaust the resources which need be applied, for alternative strategies can be consonant with a singular theory or set of hypotheses. However, in meeting the three research tasks of design, fieldwork, and written analysis, we need to consider the relative weight given to (1) quality control over each of these three tasks, (2) the time necessary to complete these tasks, and (3) the available funding for them. As wisdom and wealth are finite for every person, some trade-offs are required in any research, and these provide the mixes of which strategies are made.

Common Elements of Differing Strategies

To compare research strategies, we need to assume that some elements are common. Then we can vary the method of organizing the re-

---

[17] The "cultural equivalence" concept implied in the text is brilliantly illustrated in the science-fiction trilogy by Frank Herbert, *Dune, Dune Messiah, Children of Dune* (New York: Berkley, 1975, 1975, 1976).

search and so estimate the weights of quality control, time, and finances in each.

First, assume that we wish to organize a comparative study, that is, a theory of some scope is to be tested by analyzing a set of units. These may be subnational units to test a theory, for example, professional conflict as the energizer of American and Australian states in educational policy-making. Or these may be a set of nations, for example, value disparity and institutional isolation as theoretical factors distinguishing among school policies for ethnic groups in European democracies. In both cases, the number of units is six for purposes of illustration (the number of states in Australia and of European nations with different ethnic school policies).

Second, assume that the common research approach will be a process study to derive theoretically relevant data in each unit of analysis. This consists of field interviews and literature review of the role of governmental actors, policy processes, pressure groups, and the nature of the resulting policy. Again, these data are to test hypotheses derived from the major theory being investigated.

Third, assume that the major dissemination of these analyses will be a book, the traditional scholarly format. It will consist of six country analyses within a common design, plus a comparative analysis of the total set. Each of these seven products can be posited as 100 typescript pages long.

From these commonalities, three strategies of organizing either the federal or ethnic school policy project can be devised: single-American,[18] American-team, and mixed-team strategies.

Single-American Strategy

As often happens, one American scholar designs research within a chosen theoretical focus, spends time in other nations doing the fieldwork, and writes the book back in the United States. Based on consultation with some scholars and personal experience, I judge that the minimum time schedule would include: design stage, one summer; fieldwork, 1 academic year plus the following summer; and writing stage, 1–2 years while teaching full time. Note the emphasis on minimum time; greater time may be needed depending on personal habits or research problems.

The strengths of this strategy are several. Of the three strategies, there is the tightest quality control over theory, concept, hypothesis, data acquisition, and analysis. Hence, it is the easiest strategy in which to achieve consensus on design and administration. Also, it maximizes the

---

[18] Of course, it could be a scholar of another country dealing with the six units of analysis. I write here simply from my experience, with the understanding that it should be applicable elsewhere.

visibility of the individual scholar in the profession. As shown below, its cost is intermediate.

But there are also disadvantages. It limits severely the number of scholars with the intellectual breadth to cover more than one to two units of analysis, but six nations have been posited here. The intellectual vigor necessary for extensive and intensive fieldwork (innumerable interviews, mastery of several languages, and analysis of the literature) is staggering. Chances are strong that this strategy would require the most time at each project stage and that the single year posited for fieldwork is not feasible. But for the occasional scholar with the breadth of knowledge and language it is possible.

More problems exist. The research is limited to the breadth of one person, which cannot be as great as that of a team, whose interactive effects can stimulate ideas greater than the sum of the parts. Similarly, while one person can conduct all the stages of the project, unless there is extensive review by specialists on particular nations, quality control problems will rise. If referees are needed, why not incorporate them into a team approach? For the same reason raised here, learned journals use a referee system. Finally, we will see that this strategy has the highest per capita cost.

American-Team Strategy

An alternative approach is a set of Americans who are each specialists in one of the six units of analysis. These do the fieldwork and return to the United States for writing. All this proceeds under a common research design which members accept as a condition of joining the team; for best results they should have some input into its formulation. A seventh person originates the project, sets roughly its design elements, recruits the members, troubleshoots during the fieldwork, and provides the comparative analysis in the finished volume.

A minimum time schedule for this strategy would involve: design stage, 1 year quarter time for the seven persons; research stage, one semester for each person in the field; and writing stage, one semester while each teaches full time at his other university, plus the following summer.

The advantages which emerge here are mirror images of the disadvantages in the single-American strategy. A greater range of competence is brought to bear than in the preceding strategy; the specialist's "sunken costs" (prior knowledge of one's nation) can be utilized to good advantage here. Also, a greater intellectual breadth can result from the interactive effects of scholarly exchange of ideas and experiences. The per capita costs are lower than in the single-American strategy.

But serious problems loom. It is not easy, without much advance timing, to enlist an American specialist in each unit of analysis. It is not merely a problem of needing more time to recruit the team; rather, it is hard to find an American specialist in, say, Western Australian politics of education or Swedish school policy for the Lapps. Also, much greater administrative supervision is required than in the single-American strategy. Anyone who has assembled even a convention panel knows the attention to minutiae necessary and the way that ego concerns emerge; sometimes it seems like one is steering all the chariots in Ben Hur's race.

But note also that this factor points to a serious problem. There is greater difficulty in obtaining and maintaining consensus on the intellectual focus. Of course, the other side of this problem is that quality control is greater because so many peers are observing one another's work. But the problems of reaching agreement on the theory, hypotheses, and design elements are not minor. They can be reduced, of course, by choosing those already committed to a particular intellectual perspective, for example, liberal humanism, communism, or cultural pluralism. But even within each camp, great care is needed to arrive at an agreement on the design. Agreement on the meaning of the results is a bit easier as the peer review process of team members usually blocks out the most unfounded interpretations of data. Finally, as will be seen below, this strategy is by far the most costly.

Mixed-Team Strategy

A third strategy involves an American director who works out the design in some detail, recruits a team of foreign scholars (each a specialist in his or her unit of analysis and policy), oversees their fieldwork within this design, and writes the comparative analysis of the joint work. The foreign scholar should be paid a fee to produce the requisite chapter. In some circumstances, such as the importance of the project or its contribution to members' status, the work may be done without payment except for travel or writing expenses. Moreover, conferences held abroad, at the scholars' convenience, would be used to improve the design and to evaluate early drafts of the work.

A minimum time schedule would involve: design stage, including recruiting the team, one summer, and in the following semester the first international conference on design; research and writing of first drafts, 6 months, followed by a second international conference to evaluate these drafts; subsequent research and writing of second drafts, 6 months; final editing of the manuscript, one summer full time or one semester half time.

All the intellectual and professional advantages of the American-team strategy follow here also. A greater specialization of knowledge and a greater pool of specialists are available. Thus there will be more than one

TABLE 2

PROJECT CALENDER BY RESEARCH STRATEGY*

Basic Stages	Single American	American Team	Mixed Team
Design	1 summer full time	2 semesters quarter time	1 summer full time
Data gathering	2 semesters + 1 summer full time	1 summer + 1 semester full time	6 months part time†
Writing	1–2 academic years part time†	1 semester part time 2 + 1 summer full time	Draft 1: 6 months part time† Draft 2: 6 months part time Director: 1 semester half time
Total	2¼ years +	2¼ years	1½ years +

* This is a minimum, or "optimistic assumptions realized," estimate.
† "Part time" means working at the project while engaged full time by home institution.

Western Australian scholar who knows his state's education politics or a Swede who knows Lapp education. The "sunken cost" advantage adheres here, too, including ease of access for interviews. Consequently, the breadth of intellect brought to bear is potentially greater than with either the single-American or team strategies. It also creates the greatest international visibility for the project, which enhances the possibility of published dissemination in more than one country. And it is a remarkably economic use of funds, as will be seen.

Its problems are also those of any collaborative effort. There is likely the greatest difficulty in obtaining theoretical and design consensus, unless only adherents of one intellectual perspective are recruited. There is the greatest problem of administrative supervision, for here the director needs greater time to visit other nations to recruit, to be in the area to troubleshoot, and to spur along the progress of the writing (although the first conference should be useful in that respect). Also, the editing of the individual pieces creates the additional problem of translation misunderstandings.

Time and Cost Factors

Before we attempt a comparative evaluation of these three strategies, it would help to set out briefly the different criteria of time and cost involved. The time elements are estimated roughly in table 2. The single-American and American-team strategies take the same time, if optimistic assumptions are met; because that seems less likely for the single-American strategy, the total is probably a bit low. Clearly the mixed-team strategy is quickest, partly because scholars are in their sites already and know their specialties so well. No estimate is provided for time needed to raise the funds, but given the uncertain nature of that task, we can assume that it is about the same for each strategy.

Next, the estimation of finances introduces a major complication. It is not simply the size of the funds that is a problem, but a kind of Parkinson's law operates, whereby theory and research contract to fit the funds available. Note that earlier the two theories of federal and ethnic education policies were widely stated as possible, in order to extend their generalizability. Similarly, the combinations of units of analysis in table 1 are equally extensive. Ideally, each theory's validity would be maximized by using all possible units of analysis. But since there are never enough of the good things of life to go around, research funds are rarely available for such maximum effort. So the contraction of the cost criterion affects the scope of the theory and the analytical units to be studied, that is, optimization sets in. Too often in the past, this force accounted for use of the case study. So cost becomes a particularly crucial factor in estimating strategies and hence in testing hypotheses and theories.

To arrive at even a rough estimate of these strategies' costs, the following is assumed:

1. Some elements can be standardized in all three budgets, for example, a central U.S. location (e.g., Chicago) for estimating European air travel for the Americans, typing costs for two 700-page drafts, and miscellaneous costs.

2. Personnel costs can also be standardized, for example, director, $25,000 annually; research assistant, $400 monthly; summer income, two-ninths annual salary; an inflation factor of 6 percent for successive years; and foreign scholars as consultants preparing mongraphs at $750 each.

3. For purposes of illustration only, the ethnic conflict study is used below, selecting six European nations' approach to multiethnic or "second-language" curricula. Different governmental forms are selected to determine if this makes a policy difference. These include: formally and actually centralized (Sweden and France), formally centralized but informally decentralized (United Kingdom), formally and actually decentralized (West Germany and Switzerland), and formally decentralized (into religious structures) but informally centralized (the Netherlands). The ethnic group studied in each case will be conceptualized as the same for analytical purposes, that is, new immigrants of the last few decades coming to find work and, in some cases, permanent homes.[19]

A rough estimate of the cost factors in table 3 shows a dramatic difference among these three strategies. Single-American, American-team, and mixed-team costs differ at a ratio of 1.0:1.5:5.0. In short, mixed-team research under these terms could be carried out for five projects at the cost of one using the single-American approach.

The significant variable, as with all organizational costs, is personnel. The more that scholars are used and the more they are used full time,

[19] Other analytical factors are omitted here for brevity.

TABLE 3

COST ESTIMATES OF THREE RESEARCH STRATEGIES ($)

Budget Items	Single American	American Team	Mixed Team
Salaries, director and research assistant	52,132*	178,117†	29,192‡
Salary overhead (50%) and personnel benefits (15%)	33,885	115,776	18,975
Consultants			4,500§
Travel	2,500	4,200	5,300
Miscellaneous: telephone, postage, clerical	1,500	500	500
Manuscript preparation, 2 drafts	1,400	1,400	1,400
Total	91,417	299,993	59,867

* Director, 1 year 100%, 1 semester 25%, 2 summers × 2/9; RA, 2 years + 2 summers 100%.

† Director, 1 year 25%, 1 semester 50%, 2 summers × 2/9; team members (6 at $20,000), 1 year 25%, 1 semester 100%, 2 summers × 2/9; RA, 2 years + 1 summer 100%.

‡ Director, 1 year 50%, 2 summers × 2/9; RA, 1 year + 2 summers 100%.

§ 6 × $750.

the greater the cost. Moreover, the very high overhead costs levied by American universities on research grants (conservatively estimated here at 50 percent), as well as another levy for personnel benefits, increases personnel costs by almost two-thirds. The American team maximizes these costs. The advantage of mixed-team finances, then, is that fewer Americans with their overhead costs are used, and for lesser periods, and that more foreign scholars are used on a consultant basis at a fixed fee without overhead costs. Even providing the latter's travel to two international conferences and the usual support facilities, the mixed team is much less costly. The strategy of intermediate costs, that is, single American, has been estimated here very conservatively in terms of time. The scholar may well seek an additional quarter- or half-time leave for writing the analysis, rather than doing it while teaching full time. If so, its ratio to the mixed team would increase to 1.0:1.7 or 2.0, nearly double.

Comparative Analysis of Strategies

Cost is not the only comparative criterion, as the earlier description of these strategies noted. These criteria are set forth in table 4 in judgments which permit a rough estimate of relative benefits. On all but two criteria, the mixed team exhibits the most advantages.

But we cannot assume, as table 4 does, that each criterion is of equal weight. If we could assign even a rough but varying quantitative score for the value of each criterion, we might well find different results. Thus international visibility may well be of minor importance compared with achieving consensus on theory and design. Note that on this criterion and on administrative oversight, we face the two major control factors of research projects; more than one project has broken on these shoals.

TABLE 4

COMPARATIVE ESTIMATE OF STRATEGY UTILITIES

	Intellectual Breadth	Competencies	Administration	Theory/ Design Consensus	International Visibility	Time/ Academic Years	Estimated Cost ($)
A. Single American	Narrow	Limited	Easy	Easy	Little	2 +	91,417
B. American team	Broader	Broader	Hard	Hard	Good	2 + 1 summer	299,993
C. Mixed team	Broadest	Broadest	Hardest	Hardest	High	1 + 2 summers	59,867
Most advantageous strategy	C	C	A	A	C	C	C

More explicit tactical thinking is required to deal with this very difficult problem of optimizing theory and design unity. One tactic would be to select a director so well known internationally that her or his credentials would strongly influence agreement on theory and design and encourage its implementation among those recruited. An allied tactic is to select scholars in basic agreement on matters of theory or design, for example, Marxism or structural-functionalism. Both tactics would reduce conflict, problems so familiar when scholars assemble, but they would also narrow the intellectual breadth of the design and result. Then there is the problem of the reputable scholar who is a poor administrator. The ideal tactic, of course, is to select someone capable in both, but counsels of perfection usually are broken by unamenable reality. Hence a tactic of a codirectorship would be more workable. That is, one director is chosen for scholarly eminence to facilitate consensus building in theory and design, and another is chosen for managing the project, editing the writing, and other dull but vital tasks of collective scholarship.

Experience will be required to advise what works here. Recall that we are moving into a new generation of collaborative studies. What is new is not a group of scholars writing on a common subject; "collections" of such disjointed papers abound. Certainly it is not new for a scholar of one nationality to compare the policy experiences of other national units of analysis. Aristotle pioneered this approach 2,500 years ago, Marx essayed it over a century ago, and quantitative analysis of the ties between political forms and policy outputs of nations is most recent.[20]

Rather, what is new is the effort to mobilize specialists to work within a common design in order to extract from analyses of political processes tests of hypotheses derived from general theory. Prototypes of educational policy process studies within one nation, comparing local education authorities[21] or states,[22] have recently appeared in the United States. Currently, a multiple-nation study of school administrators' values in Europe with such a design, but using the American-team strategy from the University of Illinois, is nearing publication. Whichever team approach is used, and my preference is for the mixed team,[23] common elements are involved: (1) a team of scholars searching for answers among different

[20] E.g., Richard Hofferbert and David Cameron, "The Impact of Federalism on Education Finance: A Comparative Analysis," *European Journal of Political Research* 2 (1974): 225–58; and Jill Clark, "Correlates of Educational Policy Priorities in Developing Countries," *Comparative Education Review* 20 (1976): 129–39.

[21] Stephen Crocker et al., *Title IV of the Civil Rights Act of 1964: A Review of the Program Operations* (Santa Monica, Calif.: RAND, 1976); Gary Orfield, *Must We Bus?* (Washington, D.C.: Brookings, 1978).

[22] Joel S. Berke and Michael W. Kirst, eds., *Federal Aid to Education: Who Governs?* (Lexington, Mass.: Heath, 1972); Roald Campbell and Tim Mazzoni, eds., *State Policy Making for the Public Schools* (Berkeley: McCutchan, 1976).

[23] It is used in the project cited in n. 3 above.

units of analysis after agreeing on their theoretical purposes and empirical methods; (2) use of a specified set of research questions or hypotheses, to be answered in detail, drawn from theory and concepts; (3) an interactive, or feedback, process by which scholars evaluate members' contributions in order to stimulate further research and analysis; and (4) a subsequent integration and comparison of the findings to test hypotheses and develop theory.

Conclusions

This article seeks to trace the links among theory, hypotheses, units of analysis, and research strategies. The linkage of the first two is familiar in methodological discussions, but I add to the increasing call that comparative means comparative. Beyond that, the linkage of these two to units of analysis has not been stressed sufficiently in the comparative education literature. This emphasis developed the finite combinations of analytical units that should form a central core of any comparative study. Note, moreover, that it will be theory which guides the selection of units.

Finally, there is almost no discussion of the interaction between these first three elements and research strategies. The emphasis here is on interaction, because it is not merely theory, hypotheses, or analytical units which dictate the research strategy. What one can mobilize of different kinds of scholarly resources will expand or contract the scope of research and the utility of its findings.

While this comparative estimate of the utilities of strategies did not presume to include all resources, it is clear that no single strategy was definitively superior. Rather, one must compromise, in the sense of trading off the advantages of more coverage with lesser finances, for the disadvantages of less intellectual cohesion, as in the mixed team. In these days of much concern with cost-benefit analysis (usually defined much too narrowly), the financial advantage of one strategy may look more attractive to funding sources, while the intellectual cohesion of another strategy will attract the individual scholar.

All that this article seeks to state unequivocally is the need to be self-conscious about the interaction of these strategies with the intellectual requirements of research methods. In the process, we will understand that research, like politics, is the art of the possible and the second best, and that this can be done without loss of intellectual vigor and importance.

The Comparative Study of Classroom Behaviors

RICHARD H. PFAU

At the present time, social scientists have only vague ideas about what occurs in the classrooms of most countries of the world and how classroom behaviors vary from one part of the world to another. Given the importance of classroom occurrences, attempts to look more closely at classroom events and their relationships with other variables seem appropriate. This article has been written (1) to highlight a technique which seems especially suitable for use by scholars who wish to make precise and valid comparisons of classroom behaviors, (2) to indicate why this technique is apparently more suitable than others, and (3) to stimulate thinking leading to an increase in the number and sophistication of cross-cultural studies of classroom behaviors. Although the presentation which follows focuses mainly on the cross-national comparison of classroom behaviors, the technique discussed is applicable to comparisons of teaching associated with different cultural groups within a single country, to comparisons of teaching across time, and to other types of comparisons as well.

Reasons for making such comparisons across cultures, nations, or time include determination of the generality of classroom-related theory, generation and testing of such theory, the identification of variability across cultures to obtain otherwise unavailable experimental treatments, and the provision of information about classroom occurrences to educational planners, evaluators, and others.[1] Such reasoning, it might be noted, is based on a view that generality of theory across cultural boundaries is to be sought by researchers, and that quantitative methods may be used as a tool to help develop and test such theory. This view underlies much of what follows and is quite different from views which hold that cultures can be understood only in their own terms, and that, as a result, cross-cultural comparisons are essentially false endeavors for they compare incomparables.[2] It is realized that persons with strong leanings toward the latter views will find much of the following discussion unacceptable, while it is hoped that persons sharing the former view will find merit in the points presented and will build on them.

[1] Allen D. Grimshaw, "Comparative Sociology: In What Ways Different from Other Sociologies?" in *Comparative Social Research: Methodological Problems and Strategies*, ed. Michael Armer and Allen D. Grimshaw (New York: Wiley, 1973), pp. 1–23; Richard W. Brislin, Walter J. Lonner, and Robert M. Thorndike, *Cross-cultural Research Methods* (New York: Wiley, 1973), pp. 6–7.

[2] Walter Goldschmidt, *Comparative Functionalism* (Berkeley: University of California Press, 1966), chap. 2; Joseph P. Farrell, "The Necessity of Comparisons in the Study of Education: The Salience of Science and the Problem of Comparability," *Comparative Education Review* 23 (February 1979): 3–16.

Reprinted from *Comparative Education Review*, vol. 24, no. 3 (October 1980).

Techniques for Measuring and Comparing Behaviors

Questionnaires and Interviews

Educational researchers often use relatively indirect techniques, such as interviews and questionnaires, to gather information about classroom activities. Such techniques require that teachers or students report about what occurs in their classes. The resulting answers are then used as a basis for describing classroom occurrences and for comparing occurrences among groups of classrooms.[3]

The International Association for the Evaluation of Educational Achievement (IEA) studies of mathematics, science, and other subjects used indirect techniques in an attempt to determine what was happening in the classrooms of the countries studied. Science teachers, for example, completed a science teacher questionnaire which contained inquiries such as: "Indicate how often you give your Science students opportunities for planning and carrying out limited scientific investigations on their own."[4] Four categories of response were used for such questions: "never," "seldom," "occasionally," and "frequently." Similarly, in a major comparative study of teacher roles extensively reported in the February 1970 issue of the *Comparative Education Review*, "respondents were asked to indicate for each item the amount of emphasis given it in their own classroom teaching. Five response categories were provided: 'A great deal of emphasis,' 'Strong emphasis,' 'Moderate emphasis,' 'Slight emphasis,' and 'Little or no emphasis.' "[5] The responses to such questions were used to infer the extent of classroom occurrences in the countries studied.

Major difficulties are faced by researchers using such techniques cross-culturally, and serious questions can be raised about the validity of inferences drawn from the use of such measures. For example, does the term "frequently" mean the same thing to a British teacher and to an Indian teacher, and thus are the responses given by such teachers actually comparable? Similarly, does the term "moderate emphasis" mean the same thing to persons of differing cultural backgrounds, and does this term elicit responses implying similar meanings?

The difficulties encountered by using such indirect techniques of measurement can be appreciated by looking at the writings of researchers who

[3] E.g., see H. A. G. Paisey, *The Behavioural Strategy of Teachers in Britain and the United States* (Windsor: NFER, 1975); Aino J. Kartiovaara, "A Comparative Study of the Extent to Which the Teachers in Finland and New York State Actualize a Democratic Value System" (Ph.D. diss., State University of New York at Buffalo, 1976); and James R. Barclay and Wu-tien Wu, "Classroom Climates in Chinese and American Elementary Schools: A Cross-cultural Study" (paper presented at the biennial meeting of the Society for Research in Child Development, New Orleans, March 17-20, 1977 [ERIC Document Reproduction Service No. ED 143 457]).

[4] L. C. Comber and John P. Keeves, *Science Education in Nineteen Countries: An Empirical Study* (New York: Halsted, 1973), p. 276.

[5] Raymond S. Adams, "Perceived Teaching Styles," *Comparative Education Review* 14 (February 1970): 51.

used questionnaire responses for comparative purposes. For example, when discussing the comparative study of teacher roles referred to previously, R. S. Adams wrote that "the extent to which these reports are veridical (that is, they reflect actual teaching practices) is an open question"; "response bias was operating—in other words, some countries were being freer with their willingness to emphasize (anything) than were others"; and "the teachers, though responding to the same word cues may have placed different meaning on them. For example, 'free communication' may be semantically quite different in the United States and Australia. Again, teachers may be poor perceivers of their own performance. Thus their reports do not reflect the reality of their teaching. . . . What our respondents reported then, might represent their values rather than their practices."[6]

To appreciate further the magnitude of potential problems involved in making valid comparisons by using indirect techniques, one need only look at the many chapters relating to the use of questionnaires and interviews contained in cross-cultural and comparative research methods books.[7]

Narrative Description

If one's purpose is to describe and compare classroom behaviors, a potentially more valid technique is to have trained persons *directly* observe such behaviors, record their observations, and then use those records as a basis for making comparisons. Direct classroom observations, however, can be recorded and reported in a number of different ways.

One method, often used by educators and anthropologists, is to observe classroom teaching and then write descriptive accounts of the teaching observed. An example of a description resulting from such an approach is the following: "Teaching techniques seldom varied; the teacher might read aloud from a textbook while some children took a few notes, or the teacher or a child would chant a standard question and the class would respond by chanting a memorized answer, or the teacher would make a statement and the class would repeat it in unison."[8]

Such narrative descriptions, however, do not provide a very objective basis for comparing patterns of teaching from one country to another, or indeed from one school to another, since they furnish only very gross indications of the actual extent to which specific behaviors occur. For example, the description above gives no indication of how much time teachers spent reading aloud from textbooks—was it 50 percent of a class period, 20 percent, 1 percent?

[6] Ibid., pp. 53, 52, 58.
[7] E.g., see Brislin et al., chaps. 2 and 3; Donald P. Warwick and Samuel Osherson, eds., *Comparative Research Methods* (Englewood Cliffs, N.J.: Prentice-Hall, 1973), chaps. 6, 7, and 8.
[8] Horace B. Reed and Mary J. Reed, *Nepal in Transition: Educational Innovation* (Pittsburgh: University of Pittsburgh Press, 1968), p. 135.

Furthermore, such descriptions suffer from the problem that the descriptive words employed lack a common base for making comparisons. That is, the words used may have different meanings when written or read by different persons. Thus, as Deutscher has pointed out, the standard for the same objects or behaviors may well vary from culture to culture, from nation to nation, or, for that matter, within any given social unit—among classes, age groups, sexes, and so on. "What is 'cold' soup for an adult may be too 'hot' to give a child."[9] Similarly, what is "seldom" to one person may appear "frequent" to another.

It seems apparent that more standardized approaches for reporting classroom occurrences are required if precise descriptions and comparisons are to be made.

Rating Systems and Category Systems

Classroom observation instruments now being used are of two major types: "rating systems" and "category systems." Rating systems can usually be distinguished from category systems by the amount of inference inherent in their use and in the interpretation of their results. As Rosenshine has pointed out,

> Category systems are classified as *low-inference* measures . . . because the items focus upon specific, denotable, relatively objective behaviors such as "teacher repetition of student ideas," or "teacher asks evaluative question" and because these events are recorded as frequency counts. Rating systems are classified as *high-inference* measures because they lack such specificity. Items on rating instruments such as "clarity of presentation," "enthusiasm," or "helpful toward students" require that an observer infer these constructs from a series of events. In addition, an observer must infer the frequency of such behavior in order to record whether it occurred "constantly," "sometimes," or "never," or whatever set of gradations are used in the scale of an observation instrument.[10]

Although rating systems are no longer limited to high-inference items and high-inference items have been used in some category systems, differences can usually be seen in the types of teacher and student characteristics on which these instruments focus. That is, category systems usually focus on relatively specific, well-defined behaviors, in comparison with rating systems which usually deal with much more general characteristics of teachers and students.

An even more consistent difference in the levels of inference associated with the use of these instruments concerns how observers using them record their observations. Observers using rating systems usually estimate

[9] Irwin Deutscher, "Asking Questions Cross-culturally: Some Problems of Linguistic Comparability," in Warwick and Osherson, eds., p. 174.

[10] Barak Rosenshine, "Evaluation of Classroom Instruction," *Review of Educational Research* 40 (April 1970): 281.

the frequency of events and extent of attributes only once, at the end of an observation session. Rather than serve to provide a detailed description of what actually occurred, the ratings seem more to provide a record of recollections or general impressions about what was observed.[11] Whereas rating systems typically call for high-inference judgments, requiring that an observer integrate whatever he has witnessed over one or more periods of observation and provide a record of general impressions, observers using category systems must make specific judgments and recordings while the activities of the classroom are in progress. Depending on the particular category system being used, observers keep a record of the events being observed (a) each time they occur, (b) at very frequent intervals (e.g., every 3 sec), (c) at longer but quite precise intervals of time (e.g., exactly every 5 min), or (d) by using a stopwatch to record their duration.[12]

The characteristics of rating systems result in what Kerlinger calls an intrinsic defect of these systems, this being their proneness to constant or biased error. In addition to halo effects, which are difficult to avoid, the following types of error are often associated with rating scales: the error of severity, "a general tendency to rate all individuals too low on all characteristics"; the error of leniency, an "opposite tendency to rate too high"; and the error of central tendency, a "general tendency to avoid all extreme judgments and rate right down the middle of a rating scale."[13]

When different recording biases occur, as they are likely to, by persons with different cultural backgrounds, the utility of rating systems for making cross-cultural comparisons is seriously undermined. Add to such biases the difficulty of providing operational definitions of the high-inference concepts used in most rating systems and the very real possibility that points on the rating scale may mean different things to observers from different cultures, then it can be realized that studies which call for observers to use rating systems may result in judgments that are unreliable as well as biased.

As will be seen, it appears that category systems rather than rating systems are potentially more suitable for gathering data to be used for making cross-national comparisons. The low-inference procedures associated with the use of most category systems seem capable of being used to

[11] Barak Rosenshine and Norma Furst, "The Use of Direct Observation to Study Teaching," in *Second Handbook of Research on Teaching*, ed. Robert M. W. Travers (Chicago: Rand McNally, 1973), p. 132; Donald M. Medley and Harold E. Mitzel, "Measuring Classroom Behavior by Systematic Observation," in *Handbook of Research on Teaching*, ed. N. L. Gage (Chicago: Rand McNally, 1963), p. 252.

[12] Donald A. Jackson, Gabriel M. Della-Piana, and Howard N. Sloane, Jr., *How to Establish a Behavior Observation System* (Englewood Cliffs, N.J.: Educational Technology, 1975); Jeanne Altmann, "Observational Study of Behavior: Sampling Methods," *Behaviour* 49 (1974): 227-67.

[13] Fred N. Kerlinger, *Foundations of Behavioral Research*, 2d ed. (New York: Holt, Rinehart & Winston, 1973), pp. 548-49; Rog G. D'Andrade, "Memory and the Assessment of Behavior," in *Measurement in the Social Sciences: Theories and Strategies*, ed. H. M. Blalock, Jr. (Chicago: Aldine, 1974), pp. 161, 175.

make more standardized recordings by observers of differing cultural backgrounds. These more standardized recordings, in turn, can provide information which is more appropriate for the making of precise and valid cross-national comparisons.

Sample Category System and Comparative Data

So far the discussion of category systems and their appropriateness for cross-national comparative purposes has been a bit abstract—especially for persons not familiar with this kind of instrument. In order to provide a more concrete basis on which to judge the suitability of category systems for comparative purposes, a brief description of a category system and comparative data resulting from its use are given below.

Table 1 contains a description of a category system known as the Activity Categories Instrument (ACI), developed by Caldwell.[14] As can be seen this instrument consists of 11 categories of behavior which describe types of activities occurring in science classes. An observer using this instrument makes a record of classroom activities with the aid of a stopwatch. Every 5 sec the observer notes a single number associated with one of the ACI categories of behavior. The activity which occurs during each 5-sec interval determines which category number is recorded. Thus, if the teacher was asking a question, the observer records a 7 (teacher questioning). If a student response to the question occupied the next 5-sec interval, the number 6 (student speaking) would be recorded. In this way a series of numbers is recorded which indicates which of the 11 categories of behavior occurred during a period of observation and the relative frequency of their occurrence.

Observers using category systems such as this are usually trained until their recordings agree highly with those made by experts in the use of the instrument. This high agreement helps ensure that observations are made in a standardized way. Also, the fact that high agreement can be reached indicates that the process of assigning category numbers to describe observations is unambiguous, and that a "standard language" is being applied by the different observers to describe events being observed.

Once recordings are made, they can be analyzed in a number of ways. For example, frequency counts can be made to determine how many times each category number was recorded during the period of observation. On the basis of these, the percentage of time during which each category of behavior occurred can be estimated. If observations are made of a sample of

[14] Harrie E. Caldwell, "Evaluation of an In-Service Science Methods Course by Systematic Observation of Classroom Activities," Project no. 6-8760 (Washington, D.C.: Department of Health, Education and Welfare, Office of Education, 1967 [ERIC Document Reproduction Service No. ED 024 615]), and "Evaluation of an In-Service Science Methods Course by Systematic Observation of Classroom Activities" (Ph.D. diss., Syracuse University, 1968).

classes, means or medians can be calculated and compared with those of other samples.

These standardized recording and analysis procedures permit relatively precise statements to be made about the occurrence of specific classroom behaviors. Table 2, for example, contains statistics descriptive of behaviors occurring within the United States and Nepal. By looking at this table, we can state with some assurance that, in the science classes observed, more

TABLE 1
ACTIVITY CATEGORIES INSTRUMENT (Science)

Behavior Category	Behavior Description
1. Laboratory experiences open ended	Students are presented a problem to be solved by experimentation; the procedure may or may not be given; they are required to make observations and analyze or interpret their findings.
2. Laboratory experiences structured	Students are presented a laboratory experiment with a structured procedure; they are not required to analyze or interpret their data; they are asked to make observations.
3. Group projects	One or more groups of students are working on a science project during the class period; some may work individually (not written projects).
4. Student demonstrations	A student or group of students demonstrate a science experiment or project which they have prepared (oral report on science project would be included).
5. Library research, reporting, field trips	(a) A student or group of students give an oral report they have prepared based on reference material, (b) the class works with reference materials for purposes of writing or making reports, (c) field trips.
6. Student speaking	The student contributes verbally by asking a question, answering a question, or simply volunteering information; student writing on the blackboard is also included.
7. Teacher questioning	Students are asked a question by the teacher; silence following questions is also included.
8. Workbook work	Students work in class on workbooks, homework, questions from text, art-type work, etc.
9. Teacher demonstrations	The teacher presents materials by demonstration, models, charts, textbook pictures, film, TV, filmstrip, radio, record, etc.
10. Lecture	The teacher reads aloud, writes on blackboard, expresses his views, gives directions, makes an assignment or asks rhetorical questions; students are expected to listen; they may interrupt only when they do not understand; student reading in the text is also included.
11. Silence or general havoc	The class may be cleaning up, settling down, or doing nothing; in general, this category should be used sparingly.

NOTE.—This category system was developed by Harrie E. Caldwell and modified slightly by Richard H. Pfau and Lokendra B. Rayamajhi for use within Nepal.

TABLE 2

MEAN ACI CALCULATIONS OF NEPALESE AND U.S FIFTH-GRADE SCIENCE CLASSES

ACI Category	Nepal*	United States†
1. Laboratory experiences open ended	0	.3
	(0)	(1.2)
2. Laboratory experiences structured	0	1.6
	(0)	(3.7)
3. Group projects	0	1.3
	(0)	(6.2)
4. Student demonstrations	0	1.8
	(0)	(3.3)
5. Library research and field trips	0	5.8
	(0)	(9.4)
6. Student speaking	6.8	18.5
	(5.8)	(8.8)
7. Teacher questioning	6.7	17.1
	(6.2)	(7.4)
8. Workbook work	1.9	4.4
	(5.8)	(9.1)
9. Teacher demonstrations	.3	5.0
	(.6)	(4.1)
10. Lecture	78.3	40.2
	(12.2)	(11.0)
11. Silence or general havoc	5.9	3.9
	(4.1)	(2.3)

NOTE.—All numbers represent percentage of occurrences; numbers in parentheses are SDs.

* The Nepalese statistics shown are based on observation of classes conducted during 1974 in a representative sample of 23 schools located in central Nepal.

† The U.S. statistics shown are based on observation of classes taught by 30 teachers of the Syracuse, New York, area school system during 1966, and reported by Harrie E. Caldwell, "Evaluation of an In-Service Science Methods Course by Systematic Observation of Classroom Activities" (Ph.D. diss., Syracuse University, 1968).

student speaking occurred in the United States than in Nepal; more teacher questioning occurred in the United States; more lecture (as defined by Caldwell) occurred in Nepal; the U.S. teachers made more use of audio-visual materials than did Nepalese teachers; and no laboratory experiences, group projects, library work, and/or field trips occurred in Nepal, whereas such activities did occur in the United States. We can also realize that, of the behaviors studied, lecture occurred most frequently by far in both the Nepalese and U.S. science classes observed, and teacher questioning and student speaking were the next most frequently occurring teaching activities.

By using such procedures, then, we seem able with some precision to identify (1) aspects of behavior that are specific to particular systems, (2) behaviors that are more universal in nature, (3) differences in the extent to which behaviors occur within different systems, and, although not yet illustrated, (4) the degree to which behaviors are related to other variables found in the systems being studied. Such an ability would seem to be useful to comparative scholars, if indeed it can provide valid information.

The Meaning of Measurements Resulting from the Use of Category Systems

Some Basic Concepts and Questions

At this point, let us consider a few basic but key concepts related to this discussion. One of these is "measurement," which is considered to consist of rules for assigning numbers to objects or events in such a way as to represent quantities of attributes.[15] In the context of classroom observation, the rules associated with category systems are the explicitly stated procedures for classifying and making recordings of the behaviors observed. Application of these rules permits the extent of the occurrence of the behaviors recorded to be represented by using numbers, such as are shown in table 2.

"Validity," a second key concept, refers, in general, to the extent to which an instrument or procedure measures what was intended to be measured. Looked at in a slightly different way, validity can be thought of as referring to the appropriateness of inferences made based on measurement scores.[16] Considering the measurement of classroom behaviors, according to Medley and Mitzel, "a measure is valid to the extent that differences in scores yielded by it reflect actual differences in behavior—not differences in impressions made on different observers. For an observational scale to be valid for measuring behavior, it must provide an accurate record of behaviors which actually occurred, scored in such a way that the scores are reliable."[17]

A third key concept is that of "scalar identity." This concept is reflected by the concern that, when an instrument is used to make measurements of the same attribute in different cultures, the scores obtained be represented in terms of quantitatively identical scales.[18] That is, similar scores should indicate equal amounts or quantities of the attribute measured, and different scores should indicate differences in the amount of the attribute measured. Scalar identity, then, signifies not only that an instrument measures the same attribute in different cultures but also that the quantitative scale is the same in each culture. Such identity is considered necessary if the scores of culturally different groups are to be compared meaningfully.[19]

With these concepts in mind, let us review the techniques discussed previously for measuring and comparing behaviors. We should be able to

---

[15] Jum C. Nunnally, *Psychometric Theory*, 2d ed. (New York: McGraw-Hill, 1978), p. 3; Kerlinger, p. 426.

[16] Adam Przeworski and Henry Teune, *The Logic of Comparative Social Inquiry* (New York: Wiley-Interscience, 1970), pp. 11, 102–8.

[17] Medley and Mitzel, p. 250.

[18] Ype H. Poortinga, "Some Implications of Three Different Approaches to Intercultural Comparison," in *Applied Cross-cultural Psychology*, ed. J. W. Berry and W. J. Lonner (Amsterdam: Swets & Zeitlinger, 1975), p. 327.

[19] Andrew R. Davidson, "The Etic-Emic Dilemma: Can Methodology Provide a Solution in the Absence of Theory?" in *Basic Problems in Cross-cultural Psychology*, ed. Ype H. Poortinga (Amsterdam: Swets & Zeitlinger, 1977), p. 50.

realize that narrative descriptions do not represent measurements per se, while the use of rating systems, category systems, and indirect techniques such as questionnaires can result in measurements being made. An important question, however, is whether differences in scores yielded by these techniques actually represent differences in behavior. Considering questionnaires, interviews, and rating systems, the previous discussion strongly suggested that such may not be the case—especially in the context of cross-cultural research. In such a context the scalar identity and validity of measurements resulting from the use of each of these techniques has been seriously brought into question.

Now let us look more closely at table 2 and attempt to address the question of whether the statistics which result from the use of category systems and subsequent data analysis actually represent what occurred in the classes observed. Exactly what does 78.3 percent lecture in Nepal and 40.2 percent lecture in the United States mean? Do these statistics indeed mean that significantly more lecture, as defined by Caldwell, occurred in Nepal than in the United States? Does scalar identity for these scores exist, such that meaningful and valid comparisons between them can be made? Can similar inferences be drawn about the extent of the occurrence of the behaviors observed, equally valid for both countries, based on the measurements and analyses made?

The answer appears to be yes. By using category systems, the extent of the occurrence of many behaviors can be measured and validly compared from one country to another, from one culture to another.

This does not mean that all category systems are suitable for making comparisons between all cultures, for the concepts involved in some category systems may be too culture bound and not meaningfully comparable from one context to another. It does not mean that measurements made with apparently non–culture bound instruments provide valid comparisons in all cases, for the validity of comparisons is dependent not only on the instrument used but on factors such as observer effects on classroom behaviors, the sampling strategies used, how the instruments are used, observer honesty, and whether certain indices derived from the basic recordings are equally applicable for drawing the same kinds of inferences about the situations observed.[20] It does not mean that the use of category systems does not have limitations, because it does; perhaps chief among such limitations is the expensiveness of making direct observations and an ability, at any given time, to focus on only a relatively few specific types of classroom behaviors.

---

[20] Richard H. Pfau, "Factors Affecting the Validity of Cross-national Comparisons of Classroom Behaviors" (paper presented at the seventh annual meeting of the Society for Cross-cultural Research, New Haven, Conn., February 23-26, 1978 [ERIC Document Reproduction Service No. ED 152 658]).

However, category systems do seem to provide a potential for making precise and valid cross-national comparisons not equaled by other techniques used to measure and describe classroom behaviors. Why this seems so has been indicated previously throughout this article. A summary of the reasoning presented will now be made, and some preliminary empirical evidence will be provided in support of that reasoning.

Logical Support

Logically it seems that category systems provide the potential for making precise and valid comparisons of classroom behaviors, for they embody low-inference concepts and procedures which appear capable of lending themselves to a standardized recording of information by persons from differing cultural backgrounds. These low-inference procedures include the use of standard magnitudes of time and the explicit language of counting which, it may be recalled, are used to help measure the extent of the occurrence of specific classroom behaviors. The use of these standard magnitudes and counting procedures contrasts sharply with the use of psychological magnitudes such as "seldom" or "strong emphasis," which may vary in meaning from culture to culture and from time to time. The use of psychological magnitudes is a major factor which limits the cross-cultural usefulness of rating systems, narrative descriptions, questionnaires, and interviews.

Przeworski and Teune have stated that

> whether two or more phenomena are "comparable" depends on whether their properties have been expressed in a standard language. A language of measurement defines classes of phenomena by providing specific criteria for deciding whether an observation can be assigned to a particular class. . . . It is a standard language if it can be consistently applied to all individuals or social units . . . . Classifying observations into categories, ranking them, or counting instances serves to express observations in a language of measurement. . . . If these observations are expressed in a standard language, they are indeed comparable.[21]

Such reasoning supports the choice of category systems for making comparisons. Category systems usually do provide specific, low-inference criteria for deciding whether certain classifications of behavior have occurred or not. The decisions made are expressed in a language of measurement, by using counting or other recording procedures based on time. The extent to which the language used is a standard language is indicated by the consistency or agreement obtained between different observers who use a particular category system. That is, when different observers agree highly with respect to measurements made of the same phenomena, consistency in the use of the standard language is indicated. If this standard

[21] Przeworski and Teune, p. 93.

language is applied to describe occurrences in the classrooms of different nations, the measurements are comparable—if one accepts the logic of Przeworski and Teune. Additionally, and importantly, when such low-inference procedures are used to make measurements in different countries, interpretations of the measurements are straightforward and are not fraught with the difficulties associated with interpretation of measurements made by using other techniques, where inferential leaps are of necessity much greater and more hazardous.

Empirical Support

Even though such reasoning may seem persuasive to some readers, it should be realized that the potential validity of category system usage for comparative purposes cannot be demonstrated only by argument and logic. The ultimate test of such thinking requires empirical evidence. Such evidence is limited at the present time but not completely lacking.

Although many studies of classroom behaviors have been conducted within individual countries, few comparisons of classroom behaviors have been made between countries and cultures. For the most part, the few comparative studies made up to now, using category systems, have not closely examined the validity of comparisons made.[22]

However, a study I conducted does contain indications of the validity of measurements made within Nepal and of comparisons made between Nepalese and U.S. classroom behaviors. That study generated the data shown in table 2 and much more as well. Briefly, I learned to use the ACI and another category system called the Flanders Interaction Analysis Categories (FIAC), in standardized ways within the United States, where these instruments were first developed. I then went to Nepal and trained Nepalese observers to use the category systems until their usage while observing Nepalese classes agreed highly with my own. The observers then visited a representative sample of schools and observed the teaching of science, mathematics, language arts, and social studies in grades 2, 5, and 9. The measurements were then compared with others descriptive of U.S. classes.[23]

Before and during the survey conducted in Nepal, I observed classes taught in a number of Nepalese schools. In no case were verbal be-

[22] E.g., see R. P. Tisher, *A Study of Verbal Interaction in Science Classes and Its Association with Pupils' Understanding in Science* (St. Lucia, Brisbane: University of Queensland Press, 1970); Heathes V. Birrell, "A Comparative Study of the Verbal Behavior of Teachers in Open Education Classrooms in England and the United States" (Ph.D. diss., Syracuse University, 1974); William Caudill and Helen Weinstein, "Maternal Care and Infant Behavior in Japan and America," *Psychiatry* 32 (February 1969): 12–43.

[23] Richard H. Pfau, "A Cross-national Comparison of Classroom Behaviors: Based upon a Survey Conducted within Nepal Using the Flanders Interaction Analysis Categories and Caldwell's Activity Categories Instrument" (Ph.D., diss., University of Pittsburgh, 1977) (hereafter cited as "Cross-national Comparison), and "A Comparison of Nepalese and U.S. Classroom Behaviors" (paper presented at the annual meeting of the Comparative and International Education Society, New Orleans, February 16–19, 1977 [ERIC Document Reproduction Service No. ED 137 265]).

haviors observed which could not be meaningfully categorized using the FIAC as it was designed to be used. Also, no activities were observed which could not be classified using the ACI. When FIAC and ACI recordings were later analyzed, it appeared that elements of the classes observed were faithfully recreated, in that differences in scores seemed to represent differences in the actual classroom behaviors observed and measured. Thus both the FIAC and ACI appeared to measure what they were designed to measure when properly used. In this sense, the *face validity* of the two instruments appeared to be high when used to measure classroom behaviors in Nepal.

In addition, both the FIAC and ACI category systems overlap to some extent in their measurement of certain classroom behaviors. Both instruments measure aspects of student speaking, teacher questioning, and other teacher verbal behaviors, including lecturing, although they do so in different ways. Sufficient overlap exists so that measurements of these behaviors should vary in similar ways when the two instruments are used to observe and measure behaviors in the same classes. In fact, correlations of measurements of overlapping behaviors ranged from .68 to .87.[24] These levels seem high enough to reflect favorably on the *congruent validity* of the instruments as used in Nepal.

Finally, given the great cultural, economic, and educationally related differences existing between Nepal and the United States, classroom behaviors could indeed be expected to differ between these two countries. But specifically, how might they be expected to differ? Beeby's taxonomy of educational stages was chosen to provide a basis for making predictions about probable differences.[25] This taxonomy was developed by Beeby to describe stages in the development of primary school systems which were felt to be related to, and limited by, teacher levels of training and education. Beeby proposed, for example, that school systems with less educated and untrained or less trained teachers would have classes in which "activity methods and childish researches are shunned," "and group methods tolerated only if a group leader is satisfied . . . to ask the stock questions and accept the stock answers"; whereas classes of school systems with well-educated and well-trained teachers would be characterized by a "variety of content and methods," "activity methods, problem solving and creativity."[26]

After considering the taxonomy, the category systems to be used, and the knowledge that Nepal's teachers were relatively less trained and educated, a number of indices were selected and predictions made to determine

[24] Pfau, "Cross-national Comparison," p. 216.
[25] C. E. Beeby, *The Quality of Education in Developing Countries* (Cambridge, Mass.: Harvard University Press, 1966).
[26] Ibid., pp. 61, 72.

if classroom behaviors indeed differed between Nepal and the United States as suggested by Beeby's taxonomy. For example, on the basis of measurements with the ACI described in table 1, predictions were made that, when elementary school science classes were compared, (*a*) more student-centered activities (characterized by the sum of ACI categories 1–6) would occur in U.S. classes, and (*b*) more laboratory activities would occur in U.S. classes.

Statistical comparisons of the data gathered and summarized in table 2 supported these and a number of other predictions about differences between Nepalese and U.S. classroom behaviors. The similarity between predicted and measured differences was judged to be a favorable indication of the *construct validity* of the measurement and comparative procedures used in the investigation.[27]

In short, the logical suitability of category systems for comparative purposes was upheld by results of the investigation.

Concluding Remarks

Needless to say, favorable results from one study do not verify conclusively the general suitability of category systems for making precise and valid comparisons of classroom behaviors among countries. However, when viewed in the light of the other evidence presented in this article, they support a recommendation that researchers wishing to make valid cross-national comparisons of classroom behaviors should consider using category systems to measure behaviors of interest. It is apparent, however, that additional studies are needed to help determine the strengths and limitations of category systems when used for comparative purposes.

Further consideration and study of category systems seem especially justified given the benefits which can accrue from the use of these systems. In addition to precision and validity, which were discussed before, benefits from making standardized measurements of classroom behaviors are related to the following.

Communication: Communication among scholars is greatly facilitated when standardized languages and measures are used. Besides facilitating communication based on use of a standard language, the numerical indices resulting from measurements made with category systems make it possible to report results in finer detail than might otherwise be possible.[28]

Mathematical properties: In addition to permitting the communication of information in relatively fine detail, the numerical indices resulting from the use of category systems have another desirable property. Consider-

---

[27] For additional details see Pfau, "Cross-national Comparison," pp. 143–50, 157–78, 217–18.

[28] Nunnally (n. 15 above), pp. 6–7; Harold J. Noah and Max A. Eckstein, *Toward a Science of Comparative Education* (New York: Macmillan, 1969), p. 100.

ing the traditional classification of measurement scales, frequency and durational scores resulting from category system usage have the characteristics of ratio scales.[29] This permits a variety of arithmetic operations to be conducted with the scores, including use of powerful methods of mathematical analysis.[30] Such scores contrast with those resulting from rating systems and questionnaires which typically provide somewhat less useful ordinal data.

Objectivity: The use of standardized measuring techniques, by definition, helps take the guesswork out of scientific observation. Such techniques permit agreement to be reached on the extent of the occurrence of empirical events in an unambiguous manner.[31] In addition, they permit quantitative methods to be applied to data handling and the testing of relationships, similarities, and differences among data. Such quantitative methods can help to maintain objectivity.[32]

Testing theory: Scientific tests of many theories are not possible until adequate techniques are available to measure concerned variables. Without an ability to measure with precision, it becomes difficult to state relationships between variables in a clear-cut manner, and this hampers the development and testing of theory.[33] As indicated, category systems can be used to provide relatively precise measurements of classroom behaviors and thus should prove to be helpful in the development and testing of theory across cultures and nations.

Therefore, for these and the other reasons discussed in this article, it is felt that category systems deserve more attention and study than they have received by comparative educators and other cross-culturally oriented scholars.

[29] Richard R. Jones, "Behavioral Observation and Frequency Data: Problems in Scoring, Analysis, and Interpretation," in *Behavior Change: Methodology, Concepts, and Practice*, ed. Leo A. Hamerlynck, Lee C. Handy, and Eric J. Mash (Champaign, Ill.: Research Press, 1973), p. 132.

[30] Nunnally, pp. 18–19; Kerlinger (n. 13 above), p. 438.

[31] Nunnally, p. 6.

[32] Noah and Eckstein, pp. 99–100.

[33] Nunnally, p. 6; Beeby, p. 88; Bernard S. Phillips, *Social Research: Strategy and Tactics* (New York: Macmillan, 1966), p. 157.

Comparative Education: Challenge and Response

GAIL P. KELLY AND PHILIP G. ALTBACH

Comparative education is characterized today by a wide diversity of views, lively debates, and varying theoretical perspectives. Since *Comparative Education Review* and *Comparative Education* published their retrospective "state of the art" issues in 1977, the field has changed. In this essay, we will discuss some of these changes and the debates and research trends that have arisen since that time. Our interest is in the challenges posed to the field and the field's response.

It is our view that since 1977 many of the approaches that underlay the field, articulated so perceptively in the British and American appraisals in *Comparative Education* and *Compartive Education Review*, have come under criticism. Some have questioned the national comparisons that have traditionally characterized research and have argued cogently for world systems and regional analyses. Others have challenged the field to move beyond quantitative studies of school outcomes to qualitative research on educational processes. The theoretical assumptions that had guided the field, especially in the United States and particularly structural functionalism, have also emerged as subjects of intense debate. Some scholars have begun to explore alternative perspectives such as conflict theory, legitimation theory, and Marxism. Simultaneously, scholars challenged the field to consider subjects of inquiry that it had hitherto ignored. Among these are women's education, the concrete study of social and political institutions, and the question of how knowledge is disseminated, produced, and used. In the past decade, scholars in comparative education have also turned to reconsidering old questions, especially the role of education in bringing about modernization and social change.

The pages that follow first consider the new challenges posited to the field since 1977 and then look at the field's response. Our discussion is based on an analysis of research that has appeared in the major journals in the field, such as *Comparative Education Review*, the *International Review of Education*, *Compare*, and *Comparative Education*, as well as in some of the major books published on the field in the United States and Great Britain, including those in the series issued by Pergamon and Praeger. Our discussion is limited to the English language literature, which, for the most part, is a British and North American literature. We make no pretenses of rep-

The authors wish to thank Joseph Farrell and Stephen Klees for their criticism on an earlier draft of this article.

Reprinted from *Comparative Education Review*, vol. 30, no. 1 (February 1986).

resenting the developments in the field in Third World nations or anywhere but in the United States, Great Britain, and, to a lesser extent, Canada.

Our focus here is on new directions in the field. We will not dwell at length on traditional approaches or modes of analysis, which continue to dominate comparative education. Our purpose is to highlight challenges and to direct the field's attention to perspectives that have yet to be fully considered and that we believe are important to its vitality.

Challenges and New Directions

Since 1977, four kinds of challenges to established research traditions in comparative education have emerged. These are (1) those that question the nation-state or national characteristics as the major parameter in defining comparative study; (2) those that question the use of input-output models and exclusive reliance on quantification in the conduct of comparative research; (3) those that challenge structural functionalism as the major theoretical premise undergirding scholarship; and (4) those that direct attention to new subjects of inquiry. Some of these challenges began prior to 1977; however, before that time they scarcely entered the discourse of the field and were not promoted through the major journals or texts in comparative education. After 1977, they were increasingly and more directly articulated.

Although we have grouped the challenges to the field into four categories, we are aware that there is some overlap among them. For example, world systems analysis, which looks at international inequalities between nation-states in examining educational expansion, is guided by conflict theory and, in some instances, by Marxism. This is also the case with research that has arisen on women and sex differences in education cross-nationally, on knowledge distribution and control, and on the politics of educational planning. Regardless of the overlap, we believe it useful to discuss the challenges.

Challenges to the Nation-State as the Exclusive Research Framework

Until recently, most research in comparative education focused on the nation-state, and/or characteristics of nation-states, treated as an autonomous unit. Indeed, much of the field was comprised of studies that applied a method derived from the social sciences to the study of education in a particular nation or that simply described education in a specific country. Often research asked how education contributed to the development and maintenance of social structures within that nation-state and compared education's role in one country with its role in another.[1] When

[1] For a more complete discussion see Gail P. Kelly and Philip G. Altbach, "Comparative Education: A Field in Transition," in *International Bibliography of Comparative Education*, ed. P. G. Altbach, G. P. Kelly, and D. H. Kelly (New York: Praeger, 1981). See also "Comparative Education: Its Present

the focus was on individual attitudes, research was situated in the context of school systems in a single nation presumed to be autonomous and coequal with others. This framework predominated region-wide studies that, while dealing with Southeast Asia, Africa, Latin America, or Eastern Europe, focused on education in individual nation-states within that region that presumably shared similar cultures, histories, and economic or political structures. Topically based studies also were situated in national frameworks, asking, for example, if one national school system was more conducive to economic growth than another.

Scholars such as John Meyer, John Boli-Bennett, Francisco Ramirez, Mathew Zachariah, Martin Carnoy, Robert Arnove, and Philip Altbach challenge the use of the nation-state as the dominant category guiding comparative research. They argue that educational systems in one country are often affected more by factors outside that country than they are by factors inside it and urge research to focus on identifying these external forces. Martin Carnoy's 1974 book, *Education as Cultural Imperialism*, marked the beginning of such scholarship in the field. After 1977, the number of works of this nature in comparative education increased markedly.[2]

In 1979, John Meyer and Michael T. Hannon published *National Development and the World System*.[3] They point out that educational expansion in the post–World War II period could not be explained by reference to a single nation-state or its political structure, to the way in which it organized power, to how its economy was controlled, or to its peculiar social structure. The drive for universal primary education and the unparalleled expansion of education on the secondary and tertiary levels had little to do with national educational policies, either. Meyer and Hannon maintain that given changes in technology and communications and the internationalization of the labor market, education functions within a transnational context. They call on the field to reorient its inquiry by looking at what they call the world system rather than merely at the nation-state.

Meyer and his colleagues, as well as other scholars who focus on world systems analysis, use a range of perspectives in their work. Meyer, and

---

State and Future Prospects," *Comparative Education* 13 (June 1977): 75–150; and "The State of the Art: Twenty Years of Comparative Education," *Comparative Education Review* 21 (June/October 1977): 151–416.

[2] John W. Meyer et al., "The World Educational Revolution, 1950–1970," *Sociology of Education* 50 (October 1971): 242–58; John Meyer and Michael T. Hannon, *National Development and the World System* (Chicago: University of Chicago Press, 1979); Robert Arnove, "Comparative Education and World Systems Analysis," *Comparative Education Review* 24 (February 1980): 48–62; Philip G. Altbach, "Servitude of the Mind: Education, Dependency and Neocolonialism," *Teachers College Record* 79 (December 1977): 188–204; Mathew Zachariah, "Comparative Educators and International Development Policy," *Comparative Education Review* 23 (October 1979): 341–54; Martin Carnoy, "Education for Alternative Development," *Comparative Education Review* 27 (June 1982): 160–77; and Martin Carnoy, *Education as Cultural Imperialism* (New York: McKay, 1974).

[3] Meyer and Hannon.

his coauthors, for example, argue that an individual nation's political and economic systems have relatively little to do with either how education is organized and distributed or its content. Immanuel Wallerstein, on the other hand, discusses the nature of the world system by using Marxian frameworks, although his work is not directly dealing with education.[4] Most of the scholars directly in the field of comparative education utilize a range of explanatory frameworks in their work on specific aspects of how relationships between nations, regions, classes, or groups within and among societies affect schooling and its social, economic, and political outcomes. Altbach, Arnove, Carnoy, Zachariah, and Silva all argue that national school systems exist within the context of unequal power relations among nations.[5] They argue that either through design, historical circumstance, or the contemporary distribution of resources, including intellectual resources, the Western industrialized capitalist nations dominate the economic and educational systems of the less industrialized countries. Silva argues that educational dominance patterns parallel trading blocs. Altbach discusses how the knowledge that schools distribute in the Third World is generated, controlled, and distributed by the United States, Great Britain, and France. Carnoy contends that such controls seek to maintain existing international inequalities and keep the Third World dependent.

World systems analysis challenges comparative education to go beyond the nation-state as the major analytical category guiding research and to look at regional variations, racial groups, classes, and others that are not necessarily bound to the nation. Other scholars who have not used the world systems approach have come to similar conclusions, frequently based on microanalytic research. Notable among these are those scholars who have focused on regional variation.

Research in comparative education before 1977 focused on schooling within a nation-state; rare was the scholar whose work centered on regional variation beyond urban/rural distinctions that were applied to Third World nations and, in the case of a few studies of African nations, beyond ethnically based distinctions. Comparative work took the nation-state as the boundary for comparison and referred to it in tracing school/society relations. Comparative research did not inquire as to whether there were major regional variations in the pattern of educational diffusion or in the determinants of educational access and outcomes within a nation-state. Proponents of the analysis of regional variation argue that comparison among regions within nation-states is as significant as comparison between nations. The

---

[4] Immanuel Wallerstein, *The Modern World System* (New York: Academic Press, 1974).

[5] Philip G. Altbach, Robert F. Arnove, and Gail P. Kelly, eds., *Comparative Education* (New York: Macmillian, 1982); Carnoy, *Education as Cultural Imperialism;* Zachariah; Edward T. Silva, "Cultural Autonomy and Ideas in Transit: Notes from the Canadian Case," *Comparative Education Review* 24 (February 1980): 63–72.

challenge to pursue such a line of analysis was developed by John Craig and Margaret Archer in their works tracing the spread of education in the nineteenth century.[6] It was also advanced by Mary Jean Bowman, Phyllis Goldblatt, and David Plank.[7] All of these scholars showed that educational variance often is as great, if not greater, between regions within a nation as between nations. The determinants of women's education, for example, is not the same in northeast Brazil as in the dominant south of that country; class and ethnicity may not operate similarly in regard to educational access and outcome throughout a single nation. They have pointed to the obvious—the necessity of looking at regional variation given growing trends to decentralization of education and deconcentration of educational decision making in much of the world.

Although scholars working in the newly emergent tradition of world systems analysis and analysis of regional variation challenge established research traditions, their questions represent but one kind among those to emerge since 1977.

Challenges to Input/Output Models and Dominant Reliance on Quantification

Much research in comparative education tended to focus almost exclusively on the quantitative analysis of educational inputs and outcomes, mostly the outcomes. Research assumed that the outcomes—such as modern attitudes or mathematics achievement levels—could be attributed to whatever schools taught. With some exceptions, research—following Sadlerian traditions—assumed that whatever went on in the school was unimportant and not worthy of study. The only studies of school processes—if one could call them that—were descriptions of curricular guides, analyses of texts, and a few ethnographic studies—considered anthropology—that treated the classroom as part of the broader social order, reflecting a social consensus.

Before 1977, there were some criticisms of the field for presuming that school processes were unimportant. More recently, this criticism was extended to research such as the international achievement studies (IEA) that focused only on the quantitative measurement of outcomes and inputs (such as test scores, number of hours in the classroom, years of teacher training, and the like) to stand for the study of the educational process. Scholars such as Masemann, Weis, Heyman, and Pfau argued cogently that reliance on school outcome data failed to relate outcomes to the processes of schooling and suggested that only through qualitative methods

[6] Margaret Archer, ed., *The Sociology of Educational Expansion: Take-Off, Growth and Inflation in Educational Systems* (Beverly Hills, Calif.: Sage, 1982).

[7] See Mary Jean Bowman, "An Integrated Framework for Analysis of the Spread of Schooling in Less Developed Countries," *Comparative Education Review* 28 (November 1984): 563–83; David N. Plank, "The Determinants of School Enrollment Rates in Brazil, 1940–1980" (Ph.D. diss., University of Chicago, 1983).

could the nature of educational processes and their outcomes be under-stood.[8] They pointed out that what schools teach cannot be reduced only to the formal curriculum texts and teacher attributes; rather, student and teacher interaction, the structure of educational institutions, and the "lived culture" of the schools represented a very powerful element in producing the social, cultural, and political outcomes of schooling. Their call was for the use of qualitative means of research that focused on educational processes.

Heyman and Pfau urge comparative education to adopt ethnometh-odological techniques derived exclusively from anthropology; Masemann and Weis, in their respective works, challenge the field to go beyond anthropological traditions and to relate educational processes to broader theories of school/society relations. Weis points out that such scholarship could adopt varying theoretical perspectives, including either structural functionalism or Marxism.[9]

Although the challenge to engage in qualitative research on educational processes in light of social theory does not necessarily entail a paradigm shift for the field, paralleling interest in such studies has increased ques-tioning of the dominance of structural functionalism in guiding research in comparative education.

Challenges to Structural Functionalism

Until the 1970s, comparative education in North America was largely influenced by structural functionalism. This is not surprising given the domination of this perspective in many of the social sciences. The "state-of-the-art" volumes of *Comparative Education Review* and of *Comparative Education* are largely in this tradition.[10] The field asked either how education functioned to maintain the social fabric or how it could be made to function, in the case of the Third World, to develop a nation-state generally along Western models. It was assumed that what was good for the nation also benefited all of society. In this context, conflict, as John Bock and Rolland

[8] Vandra Masemann, "Critical Ethnography in the Study of Comparative Education," *Comparative Education* 26 (February 1982): 1–15; Lois Weis, "Educational Outcomes and School Processes: Theoretical Perspectives," in Altbach, Arnove, and Kelly, eds.; Richard Heyman, "Comparative Education from an Ethno-methodological Perspective," *Comparative Education* 15 (October 1979): 241–49; Richard H. Pfau, "The Comparative Study of Classroom Behaviors," *Comparative Education Review* 24 (October 1980): 400–14.

[9] Those that incorporate a Marxian approach include Paul Willis, *Learning to Labour: How Working Class Kids Get Working Class Jobs* (Westhead, England: Saxon House, 1977); and Pierre Bourdieu and Jean-Claude Passeron, *Reproduction in Education, Society and Culture* (London: Sage, 1977). Those who do not include John U. Ogbu, *Minority Education and Caste: The American System in Cross-cultural Perspective* (New York: Academic Press, 1978); John U. Ogbu, "Minority Status and Schooling in Plural Societies," *Comparative Education Review* 27 (June 1983): 168–90; and Karen Coffyn Biraimah, "Different Knowledge for Different Folks: Knowledge Distribution in Togolese Secondary School," in Altbach, Arnove, and Kelly, eds.

[10] See Andreas M. Kazamias and Karl Schwartz, "Intellectual and Ideological Perspectives in Comparative Education: An Interpretation," *Comparative Education Review* 21 (June/October 1977): 153–76; and Robert Koehl, "The Comparative Study of Education: Prescription and Practice," *Comparative Education Review* 21 (June/October 1977): 177–94.

Paulston so aptly point out, was considered dysfunctional at best.[11] Although many questions about functionalism were raised outside comparative education before 1977, few within the field paid much attention to debates in sociology and political science. Kazamias and Schwartz, in their essay that prefaces *Comparative Education Review*'s state-of-the-art issue, note the dominance of structural functionalism in the field and urge that scholars inform their works with different perspectives.[12] Other voices joined them. Martin Carnoy, Philip Altbach, Robert Arnove, Michael Apple, and Henry Levin began to look at how educational systems serve societal groups differentially and how social inequalities are played out at the regional and international levels.[13] Carnoy, Apple, and Levin emphasize the relationship between education and the development of capitalist relations and argue that the nature of economic systems and of state control make a difference as to what schools teach and as to the outcomes of education.

Rolland Paulston argues that reliance on functionalism has led the field away from correctly analyzing education in most social settings and places too much stress on the national setting and not on the roles that education might play in society and its myriad institutions.[14] John Bock makes a similar point.[15] He asserts that most developing societies are plural societies characterized by conflict, where dominant groups seek to legitimize their control over the state. At the same time, minorities attempt to use education to assert themselves and sometimes to unseat the dominant groups. Bock shows us that education assumes contradictory roles—it is at once oppressive and liberating. Paulston and Bock and, more recently, Hans Weiler see alternatives to functionalism in conflict theory and in legitimation theory;[16] others have adopted a classical Marxian perspective.

It is not our intention in this essay to explore in-depth these alternative theories; rather, our point here is to show that alternatives to structural

---

[11] John C. Bock, "Education and the Meaning of Development: A Conflict of Meaning," in Altbach, Arnove, and Kelly, eds. (n. 5 above); Rolland Paulston, "Conflicting Theories of Educational Reform," in *Better Schools: International Lessons for Reform*, ed. John Simmons (New York: Praeger, 1983).

[12] Kazamias and Schwartz.

[13] See, e.g., Carnoy, *Education as Cultural Imperialism;* Robert F. Arnove, "The Ford Foundation and 'Competence Building' Overseas: Assumptions, Approaches and Implications," *Studies in Comparative International Development* 12 (Fall 1977): 100–26; Robert F. Arnove, *Philanthropy and Cultural Imperialism: The Foundations at Home and Abroad* (Boston: G. K. Hall, 1980); Philip G. Altbach, "Servitude of the Mind" (n. 2 above); Henry M. Levin, "The Dilemma of Comprehensive Secondary School Reforms in Western Europe," *Comparative Education Review* 22 (October 1978): 434–51; Michael Apple, "Ideology, Reproduction and Educational Reform," *Comparative Education Review* 22 (October 1978): 367–87.

[14] Paulston.

[15] Bock.

[16] See, e.g., Hans N. Weiler, "Legalization, Expertise and Participation: Strategies of Compensatory Legitimation in Educational Policy," *Comparative Education Review* 27 (June 1983): 259–77; Hans N. Weiler, "Educational Planning and Social Change: A Critical Review of Concepts and Practices," in Altbach, Arnove, and Kelly, eds. (n. 5 above).

functionalism have been articulated in the field. These alternatives have also led to changes in research concerns, as we will now explore.

The Emergence of New Research Concerns

Comparative education until recently was a field that focused mainly on issues of education and development, on educational planning, on the individual outcomes of schooling in the context of the nation-state, and on a range of descriptive analyses and discussions of educational systems and issues. Most of the research was informed by structural functionalism or was basically atheoretical and descriptive. Few qualitative studies appeared in the field's journals that sought to understand what schools taught and that related educational processes to outcomes of education. Over the past decade the field has been challenged to study subjects that it had hitherto ignored. These ranged from including women both as a category in and as a central concern of research; to looking at the ways in which knowledge was disseminated, produced, and used; to new ways of looking at educational institutions and their relation to society. A major research challenge in all instances has been to reorient study away from preoccupation with individual outcomes and attitudes toward looking at institutions ranging from schools to the state to international agencies and finally to the relationships among them. The research challenge that emerged was to chart institutional content—that is, how institutions such as schools, planning agencies, the government, and so forth are organized and controlled and what the effect is that these institutional arrangements have on educational outcomes. We will discuss some of these challenges that have arisen in the past decade in the form of an interest in how education is planned and controlled, how educational contents are structured and distributed, and how schools shape the social reality of their pupils.

Although comparative education has a substantial literature on educational planning, much of that literature focuses on the technical aspects of planning and its outcomes—whether goals were or were not fulfilled. New scholarship has appeared that looks at the institutional context of planning—who plans what in whose interests and the relation between planning and structured inequality. Studies like Urwick's on Nigeria; McGinn, Schiefelbein, and Warwick's on planners in Chile; and Salvador's and McGinn and Street's on Mexico are in this vein.[17] Others have looked at institutional capacity to plan, the mechanisms by which plans are put

---

[17] See, e.g., Noel McGinn, Ernesto Schiefelbein, and Donald P. Warwick, "Educational Planning as Political Process: Two Case Studies from Latin America," *Comparative Education Review* 23 (June 1979): 218–39; James Urwick, "Politics and Professionalism in Nigerian Educational Planning," *Comparative Education Review* 23 (October 1983): 323–40; Noel McGinn and Susan Street, "The Political Rationality of Resource Allocation in Mexican Public Education," *Comparative Education Review* 26 (June 1982): 178–98; Weiler, "Legalization, Expertise, and Participation"; E. Mark Hanson, "Administrative Development in the Colombian Ministry of Education: A Case Analysis of the 1970s," *Comparative Education Review* 27 (February 1983): 89–107.

into practice, and the role of political parties with distinctly different ideologies in planning. Some of these institutional studies have focused on the roles of international agencies in forming and implementing national plans—for example, Linda Dove's research on Universal Primary Education in Bangladesh.[18] These works challenge the field to look at institutional processes in the context of national and international politics.

While much scholarship to emerge since 1977 has called the field's attention to the institutional processes of planning, related research has emerged on how knowledge is generated and used in educational systems to make educational policy and shape society. Much of this research—but by no means, all of it—stems from world systems or conflict analysis. Some scholars have been concerned with knowledge distribution systems. Altbach's work on transnational publishing, for example, focuses on how books are produced and distributed internationally and the implications for educational and knowledge systems within specific countries.[19] Others have been concerned with knowledge generation and control. Edward Berman's research on the role of philanthropic foundations is an example of a concern with the factors that influence research and development.[20] Other scholars have been concerned with knowledge utilization. Fry, among others, studies how educational planners use research to guide policy.[21] James Coleman has considered the role of U.S.-trained political scientists in Africa and has written on the impact of foundation assistance in Asia and Africa.[22] Hans Weiler and others have written of the impact of foreign study on education and development in the Third World. This research has looked at student flows and the students' impact on host institutions and on the students' country of origin.[23] These studies, and many others, have focused on the nature of knowledge transfer and its impact on the Third World.[24]

[18] McGinn, Schiefelbein, and Warwick. See also Linda Dove, "The Political Context of Education in Bangladesh, 1971–80," in *Politics and Educational Change*, ed. P. Broadfoot, C. Brock, and W. Tulasiewicz (London: Croom Helm, 1982).

[19] Philip G. Altbach, "The Distribution of Knowledge in the Third World," in *Higher Education in the Third World: Themes and Variations*, by P. G. Altbach (Singapore: Maruzen, 1982).

[20] Edward Berman, "Foundations, United States Foreign Policy and African Education, 1945–1975," *Harvard Educational Review* 49 (May 1979): 145–79.

[21] Sippandondha Ketudat and Gerald Fry, "Relations between Educational Research, Policy, Planning and Implementation: The Thai Experience," *International Review of Education* 27 (1981): 141–52.

[22] James S. Coleman, "Professional Training and Institution Building in the Third World: Two Rockefeller Foundation Experiences," *Comparative Education Review* 28 (May 1984): 180–202.

[23] Hans Weiler, "The Political Dilemma of Foreign Study," *Comparative Education Review* 28 (May 1984): 168–79. See also Philip G. Altbach and Y. G.-M. Lulat, "International Students in Comparative Perspective: Toward a Political Economy of International Study," in *Research on Foreign Students and International Study*, ed. P. G. Altbach, D. H. Kelly, and Y. G.-M. Lulat (New York: Praeger, 1985).

[24] Thomas O. Eisemon, "Scientific Life in Indian and African Universities: A Comparative Study of Peripheriality in Science," *Comparative Education Review* 25 (June 1981): 164–82; and Arnove, "The Ford Foundation and 'Competence Building' Overseas" (n. 13 above).

There has also been an interest in what kind of knowledge enters the classroom and how that knowledge is communicated. Heyneman's research on the role, availability, and effectiveness of textbooks in Third World nations is an example of such scholarship. There is also a growing body of research that seeks to understand the nature of social reality conveyed in textbooks used in the Third World and the relationship of this reality to development and culture.[25]

Although comparative education has traditionally been concerned with school outcomes, there has been a new concern with the detailed study of the content of schooling and with the internal workings of the school. Some of these studies have used ethnographic and participant observation research tools to search deeply into the internal life of educational institutions. Paul Willis's study of British education is an example of this trend.[26] Other studies have looked at the interaction between the formal and the "hidden" curriculum in schools in an effort to understand school cultures.[27] Some researchers have looked at a range of variables to obtain a broad picture of the impact of education on students and on society. William Cummings's work on Japan takes such an approach.[28] Susan Shirk and Jonathan Unger analyze education in China during the Cultural Revolution from this perspective.[29] The originality of this research is its concern with the internal culture of the school, the "in-school" outcomes of education, and the effect of the relationship between these factors on society.

Another important and new stream of scholarship has been gender studies. The field in the 1980s has been challenged to look at women in the context of educational and social structures that have resulted in gender-based inequalities. This scholarship has pointed out that research can no longer assume that findings based on the study of male populations are necessarily relevant for females as well. The 1980 special issue of *Comparative Education Review* challenged the field not only to include gender as a background variable in research—something almost totally neglected in comparative education—but also to make women a central research focus.[30] The field was also challenged to ask how education changed

[25] Stephen P. Heyneman, *Textbooks and Achievement: What We Know* (Washington, D.C.: World Bank, 1978). Also see Karen Coffyn Biraimah, "The Impact of Western Schools in Girls' Expectations," *Comparative Education Review* 24 (June 1980): 196–208.

[26] Willis (n. 9 above).

[27] See, e.g., Biraimah, "Different Knowledge for Different Folks" (n. 9 above).

[28] William Cummings, *Education and Equality in Japan* (Princeton, N.J.: Princeton University Press, 1980), esp. chap. 5.

[29] Susan Shirk, *Competitive Comrades: Career Incentives and Student Strategies in China* (Berkeley and Los Angeles: University of California Press, 1982); Jonathan Unger, *Education under Mao: Class and Competition in Canton Schools, 1960–1980* (New York: Columbia University Press, 1982).

[30] See, esp., Carolyn M. Elliott and Gail P. Kelly, "Perspectives on Women's Education," *Comparative Education Review* 24 (June 1980): S1–S12. See also Gail Kelly, "Women's Access to Education in the Third World: Myths and Realities," in *World Yearbook of Education 1984: Women in Education*, ed. S.

women's lives in the family and in the work force and not confine itself to asking whether educational outcomes for males and females were the same.

We have thus far detailed currents new to the field since 1977. We have by no means represented all currents in the field. Our goal has been to call attention to innovations in the field, not to the field's mainstream. Much research in the field continues to presume the autonomous nation-state and is guided by structural functionalism and its correlates like human capital theory. Research still focuses on development and on the outcomes of schooling and, as in the past, is predominantly quantitative, centered around primary through higher education.

The challenges to the field that we have outlined have, for the most part, generated some debate. They have appeared in the major journals and texts in the field; they have been presented at conferences; some have been the themes of world yearbooks of education. The last part of this essay asks how the field has responded to these challenges—what kinds of debates, if any, have they generated, and how have they affected the mainstream of the field?

Response

It is always difficult to gauge the response of a field of inquiry to challenges that it reexamine its theoretical assumptions or study phenomena through the lens of theories that contradict those that the field has traditionally used. We now ask if there have been any changes in the research published in the major journals and texts in comparative education that reflect the new challenges we have outlined thus far. Is there, for example, a greater emphasis on qualitative research that seeks to understand educational processes? Are there more studies focusing on women or on education in the context of the world system or on institutional behaviors? Has there been less reliance on structural functionalism and a greater diversity of theoretical orientations?

We will show that there have been three types of responses to the new research challenges. In many instances the field has tended to ignore new challenges. Such a response, we believe, is basically a sign of weakness in comparative education. A second response has been to confront new challenges and to attempt to refute them. In some instances scholars have contested the validity of new trends and sought to end the debates that they engendered. The third response has been to co-opt the challenges.

Acker (New York: Kogan Page, 1984). For a complete bibliography of recently generated works, see David H. Kelly and Gail P. Kelly, "Women and Schooling in the Third World: A Bibliography," in *Women's Education in the Third World: Comparative Perspectives*, ed. G. P. Kelly and C. Elliott (Albany: SUNY Press, 1982).

This has led to some changes in what scholars study but not necessarily in how they study it or in the theoretical assumptions that underlie inquiry. We will discuss these three types of responses separately.

Ignoring the Challenges

A common response to new trends is to ignore them. Comparative education is no different in this regard from other fields of inquiry. Many of the challenges we noted appeared in the field's major journals as "think pieces." For example, Vandra Masemann and Douglas Foley urged the field to engage in qualitative research that seeks to understand educational processes.[31] No debate followed, nor for that matter did much research of a qualitative nature on school processes. The field neither accepted nor rejected the challenge; it simply acted as if it were never made. *Comparative Education Review* continued to publish a very small number of ethnographies, but they, by and large, were in the tradition of anthropologically based works that did not seek to relate classroom phenomenon to social theory. Journals in Great Britain like *Compare* carried no such material; the recent *International Encyclopedia of Education* fails to mention this work as even a part of the field, although there is substantive coverage given to ethnography and to the anthropology of education.[32]

The tendency to ignore new trends extends also to challenges to attend to gender both as a variable in research and as a focus of research. Two of the major journals in the field published special issues on women's education and sex differences in education, and the *World Yearbook of Education* in 1984 focused on women.[33] Despite this, some journals in the field have yet to run research articles on either women's education or sex differences in education. The few articles that acknowledge gender that find their way into the field's journals have women as the subject of study and are written by women as well. Very rarely does research use gender as a significant background variable, even when that research does deal with other variables like class, ethnicity, and urban/rural residence. This occurs even when scholarship focuses on inequality or the determinants of academic achievement, despite the clear-cut evidence that gender is both a basis for structural inequality and a predictor of educational outcomes. At the same time that the field has tended to ignore the sizable body of research on women and gender effects that has appeared in women's studies journals, Unesco publications, and special issues in the field, there has also been little debate about the validity of such scholarship. Gender

---

[31] Masemann (n. 8 above). See also Douglas Foley, "Anthropological Studies of Schooling in Developing Countries: Some Recent Findings and Trends," *Comparative Education Review* 21 (June/October 1977): 311–28.

[32] Torsten Husen and T. Neville Postlethwaite, eds., *International Encyclopedia of Education* (Oxford: Pergamon, 1985), 10 vols.

[33] See G. P. Kelly and Carolyn Elliott, eds., "Women and Education in the Third World," *Comparative Education Review* 24 (June 1980, part 2): S1–S266. See also Acker, ed.

often becomes a nonissue, neither incorporated nor debated and then rejected.[34]

The field's reaction to the challenges to engage in the qualitative study of school processes or to make women a focus of research and gender a variable in scholarship has parallels in the case of regional analysis. A few scholars have called on the field to consider such work, and their calls so far have landed on deaf ears.

Although comparative education has ignored some new currents that have arisen since 1977, this is not the case with all new scholarship. The field has hotly debated scholarship that has directly challenged the theoretical premises underlying research. In the case of world systems analysis, the field has debated and co-opted some challenges by accepting parts of the research foci commended by such scholarship while discarding the theory that led to these very concerns. Before discussing co-optation, however, we will trace the debates that the new challenges have engendered.

Debate

Although many recent commentaries on the field have ignored the challenges posed by world systems analysis to comparative education,[35] others have attacked it on the basis of the association of world systems analysis with a Marxist problematic. Harold Noah and Max Eckstein have dubbed this approach the "new simplicitude."[36] They claim that such an approach, deriving from dependency theory and focusing on the unequal power relations between Third World and industrialized nations, has tended to look on Third World nations as passive victims of the industrialized nations and to blame the current economic hardships of these Third World nations on former colonial rulers. Noah and Eckstein deny that there is any evidence of attempts on the part of Western industrialized nations to maintain economic domination that would explain either the poverty or the evolution of school systems in much of Africa, Asia, and Latin America. Rather, they attribute the problems of the Third World solely to underdevelopment, which predated colonialism and which industrialized nations are, through their aid programs, seeking to remedy. Additionally, Noah and Eckstein point out that if world systems analysis had any validity, it would be impossible to explain social revolutions in parts of the Third World or development in other parts.

Attacks on world systems analysis, similar to those initiated by Noah and Eckstein, were mounted by Keith Watson and Jon Lauglo in British

---

[34] Husen and Postlethwaite. See also Keith Watson and Raymond Wilson, eds., *Contemporary Issues in Comparative Education: A Festschrift in Honor of Professor Emeritus Vernon Mallinson* (London: Croom Helm, 1985).

[35] Watson and Wilson.

[36] Harold Noah and Max Eckstein, "Dependency Theory in Comparative Education: The New Simplicitude," *Prospects* 15, no.2 (1985): 213–25.

journals.[37] Watson does not dispute the existence of the international ties documented by Arnove, Altbach, and others. He simply disagrees with world systems analysts' interpretation of what these ties mean. Watson, for one, sees dependency as a stage in the development of autonomous nation states.

The debates over world systems analysis do not only concern the interpretation of underdevelopment. One study has attempted to generate data to refute world systems analysis and the application of dependency theory to the evolution of schooling in the Third World. Sica and Prechel ask if there is any relation between the spread of Western-style education and economic dependency (they note the lack of relation between educational expansion and economic development).[38] They find no significant relation between measures of educational enrollments and dependency. Whether such a statistical analysis has validity is open to question—the authors themselves point out that the fact that they have found no statistically significant relation cannot be taken to mean that no relation at all exists.

The debates surrounding world systems analysis are related to those that challenges to structural functionalism have generated. Not only have scholars working in the tradition of world systems analysis questioned structural functionalism but so also have some scholars who focus their studies on education and inequality and on the role of education as an institution in maintaining existing social and political injustice. These scholars have been openly critical of structural functionalism and have applied conflict, Marxist, and/or other nonmainstream theories to the study of education. Within comparative education there have been few, if any, outright defenses of structural functionalism; rather, there have been critiques of alternative approaches, especially those identified as Marxist. Some scholars have dismissed such approaches out of hand as ideological and "biased."[39] Others, like Erwin Epstein, have tried to moderate the debate and strive for consensus in the field. In his Presidential Address to the Comparative and International Education Society, Erwin Epstein implied that the strident debates that Marxist and conflict theories had brought to the field put comparative education's future at risk.[40] He claimed that "neo-Marxism," "neo-positivism" (which he identified with functionalism), and "neo-relativism" (which he associated with Brian Holmes and his "problem approach" first articulated in the 1960s) divided the

[37] Keith Watson, "Dependence or Independence in Education: Two Cases from Post-colonial Southeast Asia," *International Journal of Educational Development* 5 (1985): 83–94. See also Jon Lauglo, "Mass Schooling: A Tool of Capitalist Domination?" *Compare* 15, no. 1 (1985): 21–27.

[38] Alan Sica and Harland Prechel, "National Political-Economic Dependency in the Global Economy and Educational Development," *Comparative Education Review* 25 (October 1981): 384–402.

[39] See Brian Holmes, *Comparative Education: Some Consideration of Method* (London: Unwin Educational, 1981).

[40] Erwin Epstein, "Currents Right and Left: Ideology in Comparative Education," *Comparative Education Review* 27 (February 1983): 3–27.

field into hostile camps. Each position generated its own data sets, none of which were comparable. Because of this, the field had reached a point where it was unable to provide "objective" evidence to guide policy. Epstein felt that comparative education would be better off if theoretical divisions were muted and attention focused on generating a knowledge base that all could use.

Epstein did not directly attack Marxian theory—his plea was one for greater consensus in the field. Paulston, in his article that outlines the divergent theories in the field, also argues for consensus.[41] He suggests that Marxian theories could be used to "diagnose" educational problems and consensual functionalist theories to arrive at reform strategies. Whether such a strategy is viable is open to question.

Not only has the application of conflict and Marxist theories been criticized for being divisive but there have also been some works that seek to disprove empirically the findings of such studies. Among these is William Cummings's book, *Education and Equality in Japan.*[42] Cummings characterizes Marxist-based theories of social/cultural reproduction as refusing to posit the possibility of social transformation other than through a revolution that drastically alters the way production is organized and the ownership of the means of production. Despite a highly differentiated system of higher education and evidence that socioeconomic status closely predicts educational levels and future income, Cummings contends that the schools are making Japanese society more egalitarian than is the case in any other country, including those countries that have undergone socialist revolutions. He bases this on an analysis of attitudes of students and corporate employees, which are egalitarian. He argues that because students and corporate executives place little emphasis on social mobility and show sympathy toward income equalization, the transformation of Japanese society will soon occur. He maintains that such a change is inevitable, since individual attitudes shape social structures. He interprets his study as refuting Bowles and Gintis and other Marxist scholars of education who argue that without structural transformation there can be no social change.

Cummings's study and the other critiques of conflict and Marxist alternatives to structural functionalism represent a set of responses to the scholarship generated in recent years. Debate, however, has not been the only active response. In some instances the field has co-opted some of the recent challenges.

Co-optation

Although the field has debated and ignored many of the new currents, some have been co-opted into the field. This co-optation has followed a

---

[41] Paulston (n. 11 above).
[42] Cummings (n. 28 above), esp. chap. 1.

distinct pattern. For example, world systems analysis has suggested a research agenda that includes study of international aid agencies and linkages among Third World and industrialized nations with a view toward understanding the mechanisms through which the world system is maintained. A host of studies have appeared on topics suggested by world systems analysis; most are devoid of the theoretical frames from which they initially arose. For example, the journals in the field have devoted considerable coverage to the activities of international aid agencies, most recently to the World Bank.[43] This work has, for the most part, described the policies of these agencies and changes in them over time. Some of this scholarship has not sought to explain the impact of such policies. More often than not, the assumption is that these institutions exist outside the frame of international politics and serve simply to develop Third World nations.

Another example of co-optation of world systems analysis is renewed interest in "institutional transfers." The British journal, *Compare*, for example, ran a special issue on this topic in 1980.[44] The studies that it included, aside from Robert Arnove's on the Ford Foundation, attacked the very concept of world systems analysis and focused on transfers instead. The articles, by implication, likened educational borrowing between Great Britain and the United States to that between the United States and Latin America or between Great Britain and Africa. They criticized the presumption that educational borrowing takes place within the context of either international politics or unequal relations between nation-states.

World systems analysis is not the only new challenge to be co-opted in comparative education and transformed in the process. This is also the case for research emanating from scholarship on women. We pointed out earlier that the field for the most part has ignored the challenge to focus on women as a central concern and a variable in research. However, the field has begun to focus to some extent on issues raised by this challenge. Such research has not focused on women as such or on the social construction of gender. Rather, it has centered on issues presumed to be the province of women—fertility, nutrition, health, and the generation of

---

[43] See Wadi D. Haddad, "The World Bank's Education Sector Policy Paper: A Summary," *Comparative Education* 17 (June 1981): 127–39; Milagros Fernandez, "The World Bank and the Third World: Reflections of a Sceptic," *Prospects* 11 (1981): 294–301; Martin Carnoy, "International Institutions and Educational Policy: A Review of Education-Sector Policy," *Prospects* 10 (1980): 265–83; Seth Spaulding, "The Impact of International Assistance Organizations on the Development of Education," *Prospects* 11 (1981): 421–33; Paul Hurst, "Aid and Educational Development: Rhetoric and Reality," *Comparative Education* 17 (June 1981): 117–25; A. R. Thompson, "How Far Free: International Networks of Constraint upon National Education Policy in the Third World," *Comparative Education* 13 (October 1977): 155–68; George Psacharopoulos, "The World Bank in the World of Education: Some Policy Changes and Some Remnants," *Comparative Education* 17 (June 1981): 141–46.

[44] Ronald Goodenow, "To Build a New World: Toward Two Case Studies on Transfer in the 20th Century," *Compare* 13, no. 1 (1983): 43–60. See also "Educational Transfer" (special issue), *Compare* 13, no. 1 (1983): 1–88.

basic needs for poor families in which the male is not able to be the sole provider.[45] The focus of this research is on women in the narrowly defined roles of childbearers and child rearers in the family. Women are not the center of study or necessarily the subject of research so much as its object. In the process of co-optation the very issues initially raised about the necessity of studying women and their education have disappeared.

The ways in which the field has co-opted world systems analysis and, to an almost unrecognizable degree, the study of women stand as examples of how the field has responded to new challenges that it has not attacked or totally ignored. These forms of co-optation exemplify the approaches that the field has taken to other issues and theoretical challenges posited over the past decade. What we have suggested about world systems analysis and the study of women's education also extends to the field's treatment of the challenge to study educational institutions and their processes.

Conclusion

We understand that our discussion of new currents and comparative education's response to them is far from complete. We have attempted in this essay to provide an overview of recent challenges and to outline the ways in which the field has responded. We hope that the reluctance with which the field has greeted many of these challenges is but a temporary phase. We do not believe it is healthy for a field of inquiry to ignore questioning about the frameworks, theories, and methods that it has used to generate research or to dismiss challenges out of hand. To do so is to consign the field to stagnation and to rehashing old questions.

Although our focus in this essay has been on new challenges, comparative education has, as a field of study, shown considerable continuity both in its approaches to research and in the theory underlying such research. Since 1977, however, this continuity has also shown some signs of change. The optimism that education could be a force for social equality, which pervaded the field in the 1960s and 1970s, has been muted by years of not always successful attempts to reform both schools and society. This sober mood has especially appeared in the scholarship on comprehensive school reforms in Western Europe, on the Chinese experiments during the Great Proletarian Cultural Revolution, and on evidence drawn from the Soviet Union, Eastern Europe, and the Third World.[46] The

[45] See, e.g., Susan Cochrane, *Education and Fertility: What Do We Really Know?* (Baltimore: Johns Hopkins University Press, 1979).

[46] Henry Levin (n. 13 above); Lois Weis, "Education and the Reproduction of Inequality: The Case of Ghana," *Comparative Education Review* 23 (February 1979): 41–50; Torsten Husen, *The School in Question* (New York: Oxford University Press, 1979); Joseph P. Farrell, "Educational Expansion and the Drive for Social Equality," in Altbach, Arnove, and Kelly, eds. (n. 8 above); Gail Lapidus, *Women in Soviet Society* (Berkeley and Los Angeles: University of California Press, 1981); Joseph R. Fiszman, "Education and Equality of Opportunity in Eastern Europe," in Altbach, Arnove, and Kelly,

thought that expanded enrollments and common schooling would change social structures or the effects of parental education and income, gender, and race on children's life chances has become a subject of debate.

Much of this discussion was stimulated by a radical critique of structural functionalism that assumed that over time the transformation of society could occur without changes in social structures. The radical critique was clearly articulated, for example, by Weis in her study of Ghanaian secondary schools. Levin, in his study of Western Europe, argued that without changes in social structures the schools could only reproduce existing social relations and the inequalities currently structured into them. Others in comparative education maintained that inequality was difficult, indeed almost impossible, to eradicate, even if basic social structures were changed. Such was the argument made by Court's study of educational expansion and inequality in Kenya and Tanzania, Morrison's work on Tanzania, and Dobson's studies of the Soviet Union.[47]

Comparative educators have, to some extent, become more pessimistic—some would say, realistic—about the role of education in shaping social change and in contributing to economic development and modernization. This "new realism" has been stimulated to a considerable degree by the insights of radical critics of the past decade as well as by the failure of many of the educational efforts of the 1960s and 1970s. The fiscal crisis of the 1980s as well as the lowered expectations of the current period have stimulated further critique and analysis, this time from a more conservative stance. Scholars like Philip Coombs, George Psacharopoulos, and Mateen Thobani have questioned the viability and, to some extent, even the desirability of the vision of universal, free primary education and total literacy for Third World nations.[48] Some have argued that not only is universal primary education a luxury but in some cases it may be harmful to economic development and to social well being, since it discourages the efficient use of resources. In the 1980s, some scholars in the field have turned increasingly to the concept of privatization as a means to improve economic efficiency in the provision of education and to enhance

---

eds. (n. 5 above); W. D. Halls, "A Comparative Political and Sociological Analysis of Educational Opportunity in Western Europe, 1960–80," in Watson and Wilson, eds. (n. 34 above).

[47] David Court, "Education as Social Control: The Response to Inequality in Kenya and Tanzania," in *Education and Politics in Tropical Africa*, ed. V. C. Uchendu (Owerri and New York: Conch, 1979); Richard Dobson and Michael Swafford, "The Educational Attainment Process in the Soviet Union: A Case Study," *Comparative Education Review* 24 (June 1980, part 1): 252–69; David Morrison, *Education and Politics in Africa: The Tanzanian Case* (Montreal: McGill-Queens University Press, 1967).

[48] See George Psacharopoulos, "The Perverse Effects of Public Subsidization of Education, Or How Equal if Free Education?" *Comparative Education Review* 21 (February 1977): 69–90; Mateen Thobani, "Charging User Fees for Social Services: Education in Malawi," *Comparative Education Review* 28 (August 1984): 402–23; Steven J. Klees, "The Need for a Political Economy of Educational Finance: A Response to Thobani," *Comparative Education Review* 28 (August 1984): 424–40; and W. Van Vliet and J. A. Smyth, "A Nineteenth Century French Proposal to Use School Vouchers," *Comparative Education Review* 26 (February 1982): 95–103.

educational quality.[49] The recent debates on educational vouchers and on the imposition of school fees represent a return to some of the debates of the 1950s.

The field has recently reconsidered with increasing frequency the role of education of any sort—formal or nonformal, vocational or general—in development. In the 1960s and 1970s, many hoped that given the proper form and content of education and its widespread diffusion, Third World countries would industrialize and become modern, and the poverty and accompanying ills that were associated with underdevelopment would be eradicated. The vision was development, and the field assumed that no matter how poor a country was, education would lead to the creation of human capital, which in turn would develop the nation to the levels of most Western countries.[50] Much empirical research has shifted its major focus from modernization to education's relation to the provision of basic needs: to crop production, small-scale technology, marketing, and family health and nutrition. Education is increasingly being looked to for survival or as a means of stemming a demographic and ecological disaster. In short, the vision of what it means to develop human capital is undergoing modification.

In this essay we have been critical of the field for the ways in which it has responded to new ways of thinking about comparative education and treated alternative theories. Unlike some who have openly attacked some of the new challenges for their divisiveness, we believe that the new strains are a sign of vitality for the field of comparative education. It strengthens the field to have more than one way of viewing the role of education in society and to debate alternatives for studying education and its context. To ignore new challenges, many of which arise from changing contexts and advances in scholarship both in comparative education and sister disciplines, is to consign the field to irrelevance in the long run. It is commendable that the field has taken time to reflect on issues that it considered in the past. Nonetheless, it is important that it explores new ones. The challenge of the next decades will be not only to explore the issues raised in the field since 1977 and to take them seriously but also to identify new areas for investigation that will bring continuing debate and vitality to research in comparative education.

---

[49] Estelle James, "Benefits and Costs of Privatized Public Services: Lessons from the Dutch Educational System," *Comparative Education Review* 28 (November 1984): 605–24. See also Thobani.
[50] See Philip H. Coombs, *The World Crisis in Education: The View from the Eighties* (New York: Oxford University Press, 1985); Irvin Sobel, "The Human Capital Revolution in Economic Development," in Altbach, Arnove, and Kelly, eds. (n. 5 above); Hans Weiler, "Educational Planning and Social Change" (n. 16 above); Hans Weiler, "Towards a Political Economy of Educational Planning," *Prospects* 8 (1978): 247–67; George Psacharopoulos, "The State of Educational Planning Revisited," *Prospects* 11 (1981): 154–58.

CONTRIBUTORS

PAUL P. W. ACHOLA is a member of the staff of the Educational Research Bureau, University of Zambia.

PHILIP G. ALTBACH is professor and director of the Comparative Education Center, State University of New York at Buffalo. He is also editor of the *Comparative Education Review*.

MICHAEL W. APPLE is professor in the Department of Curriculum and Instruction, University of Wisconsin—Madison.

FRANCIS MUSA BOAKARI is a doctoral candidate in education at the University of Iowa.

JOHN BOLI is on the staff of the Department of Sociology, University of Lund, Sweden.

MARY JEAN BOWMAN is professor emerita of education and economics at the University of Chicago.

MARTIN CARNOY is professor of education at the Stanford International Development Education Center, Stanford University.

MAX A. ECKSTEIN is professor of education at Queens College, City University of New York. He is a past president of the Comparative and International Education Society.

ERWIN H. EPSTEIN is professor of social sciences at the University of Missouri— Rolla. He is a past president of the Comparative and International Education Society.

JOSEPH P. FARRELL is professor in the Department of Adult Education at the Ontario Institute for Studies in Education, Toronto, Canada. He is a past president of the Comparative and International Education Society.

BRIAN HOLMES is professor emeritus in the Department of Comparative Education, University of London.

GAIL P. KELLY is professor in the Department of Educational Organization, Administration, and Policy, State University of New York at Buffalo. She is president of the Comparative and International Education Society and is associate editor of the *Comparative Education Review*.

LÊ THÀNH KHÔI is professor at the University of Paris—Sorbonne.

VANDRA LEA MASEMANN works with Masemann and Mock, Consultants, Toronto, Canada.

JOHN W. MEYER is professor and chair in the Department of Sociology, Stanford University.

HAROLD J. NOAH is Cowles Professor of Education at Teachers College, Columbia University. He is a past president of the Comparative and International Education Society.

CONTRIBUTORS

RICHARD H. PFAU is associate extension professor in the Institute of Public Service, University of Connecticut.

FRANCISCO O. RAMIREZ is professor of sociology at San Francisco State University.

REIJO RAIVOLA is associate professor of education at the University of Tampere, Finland.

GARY L. THEISEN is on the staff of the U.S. Agency for International Development, Washington, D.C.

FREDERICK M. WIRT is professor of political science at the University of Illinois at Urbana-Champaign.

MATHEW ZACHARIAH is professor of comparative education at the University of Calgary, Calgary, Canada. He is a past president of the Comparative and International Education Society.

Index

Academic achievement: as a model, 56–57; comparative studies of, 6, 9, 27–49; in relation to expenditure, 7. *See also* Family

Adorno, Theodor, 61

Africa, 92, 94, 115, 317

Agency for International Development (AID), 8

Alienation: among students, 23; characterizing communication in schools, 24

Altbach, Philip G., 20, 100, 234, 311, 315, 317, 322

Althusser, Louis, 229

Anderson, C. Arnold, 4, 238, 239, 240, 241, 242, 244

Anthropology and educational research, 13–15, 266, 320

Apple, Michael W., 9, 22, 101, 315

Archer, Margaret, 21, 235, 239, 243, 244, 313

Arnove, Robert, 20, 23, 247, 311, 315, 322, 324

Asia, 92, 317

Austria, 114, 157

Bangladesh, 317

Banks, Arthur S., 122

Barber, B. R., 206, 211

Baudelot, C., 84

Bendix, Reinhart, 110

Bennett, Nicholas, 38

Bereday, George, 4, 182, 197, 209, 262, 270

Berman, Edward, 317

Bernstein, Basil, 16, 21, 55, 58, 59, 68

Bibby, John, 38

Bills, David B., 19, 248

Bock, John, 315

Boli, John (Boli-Bennett), 9, 124, 311

Bottomore, Thomas, 13

Bourdieu, Pierre, 20, 55, 58, 59, 60, 68, 100

Bowles, Samuel, 19, 20, 58, 59, 68, 84, 85, 248, 323

Bowman, Mary Jean, 9, 313

Brazil, 102, 131, 137, 141–42, 146–48

Bronfenbrenner, Urie, 3

Canada, 7, 20

Canadian and International Education, 2

Capitalist society: cultural and economic reproduction in schooling, 62; and problematic of educational reform, 74–76, 81–85

Carnegie Foundation for the Advancement of Teaching, 156

Carnoy, Martin, 9, 235, 237, 238, 311, 315

Chile, 75, 102, 316

China, 2, 46, 89, 92, 154, 318

Class and educational access and outcome, 5, 6, 19, 30, 33, 35, 54, 55, 58–59, 66, 74–76; as a research variable, 320

Classroom life: new interpretations of, 16–17, 21, 87, 293–307, 318, 320; impact on achievement, 36, 41–42

Clignet, Remi, 21, 168, 253

Cobb, Stanwood, 54

Coffman, William E., 47

Cohen, David K., 97, 98

Cohen, Yehudi, 127

Cole, Michael, 4

Coleman, James S., 38, 207, 317

Colonialism: colonial education, 17, 231; and comparative education, 3, 20; studies of former colonies, 14, 17, 20, 43–45; and underdevelopment, 95

Comparative and International Education Society (CIES), 91, 97, 201, 204, 263, 323

Parsons, Talcott, 186, 190
Paulston, Rolland, 235, 258, 315, 323
Peil, Margaret, 38
Pfau, Richard H., 10, 313
Phenomenology, 15, 16, 53
Philanthropic agencies, 317, 324
Philosophy and educational research, 15, 181–83
Piaget, Jean, 171–73, 253
Plank, David, 313
Political economy of education, 51–55, 101, 103
Popper, Karl, 61, 180, 182, 183, 205, 210, 253
Portugal, 75
Positivist social science: discussion of, 11–12, 98, 182, 196–97, 236, 237, 238–43
Prechel, Harland, 168, 322
Primary education, 17, 18, 37–38, 122, 311
Private education, 17, 101, 326
Production, 5, 19, 75, 77, 82–85, 101, 134, 225–26
Progressive education, 17, 18
Progressive Education Association, 54
Prussia, 114, 120, 125
Psacharopoulos, George, 168, 326
Psychology and educational research, 14, 55, 56
Psychometrics, 6, 261
Publishing, 317

Quality of education, 6, 39

Race, 5, 36, 80–81
Racial minorities, 6
Radcliffe-Brown, A. R., 12
Raivola, Reijo, 10
Ramirez, Francisco, 311
Ravitch, Diane, 161
Redfield, Robert, 186
Reissman, L., 203, 208
Religious institutions and groups: and educational development, 125, 126

Reproduktion des Kulturkapitals als Funktion der Erziehung, 20, 51–71, 75, 81, 86, 216, 323
Research: directions, 1–7, 121–22, 310–19; funding of, 7–8; implications of the various approaches, 12–25; parameters (national, regional, worldwide), 310–13; utilization of, 3, 97–104, 154–57
Resistance: among working-class students; among teachers, 21, 22; strategies for, 85–87
Richards, I. A., 177
Rossello, P., 261
Rugg, Harold, 185
Rural education, 33, 73, 76, 88–90, 102, 107
Russian education, 154
Ryan, Doris, 42

Sadler, Michael, 92, 154, 234, 253, 261
Scandinavia, 123
Schiefelbein, Ernesto, 316
Schneider, Friedrich, 181, 182, 197
Scholarship: dominance of English-speaking countries, 2; Third World scholars, 2; politics and strategies, 97, 283–92
School structure and organization: seen as means of control, 16
Schwab, Joseph, 55
Schwartz, Karl, 315
Scotland, 114
Secondary education, 17, 36, 37, 105, 122, 311
Senegal, 38
Sharp, Rachel, 21
Shirk, Susan, 318
Sica, Alan, 168, 322
Silva, Edward T., 312
Silvert, K., 203, 208
Smelser, Neil, 264
Socialist countries, 46, 103
Socialization, 14, 56–57, 68, 109, 117, 124
Social relations, 5, 19, 21, 101